OXFORD EARLY CHRISTIAN STUDIES

Henry Chadwick   Rowan Williams

THE OXFORD EARLY CHRISTIAN STUDIES series
will include scholarly volumes on the thought and history of
the early Christian centuries. Covering a wide range of
Greek, Latin, and Oriental sources, the books will be of
interest to theologians, ancient historians, and specialists in
the classical and Jewish worlds.

Pelagius's Commentary on St Paul's Epistle to the Romans

Translated
with Introduction and Notes

THEODORE DE BRUYN

CLARENDON PRESS · OXFORD

Oxford University Press, Great Clarendon Street, Oxford OX2 6DP

Oxford New York
Athens Auckland Bangkok Bogota Bombay
Buenos Aires Calcutta Cape Town Dar es Salaam
Delhi Florence Hong Kong Istanbul Karachi
Kuala Lumpur Madras Madrid Melbourne
Mexico City Nairobi Paris Singapore
Taipei Tokyo Toronto Warsaw
and associated companies in
Berlin Ibadan

Oxford is a trade mark of Oxford University Press

Published in the United States
by Oxford University Press Inc., New York

British Library Cataloguing in Publication Data
Data available

Library of Congress Cataloging in Publication Data
Pelagius on St. Paul's Epistle to the Romans: a translation with
introduction and notes of Pelagius's commentary on Romans
Theodore de Bruyn.
Includes bibliographical references and indexes.
1. Bible. N.T. Romans–Commentaries. 2. Pelagius.
3. Pelagianism. I. Title, II. Title: Pelagius on Saint Paul's
Epistle to the Romans. III. Series.
BS2665.D38   1993   227'.107–dc20
ISBN 0-19-826980-3

1 3 5 7 9 10 8 6 4 2

Typeset by Joshua Associates Ltd., Oxford
Printed in Great Britain on acid-free paper by
Bookcraft (Bath) Ltd., Midsomer Norton

To
the Faculty of
Atlantic School of Theology

Preface

DESPITE the importance of Pelagius for the history of western theology, his writings have not been available in English. As a result his work has been inaccessible to many, and his thought usually presented in the terms of his opponent Augustine. Happily, this deficiency has been remedied for the letters with the recent translation by B. R. Rees. The present work turns to the commentaries on the Pauline epistles, the largest of Pelagius's extant works, and offers an English translation of the commentary on Romans.

The translation is prefaced by an introduction and accompanied by notes. Those reading Pelagius for the first time will find in the introduction an account of the events and issues which shaped his interpretation of Romans. In approaching the commentary, I have relied heavily on the commentaries Pelagius himself used, as well as other contemporary writings. For this the papers of A. J. Smith have been indispensable. The parallels discovered by Smith, and those I have found, have been adduced in the notes to the translation. Regrettably, I did not have access to Lommatzsch's edition of Origen on Romans when I undertook this study, and consequently resorted to Patrologia Graeca. The first volume of the new edition of Origen's text by C. P. Hammond Bammel in the Vetus Latina series 'Aus der Geschichte der lateinischen Bibel' appeared when the study was in its last stages.

The translation follows Alexander Souter's edition for Pelagius's comments, but replaces Souter's lemmata with a new recension of the biblical text (see Introduction and Appendix). In general the English remains close to the Latin, but because Pelagius's remarks are elliptical I have found it necessary on occasion to elaborate. With Pelagius's language for human beings I have tried to be inclusive of both sexes, but the constraints of ancient discourse have led me to use the masculine pronoun when referring to both.

This work had its beginnings in a doctoral dissertation at the University of St Michael's College in the Toronto School of Theology. I am much indebted to Professors J. E. McWilliam and C. J. McDonough, my directors, for their time and advice. Further improvements are owing to the comments which Professors W. H. Principe and W. S. Babcock offered at the defence. The Social Sciences and Humanities Research Council of Canada and the Government of Ontario provided financial support during my doctoral studies, and the libraries of the Pontifical Institute of Medieval Studies in Toronto and St Paul University in Ottawa gave me all I could desire in a library. At Atlantic School of Theology, where it has been my good fortune to teach, Alison Grantham has been a great help with interlibrary loans, and the Administration and the Board generous in allowing me time for research.

I am grateful to Professor M. Wiles for reviewing the manuscript with a view to publication, and to Professor H. Chadwick and Dr R. Williams for including it in the present series. My thanks go as well to Professor H. J. Frede for his kind reply to some queries. The book has benefited greatly from the suggestions of Professor Chadwick and the careful editing of Dr John Waś. At the Press Hilary O'Shea has been unfailing with her advice and assistance, and Lucy Kentfield saw the book through its final stages of production. I alone, of course, remain responsible for the contents of the volume.

Throughout this time I have enjoyed the unfailing support of my family, especially my parents, and the company of many friends. Much of the pleasure of the original writing was due to the friendship of Robert Black, Luigi Girolametto, Rosanne Lopers, Nancy McElwee, Priscilla Reimer, Lyndon Reynolds, Lesley Smith, Robert Sweetman, and Agnes Vandergang. From the Faculty of the Atlantic School of Theology I have learnt more than could appear between the covers of a book, but I trust they will accept the dedication as a sign of my affection and respect.

T. DE B.

Contents

Abbreviations

For abbreviations of ancient authors and writings see the sources listed in the Bibliography.

ACO	Acta Conciliorum Oecumenicorum
BALCL	*Bulletin d'ancienne littérature chrétienne latine*
CCSL	Corpus Christianorum, series latina
CLA	Codices Latini Antiquiores
CSEL	Corpus Scriptorum Ecclesiasticorum Latinorum
FP	Florilegium Patristicum
GCS	Die griechischen christlichen Schriftsteller der ersten drei Jahrhunderte
LCL	Loeb Classical Library
OCT	Oxford Classical Texts
PG	Patrologia Graeca
PL	Patrologia Latina
PLS	Patrologiae Latinae Supplementum
SC	Sources Chrétiennes
TU	Texte und Untersuchungen zur Geschichte der altchristlichen Literatur

Introduction

1. THE CONTEXT OF THE COMMENTARY

Literary Traditions

The latter half of the fourth century witnessed what some have called a 'renaissance' of interest in the Pauline epistles in the Latin church.[1] The works produced in these decades include commentaries by Ambrosiaster, an anonymous writer, and Pelagius on all the epistles; commentaries by Marius Victorinus, Jerome, and Augustine on select epistles; and Rufinus of Aquileia's translation of Origen's commentary on Romans[2]—in addition to the attention given to the epistles in the letters and tracts of the time.[3] This wealth of commentaries, investing so much in the writings of the apostle,[4] is all the more striking because as a genre the commentary appeared relatively late in the west. We know of Greek commentaries on Scripture already in the second century, and in the third century the monumental work of Origen looms

---

[1] Lohse, 'Beobachtungen zum Paulus-Kommentar', 351–3.

[2] For editions of these commentaries see the sources listed at the end of this volume. The dates of the commentaries, in sequence, are as follows (with references in parentheses): Marius Victorinus, within a few years after 363, in the following order: *Eph.*, *Gal.*, *Phil.* (Hadot, *Marius Victorinus*, 285–6; Erdt, *Marius Victorinus Afer*, 82–5); Ambrosiaster, between 366 and 384 (Souter, *Earliest Latin Commentaries*, 42–3; cf. id., *Study of Ambrosiaster*, 166–74); Jerome, May–Oct. 386, in the following order: *Phil.*, *Gal.*, *Eph.*, *Tit.* (Nautin, 'La date des commentaires', 5–12; but cf. Jay, *L'Exégèse de saint Jérôme*, 407–9); Augustine, beginning in 394 and probably finishing before May 395 (the date of his episcopal consecration), in the following order: *Exp. prop.*, *Gal.*, *Exp. inch.* (Divjak, CSEL 84: vii–ix; cf. Mutzenbecher, CCSL 44: xxx–xxxiii); the anonymous commentary, between 396 and 405, before Pelagius's commentary (Frede, *Ein neuer Paulustext*, i. 215–17; cf. ii. 9–10 for the sigla which distinguish the 'anonymous' comments from the 'pseudo-Jerome' comments written between 412 and 432); Origen–Rufinus on Romans, *c.*405–6 (Bammel, 'Last Ten Years', 403–6); Pelagius, between 405–6 and 410 (see nn. 64–5 below).

[3] Ambstr. *Quaest.*, *passim* (CSEL 50); Tycon. *Lib. regul.* 3 (Burkitt 12–31); Ambr. *Iac.* 1. 4. 13–16 (CSEL 32: 13. 2–15. 20); Prisc. *Canones* (CSEL 18: 109–47); Aug. *Diu. quaest.*, qq. 66–8 (CCSL 44A: 150–83), *Ad Simpl.* 1. 1–2 (CCSL 44: 7–56); Jer. *Ep.* 85 (CSEL 55: 135–8), *Ep.* 120. 10 (CSEL 55: 500–6), *Ep.* 121. 7–9 (CSEL 56: 27–41).

[4] See pp. 15–16 below.

large.[5] The earliest Latin commentator, by contrast, wrote in the latter half of that century, and his work is more Greek than Latin in spirit.[6] But by the beginning of the fifth century all this has changed, and Latin writers from several distinct traditions have achieved a considerable maturity in the genre.

The succession of Pauline commentaries in which Pelagius's stands may be called 'Roman' on the strength of its location and pedigree. It is not insignificant that three, if not four, of the commentators who undertook to comment on the entire Pauline corpus worked in Rome. We know that Marius Victorinus (who intended to comment on all the epistles but did not in fact complete the project),[7] Ambrosiaster, and Pelagius wrote in Rome, and there is evidence to suggest that the anonymous commentator did as well.[8] As each in turn contributed to the succession of commentaries, his work combined independence with tradition. Ambrosiaster was at least acquainted with Marius Victorinus, and Pelagius was indebted to Ambrosiaster and the anonymous commentator.[9] The result, however, was not mere imitation. Each commentary is distinctive, reflecting the interests of its author and the influences of his times.

A thread of continuity amid the variations from one commentator to the next in this Roman tradition is the style of commentary. It is a literal one, beginning and often remaining with the historical and grammatical meaning of the biblical text. This approach probably had its beginnings in Latin rhetorical training. Marius Victorinus had been professor of rhetoric in Rome, and when late in life he began work on the Pauline epistles he approached Paul in much the same way as he had taught Cicero.[10] His commentaries are expressly pedagogic in style and suggest a lecture with students in view. They offer simple explanations of the text, summarize the train of thought, elucidate the syntax of the longer sentences, and generally adhere closely to Paul's language. The approach of Ambrosiaster and Pelagius is similar, but their comments are briefer than Marius Victorinus's. And although by the time of Pelagius influences from the

[5] Turner, 'Greek Patristic Commentaries', 488–96.

[6] Bardy, 'Victorin de Pettau', 2882–7.

[7] Gori, CSEL 83. 2: viii n. 5.

[8] de Bruyn, 'Constantius the *tractator*', 39–40.

[9] See Souter, *Earliest Latin Commentaries*, 21–7 and 63–7, on the commentaries of Marius Victorinus and Ambrosiaster. For Pelagius's debt to Ambrosiaster see Smith, 'Latin Sources', 19: 167–230. For Pelagius's use of the anonymous commentary see Frede, *Ein neuer Paulustext*, i. 196–205.

[10] See Erdt, *Marius Victorinus Afer*, 93–6; Hadot, *Marius Victorinus*, 289–90.

Greek schools of commentary were more extensive in the west, this foundation in Latin rhetoric was still not negligible: Jerome acknowledged his debt to it even after many years in the east.[11]

The preference for literal commentary was, of course, a hallmark of the Antiochene school in the east, prompting speculation about the influence of this school on Pelagius. Theodore of Heraclea and Diodore of Tarsus are regarded as founders of the school, but unfortunately little remains of their work.[12] We know more of subsequent Antiochene commentators on Paul—Apollinaris of Laodicea, John Chrysostom, and Theodore of Mopsuestia. However, they, unlike their western contemporaries, did not envisage a single commentary on the whole of the Pauline corpus.[13] Theodore of Mopsuestia's commentaries on the epistles, for example, were the work of several decades and were too voluminous to appear in a single volume.[14] Moreover, despite parallels to Pelagius's comments in the homilies of John Chrysostom and the commentaries of Theodore of Mopsuestia,[15] it is doubtful whether the latter were used directly by Pelagius. Henry Swete concluded from his study of the parallels between Theodore and Pelagius that Theodore was indebted to Pelagius, and his view has gained general acceptance.[16] It is also unlikely that Pelagius read Chrysostom's homilies on the Pauline epistles, since Pelagius's Greek was not strong at the time he wrote his commentary,[17] and we know of no Latin translation of the homilies available in the first decade of the fifth century.

[11] Jer. *Contra Rufin.* 1. 16 (CCSL 79: 14. 11–15. 33); on the influence of Jerome's teacher, the grammarian Donatus, on Jerome's exegesis see Jay, 'Jérôme et la pratique de l'exégèse', 535–6.

[12] Turner, 'Greek Patristic Commentaries', 497–8, 500–1.

[13] Ibid. 485, 500, 509; for a list of extant commentaries and fragments of commentaries see Geerard, *Clavis Patrum Graecorum*, v. 140–7.

[14] Turner, 'Greek Patristic Commentaries', 509–11.

[15] Souter, *Expositions*, i. 193–9.

[16] *Theodori Episcopi Mopsuesteni in epistolas b. Pauli Commentarii*, vol. i, pp. lxxiv–lxxvi. Turner, 'Greek Patristic Commentaries', 512, inclined to the opposite conclusion, stating that 'it would be unusual to find a Greek writer using a Latin authority, and in at least two of the parallels (Gal. 3: 20, 2 Tim. 2: 20), while Theodore states his own view and no other, Pelagius prefixes to the view that coincides the formula "*ut quidam putant*"'. A more likely source for Pelagius in these two instances, however, is Ambrosiaster; cf. Pel. *Gal.* 3: 19 and *2 Tim.* 2: 20 (Souter, *Expositions*, ii. 322. 1–2, 515. 10–15), with Ambstr. *Gal.* 3: 19 and *2 Tim.* 2: 20 (CSEL 81. 3: 38. 14–22, 308. 4–5); Ambrosiaster is not the source, though, for the remaining passages listed by Swete.

[17] Chapman, 'Pélage et le texte de s. Paul', 18: 472–3. See also Pel. *Rom.* 11: 11 n. 13 below. On the basis of Chapman's article Souter, *Earliest Latin Commentaries*, 225, qualified his earlier opinion of Pelagius's debt to Greek authors; cf. Plinval, *Pélage*, 85–6, 134, 140 n. 1, 206 n. 2.

The Antiochene style may, however, have been conveyed indirectly to Pelagius by the anonymous commentary on the Pauline epistles. This commentary has been preserved partly in a Budapest manuscript, partly in manuscripts of Pelagius's commentary.[18] It was written some time between 396 and 405, possibly in Rome, though it has also been assigned to Aquileia.[19] It may have been the work of Constantius, a bishop with whom Pelagius at one time corresponded and who later was vociferous in his opposition to the Pelagians in Rome.[20] The author was proficient in Greek and familiar with the Greek exegetical traditions; the work shows the influence of Origen in substance, but resembles the Antiochenes in style.[21] Pelagius was indebted to his interpretation at a number of points, but the debt does not appear to be as extensive as that to other commentaries.[22] It is the similarity in style between the anonymous work and Pelagius's that is most striking, a similarity which suggests that the former may have served as a model for the latter. In both commentaries short comments on a portion of the text predominate: sometimes a brief paragraph, sometimes a sentence, sometimes merely a phrase.[23]

Pelagius's commentary resembles the anonymous commentary in another aspect as well. Both authors drew on Origen, whose exegetical writing had guided so many in the east.[24] The debt marks something of a change from the practice of Marius Victorinus and Ambrosiaster. There are few echoes of other exegetes in the commentaries of Marius Victorinus,[25] and although there are some parallels to the Greek tradition in Ambrosiaster's commentaries, perhaps derived from Greek catenae, Ambrosiaster was himself suspicious of Greek authorities.[26] On the other hand, the debt to the east in such interpreters as

[18] Frede, *Ein neuer Paulustext*, i. 164–85.

[19] de Bruyn, 'Constantius the *tractator*', 38–40; cf. Frede, *Ein neuer Paulustext*, i. 247–59.

[20] de Bruyn, 'Constantius the *tractator*', 40–51.

[21] Frede, *Ein neuer Paulustext*, i. 205–15. Frede acknowledges that the scarcity of the remains makes it difficult to identify early sources in the Antiochene tradition precisely.

[22] Ibid. 196–205.

[23] The commentary is not preserved in full; only extracts remain in the Budapest MS and interpolations in Pelagius's commentary. Consequently we cannot be sure that it was as continuous as Pelagius's commentary, though the comments individually are similar in form.

[24] On the anonymous commentator's use of Origen see Frede, *Ein neuer Paulustext*, i. 205–6.

[25] Erdt, *Marius Victorinus Afer*, 94; cf. Hadot, *Marius Victorinus*, 289; Souter, *Earliest Latin Commentaries*, 26–7.

[26] Ambstr. *Rom.* 5: 14. 4e–5 (CSEL 81. 1: 177. 10–22); see Souter, *Earliest Latin Commentaries*, 65–6.

Ambrose and Jerome was considerable, and the regard they had for Greek commentators, especially Origen, was shared by others.[27] By the end of the fourth century constant demands were made on those fluent in Greek for translations of Greek commentaries and for original Latin works written with a knowledge of Greek exegesis.[28] Pelagius was among those who benefited from the translators: he read Origen's commentary on Romans in the abridged translation by Rufinus of Aquileia.[29]

The extent of Pelagius's debt to Rufinus's translation of Origen has been well documented.[30] Pelagius frequently includes an interpretation from Origen as one of two or three alternatives, which he introduces, as is his custom, with a formulaic 'or' (*siue*). More generally, he draws on Origen's—or rather, Origen–Rufinus's—view of the human condition, particularly for his defence of human freedom and his understanding of divine grace.[31] This sympathy with Origen, revealed in details of interpretation and yet more than a matter of detail,[32] is especially noticeable in Pelagius's commentary when the Origenist tradition is compared with the third of the exegetical traditions that converge in Rome, the African tradition represented chiefly in Tertullian, Cyprian, and Augustine.

Pelagius's relation to the African tradition is mixed. Inasmuch as it was bequeathed to him as part of the general theological legacy at Rome, he appears to have absorbed African writers along with other western writers. Thus, for example, one can mark the lineaments of second- and third-century *testimonia*, or catalogues of biblical texts, in the scriptural references that figure in his comments.[33] These catalogues gathered passages from Scripture and arranged them under headings with little or no comment for catechetical and polemical

---

[27] On Ambrose's debt to Philo and to Origen see Savon, *Saint Ambroise devant l'exégèse de Philon le juif*, 377–85, and auf der Maur, *Das Psalmenverständnis des Ambrosius von Mailand*, 295–309. On Jerome's formation in Greek exegesis see Jay, 'Jérôme et la pratique de l'exégèse', 524; on Jerome's debt to Origen in particular, which proved so aggravating in the Origenist controversy, see Schatkin, 'The Influence of Origen', 49–58. See also Doignon, 'Les premiers commentateurs', on the work of Hilary of Poitiers prior to Ambrose and Jerome.

[28] Jay, 'Jérôme et la pratique de l'exégèse', 534; Bammel, 'Last Ten Years', 386–7, 393–4, 403.

[29] On Rufinus's method of translation and on his faithfulness to Origen see now Bammel, *Römerbrieftext*, 43–58.

[30] Smith, 'Latin Sources', 20: 127–77.

[31] Bammel, *Römerbrieftext*, 45–7.

[32] Cf. e.g. the parallels from Origen–Rufinus cited at Pel. *Rom.* 1: 24, 5: 19, 11: 8.

[33] On Latin *testimonia* see Saxer, 'La Bible chez les Pères latins', 345–55.

purposes. In the west in the fourth century the two collections of Cyprian, *For Quirinus* and *For Fortunatus*, were the best known, but older Latin collections, which Tertullian drew on for his *Against the Jews* and *Against Marcion*, were also influential. In Pelagius's treatment of Romans patterns of association set by Cyprian in his *testimonia* are apparent, and though these patterns would also have been mediated to Pelagius in other writers and in sermons and lectionaries, he probably had first-hand knowledge of the *testimonia* themselves.[34]

Pelagius appears likewise to be indebted to the considerable body of apologetic literature which had accumulated by his time, including a number of African writings. This is hardly surprising, since Christian apology in the second and third centuries was largely a claim for or from the Scriptures. It was the genre in which most interpretations of Scripture were preserved for subsequent generations. Furthermore, one of the main themes of the epistle to the Romans, the relation of Jews and Gentiles to God, had also become one of the chief preoccupations of Christian apology. Thus, when discussing Paul's argument regarding the Jews in Romans, Pelagius draws on the Latin *aduersus Iudaeos* tradition represented in (among others) Tertullian's *Against the Jews*, Cyprian's *testimonia*, the *Consultationes Zacchaei et Apollonii*, and Zeno's *Sermons*.[35] Likewise, there are points where Pelagius's comments on Paul's argument regarding the Gentiles echoes Latin apology to pagans, in particular Tertullian's *Apology*, Lactantius's *Epitome*, and Rufinus of Aquileia's translation of the *Sentences of Sextus*.[36] And on some matters of Christology there are parallels to Pelagius's comments in Tertullian's anti-Marcionite treatise *On the Flesh of Christ*.[37]

But the African writer whose relation to Pelagius is of greatest interest is, of course, Augustine. It is clear from his commentary on Romans that Pelagius was familiar with the several works which Augustine produced on the same epistle between 394 and 397: the *Propositions from the Epistle to the Romans*, the *Unfinished Commentary on the Epistle to the Romans*, and the relevant questions of the *Eighty-Three Questions* and *To Simplician*.[38] In the course of these works Augustine's

---

[34] Parallels are noted at Pel. *Rom.* 1: 30 n. 52, 2: 4 nn. 6–7, 10: 21 n. 11. For instances where Ambrosiaster may have mediated Cyprian to Pelagius see Pel., *Rom.* 5: 6 n. 10, 8: 15 n. 22, 8: 37 n. 52.

[35] *Rom.* 2: 25 nn. 35–7, 2: 26 n. 39, 2: 29 nn. 46–7, 10: 21 n. 12.

[36] *Rom.* 1: 19 nn. 34 and 36, 1: 27 n. 49.   [37] *Rom.* 1: 16 n. 24, 5: 14 n. 29.

[38] Smith, 'Latin Sources', 20: 55–65; Souter, *Expositions*, i. 187; Smith, 'Pelagius and Augustine', 21–35.

views on human freedom and divine grace undergo a number of significant changes, and once he arrives at the view he sets out for Simplician he has lost Pelagius's sympathy. Pelagius repudiates Augustine's views at corresponding points in his own commentary, and distances himself from those at Rome who favour the African tradition on the consequences of the fall.[39]

There remains one last dimension of the work of the commentators in Rome—in addition to the model of Latin rhetoric, the style of Antioch, the growing knowledge of Origen, and the influence of Africa—which should be noted. This is the version of the epistles, along with its prologues, on which the commentaries were based.[40] At the turn of the century what we know as the Vulgate version of the epistles was produced in Rome. According to the current consensus, its author was Rufinus of Syria, who had kept company with Jerome in Bethlehem and had been dispatched by him on a mission to the west in 399.[41] Rufinus undertook to do for the Pauline epistles (as well as the Catholic epistles and perhaps the whole of the New Testament outside the Gospels) what Jerome had done for the Gospels, namely, to revise the existing Latin text so that it corresponded to the Alexandrian Greek text. With the growing interest in Greek exegesis, in part as a result of the dispute over Scripture in the Arian controversy, the latter had come to be preferred over the western Greek text on which earlier Latin versions (*uetus latina* or Old Latin) had been based. The particular text which Rufinus revised was one which combined two Old Latin traditions, a European tradition (D-type text) and an Italian tradition (I-type text); a form of it stands behind the text of the Book of Armagh. The earliest traces of the I-type text may be found in Novatian, but it emerged most clearly around the middle of the fourth century in Marius Victorinus. Thereafter evidence of it may be found elsewhere in Italy, Illyria, Gaul, and Spain; its witnesses include Ambrosiaster, Ambrose, and Rufinus of Aquileia. This I-type text originally derived from an older African one (K-type text) first attested in the writings of Cyprian and pseudo-Cyprian. Extensive remains of this tradition are found in the writings of the Donatists, Augustine, and other African writers, as well as in Gaul, Ireland, Spain, and Italy. It and the D-type text share a Latin ancestor for the thirteen epistles

[39] See pp. 18–24 below.

[40] The following summary of the Old Latin text types and their relation to the Vulgate relies upon Fischer, 'Das Neue Testament in lateinischer Sprache', 24–6; cf. Frede, *Vetus Latina*, xxiv. 1. 29*–38*; Bammel, *Römerbrieftext*, 142–3.

[41] Fischer, 'Das Neue Testament in lateinischer Sprache', 25, 73.

commonly attributed to Paul, though the K-type text seems the more
primitive of the two. Hebrews alone is excepted; it was not regarded as
canonical in Africa well on into the fourth century, and consequently
the ancestor to the Latin version of Hebrews is to be found sooner in
Italy than in Africa.

Pelagius's Pauline text corresponds largely to the Vulgate, but
includes certain variants of the I-type text. It has been the subject of
considerable debate in this century. The correspondence of the text in
the Karlsruhe manuscripts, one of the principal witnesses of Pelagius's commentary, to the Vulgate is such that, after Alexander
Souter first noted it in the course of preparing his edition of the commentary,[42] it was suggested that Pelagius was the author of the Vulgate.[43] This proposal provoked a flurry of papers, including a
reconsideration from Souter.[44] Another manuscript, the Balliol manuscript, had come to Souter's attention, in which the text of the comments matched that of the Karlsruhe manuscript, but whose biblical
text had more affinity to the Old Latin I-type text.[45] Because the biblical text of the Balliol manuscript had more ancient corroboration than
that of the Karlsruhe manuscript, Souter followed it in his edition and
accordingly abandoned the view that Pelagius had commented on the
Vulgate.[46] When his edition appeared, however, critics pointed out
that the comments themselves support the biblical text of the Karlsruhe manuscript.[47] The more recent studies of Hermann Frede have
confirmed this observation with greater technical accuracy, but have
not ended the debate on the precise relation of the biblical text of the
Karlsruhe manuscript to the Vulgate.[48] Do the I-type readings which
are still present in the Karlsruhe text indicate that Pelagius's text was a
close precursor to the Vulgate but not yet the Vulgate,[49] or should they

---

[42] Souter, 'The Commentary of Pelagius on the Epistles of Paul', 425–6.

[43] De Bruyne, 'Étude sur les origines de notre texte latin de saint Paul'.

[44] Arguing particularly against Pelagius as author of the Vulgate were Buonaiuti,
'Pelagius and the Pauline Vulgate'; Mangenot, 'Saint Jérôme ou Pélage'; Chapman,
'Pélage et le texte de s. Paul'; for other aspects of the debate see Metzger, *Early Versions*,
357–8. The hypothesis was revived by Plinval, 'Précisions sur l'authenticité d'un
prologue', but again refuted by Frede, *Vetus Latina*, xxiv. 2. 303–4.

[45] Souter, 'Pelagius and the Pauline Text in the Book of Armagh'; 'The Character
and History of Pelagius' Commentary on the Epistles of St Paul'; cf. *Expositions*,
i. 155–8.

[46] Souter, *Expositions*, i. 343.

[47] Vogels, 'Der Pelagiuskommentar', 124–5; De Bruyne, *BALCL* 1 (1921–8), No. 589
(p. 243).

[48] Frede, *Pelagius*, 9–58; see the appendix below.

[49] Frede, *Palagius*, 43–7; *Vetus Latina*, xxiv. 1. 36*–37*, xxiv. 2. 40–2.

be regarded as occasional reversions from the new Vulgate text to its more familiar Old Latin predecessor?[50] The latter view seems preferable. As Frede has argued, the Vulgate is too homogeneous and systematic a revision to have been produced by gradual modification of the Old Latin, and the number of Old Latin readings found in Pelagius's text is no greater than the number introduced into manuscripts of the Vulgate.[51]

The text of the epistles in these various biblical manuscripts of the fourth century was commonly prefaced by prologues both to the Pauline corpus as a whole and to individual epistles. Three prologues, or sets of prologues, were known in Rome before or at the time Pelagius wrote his commentary. The oldest are the so-called Marcionite prologues, a series on all the epistles except Hebrews, named because of their attribution to Marcion—an attribution which is still disputed.[52] These prologues appeared in an edition of the Scriptures in I-type text, and were used by Marius Victorinus and Ambrosiaster.[53] They are the ancestor of a second set of prologues which was prepared for an edition of the Scriptures that appeared in north Italy or Rome after Ambrosiaster but before the Vulgate.[54] Pelagius consulted them for at least his commentaries on Ephesians, Philippians, and 1 Timothy.[55] Finally, there is a prologue *Primum quaeritur* which was prepared by the author of the Vulgate as a general preface to the Pauline corpus.[56] It was used by Pelagius in a second recension, wherein the sequence of the epistles in the prologue was altered to match their sequence in Pelagius's commentary.[57] A fourth prologue which has traditionally prefaced Pelagius's commentary on Romans was, according to Frede, in fact not by Pelagius, but rather attached to his commentary early on in its transmission.[58]

All these various currents—the concise literal style which was grounded in Latin rhetorical training and corresponded to Antiochene approaches, the theological perspective derived from Origen,

---

[50] Schäfer, 'Der Paulustext des Pelagius', 458–9; Tinnefeld, *Untersuchungen*, 107; Nellessen, *Untersuchungen*, 253; cf. De Bruyne, *BALCL* 1 (1921–8), No. 115 (p. 58).

[51] Frede, *Vetus Latina*, xxiv. 1. 36*, xxiv. 2. 41.

[52] Ibid. xxv. 1. 108–9; see esp. p. 109 n. 1 for the literature on the origin of the prologues.

[53] Erdt, *Marius Victorinus Afer*, 198–208.

[54] Frede, *Vetus Latina*, xxv. 1. 109–11.

[55] Ibid. 109, 110 n. 6.

[56] Ibid. 99–101.

[57] Ibid. 100; cf. Souter, *Expositions*, ii. 3–5, for the second recension.

[58] Frede, *Vetus Latina*, xxv. 1. 101; cf. Souter, *Expositions*, ii. 6–7.

the weight of the Latin tradition of North Africa, the older Italian version and the new Vulgate version of the epistles, and the lineaments of interpretation put forward by the prologues to these versions—flowed into the stream of Pauline commentaries at Rome and into the work of Pelagius. Pelagius manages them, as one might expect, both inadvertently and deliberately, depending on the issues which preoccupy him as he explicates the text. A number of these may be discerned both from his comments and from what we know generally about the church in Rome at the beginning of the fifth century.

Controversies in Rome

Pelagius was active in Rome during the last two decades of the fourth century and the first decade of the fifth. We know little of his life prior to his arrival in Rome in the early 380s.[59] It is now agreed that he was born in west Britain around the middle of the fourth century.[60] His writings show the benefit of a good education.[61] On the basis of a disputed characterization in a letter by Jerome some have held that he studied law before turning to the church.[62] He was not ordained, but was known for his asceticism, which was moderate: he followed a discipline which did not oblige him to withdraw entirely from the life of the church and the city.[63] The Pauline commentary dates from his

[59] On Pelagius's early life see Souter, *Expositions*, i. 1–5; Plinval, *Pélage*, 47–71; Myres, 'Pelagius', 21–2; Ferguson, *Pelagius*, 39–45. For a review of the evidence see now Rees, *Pelagius*, pp. xii–xiv.

[60] On the question of Pelagius's origin see now Hanson, *Saint Patrick*, 35–8; cf. Zimmer, *Pelagius in Irland*, 18–21; Bury, 'The Origins of Pelagius'; Williams, *Christianity in Early Britain*, 200–3.

[61] Souter, *Expositions*, i. 3–4; Plinval, *Pélage*, 61–3, 72–4.

[62] Jer. *Ep.* 50. 2 (CSEL 54: 389. 18–390. 6). The identity of the unnamed monk in this letter is disputed; for the arguments in favour of identifying him as Pelagius see Plinval, *Pélage*, 50–6, 65–8, and Evans, *Inquiries and Reappraisals*, 31–7; and against, Duval, 'Pélage est-il le censeur inconnu?' For a summary of the debate, inclining to the side of Plinval and Evans, see Rees, *Pelagius*, 4–5.

[63] The testimony about Pelagius's status is varied and apparently conflicting. For two recent reviews of the evidence and the literature see Hanson, *Saint Patrick*, 144–5, and Rees, *Pelagius*, p. xiv. Orosius, *Lib. apol.* 4 (CSEL 5: 607. 23–4), and Zosimus, *Ep.* 46. 6 (CSEL 35: 104. 20), refer to him as *laicus*. Augustine, *Pecc. merit.* 3. 1. 1 (CSEL 60: 129. 7), remarks on his exemplary life, and later, in *De gest. Pel.* 36 (CSEL 42: 92. 12) and *De haer.* 88 (CCSL 46: 340), refers to him as *monachus*; likewise Marius Mercator, *Lib. sub.*, praef. 2 (PL 48: 111A 10–11). Pelagius himself, however, nowhere describes himself as *monachus*, a term which, if he is the author of *De diuina lege*, he reserved for those who withdrew in solitude: 'Ego te Christianum uolo esse, non monachum dici, et uirtutem propriae laudis possidere magis quam nomen alienum. Quod frustra a Latinis in turba

last years in Rome. He began it some time after 405 or 406 and completed it before 410, when at the approach of Alaric's army he joined the exodus from the city.[64] Alaric's attack may have brought the work to an abrupt end, preventing Pelagius from commenting on Hebrews, a book he regarded as Pauline but did not include in his commentary.[65]

The Pauline commentary probably grew out of Pelagius's work as a teacher to the Christian aristocracy at Rome.[66] Relations of this kind, whereby the aristocracy took mentors to guide them in theological understanding and spiritual discipline, were not uncommon in the last decades of the fourth century.[67] Jerome's long association with Marcella and Paula comes immediately to mind, as well as Rufinus of Aquileia's friendship with Melania the Elder and her relatives, and Priscillian's association with Euchrotia in Gaul.[68] It was a time when, having at long last decided for the Christian faith, these noble converts

commorantibus imponitur, cum a Graecis solitarie uiuentibus legitime deputetur' (*De diu. leg.* 9, PL 30: 115C 11–15). Nevertheless, from the same passage it is evident, as ps.-Firm. Mat. *Consult.* 3 (FP 39: 101. 20–36) observes, that the term *monachus* did not for Latin writers refer only to hermits, but included those who, while leading a chaste life, were not otherwise distinct from other Christians. It appears, in fact, that *monachus* originally meant 'unmarried'; only later was its meaning narrowed to refer to anchorites, then subsequently widened to include coenobites: see *RB 1980*, app. 1, 'Monastic Terminology: Monk, Celibate, Nun', 310–17. The conclusion of Hanson, *Saint Patrick*, 145, then, is surely right: 'It seems entirely probable that, while Pelagius joined no monastic community, he did adopt a monastic or ascetic kind of regimen in his own life, at a time when in the West the distinction between this kind of individual, unorganized, monasticism had not yet become clearly defined.'

[64] Souter, *Expositions*, i. 4–5, 188–9; Bammel, 'Last Ten Years', 403–6, dates Rufinus's translation of Origen's commentary on Romans, the *terminus a quo* for Pelagius's commentary, around 405–6.

[65] The prologue *Primum quaeritur*, which was attached to Pelagius's commentary in a slightly altered form, argued for the Pauline authorship of Hebrews, and Pelagius himself attributes the epistle to Paul in his comments (see e.g. *Rom.* 6: 9). Nevertheless, Pelagius did not comment on the epistle—a puzzling lacuna, as Frede, *Vetus Latina*, xxv. 2. 1019, observes. Opinion on Hebrews in the west, where Pauline authorship had long been contested, was beginning to change in the latter half of the 4th cent. The anonymous commentary was, in fact, the first to include comments on Hebrews. Pelagius himself cited Hebrews often, but, despite the precedent set by the anonymous commentary, he did not comment on the epistle. Frede suggests that perhaps Alaric's descent on Rome aborted this final section of the commentary, or that the older western tradition against Pauline authorship was still strong enough to prevent Pelagius from finishing with a commentary on the epistle.

[66] See Jer. *Ep.* 50. 3 (CSEL 54: 390. 17–19); but cf. n. 62 above.

[67] Brown, 'Pelagius and his Supporters', 97.

[68] On Jerome see Kelly, *Jerome*, 91–103. On Rufinus see Brown, 'The Patrons of Pelagius', 57–8; Bammel, 'Last Ten Years', 378–82. On Priscillian see Chadwick, *Priscillian*, 36–7.

were in search of a way of life to express their commitment.[69] They joined in small circles devoted to the study of Scripture and to prayer, and when they encountered obscure passages in the Scriptures they sought explanation from the experts. Thus Jerome and Rufinus of Aquileia received a steady flow of letters requesting clarification of some difficulty or other, or urging them to provide commentaries on entire books.[70]

The degree of asceticism of these circles, and relations between their adherents and the larger church, varied. For most Christians, both clergy and laity, the regime advocated by zealots was too severe.[71] Even those who approved of asceticism in general were disturbed by extreme manifestations, while those who remained unconvinced of the need for ascetic discipline found the new movement offensive. A notable skirmish occurred in 383, when a certain Helvidius responded to a tract in which the monk Carterius, arguing from the conviction that Mary remained a virgin after the birth of Jesus, asserted the superiority of virginity over marriage.[72] Appealing to evidence in the Gospels, Helvidius argued that after the birth of Jesus Mary had regular marital relations with Joseph and bore children fathered by him, and therefore could not be held up as the paradigm of virginity alone. The view and its implications were scandalous to Jerome, whose reply reveals more about his convictions concerning virginity than it does about the kindred of Jesus.[73] In the next few years Jerome, cultivating his version of asceticism in the company of Marcella and Paula, grew ever more shrill in denouncing those who continued regular habits in food, dress, and conversation. His satires of clergy and laity won him few friends.[74] After the death of Blesilla, who had undertaken a regime of severe mortification at Jerome's direction, the undercurrent of anger swelled into the open.[75] Within months of the

[69] Brown, 'Pelagius and his Supporters', 95–8.

[70] Kelly, *Jerome*, 94–5, 145, 212–13, 220–2, 290–1; Bammel, 'Last Ten Years', 413–14.

[71] For what follows see Coyle, *Augustine's 'De moribus ecclesiae catholicae'*, 224–36; Kelly, *Jerome*, 104–15.

[72] Not much is known about Helvidius; for a discussion of his background, his pamphlet against Carterius, and his audience see Jouassard, 'La personnalité d'Helvidius', 139–56.

[73] Jer. *Heluid.* 2 (PL 23: 194A 3–B 2). Jerome asserts that Mary remained a virgin before and after Jesus's birth, but not, interestingly, while giving birth to Jesus; see *Heluid.* 18 (PL 23: 202B 5–8). The latter was not yet an issue for him, nor was it one, apparently, for Carterius, who argued only for Mary's virginity *post partum*. Cf. Neumann, *The Virgin Mary*, 146–8.

[74] Wiesen, *St. Jerome as a Satirist*, 68–74.

[75] Jer. *Ep.* 39. 6 (CSEL 54: 306. 7–14).

death of his patron Damasus, Jerome had little choice but to leave the city.

Jerome's departure may have relieved, but did not eliminate, tension over the rise of asceticism in the church. A decade later there was another eruption. It was occasioned by the views of Jovinian, a monk who acknowledged the value of asceticism, but resisted the tendency of its advocates to depreciate the ordinary way of life of most Christians.[76] The distinctions which Jovinian tried to introduce into the debate about asceticism were not well received, however, and once again Jerome was called on to reply.[77] But Jerome's rebuttal was so violent and extreme, particularly in its description of marriage, that even his partisans were appalled. They tried, without success, to withdraw the tract from circulation. Again there was an outburst of feeling against Jerome and his ascetic ideology.

It may be that Pelagius was among Jerome's critics.[78] If so, he probably steered a middle course between the two parties of the debate.[79] Certainly this is his approach later, when he discusses the question of abstaining from meat in his commentary on Romans.[80] There he begins by advising that neither party in the dispute should pass judgement on the other, because the law does not explicitly enjoin abstinence. He also allows that some may have good reason not to abstain.[81] But eventually he reveals his preference for restraint in the use of meat and wine, countering those who deny the value of such restraint altogether (the most notorious of these being Jovinian).[82] In short, he advocates a moderate asceticism not unlike that commended by Augustine in an early tract against the Manichaeans, eschewing the extremes represented by Jerome and Jovinian.[83]

Throughout the controversy over asceticism the spectre of Manichaeism hovered close at hand. Jerome noted that to Jovinian certain

---

[76] For a general account see Kelly, *Jerome*, 180–9.

[77] For two recent interpretations see Hunter, 'Resistance to the Virginal Ideal', 50–61, and Markus, *The End of Ancient Christianity*, 38–40, 75–6.

[78] If, that is, Pelagius is the unnamed monk of Jerome's *Ep.* 50; see n. 62 above.

[79] Jer. *Ep.* 50. 2, 5 (CSEL 54: 390. 6–11, 394. 12–15); cf. Hunter, 'Resistance to the Virginal Ideal', 62.

[80] See pp. 51–2 below.

[81] See *Rom.* 14: 1.

[82] See *Rom.* 14: 15–19; cf., on the gluttony of the Jovinianists, *Phil.* 3: 18 (Souter, *Expositions*, ii. 409. 10–12). For other references to Jovinian or the Jovinianists in Pelagius's commentary see *1 Cor.* 3: 8 (denial of distinctions in future rewards), *2 Cor.* 9: 6 (*idem*), *1 Thess.* 2: 3 (disregard for chastity) (Souter, *Expositions*, ii. 142. 11–12, 281. 12–13, 421. 3–4).

[83] *De mor.* 1. 33. 71–3 (PL 32: 1340–1).

ascetics appeared to be 'followers of the Manichaeans', for they, like the Manichaeans, forbade marriage and rejected food. This opinion was sufficiently compelling for Jerome to feel it necessary to respond that he, unlike those *de facto* Manichaeans, did not disparage marriage.[84] It was no light matter to be accused of Manichaeism. The church in the west was taking an increasingly active part in suppressing Manichaeans, particularly those who passed themselves off as Christians.[85] The potency of the charge is clear from the fate of Priscillian. Suspect on account of his habits and teachings, and disliked for his following and influence, Priscillian was eventually brought to trial before the emperor Maximus on charges that included Manichaeism.[86] Though he denied the accusation, it remained with him long after his execution.[87] There were, admittedly, other factors involved in his condemnation, but his fate nevertheless highlights the considerable animus and anxiety surrounding Manichaeism in the minds of leaders and writers in the church.

The contest between the two groups was not merely doctrinal. For those in search of friendship and direction, the Manichaean cell provided a hospitable and distinctive community.[88] About the time that Pelagius arrived in Rome, the emperor Theodosius issued a number of edicts which deprived Manichaeans of legal rights of testation and left them vulnerable to anonymous accusation.[89] Yet despite this official condemnation there were still Manichaeans among the Roman aristocracy. Augustine tells of a wealthy and learned Manichaean Hearer, Constantius, who tried unsuccessfully to gather a company of the Elect in his home in the 380s.[90] Augustine was himself taken in by a Manichaean (perhaps this same Constantius) upon his arrival in Rome.[91] He also reports later, after renouncing Manichaeism, that weak and unwary Catholics were from time to time drawn into Manichaean circles.[92] Indeed, the appeal of Manichaeism was

[84] Jer. *Iouin.* 1. 3, 5 (PL 23: 213A 4–9, 217C 5–8).

[85] Brown, 'The Diffusion of Manichaeism in the Roman Empire'; Lieu, *Manichaeism*, 161–4.

[86] Chadwick, *Priscillian*, 20–56, 111–48.

[87] On Priscillian's disavowal of Manichaeism see ibid. 96–8. For a brief account of Priscillian's reputation after his execution, with a shift in emphasis in the estimate of his heresy, see Chadwick, 'Priscillien', 2355–8.

[88] Lieu, *Manichaeism*, 133–8.

[89] Ibid. 111–14.

[90] Aug. *De mor.* 2. 20. 74 (PL 32: 1376. 22–1377. 20).

[91] *Conf.* 5. 18–19 (CCSL 27: 67–8); cf. Lieu, *Manichaeism*, 137–8.

[92] *De mor.* 1. 34. 75, 35. 80 (PL 32: 1342. 21–3, 1344. 44–7).

sufficiently threatening to the Catholic church in Rome to occasion a reaction in the last decades of the fourth century and the first decades of the fifth.[93]

In practice there was little to distinguish the ascetic Manichaean from the ascetic Christian.[94] Both were noted for their chastity, their abstinence from wine and meat, their avoidance of the baths. Even in their teachings there were superficial similarities. Manichaeans argued that in fulfilling the injunctions of the Gospels they were in fact the authentic disciples of Christ,[95] while, as we have already seen, some Christians suspected that Catholic ascetics actually held Manichaean views. But officially Manichaeans and Christians diverged on the doctrines which undergirded their practices. Manichaeans regarded the body as a prison for all but the Elect, who could hope for release from material existence by way of their ascetic discipline.[96] Christians, on the other hand, affirmed the goodness of physical creation in general and of the body in particular. Their ascetic programme envisaged not the end of corporeal existence, but rather the extirpation of the passions which obscured the vision of God. The line between the two approaches was at times a fine one: the spirituality of Origen, for example, might seem practically to eliminate it.[97] But it was a line which Catholics drew with increasing emphasis towards the end of the fourth century, discarding in the course of the polemic earlier views of the body which hindered the demarcation of Christian doctrine over against Manichaean teaching.

The conflict with the Manichaeans may, in fact, have contributed to the 'renaissance' of Pauline studies in the latter half of the fourth century. In the first two centuries of the Christian era Paul was recognized as the missionary to the Gentiles, the founder of churches, and the combatant against heresy, but a full appreciation of his theology was precluded by a heavy emphasis on morality in early Christian writings.[98] In response to Marcion's peculiar use of Paul, however, Catholic writers came to see that it was not adequate merely to cite Paul as an authority, but that it was necessary also to interpret his

---

[93] *Lib. pont.* 50. 3, 51. 2 (Duchesne i. 216, 218); cf. Lieu, *Manichaeism*, 165; Pietri, *Roma Christiana*, ii. 913–14, esp. p. 913 n. 7.

[94] Lieu, *Manichaeism*, 143–9.

[95] Aug. *Faust.* 5. 1 (CSEL 25: 271. 8–272. 7).

[96] Lieu, *Manichaeism*, 5–24, esp. pp. 18–21; cf. Coyle, *Augustine's 'De moribus ecclesiae catholicae'*, 194–201.

[97] Brown, *The Body and Society*, 160–77.

[98] Lindemann, *Paulus im ältesten Christentum*, 112–13, 401–2.

meaning.[99] Likewise, frequent recourse to Paul's letters among Manichaeans obliged Catholic apologists to argue for what they held to be the right understanding of Paul's thought.[100] Thus, attention was given to Paul's letters as a whole, and the commentary became a means to set forth an interpretation of Paul's theology which precluded the errors of, among others, the Manichaeans.

An anti-Manichaean thrust is apparent in the Pauline commentary by Ambrosiaster, as well as in his collection of various theological and exegetical *quaestiones*.[101] It is even more marked in Pelagius's commentary. Again and again in the comments on Romans Pelagius contradicts the Manichaean interpretation of 'the flesh' because of the determinism it entails.[102] In fact, Pelagius appears to have developed his theological tenets precisely to counter Manichaean (or virtually Manichaean) notions of creation, sin, redemption, and beatitude.[103] The goodness of creation, the capacity of all human beings to choose between good and evil, the endurance of that capacity despite the accumulation of sinful habits, the accounting for that capacity in God's plan of salvation—these are basic to Pelagius's understanding of human destiny, and in his stark formulation they are rid of any shadows which to his mind blur the contrast between Manichaean determinism and Christian freedom.

If a moderate asceticism was the ethos of Pelagius's exegetical reflections, and if Manichaean determinism was the foil for his sense of human freedom and responsibility, then the older Christian tradition concerning the freedom of the will provided him with the substance of his theology. The assertion of human freedom, and particularly of the freedom of the will, was common in theological writing of the second and third centuries, when Christian writers

---

[99] Lindemann, *Paulus im ältesten Christentum*, 378–95.

[100] Mutzenbecher, CCSL 44: xv–xvi; for the literature on the Manichaean appropriation of Paul see p. xvi n. 1. Decret, *Aspects du manichéisme*, 169–74, shows that letters of Paul figure prominently in Augustine's debates with Manichaeans at the end of the 4th cent.

[101] *1 Cor.* 1: 2. 2 and 6: 20, *Gal.* 1: 1. 2, *Phil.* 1: 1. 1, *1 Tim.* 4: 1–5. 1, *2 Tim.* 3: 6–7. 1–2 and esp. 4: 3–4. 1–3, *Tit.* 3: 9. 2 (CSEL 81. 2: 6. 5–6, 69. 23–71. 2; CSEL 81. 3: 5. 21–7. 3, 130. 5–6, 272. 10–21, 312. 4–24, 315. 22–316. 10, 333. 9–11); *Quaest.* 3. 1, 76. 1, 127. 18 (CSEL 50: 21. 21–5, 129. 17–21, 406. 23–407. 9); cf. Mundle, *Die Exegese der paulinischen Briefe*, 72; Bohlin, *Die Theologie des Pelagius*, 58–60.

[102] See *Rom.* 5: 10, 6: 19, 7: 15, 7: 17, 7: 18, 8: 3, 8: 7, and 8: 8. At *Rom.* 1: 2, 7: 7, and 9: 5 Pelagius also contests the Manichaean disjunction between the Jewish and Christian eras in Scripture.

[103] Bohlin, *Die Theologie des Pelagius*, 12–14 and *passim*.

encountered a variety of deterministic world-views.[104] The tradition persisted well into the fourth century. The principal writers Pelagius consulted in preparing his commentary—Ambrosiaster, the early Augustine, the anonymous commentator, Origen–Rufinus—all regarded the freedom of the will as a given of theological anthropology.[105] Attention has been drawn in particular to Augustine's discussion of the nature and exercise of the will in *On the Freedom of the Will*, and to the larger echoes of Origen's theology as conveyed in Rufinus's translation of the commentary on Romans.[106] The latter affinity, even if shorn of Origen's original subtlety,[107] is significant, for it came at a time when the older tradition concerning human freedom, and particularly Origen's contribution to that tradition, was under reconsideration. It came during the Origenist controversy and the traducianist debate at Rome.

Rome was a secondary theatre for the Origenist controversy.[108] The main battles were in the east, between Epiphanius of Salamis and John of Jerusalem, and later between Theophilus of Alexandria and the monks of Nitria. But appeals from the disputants to the bishop of Rome, and the involvement of Jerome and Rufinus of Aquileia, each of whom had their allies in Rome, carried the debate to the west. The issues at Rome were complex. Ostensibly the debate was about certain teachings of Origen—the subordination of Son and Spirit in the Trinity, the fall of souls, the nature of the resurrected body, the universality of salvation[109]—and about Rufinus of Aquileia's translation of the chief source of these errors, the treatise *On First Principles*. But the polemic so aroused old rivalries and nagging grievances between Rufinus and Jerome and their supporters that when the focus of the debate shifted from the errors of Origen—all agreeing that on certain points Origen was not to be followed—to the condemnation of Chrysostom, the old parties nevertheless remained intact.[110] Each in turn enjoyed the favour of the pope, first Jerome's party under Anastasius, then Rufinus's under Innocent.

[104] Pelikan, *The Christian Tradition*, i. 280–4.

[105] Bohlin, *Die Theologie des Pelagius*, 47–53, 58–9, 89–90; Frede, *Ein neuer Paulustext*, i. 225.

[106] Bohlin, *Die Theologie des Pelagius*, 47–53, 87–103, 106–8; cf. Bammel, *Römerbrieftext*, 45–6. Bohlin does not discriminate between Augustine's position in the first book of *Lib. arb.* (388 CE) and the remaining two books (*c.* 391–5 CE). See n. 136 below.

[107] See the Introduction at n. 149 and ff.

[108] On the Origenist controversy see Kelly, *Jerome*, 195–209, 227–63; Lardet, 'Introduction', 1*–75*.

[109] Jer. *Ioan.* 7 (PL 23: 376B 1–377A 2).　　[110] Bammel, 'Last Ten Years', 373–8.

Pelagius had links with members of both parties. He shared with Rufinus of Aquileia a number of connections among the Roman aristocracy,[111] and clearly did not scruple to avail himself of Rufinus's translations of Origen's writings.[112] On the other hand, he was also acquainted with Rufinus of Syria, who, having been sent west by Jerome, enjoyed the hospitality of Pammachius, Jerome's principal defender in Rome, and reiterated Jerome's vehement anti-Origenism in his tract *On the Faith*.[113] Apparently, Pelagius was comfortable with denouncing the errors of Origen without proscribing his works altogether.[114] For Pelagius, as for Rufinus of Aquileia, Origen's works were still helpful in answering troublesome questions about divine providence and human freedom.[115] And though Pelagius associated with Rufinus of Syria in Rome, the connection did not necessarily extend to Jerome in Palestine or to Jerome's party in Rome.[116] In fact, when Pelagius later sparred with Jerome in Palestine, he recalled the arguments of Jerome's opponents in Rome during the Origenist controversy, reviving, as had Rufinus of Aquileia, the spectre of Origenism in Jerome's own early writings.[117]

A spin-off of the Origenist controversy in Rome was a debate about the origin of the soul and the consequences of the fall. After Origen's notion of the pre-existent fall of the soul had been rejected, there remained a number of alternatives. Rufinus of Aquileia, having retreated a safe distance from the unfriendly Anastasius, confessed to be undecided as to the three opinions current in Rome—as to whether the soul is conveyed by human seed along with the body, created by God when the body is being formed in the womb, or created by God in the beginning and bestowed when the body is being formed.[118] But others in Rome drew the lines rather more sharply, among them Rufinus of Syria and his follower Caelestius. For Rufinus of Syria

[111] Brown, 'The Patrons of Pelagius', 59–61.

[112] We know that, in addition to the translation of Origen's commentary on Romans, Pelagius used Rufinus's translation of the *Sentences of Sextus*; see Evans, *Pelagius*, 48–65; cf. Pel. *Rom.* 1: 27 n. 49. Pelagius probably read Rufinus's translation of *On First Principles*, whose view of the human capacity for good and evil resembled his own; cf. *Princ.* 3. 20 (19) (GCS 22: 235. 20–4). He may also have had recourse to Rufinus's translation of the *Dialogue of Adamantius*, which Rufinus erroneously attributed to Origen; cf. Pel. *Rom.* 1: 16 n. 24 and Bammel, 'Last Ten Years', 391 n. 2.

[113] Bonner, *Augustine and Modern Research*, 19–31.

[114] Pel. *Rom.* 11: 8 n. 9.

[115] Bammel, 'Last Ten Years', 423–4.

[116] See Brown, 'The Patrons of Pelagius', 67–9.

[117] Evans, *Pelagius*, 6–25.

[118] *Ad Anast.* 6 (CCSL 20: 27. 1–19); cf. Aug. *Lib. arb.* 3. 21. 59 (CCSL 29: 309. 1–310. 9).

there remained only two options: the view that the soul is created and endowed some time between conception and birth, and the view that the soul is passed on from parent to child (traducianism). The third option, that the soul is created in advance, he regarded as an error of Origen, to be dismissed summarily.[119] The traducianist view exercised him most.

What Rufinus of Syria objected to in the traducianist view was the notion of hereditary sin associated with it: the belief that the whole human race inherits the sin of the first human beings, and that on account of this inherited sin unbaptized infants are damned. To him it was a contradiction of the justice and omnipotence of God, and of the free will and accountability of each human being, to assert that because of the sin of Adam and Eve all people are guilty of sin.[120] He held that the fall did not so vitiate human nature that people are unable not to sin, and cited evidence from Scripture that after the fall Adam and Eve and others in fact did not sin.[121] The common human condition of physical mortality is indeed a result of the fall; the bodies of Adam and Eve, created mortal, would not have died had they obeyed the command of God.[122] But it is not a punishment for sin, since it is visited even on the righteous. Rather it is a means to restrain evil and eventually to release one from the struggle with evil in this life.[123] Furthermore, since even baptized infants, who presumably have been cleansed of Adam's sin, die, it is manifest that they do not die because of Adam's sin and that baptism is not a remedy for Adam's sin.[124] Infants are baptized not because of sins, but so that they may undergo a spiritual birth in Christ and share in the reign of his kingdom.[125]

The origins of the traducianist view, and Augustine's particular contribution to its development and dissemination, has been a matter of considerable discussion.[126] A recent study has argued that the idea of a hereditary guilt conveyed by physical generation had its origins in Jewish and Christian Encratism, which deeply influenced African theology from the second century onward, in contrast to the east,

[119] *Lib. fid.* 27 (Miller 88. 8–90. 11).
[120] Ibid. 37, 39 (Miller 110. 5–10, 112. 6–15).
[121] Ibid. 39 (Miller 112. 17–33).
[122] Ibid. 29 (Miller 94. 6–10).
[123] Ibid. 32–4 (Miller 100. 1–104. 13).
[124] Ibid. 40 (Miller 114. 9–13).
[125] Ibid. (Miller 114. 23–9).
[126] For reviews of the literature see Beatrice, *Tradux peccati*, 29–38, and Rigby, *Original Sin in Augustine's* Confessions, 7–14.

where the idea was explicitly rejected or at least significantly qualified.[127] Rufinus of Syria's opposition to traducianism, then, may well represent a general critique of the idea in the east, which Rufinus drew from to counter the more prevalent acceptance of the idea that he found in the west.[128] But it is difficult to go beyond the evidence of a general clash of theological cultures to ascertain a particular occasion for Rufinus's outburst. A tangential reference to *tradux peccati* in Augustine's reply to some questions from Simplician of Milan about Romans has been tantalizing, since Pelagius, when he summarizes the arguments against the traducianists, echoes Augustine's phrase.[129] However, this aspect of Augustine's answer to Simplician does not seem to exercise Pelagius most in his commentary on Romans; rather, he, like others at the time, focuses on Augustine's understanding of the relation between divine election and human freedom.[130] Furthermore, the extent to which Augustine's later articulation of the doctrine of original sin informs this admittedly pivotal but nevertheless early formulation of the problem—Augustine wrote it by 397 or early 398—is disputed.[131]

Augustine's reply to Simplician concluded a series of interpretations of Romans in the first decade of Augustine's priesthood, and marked a shift in Augustine's definition of the priority of grace.[132] For the first time Augustine broke altogether with the sense of justice that figured in prior discussions of Romans, and denied that anyone merits the grace of God either by works or by faith.[133] Augustine had come to the priesthood in 392 with a conventional sense of justice, according to which only those who are free to choose for good or ill may be held accountable for their actions, meriting either reward or punish-

---

[127] Beatrice, *Tradux peccati*, 205–303; cf., however, the reviews by Lorenz, *Zeitschrift für Kirchengeschichte*, 91 (1980), 411–12; Bonner, *Journal of Ecclesiastical History*, 32 (1981), 87; and De Simone, 'Modern Research'.

[128] The suggestion is made by Bonner in his review of Beatrice, p. 86.

[129] Cf. Aug. *Ad Simpl.* 1. 2. 20 (CCSL 44: 51. 697–9): 'Tunc facta est una massa omnium ueniens de traduce peccati et de poena mortalitatis, quamuis Deo formante et creante quae bona sunt', and Pel. *Rom.* 5: 15 (Souter, *Expositions*, ii. 46. 25–6): 'hi autem qui contra traducem peccati sunt, ita illum impugnare nituntur'. See also TeSelle, 'Rufinus the Syrian', 79–82.

[130] See Pel. *Rom.* 9: 16 n. 16; cf. Jer. *Ep.* 85. 2 (CSEL 55. 7–10) (from Paulinus of Nola) and *Ep.* 120. 10 (CSEL 55: 500. 7–506. 7) (from Hedybia in Gaul); Anon. *De indur. cord.* 2 (Plinval 139. 1–7). For a discussion of the reaction to Augustine's interpretation see Martinetto, 'Les premières réactions', 106–9; but cf. Nuvolone, 'Problèmes d'une nouvelle édition', 115–16.

[131] TeSelle, 'Rufinus the Syrian', 85–7; Beatrice, *Tradux peccati*, 110–12.

[132] Babcock, 'Augustine's Interpretation of Romans', 55–67.

[133] *Ad Simpl.* 1. 2. 2–7 (CCSL 44: 24. 12–32. 215).

ment.[134] This sense of justice is not unlike that held by Pelagius; indeed, it may have been an aspect of the theology Augustine acquired or at least maintained without question in Italy.[135] He continued to adhere to it when he began to distinguish between the human condition before the fall and after the fall, and acknowledged the complications of ignorance and habit which characterize the latter.[136] Thus in his dispute in 392 with the Manichaean Fortunatus he affirmed that we, like Adam, have freedom of choice, but that as a result of Adam's sin we are plunged into the 'necessity' of habit—not to the point that we lose our capacity for freedom of choice, but rather that we require the grace of God to turn us by illumination and love from our sinful habits.[137] As Augustine studied the epistle to the Romans over the next few years, he continued to protect this notion of freedom of choice. In his *Propositions from the Epistle to the Romans*, written about 394, he observes that divine election would be wholly arbitrary if there were no correlation between divine election and human merit, and accordingly argues that God chooses on the basis of faith, an act of free will whereby the believer is fairly distinguished from the unbeliever.[138] Though Augustine also observes that grace by definition precedes merit, and that God's call precedes the believer's faith,[139] he is nevertheless still prepared to speak of faith as the believer's act, and to regard it as the basis upon which God in foreknowledge chooses the believer.[140] But when Augustine reconsiders the passage once more in order to answer Simplician's questions, there is no mention of election on the basis of foreknowledge of faith, but rather the bold assertion that grace comes before all merits, including the merits of faith.[141] And with this stronger assertion of divine grace comes a new assertion of human sinfulness. For the first time Augustine speaks of *poena originalis peccati* and of *una quaedam massa peccati*—of the whole human race bearing corporately the penalty for the first sin.[142]

[134] See *Lib. arb.* 1. 1. 1, 1. 12. 26 (CCSL 29: 211. 8–23, 228. 52–66).

[135] Cf. Brown, *Augustine of Hippo*, 146–8.

[136] On the change in the human condition as a result of the fall see *Lib. arb.* 3. 18. 52–19. 53 (CCSL 29: 305. 41–306. 22). On freedom of choice as necessary for responsibility (though not sufficient for beatitude) see ibid. 2. 1. 3, 2. 19. 53, 3. 3. 7, 3. 10. 29, 3. 16. 45–6 (CCSL 29: 236. 35–237. 58, 272. 57–75, 279. 61–83, 292. 1–28, 302. 1–303. 46).

[137] *Fort.* 22 (CSEL 25: 103. 24–106. 10); cf. Pel. *Rom.* 7: 15 n. 21.

[138] *Exp. prop.* 52 (60). 8–9 (CSEL 84: 34. 16–21).

[139] Ibid. 14 (CSEL 84: 35. 13–15).

[140] Ibid. 11, 15 (CSEL 84: 34. 24–35. 5, 35. 35–20); cf. *Diu. quaest.* 68. 8 (CCSL 44A: 177. 78–178. 85).

[141] *Ad Simpl.* 1. 2. 7 (CCSL 44: 32. 208–10).

[142] Ibid. 16, 20 (CCSL 44: 41. 467–42. 471, 51. 704–52. 707).

When he explains what these phrases mean, Augustine does not yet speak, as he would in his arguments against the Pelagians over the baptism of infants, of the guilt of original sin which alone renders one liable to damnation.[143] Rather, he refers to the mortality of the flesh (the penalty of the first sin) and the persistence of sinful desire (the penalty of repeated sinning), which together over time render concupiscence invincible,[144] so that the sinful condition of the first human being persists in the whole race—*originali reatu in omnia permanente*.[145] Nevertheless, by the next decade the phrase *tradux peccati* had in Roman circles come to signify the view that all human beings bear the sin of Adam and Eve and are liable to its penalty.[146] From charges brought later at the Council of Carthage it appears that among the associates of Rufinus of Syria Caelestius was especially preoccupied with the question of the consequences of Adam's sin and the status of newborn infants.[147] But others not so closely associated with Rufinus of Syria were concerned as well. In a letter to Jerome written some time after 399 Paulinus of Nola enquired as to how, in the words of 1 Cor. 7: 14, children of believers are 'holy', since, despite their parentage, they must receive and preserve the gift of grace in order to be saved.[148] What was at issue here was not that infants should be baptized; it was rather what the baptism of infants implies about their spiritual condition. Are children sinful from birth and, if so, what is the nature of their sin?

It is instructive to compare Pelagius's answer to this question with the answer of the tradition on which he drew.[149] Ambrosiaster asserted the solidarity of the whole human race with Adam in the fall, inasmuch as everyone is physically descended from Adam, and held that as a result all human beings succumb to physical death, concupiscence, and sin.[150] However, the heaviest penalty for sin, damnation, is

---

[143] See e.g. *Serm.* 294. 5–6 (PL 38: 1338–9). On the development of Augustine's doctrine of original sin see Sage, 'Péché originel' and 'Le péché originel'; but cf. Rigby, *Original Sin*, 7–28.

[144] *Ad Simpl.* 1. 1. 10 (CCSL 44: 15. 172–80); cf. Sage, 'Péché originel', 218–21; Beatrice, *Tradux peccati*, 73–5.

[145] *Ad Simpl.* 1. 2. 20 (CCSL 44: 51. 704–52. 707).

[146] Pel. *Rom.* 5: 15 (Souter, *Expositions*, ii. 46. 25–47. 13).

[147] Wermelinger, *Rom und Pelagius*, 9–18; Bonner, *Augustine and Modern Research*, 35–8; TeSelle, 'Rufinus the Syrian', 73–8.

[148] Jer. *Ep.* 85. 2 (CSEL 55. 11–13); cf. Cavallera, *Jérôme*, i/2. 89.

[149] On what follows see de Bruyn, 'Pelagius's Interpretation of Rom. 5: 12–21'; cf. also Beatrice, *Tradux peccati*, 212–21, and Bammel, 'Adam in Origen', esp. pp. 80–3.

[150] *Rom.* 51: 12. 3 (CSEL 81. 1: 165. 11–19); cf. *Rom.* 7: 14. 4–5, 7: 18. 1–2, 7: 22 (CSEL 81. 1: 235. 9–26, 237. 19–239. 6, 241. 18–24). See also Gaudel, 'Péché originel', 368–9.

reserved for deliberate and unrepentant sinners; unbaptized infants are spared such torment.[151] Similarly, in Rufinus of Aquileia's translation of Origen's commentary on Romans Pelagius would have read that all bear the pollution of Adam's sin from birth, a sinful tendency which, along with physical mortality and corruption, is a result of Adam's fall.[152] In addition, all are influenced by the sinful teaching and example of their forebears, which they follow unthinkingly until they arrive at an age of discretion.[153] However, at that point all become responsible for their own actions, so that spiritual death, having entered into all, reigns only in those who of their own choice persist in the way of their forebears.[154] This view is echoed by the anonymous commentator, who, like Origen, asserts that though infants do not, like adults, deliberately transgress the law, they are nevertheless guilty of sins on account of the feebleness of their nature.[155] The habits they develop in their early years subsequently result in spiritual death when they reach the age of reason.[156] A similar view is taken by Jerome in a letter he wrote in 407 in response to questions about Romans 7: 7–25 from a woman in Gaul.[157]

In contrast, when Pelagius discusses the question of the transmission of sin he is silent about those effects of the fall which are conveyed irrespective of choice from one generation to the next—ignorance, weakness, mortality, concupiscence—and he repudiates any notion of the transmission of guilt. He speaks only of the influence of Adam's example followed voluntarily by each generation in succession.[158] He does acknowledge the effect of ignorance and concupiscence when he discusses the problem of habitual sin at Romans 7: 7–25, but then he repeatedly asserts, in a way that is reminiscent of Augustine's discussion of habit in *Against Fortunatus*, that any enslavement to sin originates in a choice which becomes habitual through repetition.[159] Pelagius will not in any way compromise the capacity granted to each person to choose between good and evil, because his notion of justice is based on this capacity. Thus, when treating the question of election

---

[151] *Rom.* 5: 14. 3a, 4b–c (CSEL 81. 1: 173. 11–22); cf. *Quaest.* 47. 4–5 (CSEL 50: 93. 12–15, 94. 7–14).

[152] *Rom.* 5. 1 (PG 14: 1009C 13–1010A 8); 5. 9 (PG 14: 1046B 9–1047C 3).

[153] *Rom.* 5. 2 (PG 14: 1024A 13–C 15).

[154] *Rom.* 5. 1 (PG 14:. 1012C 10–1013A 6, 1016C 3–1017C 4).

[155] *Rom.* 43A, 44A (Frede ii. 39).

[156] *Rom.* 054, 059 (Frede ii. 45–7).

[157] *Ep.* 121. 8 (CSEL 56: 33. 19–34. 4).

[158] See *Rom.* 5: 12–21, and pp. 40–2 below.

[159] See *Rom.* 7: 15, 7: 17, 7: 20, and pp. 43–4 below.

at Romans 8: 28, he invariably predicates election on God's fore-knowledge of the believer's response, resolving the problem of merits by resorting to the solution held by Augustine in his *Propositions from the Epistle to the Romans*.[160]

In short, we have in Pelagius a one-sided appropriation of tradition. With his predilection for a voluntary ascetic discipline, and his animus towards the fatalism of the Manichaeans, Pelagius repudiated any suggestion that sin is an inevitable aspect of human existence. Though he acknowledged that most people do in fact sin, and that it is difficult to achieve perfection, he was convinced that the latter was essentially possible even in this life.[161] For all his moderation with regard to details of ascetic practice, Pelagius, as Peter Brown has observed, was more demanding than those who acknowledged that champions of holiness would always be few in the church.[162] He called each baptized Christian to follow the example of Christ without fail.[163] Even though the pattern is hortatory rather than descriptive, the expectation is great.

The Career of the Commentary

While they were in Rome, Rufinus of Syria, Caelestius, and Pelagius were able to express their views without hindrance, though there are indications that already then they were attracting notice: Pelagius later recalled that about this time he wrote to Paulinus of Nola and to a certain Constantius to affirm the priority of divine grace (as he understood it) in cultivating a good life.[164] However, once the scene shifted from Rome to Carthage, the position of Pelagius and Caelestius was more precarious. In the autumn of 411 Caelestius was summoned before a council in Carthage to answer to a list of

---

[160] See *Rom.* 8: 29–30 and pp. 45–6 below.

[161] See *Rom.* 1: 21, 2: 20, 3: 18, 6: 2, 6: 7.

[162] 'Pelagius and his Supporters', 101–13; and see now Markus, *The End of Ancient Christianity*, 40–3.

[163] See pp. 42–3 below.

[164] Pelagius noted these letters, along with the letter to Demetrias, in his petition to Innocent in 417. All three are cited by Augustine at *De grat. Chr.* 1. 35. 38, 36. 39, 37. 40 (CSEL 42: 154. 8–12, 23–5, 155. 1–4) which Augustine wrote around the middle of 418. The first, to Paulinus of Nola, was written 'about twelve years' earlier and may thus be dated about the time Pelagius began his commentary. The letter to Constantius probably belongs to that period as well, since it is cited after the letter to Paulinus but before the letter to Demetrias, which is distinguished from the preceding letters as having been written while Pelagius was in the east, i.e. some time between 413 and 414. See de Bruyn, 'Constantius the *tractator*', 43–4.

questionable teachings. Opposition to Caelestius was not exclusively African: his accuser was a deacon from Milan.[165] Nevertheless, the African church, whose tradition concerning the transmission of sin and baptismal regeneration had been sharpened in the course of the Donatist controversy, provided a climate in which formal charges could be brought and condemnation secured.[166]

When the views attributed to Caelestius were condemned by the council, he appealed against the judgement to Rome and departed for the east. Pelagius had already left before the council was convened, and eventually settled in Palestine. There he fell foul of Jerome and the Spanish priest Orosius, who, along with the Gallic bishops Heros of Arles and Lazarus of Aix, continued to press the African position against him.[167] The case against him was heard twice by John, Bishop of Jerusalem, in 415—first at a synod in Jerusalem and subsequently at one in Diospolis—and both times Pelagius was acquitted. In the following year, however, councils at Carthage and Milevis reiterated the African judgement against him and Caelestius. The African church also prevailed upon the pope, Innocent I, to excommunicate Pelagius and Caelestius, though not without the pope asserting his prerogative to come to an independent judgement. Pelagius and Caelestius both appealed to the pope to reverse his judgement, Pelagius in writing, Caelestius in person. Innocent's successor, Zosimus, gave them a favourable review at first, but in time succumbed to the pressure of the opposition both in Africa and in Rome. After a violent clash between the opposing parties in Rome in 418, the emperor Honorius published a rescript banishing Pelagius, Caelestius, and their adherents from the city, and Zosimus followed suit by reversing his previous judgement and excommunicating Pelagius and Caelestius.

Of Pelagius's end we know little. He was expelled from Jerusalem, and then from Antioch.[168] It is probable that he sought refuge in Egypt, though some still argue that he returned to Britain.[169] His writings

---

[165] Bonner, 'Les origines africaines', 102, and *Augustine and Modern Research*, 37; but cf. Lorenz, 'Zwölf Jahre Augustinusforschung', 145–6, for the view that the Milanese opposition to Pelagianism derives from Augustine's *Ad Simplicianum*.

[166] Beatrice, *Tradux peccati*, 260–78; Scheffczyk, *Urstand, Fall und Erbsünde*, 89–103.

[167] For the most thorough account of the events in Palestine and Rome see Wermelinger, *Rom und Pelagius*, 29–218; cf. Plinval, *Pélage*, 270–332; Ferguson, *Pelagius*, 72–115; and Rees, *Pelagius*, 1–20.

[168] Mar. Merc. *Comm. super nom. Cael.* (ACO 1. 5. 1: 68. 44–69. 5); cf. Nuvolone, 'Pélage', 2898.

[169] For Egypt see Ferguson, *Pelagius*, 114; Myres, 'Pelagius', 23; Wermelinger, *Rom und Pelagius*, 210; Nuvolone, 'Pélage', 2898; Rees, *Pelagius*, xii n. 13. Eus. Crem. in *Coll.*

suffered the fate that befell the *œuvre* of most heretics. Few works have been preserved intact, and those which are complete were transmitted pseudonymously.[170] The Pauline commentary is one of the latter. It is the largest extant work by Pelagius, and one of the few whose Pelagian authorship is now undisputed. For this reason, and also because it antedates the polemics of the Pelagian controversy, it is a most important document of Pelagius's views.

In the decades following its appearance the commentary circulated among both supporters and opponents of Pelagius. Several anonymous works of Pelagian or semi-Pelagian ethos show an acquaintance with it. The earliest of these is a treatise on the use of wealth, belonging to a collection of works written between 411 and 413 and now attributed to the 'Sicilian Briton'.[171] In addition, two letters from the same half of the century, thought by some to have been written by Pelagius himself, quote the commentary on 1 Corinthians.[172]

The first record of knowledge of the commentary among Pelagius's opponents comes from Augustine. It was brought to his attention in 412, shortly after the council at Carthage.[173] Upon reading the objections to the traducianist understanding of the transmission of sin in the comment at Romans 5: 15—objections which, Augustine cautiously noted, Pelagius cites without giving his own assent— Augustine added a third book to his treatise *On the Merits and the Forgiveness of Sins* in rebuttal.[174] Later, Marius Mercator quoted a more

Auell. 49. 2 (CSEL 35: 114. 5–12) reports that Alexandria alone among eastern sees was still receiving Pelagians into communion after their condemnation by Innocent. For Britain—improbable, in my view—see M. Forthomme Nicholson, 'Celtic Theology', 392–4.

[170] For a bibliography of Pelagius's works see now Nuvolone, 'Pélage', 2899–901. Listings of the authentic works have varied widely, ranging from the generous estimate of Plinval, 'Recherches', 41–2 (cf. id., *Pélage*, 44–5), to the more conservative estimates of Morris, 'Pelagian Literature', and Evans, *Four Letters*, 34–5 (cf. Hanson, *Saint Patrick*, 40–4).

[171] Cf. *De diu.* 11. 6 (Caspari 46. 4–9) and Pel. *Rom.* 16: 23 (Souter, *Expositions*, ii. 125. 14–18). For a review of the discussion of the authorship of this treatise and its companions see Nuvolone, 'Pélage', 2915–17. In addition to the above passage, Evans, *Four Letters*, 25–6, cites looser parallels between Pelagius's commentary and *De diu.* and *De cast.*

[172] Cf. ps.-Hi. *Ep.* 7. 7 (*De diuina lege*) (PL 30: 113A 11–B 4) and Pel. *1 Cor.* 15: 41 (Souter, *Expositions*, ii. 223. 5–8); and ps.-Hi. *Ep.* 13. 7 (*Virginitatis laus*) (PL 30: 168B 5–23) and Pel. *1 Cor.* 7: 34 (Souter, *Expositions*, ii. 169. 5–11). For a summary of the debate regarding the author of these letters see Evans, *Four Letters*, 13–31; cf. Plinval, 'Recherches', 21–2, 26, *Pélage*, 32–42; Morris, 'Pelagian Literature'; Hanson, *Saint Patrick*, 44–6; Frede, *Kirchenschriftsteller* (1981), 371–2; Nuvolone, 'Pélage', 2900–1.

[173] *Pecc. merit.* 3. 1. 1, 3. 2. 2, 3. 3. 5 (CSEL 60: 129. 6–14, 18–22, 132. 2–14).

[174] Ibid. 3. 2. 2, 3. 3. 4 (CSEL 60: 129. 18, 131. 15); cf. Wermelinger, *Rom und Pelagius*, 21–4.

extended portion of the same chapter in a brief prepared for the church in Constantinople, where he resided between 428 and 433.[175] Having been among those in Rome who had urged the pope to condemn Pelagius and Caelestius, he continued to press the case against them in the east, where they had sought refuge.[176]

Pelagius's commentary was also revised twice. The first of these revisions occurred early on, between 412 and 432, and appears to have proceeded in two stages.[177] Within a few years of its appearance, a compilation of Pelagius's commentary and the anonymous Pauline commentary was produced, interleaving comments from both commentaries without any obvious polemical intent.[178] Subsequently this compilation was edited by a Pelagian—perhaps Caelestius[179]—to sharpen the Pelagian perspective of the work. His concerns are particularly evident in comments interpolated at Romans 5: 12–15, where the editor stresses the voluntary character of sin, both in the fall of Adam and Eve and in the spiritual death of their descendants.[180] The interpolations which this Pelagian introduced are preserved in the pseudo-Jerome tradition of Pelagius's commentary.[181] This was the version of the commentary which the author of the treatise *Praedestinatus*, generally believed to have been Arnobius the Younger, cited some time between 432 and 435.[182]

Over a century later the original commentary was revised once again by Cassiodorus and his students. Unaware that Pelagius was the author of the commentary, Cassiodorus reports in his *Institutiones* that the work was widely known and much admired, and was thought to have been written by Pope Gelasius. Upon closer scrutiny, however,

---

[175] *Comm. super nom. Cael.* (ACO 1. 5. 1: 67. 5–68. 9). The version which appears here is a Latin translation of a Greek translation of the original Latin text; cf. Souter, *Expositions*, i. 44.

[176] Wermelinger, 'Marius Mercator', 610–12.

[177] For the following reconstruction see Frede, *Ein neuer Paulustext*, i. 193–6.

[178] Ibid. 196–7.

[179] Souter, *Expositions*, i. 266, considered attributing the work to Caelestius, having rejected Julian of Aeclanum on stylistic grounds. Frede, *Ein neuer Paulustext*, i. 224 and 226, entertained either Caelestius or Julian, but preferred Julian on stylistic grounds. More recently, however, Frede, *Kirchenschriftsteller* (1981), 375, has decided in favour of Caelestius; so also Nuvolone, 'Pélage', 2894.

[180] Frede, *Ein neuer Paulustext*, i. 224–4; cf. de Bruyn, 'Constantius the *tractator*', 48–9.

[181] The interpolations were first presented by Souter as the third part of his edition: *Pseudo-Jerome Interpolations*. They have subsequently been catalogued with greater precision by Frede, *Ein neuer Paulustext*, i. 164–85.

[182] *Praed.* 1. 88 (PL 53: 613C 7–614C 9); cf. also ibid. 3. 2, 14 (PL 53: 634A 3–9, 653D 7–654A 8) and ps.-Hi. *Rom.* 70II, 96 (Frede ii. 51–2, 66). See von Schubert, *Der sogennante Praedestinatus*, 33–6; Souter, *Expositions*, i. 266; Abel, 'Le "Praedestinatus"', 5–6.

the comments seemed to him to be marred by Pelagian errors. Accordingly he set out to revise the commentary, completing the task himself for Romans and leaving the remainder to his less original students.[183] The version thus produced was subsequently attributed to Primasius, and its actual origin in the school of Cassiodorus was recognized only in this century.[184]

From the seventh century to the ninth evidence of the commentary emerges at intervals in Ireland, England, and the Continent.[185] The prominence of the Irish in these circles, particularly in the eighth century, when most of the works which use the commentary are Celtic,[186] led scholars to believe that the Irish were pivotal in the transmission of the commentary. Zimmer introduced the hypothesis in his seminal study *Pelagius in Irland*, relying not only on the Irish sources which used Pelagius, but also on the newly discovered St Gall manuscript of the commentary, Stiftsbibliothek 73. Zimmer believed that this manuscript presented a uniquely Irish transmission of the commentary, clearly distinguished from the continental transmission represented in the pseudo-Jerome and pseudo-Primasius traditions.[187] Zimmer's sharp distinction between these two traditions was challenged by Hellmann, who demonstrated that the St Gall manuscript and the pseudo-Jerome traditions were related.[188] Nevertheless, after comparing pseudo-Jerome, pseudo-Primasius, and the Irish sources which cite Pelagius, Hellmann still held with Zimmer that the route of transmission of the most authentic version of the commentary was by way of the Irish.[189] Bischoff likewise maintained the thesis in his

---

[183] *Inst.* 1. 8. 1 (PL 70: 1119C 4–1120A 2). Shortly before publication of this book D. F. Wright brought to my attention the dissertation of D. W. Johnson, 'Purging the Poison: The Revision of Pelagius' Pauline Commentaries by Cassiodorus and his Students' (Princeton, 1989), which regrettably I was unable to consult.

[184] Turner, 'Pelagius' Commentary'; Souter, 'The Commentary of Pelagius on the Epistles of Paul'; id., *Expositions*, i. 30–1, 318–26.

[185] See Frede, *Kirchenschriftsteller* (1981), 477, and *Vetus Latina*, xxv. 2. 1026, for works which are indebted to Pelagius's commentary, with particular emphasis on continental transmission. For a survey of the use of Pelagius among the Irish see Kelly, 'Pelagius'. On early Anglo-Saxon evidence of the commentary see Dumville, 'Late-Seventh- or Eighth-Century Evidence'. On the *Book of Armagh* and Sedulius Scottus in particular see Souter, *Expositions*, i. 126 and 136–9; Frede, *Pelagius*, 59–105; Nellessen, *Untersuchungen*, 274–6, 288; Thiele, 'Review of Karl Th. Schäfer *et al.*', 366; Nellessen, 'Der lateinische Paulustext'; Thiele, 'Zum lateinischen Paulustext'.

[186] Kelly, 'Pelagius', 108–12; see also Dumville, 'Late-Seventh- or Eighth-Century Evidence', and *Flor. Frising.* (CCSL 108D: vii–xxxix, 139).

[187] *Pelagius in Irland*, 229–30; cf. Souter, *Expositions*, i. 24–30.

[188] *Sedulius Scottus*, 153–8.

[189] Ibid. 159–70.

studies of Hiberno-Latin exegesis.[190] Recently, however, Frede has
contested the hypothesis, noting evidence of the use and transmission
of Pelagius's commentary on the Continent independently of the
Irish.[191] He includes the St Gall manuscript, whose anonymous commentary on Hebrews, a relative of that found in the pseudo-Jerome
tradition, is interpolated with comments from a seventh-century
Merovingian gloss on the Psalms.[192] Frede's observations call for a
reconsideration of the transmission of the commentary, and for
caution in assuming that reference to Pelagius is by itself evidence of
Irish provenance.

From even such a brief review of the transmission of the commentary it will be apparent that the task which Souter faced when he
began his edition was formidable. The credit for organizing the manuscripts into groups as we now know them is largely his. The manuscript witnesses with which he worked included several early
fragments;[193] two relatively complete manuscripts based on fifth- to
sixth-century archetypes (Augiensis CXIX at Karlsruhe (A) and
Balliol College 157 at Oxford (B), the latter reproduced in Merton
College MS 26 (O));[194] the version by Cassiodorus and his students
(Cas);[195] two families of pseudo-Jerome manuscripts (H), the one a
shorter Anglo-Saxon version (H₁),[196] the other a longer Irish version
(H₂);[197] an unusual Paris manuscript, Bibl. Nat. lat. 653 (V);[198] and the
St Gall manuscript, Stiftsbibliothek 73 (G).[199] Several additional wit-
nesses subsequently came to light, two fragments at Göttingen and
Berlin belonging to the shorter pseudo-Jerome family[200] and two
manuscripts at Göttweig and Ivrea belonging to the longer pseudo-
Jerome family.[201]

[190] 'Wendepunkte', 210, 265.
[191] *Vetus Latina*, xxv. 2. 1026.
[192] Ibid. 1023–5.
[193] These are the 6th-cent. interpolation of material from Pelagius into certain MSS
of Ambrosiaster's commentary at *1 Cor.* 15: 44 to *2 Cor.* 1: 5 (Souter, *Expositions*, i. 51–9);
the 7th-cent. Vatican fragment (Mercati, 'Two Leaves of a Sixth-Century MS', 529–35;
Souter, *Expositions*, i. 48–51, 226–8; Lowe, *CLA* 1: 58); and the Freiburg fragments from
an 8th- to 9th-cent. MS (Souter, *Expositions*, i. 229–31; Lowe, *CLA* 8: 1193).
[194] Souter, *Expositions*, i. 34–48, 200–26.
[195] Ibid. 318–26.
[196] Ibid. 268–94; cf. Dumville, 'Late-Seventh- or Eighth-Century Evidence', 40, 52.
[197] Souter, *Expositions*, i. 294–318.
[198] Ibid. 245–64; Lowe, *CLA* 5: 527; Frede, *Vetus Latina*, xxv. 2. 1002–3.
[199] Souter, *Expositions*, i. 232–45; Frede, *Vetus Latina*, xxv. 2. 1022–6.
[200] Lowe, *CLA* 8: 1203 and *CLA* Supplement, 1676; cf. Frede, 'Eine neue Handschrift' and *Ein neuer Paulustext*, i. 246 n. 1.
[201] Souter, *Expositions*, iii, pp. xi–xii; Frede, *Ein neuer Paulustext*, i. 246 n. 1, ii. 10–12.

By comparing the manuscripts with the citations of Pelagius's commentary from Augustine and Marius Mercator, Souter determined that all but the Karlsruhe and Balliol manuscripts were heavily interpolated.[202] This judgement was confirmed by a further comparison of these two manuscripts with the Vatican and Freiburg fragments, as well as with the material from Pelagius' commentary interpolated into certain manuscripts of Ambrosiaster's commentary.[203] Souter accordingly established his edition on the witness of the Karlsruhe and Balliol manuscripts, granting priority to the Karlsruhe text of the comments because it offered a slightly shorter and earlier version. For the text of the epistles he relied on the Balliol manuscript, whose lemmata he judged to be closer to Pelagius's than those of the Karlsruhe manuscript.[204]

Souter's edition, though widely admired, was not received without criticism. This focused for the most part on the lemmata,[205] but there were misgivings about the comments as well. The sharpest review came from Donatien de Bruyne, who criticized Souter for presenting material omitted by the Karlsruhe or the Balliol manuscript in square brackets without editorial discrimination, and reiterated his arguments for giving more weight to the longer form of the pseudo-Jerome tradition (H_2).[206] Several decades later Célestin Charlier called for a new edition based on a revised stemma.[207] Charlier claimed that Souter had not given sufficient attention, on the one hand, to similarities among the manuscripts of the group ABHG (using Souter's sigla)—similarities which narrowed the distance which Souter placed between interpolated and uninterpolated manuscripts—and, on the other hand, to unique characteristics of the Paris manuscript V. Charlier argued that ABHG and V present two distinct but related forms of Pelagius's commentary, and by comparing both of them with Cassiodorus's revision he found that the tradition represented in the Paris manuscript antedated that represented in ABHG and Cassiodorus's revision. Thus, whereas Souter concluded that the Paris manuscript had been contaminated by Cassiodorus's revision,[208] Charlier maintained that

[202] *Expositions*, i. 34–48.

[203] Ibid. 48–60.

[204] Ibid. 343.

[205] See pp. 8–9 above.

[206] De Bruyne, *BALCL* 1 (1921–8), No. 589 (pp. 242–4); cf. No. 115 (pp. 57–8). But on the evidence of the prologues see now Frede, *Vetus Latina*, xxv. 1. 102–3, 117 (PROL Paul 4 and PROL 1 Cor 38d).

[207] 'Cassiodore, Pélage et les origines de la vulgate paulinienne', 461–5.

[208] *Expositions*, vol. ii, p. viii; cf. i. 255.

the Paris manuscript, along with the group ABHG, formed the basis for Cassiodorus's revision and, furthermore, that as a witness to the original text of Pelagius the Paris manuscript is prior to the group ABHG.

Charlier's hypothesis has not stood up well to scrutiny. In his study of the *uetus latina* of 1 Thessalonians Ernst Nellessen examined the relation between the Paris manuscript and Cassiodorus's revision, and found that the former is influenced by and posterior to the latter.[209] A similar investigation of the problem in the commentary on Romans has likewise found no grounds for believing that the Paris manuscript is, as Charlier suggested, derived from Pelagius's autograph.[210] Rather, it appears that the Paris manuscript, though at times agreeing with Cassiodorus, for the most part represents a tradition which stands between the manuscripts ABHG and Cassiodorus.[211]

Where the manuscripts ABHG disagree, the Paris manuscript can be helpful. There are instances where A is at variance with BHG but agrees with the Paris manuscript. These variants arise when the Balliol manuscript includes pseudo-Jerome interpolations of which the Karlsruhe and Paris manuscripts are free. Since the Paris manuscript normally supports BHG against A,[212] its agreement with A in these instances is strong evidence that the witness of A is more authentic than that of BHG. Souter in fact suspected the authenticity of the Balliol manuscript at these points. His suspicions have been confirmed by Frede's study of the Budapest manuscript, Hungarian National Museum Codex Latinus Medii Aevi 1.[213]

[209] *Untersuchungen*, 232–5.

[210] Charlier believed that the marginal glosses in the Paris MS reflected the form of Pelagius's autograph, which he supposed to consist of marginal and interlinear glosses on a manuscript of the Pauline epistles. He failed to note, however, that both Souter and De Bruyne had initially entertained a similar view but subsequently abandoned it; see Souter, *Expositions*, i. 49–50, 120, 268; De Bruyne, *BALCL* 1 (1921–8), No. 589 (p. 243). Souter and De Bruyne rejected the hypothesis because of Pelagius's comment at *Eph.* 3: 19 (Souter, *Expositions*, ii. 468. 22–469. 1): 'sicut ad Ephesios plenius subnotatum est'. This reading is confirmed by the arrangement of the Vatican fragments. In the Paris MS and in Cassiodorus, however, the comment reads *an(d)notatum est*.

[211] A comparison of the marginal glosses in the Paris MS with the MSS ABHG and Cassiodorus reveals that the marginal glosses incorporate material from both the MSS ABHG and from Cassiodorus, but that in general the Paris MS stands closer to the former than the latter; see de Bruyn, 'Pelagius's Commentary on Romans', 19–25.

[212] Cf. the following marginal glosses in the Paris MS with their equivalent in the MSS BGH, the former noted by folio and line, the latter noted in parentheses by reference to Souter's edition: 13^v 4–5 (*Rom.* 1: 28, Souter, ii. 16. 24–17. 2); 37^r 14–18 (*Rom.* 6: 14, Souter, ii. 52. 1–6); 44^r 18–19 (*Rom.* 8: 2, Souter, ii. 60. 21–3); 59^v 6–7 (*Rom.* 10: 19, Souter, ii. 84. 3–4); 82^r 4–8 (*Rom.* 16: 20, Souter, ii. 124. 21–125. 9). When comparing Souter, the apparatus must also be consulted.

[213] *Ein neuer Paulustext*, i. 193–6.

Variants of a second sort, in which A, sometimes together with G, is at variance with BH(G)V, are more problematic. Here the Karlsruhe manuscript either preserves original material or introduces new material. A number of these variants are theologically significant, qualifying a comment in a way that could be considered 'Augustinian' rather than 'Pelagian'. Because they are important to one's interpretation of Pelagius's theology as a whole, as well as to one's estimate of Souter's edition, it will be useful to review them here. Where the evidence is complicated, reference is made to the notes to the translation; otherwise, one may consult the text and apparatus of Souter's edition.

Several of the variants have to do with the ability to refrain from sin. At *Rom.* 3: 18 the Karlsruhe manuscript softens the expectation that those who truly fear God will not sin by inserting the qualification 'so seriously' (*tam grauiter*). Likewise, the assertion at *Rom.* 6: 2 that one may be unable to sin—*peccare non posse*, an expression which occasioned considerable debate in the Pelagian controversy[214]—is tempered by the Karlsruhe manuscript with the words 'in a way' (*quodam modo*).[215] Similarly, at *Rom.* 8: 3 the Karlsruhe manuscript casts a conditional comment on the possibility of sinlessness in the imperfect rather than the present tense, thereby removing the potential from realization.[216] Nevertheless, the Karlsruhe manuscript does not regard sin as inevitable. In discussing the strength of sinful habit in one who knows what is good but does what is evil—the theme of Romans 7—the Karlsruhe and St Gall manuscripts introduce a couple of variants which underscore the contention that no one actually sins against his or her will, despite the force of habit. One acts only 'in a way' (*quodam modo* at v. 15) or 'as it were' (*uelut* at v. 20) against one's will.

Another issue which emerges in the variants of the Karlsruhe manuscript is the manner in which God works to perfect the believer. To the two means which Pelagius usually mentions—teaching and example—the Karlsruhe and St Gall manuscripts at *Rom.* 6: 14 refer additionally to the power of the Holy Spirit—*et insuper uirtutem per spiritum sanctum*. A similar addition is inserted at *Rom.* 8: 3 to explain what the carnal person lacked in attempting to overcome the temptations of the sinful nature. Where the other manuscripts name only example, the Karlsruhe manuscript speaks of example and grace. A third instance of this kind of variation may be found at *Rom.* 8: 26. There the Karlsruhe manuscript specifies illumination—*illuminatio* in

---

[214] Evans, *Pelagius*, 21–5.   [215] See *Rom.* 6: 2 n. 1.   [216] See ibid. 8: 3 n. 10.

the original hand, *illuminatione* in a subsequent correction—rather than teaching as the way in which the Holy Spirit assists the human faculties.

In several variants the Karlsruhe manuscript also refers more generally to the need for and priority of God's action. The long comment at *Rom.* 9: 16—'Then it does not depend on the one who wills or the one who runs, but on God who has mercy', a verse which perplexed many around the turn of the fourth century[217]—may be divided into three parts according to the witness of the manuscripts.[218] The first part casts the verse as the argument of some opponents, and adduces testimony from other letters of the apostle to the contrary. This part is omitted by the Karlsruhe manuscript. Then follows a comment which, referring indirectly to Augustine's interpretation of the passage in his letter to Simplician, contests the view that all depends on the will of God to the exclusion of human initiative. This remark is attested by all the manuscripts. Lastly, there is an alternative comment which stipulates that divine assistance is necessary in addition to human initiative. This is found in the Karlsruhe manuscript alone. We find a similar concern at *Rom.* 12: 6, where the Karlsruhe manuscript underscores the priority of divine action. To a comment in which Pelagius explains that the gifts of the Spirit are granted in proportion to one's faith, the Karlsruhe and St Gall manuscripts add a clause which reiterates what has already been stated, namely, that the gift depends on the decision of God—*quam deus ei donare uoluerit*.

There remain a few other variants. In the first four chapters of Romans Pelagius often asserts that the convert comes to God in faith alone but that the believer subsequently cultivates a life of holiness which may be meritorious in God's sight. At *Rom.* 3: 28 the Karlsruhe manuscript twice specifies that baptism is the threshold whereby one passes from the former to the latter. In the second of these instances the Karlsruhe manuscript is supported by the St Gall manuscript. A Christological concern surfaces in a variant at *Rom.* 8: 3. By adding the phrase 'as far as the nature is concerned' (*quantum ad naturam*), the Karlsruhe manuscript takes care to point out that the human nature which Christ assumed is free of the sin which is now part of human experience; it is a nature true to that originally created by God.

Are these variants in the Karlsruhe manuscript from Pelagius's original commentary, or are they later additions from the hand, say, of a writer of the ethos of Faustus of Riez, chastened perhaps by the

---

[217] See n. 130 above.   [218] See *Rom.* 9: 16 nn. 15–17.

Council of Orange in 529?[219] It is now my view that they are original to Pelagius.[220] Initially I entertained the notion that they might be interpolations for two reasons. First, the Vatican fragment, which happily includes a portion of the comment on *Rom.* 8: 3, does not agree with the readings of the Karlsruhe and St Gall manuscripts. In one instance Souter suggested that the reading of the fragment should perhaps be preferred.[221] Secondly, where the variants can be compared with other comments in Romans, they appear to be anomalous.[222] But upon further consideration the weight of the evidence seems to shift. Most importantly, there are parallels to the variants in the remaining commentaries on the epistles.[223] Moreover, the Vatican fragment, though early, is not unrelated to the pseudo-Jerome tradition and cannot be taken as an unbiased standard.[224] It now seems more plausible to suggest that the Pelagian revisor, as Frede has named him, or another reader eliminated phrases from the commentary which seemed out of step with the Pelagian position as it hardened after the condemnation of Pelagius and Caelestius,[225] and that these alterations are less faithfully represented in the St Gall

---

[219] See Markus, 'Legacy', 220–7, and the literature cited for a nuanced discussion of Gallic orthodoxy and the pressures exerted by the events leading up to the Council of Orange.

[220] A reversal of the position I took in an unpublished communication given at the Eleventh International Conference on Patristic Studies at Oxford in Aug. 1991.

[221] See *Rom.* 8: 3 n. 10. The Vatican fragment generally supports BHV against AG. See the data in Souter's apparatus for '*Venundatus quasi*' at *Rom.* 7: 15 (Souter, *Expositions*, ii. 58. 15); '*quo hominem*' at *Rom.* 8: 3 (Souter, *Expositions*, ii. 61. 15); '*substantiae*' at *Rom.* 8: 5 (Souter, *Expositions*, ii. 62. 9).

[222] At *Rom.* 1: 28 and 2: 20 (Souter, *Expositions*, ii. 16. 20–4, 24. 18–19) the expectation that those whose minds are fixed on God will refrain from sin is expressed without such allowance for gradation in sin as the variant *tam grauiter* at *Rom.* 3: 18 suggests. Similarly, the view that one who has been baptized will be so altered in affections as to be unable to sin is stated with less hesitancy at *Rom.* 6: 7 (Souter, *Expositions*, ii. 50. 18–20) than at *Rom.* 6: 2. So too, the comment at *Rom.* 6: 17 (Souter, *Expositions*, ii. 52. 20–1) speaks only of the teaching and example of Christ, and makes no mention of the additional power of the Holy Spirit, as do the Karlsruhe and St Gall MSS at *Rom.* 6: 14.

[223] Cf. *Rom.* 6: 14 (Souter, *Expositions*, ii. 52. 6–8) with *2 Cor.* 3: 3, *Eph.* 6: 10, and *2 Thess.* 1: 11 (Souter, *Expositions*, ii. 244. 8–12, 382. 12–13 (where it is noteworthy that the omission of *in uirtute* in the St Gall MS was corrected), 442. 5–7). Cf. *Rom.* 8: 3 (Souter, *Expositions*, ii. 60. 23–61. 1) with *2 Cor.* 1: 21, *1 Thess.* 5: 23, and *2 Thess.* 3: 3 (Souter, *Expositions*, ii. 237. 10–13, 437. 9–10, 448. 1–2). Cf. *Rom.* 8: 26 (Souter, *Expositions*, ii. 67. 12–16) with *Eph.* 3: 16 (Souter, *Expositions*, ii. 360. 6–9). Cf. *Rom.* 9: 16 (Souter, *Expositions*, ii. 76. 15–16) with *Col.* 1: 10 (Souter, *Expositions*, ii. 452. 16–453. 17).

[224] For agreement between the Vatican fragment and the shorter pseudo-Jerome tradition (H₁) see the data in Souter's apparatus for '*Marcionistas*' at *Rom.* 7: 12 (Souter, *Expositions*, ii. 57. 22); '*prudentiae*' at *Rom.* 8: 6 (Souter, *Expositions*, ii. 62. 13–14).

[225] This could account for the addition of *suo exemplo* at *Rom.* 5: 16; cf. ps.-Hi. *Rom.* 41, 45 (Frede ii. 40–1, and see i. 223–4).

manuscript than in other manuscripts belonging to the pseudo-Jerome tradition.[226]

Accordingly, the translation below follows Souter's edition for Pelagius's comments, and the reader is alerted to doubtful or divergent readings in the notes. Because Souter's device of square brackets still serves to indicate variants in the Karlsruhe manuscript, they have been incorporated into the translation, though they do not always fit as easily with the English as with the Latin. The lemmata of the translation, however, are not based on the lemmata of Souter's edition. A new text of the epistle has been prepared according to the principles established by Frede, and is printed in the appendix below.

2. PELAGIUS'S INTERPRETATION OF ROMANS

Pelagius's commentary is remarkable for the alternative interpretations—often two, sometimes three—it offers as it pauses over a clause or a verse. This combination of riches and brevity was unprecedented in the west. At first glance it may suggest that Pelagius approached the epistle to the Romans with no guiding interpretation of his own, but merely provided a synopsis of the comments of others. Such an impression would belie the truth, however. From the many comments one can discern the lineaments of an interpretation born, on the one hand, of Pelagius's attention to the text of the epistle and, on the other, of his theological interests.[227]

Pelagius's interpretation of Romans falls into four thematic sections. The first, chapters 1–4, treats the histories of the Gentiles and the Jews in order to show that their response to the revelation of God has been the same and that consequently they are on an equal footing before God. The second section, chapters 5–8, considers the transition from the

[226] The affinity of the St Gall MS to the pseudo-Jerome tradition is uneven. It contains an uninterpolated version of Pelagius's commentary on 1 Cor. with lemmata akin to those of the Balliol MS, and an interpolated version of the anonymous commentary on Hebrews, also found in the Karlsruhe MS. See Souter, *Expositions*, i. 239–41; Frede, *Ein neuer Paulustext*, i. 233–9; Frede, *Vetus Latina*, xxv. 2. 1023.

[227] For one evaluation of the adequacy of Pelagius's interpretation of Paul see Esser, 'Thesen und Anmerkungen', a summary of the author's more detailed dissertation, 'Paulusverständnis'. What follows here is more modest: a synopsis of Pelagius's interpretation of Romans based on a comparison of his comments with the traditions out of which he wrote. References to parallels in these traditions, along with discussion of some details of interpretation, may be found in the notes to the translation of the commentary.

'death' of sin to the 'life' of righteousness. The pivotal point in this
transition is baptism, which incorporates the believer into Christ. On
either side of this transition there lies a deliberate way of living: on the
one side, a 'carnal' life, in which a person, following the pattern set by
Adam, commits sinful acts, first by choice and subsequently by habit;
on the other side, a 'spiritual' life, in which a person, following the
example of Christ, resists the temptation to sin and cultivates the virtues. The third section, chapters 9–11, considers the status of the Jews
in the Christian era of salvation. The burden of the argument, with a
view first to the past and then to the present, is to show that the condition for salvation is the same now as it was before, namely, a believing
response to divine revelation. The final section, chapters 12–16, discusses various practical matters in a hortatory mode, always to the end
that the Christian should better imitate Christ.

Justification by Faith Alone, for Gentile and Jew Alike

Introduction (Rom. 1: 1–17)

In his comments on the first four chapters of Romans Pelagius is
concerned chiefly to demonstrate the equality of Gentile and Jew
before God. For Pelagius this is the central issue of Romans, and he
anticipates it in his comments on the introductory verses of the epistle.
At Paul's salutation he calls attention to God's impartiality towards
Jew and Gentile (*Rom.* 1: 7). He points out that it is God who has
called and forgiven both peoples, and urges them in response to live
justly and peacefully with one another. And when the theme of the
righteousness of God is introduced later, Pelagius invokes Abraham,
who incorporates in himself both Gentile and Jew, as a paradigm of
the way in which all are saved (*Rom.* 1: 17).

The Case of the Gentiles (Rom. 1: 18–2: 16)

After the introduction Paul, according to Pelagius, turns his attention
to the case of the Gentiles (*Rom.* 1: 18). His aim with them, as with the
Jews, is to eliminate any claim to special status before God. Against a
supposed defence of ignorance, Paul argues that God was indeed
revealed to the Gentiles and that therefore they have no excuse for
their idolatry. The source of their knowledge of God is twofold,
creation and conscience (*Rom.* 1: 19–21). From this revelation the
Gentiles knew, or could have known, that God exists, that God is the
author of creation, and that God is just. This knowledge is sufficient to

hold the Gentiles accountable for their idolatry, since from it they should have recognized that God, whose will is supreme in establishing and governing creation, is alone deserving of worship, and that failure to honour God, whose justice is patent, would result in condemnation (*Rom.* 1: 26–32). That the Gentiles in fact failed to come to these conclusions is a consequence of their own free choice (*Rom.* 1: 21). This choice led them into increasingly greater turpitude, to the point that they became ignorant not only of God, but also of their own position in the natural order, the order created by God (*Rom.* 1: 26–7).

The Case of the Jews (*Rom. 2: 17–3: 31*)

As Pelagius comes to the end of the case of the Gentiles, he intimates that the position of the Jews is no better than that of the Gentiles (*Rom.* 2: 13). The Jews fell as short of the law of Moses as did the Gentiles of the law of nature.

Pelagius's case turns on the definition of a Jew (*Rom.* 2: 17–29). He argues that the Jews addressed by Paul, who claim to be superior to the Gentiles, are not 'real' Jews. First he shows that these Jews did not keep the very law on which their claim is based (*Rom.* 2. 17–24). Then he argues that the mark of a 'real' Jew is not the external feature of circumcision, but rather an inner attitude that is manifest in outer holiness (*Rom.* 2: 25–9).

Much of this reasoning is commonplace in the Christian *aduersus Iudaeos* tradition. Pelagius's debt to this tradition is especially apparent in his remarks on circumcision. Origen is the most proximate source for the distinction between physical and spiritual circumcision and between the inner and outer person (*Rom.* 2: 27 n. 43, 2: 28–9 n. 45). Ambrosiaster frequently insists that faith in Christ is the fulfilment of the law (*Rom.* 2: 27 n. 44; cf. *Rom.* 2: 12 n. 21). And the several explanations of the purpose of circumcision are present in various other Christian writers (*Rom.* 2: 25 nn. 35–7). All of this serves to subordinate circumcision to righteousness, and physical descent from Abraham to faith in Christ.

In discussing the Jewish observance of the law, however, Pelagius pursues an independent course. Central to his comments is the tenet that to know God is to obey God's will (*Rom.* 2: 18; cf. *Rom.* 1: 19). Again and again Pelagius speaks of the contrast between ignorance and knowledge, of the role of the teacher in bringing others to knowledge, and of the importance of example, or manifest obedience to the will of God, as the sole test of true knowledge of God (*Rom.* 2: 20–1).

According to Pelagius, the Jews, like the Gentiles, knew or could have known the law of God (cf. *Rom.* 1: 21, 3: 11, 3: 19), but disregarded that law or neglected to seek it (cf. *Rom.* 1: 21, 28). They are therefore responsible for their contempt for God (cf. *Rom.* 3: 2).

Having set out the case of the Jews in chapter 2, the apostle, according to Pelagius, responds to some objections from the Jews in chapter 3. The opponent—or opponents—claim that the history of the Jews is foreordained by God and that the Jews have sinned merely to show that God is just (*Rom.* 3: 1–8). (The argument anticipates the debate about divine election in chapter 9.) This strikes Pelagius as patently false, and he says as much even as he represents the position of the opponents (*Rom.* 3: 4–5). Then he turns to the reply of the apostle, who, he explains, supplements arguments based on reason with authority from Scripture (*Rom.* 3: 9).

Three things are noteworthy in Pelagius's comments on the verses which follow. The first is the way in which he qualifies Paul's portrayal of the Jews. For Pelagius this portrayal is not true of them throughout their history, but rather describes their condition at the end of the Mosaic period (*Rom.* 3: 12). Pelagius implies that there was a time when some Jews were righteous, though by the time of Christ almost none were found to be so (cf. *Rom.* 5: 12). Secondly, Pelagius indicates that failure to know God's will is the result of failure to seek God's will (*Rom.* 3: 11). This is consonant with the view that Jews were righteous at one time and capable of righteousness at all times. It recalls Pelagius's discussion of the observance of the law above (cf. *Rom.* 2: 20, 3: 18). Finally, the emphasis on instruction and, to a lesser extent, example is striking (*Rom.* 3: 16 n. 17). Instruction and example are for Pelagius the chief ways in which salvation is communicated, and correspond to the human ability to know and to act according to God's will—an ability, Pelagius emphasizes, which is characteristic of the Jews as well as the Gentiles, and throughout their history.

The chapter concludes with a synopsis of the salvation that is available to all without distinction in Christ (*Rom.* 3: 21–30). Paul has demonstrated, according to Pelagius, that the Jews as well as the Gentiles have failed to live in accordance with the law that was revealed to them (*Rom.* 3: 29; cf. *Rom.* 2: 12–13). In the course of human history God waited patiently for the human race to reform (*Rom.* 3: 26), and remedied the decline of the law of nature with the revelation of the law of Moses (*Rom.* 3: 20). But all this had been of no avail, and the ultimate outcome would have been spiritual death for both Gentile and Jew, had not Christ offered his death as a substitution for the punishment due to the human race (*Rom.* 3: 24). God now declares both Gentile and Jew righteous not on the basis of their obedience to the law—since on that basis neither would be declared righteous (cf. *Rom.* 4: 5)—but rather freely on the basis of Christ's death. This universal offer of salvation is rooted in Pelagius's doctrine of creation (*Rom.* 3: 29). As Pelagius explains, the work of salvation is an extension of the work of creation (cf. *Rom.* 1: 16, 3: 24, 5: 8). Inasmuch as all people belong to God as creatures of God, but have been alienated by sin, God's offering in redemption extends to all. Nothing in the histories of the Jews and the Gentiles obviates this original and enduring bond of both peoples to God.

In this synopsis Pelagius, like Ambrosiaster and Origen, emphasizes that righteousness in Christ is freely given (*Rom.* 3: 24 n. 33). It is not granted on the basis of merit, or on the basis of works of the law, but rather bestowed on those who believe that they need to be freed by the death of Christ—in other words, by faith alone (*Rom.* 3: 25–6). However, unlike Ambrosiaster and Origen, Pelagius adds that righteousness 'by faith alone' applies strictly to the past sins which are forgiven in baptism of one who has come to believe in Christ (*Rom.* 3: 28). Thereafter the Christian, having been incorporated into Christ, is expected to live as Christ did. This aspect of the salvation of the Christian, from baptism to eternal life, is the focus of Pelagius's comments on chapters 5–8. That Pelagius anticipates that discussion here indicates that for him the review of the past in chapters 1–4 is preliminary to the exhortations for the present in chapters 5–8.

The Archetype of Abraham (*Rom. 4: 1–24*)

With chapter 4 Pelagius turns to consider the figure of Abraham in relation to both Gentiles and Jews. For Pelagius, as for patristic interpreters in general, Abraham is an archetype of the Christian. He typifies every believer, whether Gentile or Jew, because he is saved by faith alone (*Rom.* 4: 9). It is no surprise, therefore, that Pelagius's comments on this chapter echo themes from the preceding chapters. We are reminded of the failure of all people to keep the law; of the punishment that consequently awaits them; of the offer of forgiveness and declaration of righteousness that is unmerited by works but is received freely, by faith alone; of the works of love which follow upon faith; and of the universality of salvation by faith throughout human history (*Rom.* 4: 3, 5, 6, 16).

As an archetype of the Christian, Abraham is also a model for Christians. This is implicit in many of Pelagius's comments (*Rom.* 4: 3, 11, 19–24). Pelagius calls attention not only to Abraham's superlative faith, but also to his great love (*Rom.* 4: 3). Here again Pelagius anticipates the discussion of chapters 5–8, evoking Abraham as an example of the sort of life that should characterize one who has come to believe in Christ.

The Life of the Christian

The Pursuit of Holiness (*Rom. 5: 1–11*)

After briefly summarizing the argument of the previous chapters, Pelagius turns in chapter 5 to the pursuit of holiness (*Rom.* 5: 1). The chief motivations to which he appeals, and by which he measures the effort to refrain from sin, are two. The one, eternal life, stands before the Christian; the other, the death of Christ, stands behind. Both are vantage-points from which one gains a perspective on the course of the life of the Christian.

The first of these, the hope of eternal life, occasions a long comment encouraging those who suffer in this life with a vision of the incomparable glory of eternal life (*Rom.* 5: 3–4; cf. *Rom.* 2: 7). What is most striking in the rhetoric is the disparity between temporal and eternal life. Every mundane analogy fails because it cannot cross the divide between corruptible and incorruptible existence (*Rom.* 5: 4). Nevertheless, the glory of eternal life—likeness to Christ—is achieved by imitating Christ in this life (*Rom.* 5: 10–11).

The second motivation for the Christian to be holy is the love which God has shown in Christ (*Rom.* 5: 5–9). The Christian's love for God, according to Pelagius, is a response to God's love for the Christian, which God has manifested both in the redemptive death of Christ and in the gift of the Holy Spirit (*Rom.* 5: 5). It is God who acted first in Christ—gratuitously and generously (*Rom.* 5: 6, 8). Now it is incumbent on the Christian to live worthily, to live righteously (*Rom.* 5: 8–9).

Adam and Christ (*Rom. 5: 12–21*)

Christ, it is clear, is the beginning of the life of the Christian. But over against Christ stands Adam, who began the life of the sinner. In the remainder of the chapter Pelagius discusses the significance of Adam and Christ as the two initiating figures in human history, repudiating along the way the fatalist connotations of the traducianist understanding of the transmission of sin.

Adam and Christ are, according to Pelagius, antithetical types—*forma a contrario*—for the human race (*Rom.* 5: 14). Adam is the *forma* of sin, leading his descendants to spiritual death by his pattern of transgression (*Rom.* 5: 12). Christ is the *forma* of righteousness, offering forgiveness of sins to those who believe and setting an example of righteousness to enable them to avoid transgression (*Rom.* 5: 16–17, 20). All human beings join Adam in sin or Christ in righteousness by choice. They suffer the ultimate consequence of sin, spiritual death, only in so far as they deliberately follow Adam in transgression of the will of God (*Rom.* 5: 14, 16, 21). Likewise, they enjoy the ultimate benefit of righteousness, the glory of eternal life, when they accept the offer of forgiveness in Christ and follow his example of righteousness (*Rom.* 5: 21; cf. *Rom.* 6: 4).

Adam and Christ are not, however, equal as antetype and type. Pelagius, following Paul, observes that Christ has begun something immeasurably greater than Adam. Whereas Adam led only himself and his descendants into death, Christ frees not only those who have lived after him, but also those who were born before him and were alive in his lifetime (*Rom.* 5: 15). Furthermore, whereas Adam destroyed righteousness by his example of sin, Christ not only provides an example of righteousness, but also has the power to forgive past sins (*Rom.* 5: 16).

Pelagius's comments are evidently coloured by the reaction in Rome to the traducianist notion of the transmission of sin from Adam to his descendants (see the Introduction at n. 120 and ff.). Pelagius refers to this reaction in his comment on v. 15, but its influence is felt in his other comments as well. Whereas previous and contemporary interpretations of the fall included aspects that do not depend on human volition, such as corruptibility, mortality, ignorance, and concupiscence, Pelagius focuses only on the volitional appropriation of Adam's pattern of transgression, the outcome of which is spiritual death (see the Introduction at n. 149 and ff.). For Pelagius, as for Ambrosiaster and Origen, spiritual death is a consequence of actual sin, that is, sin which like Adam's is a deliberate act of the will (*Rom.* 5: 14). Since it follows from this view that the righteous will not experience spiritual death, Pelagius qualifies Paul's language, as do Ambrosiaster and Origen, to allow for this possibility (*Rom.* 5: 12 n. 25). However, this allowance for righteousness prior to Christ does not eliminate the need for Christ in the history of salvation. It is precisely because most people sinned to the point that there was almost no knowledge of what is right that Christ's coming was necessary for salvation (*Rom.* 5: 12).

From Death to Life (*Rom. 6: 1–23*)

In his last comment on chapter 5, Pelagius indicates that unceasing righteousness should follow upon forgiveness of sins (*Rom.* 5: 21). This uncompromising pursuit of holiness is the subject of his comments on chapter 6. Pelagius's expectation of the Christian is a high one. It is no less than to live '[as one who in a way cannot sin]' (*Rom.* 6: 1 and n. 1).

The foundation for this expectation lies in Paul's discussion of baptism. In his comments Pelagius evokes two dimensions of this pivotal event. The first is the sacramental act whereby one participates in the death of Christ and is incorporated into Christ. The second is the lifelong process whereby one strives to live like Christ and hopes for the glory of the resurrection. Pelagius refers to the sacramental act when he says that 'through the mystery we are buried with Christ, dying to our offences and renouncing our former life' (*Rom.* 6: 4); that 'through baptism you, who have been made a member of his body, were crucified with Christ' (*Rom.* 6: 6); that 'if we have not died with him, we shall also not live with him, because we are not his members' (*Rom.* 6: 8); that you are 'members of him . . . having died with him once for all' (*Rom.* 6: 11). He refers to the lifelong process when he says that 'just as [the Father] is glorified in the resurrection of the Son, so too on account of the newness of our way of life he is glorified by all, provided that not even the signs of the old self are recognizable in us' (*Rom.* 6: 4); that 'if we have become new and been changed [in] our way of life, we shall be likewise new and changed in glory' (*Rom.* 6: 5); that Christ 'hangs his innocent body, so that [you] may restrain your guilty body from vices' (*Rom.* 6: 6); that '"one who is born of God does not sin" . . . for because he has been crucified, and all his members are filled with sorrow, he will hardly be able to sin' (*Rom.* 6: 7); that Christ '"carried our sins" and suffered for us, so that in future we might not sin' (*Rom.* 6: 10); that 'having died with him once for all, you ought now always to live for God in Christ . . . since we have been clothed with him, we should follow his example' (*Rom.* 6: 11). These two dimensions of baptism are united, clearly, in Christ, whose death becomes a way of life for the Christian. Indeed, though physical death and resurrection still await the Christian, the Christian should live as if he or she has passed through physical death to eternal life, where there will be no occasion for sin because the resurrected body, unlike the present corrupt body, will present no temptation to sin (*Rom.* 6: 12; cf. *Rom.* 8: 10).

Pelagius is aware that this is easier said than done. He follows Paul in moving from the indicative to the hortatory, and with the latter mode implicitly acknowledges the difficulty of what is expected. It is telling that his counsels have as much to do with eliminating vices as with fostering virtues (*Rom.* 6: 4–5), and that Christ is exemplary not merely for the pursuit of holiness but also for the restraint of vice (*Rom.* 6: 6, 11). Moreover, for those who fail there remains the remedy of penance (*Rom.* 6: 9).

But, having noted this allowance for difficulty and even failure, one cannot but observe that Pelagius stresses the potential for a complete change of life. In his comments towards the end of the chapter Pelagius alludes several times to the freedom one has either to sin or to refrain from sin (*Rom.* 6: 12, 13, 16, 19). 'It is through freedom of choice', he asserts, following Origen, 'that a person offers his members for whatever side he wishes' (*Rom.* 6:13). Sin cannot be imputed to the body, as the Manichaeans suggest, or to the desires of the body; it remains the responsibility of the soul, which is free to choose whether or not to act in accordance with the desires of the body (*Rom.* 6: 19). It is this freedom which sharpens Pelagius's expectation of a radical change of life. One may be called to live without sin because one has a will which is free (*Rom.* 6: 20). Knowledge of good, together with shame for past sin, should keep one from sinning (*Rom.* 6: 21–2). And knowledge of good is precisely what Christ provides by his teaching and example (*Rom.* 6: 14, 18).

The Dilemma of the 'Carnal Person' (*Rom.* 7: 1–25)

Having described the radical change which is effected in baptism, Paul, according to Pelagius, contrasts life under the law with life in Christ (*Rom.* 7: 1–6). The persona which he assumes to articulate this difference is the 'carnal person', someone who at one time gave in to sin, but has since been made aware of it by the law and now struggles to overcome sin (*Rom.* 7: 7). Three aspects of this person's dilemma stand out in Pelagius's comments. The first is the force of habit (*Rom.* 7: 7, 15, 18, 20, 23, 24). Pelagius recognizes the power it has over the sinner. Under its influence the sinner is like a drunk who no longer knows what he is doing (*Rom.* 7: 15), or a profane individual who sins even when he does not wish to (*Rom.* 7: 19). Pelagius even goes so far as to call habit a 'compulsion' (*necessitas*) which leads one to act '[as it were] against one's will' ([*uelut*] *inuitus*) (*Rom.* 7: 20).

But even while he recognizes the force of habit, Pelagius notes that the sinner is nevertheless responsible for habitual sin. Pelagius contests the (Manichaean) view that sin is the inevitable result of incarnate existence (*Rom.* 7: 17, 18, 20). Again and again he points out that habitual sin originates in the free choice of the sinner (*Rom.* 7: 15, 17, 20). The will, not the body, is the source of sin, and though habit interferes with volition, it never eliminates the will (*Rom.* 7: 18). Thus the sinner acts only 'in a way' ([*quodam modo*]) against his or her will (*Rom.* 7: 15); as with the drunk, the faculties are still present, even if they no longer function as they should.

The limitations of the law as a means for salvation, when added to this picture of someone who retains the capacity to choose but is frustrated by a habit of sinning, completes the dilemma of the 'carnal person'. Against the Marcionites and the Manichaeans (*Rom.* 7: 7, 12), Pelagius affirms that the law is good and that it could have led to eternal life (*Rom.* 7: 10, 13). However, because of sin the law serves only to condemn, since it does no more than to make the sinner aware of his or her sin (*Rom.* 7: 14). The law does not have the power to prevent the sinner from sinning, but only adds the knowledge that sin is reprehensible (*Rom.* 7. 7, 9, 14). In effect, then, the law leads to death, because to sin knowingly is to die spiritually (*Rom.* 7: 10, 13, 16). The habitual sinner thus knows what is good and desires to do it, but is frustrated by the consequences of prior choices for evil.

This is the dilemma of the 'carnal person'. It is a dilemma which, according to Pelagius, is resolved only 'by grace' (*Rom.* 7: 25). To such a one, who has been freed 'by grace', Pelagius turns, with Paul, in chapter 8, explaining what he means by the phrase.

Living 'according to the Spirit' (*Rom. 8: 1–39*)

The first verses of chapter 8 elaborate what was announced in the last verse of chapter 7 to show how Christ frees one from sin and enables one to be righteous—neither of which the law was able to effect (*Rom.* 8: 1–4). By his death Christ makes it possible for the sins of the 'carnal person' to be forgiven, and by his life Christ provides an example of the way sin can be overcome (*Rom.* 8: 3). As a result one is expected to refrain from sin and increase in holiness, embarking on a process of sanctification whose end, anticipated *en route* in the gifts of the Spirit, is the glory of eternal life (*Rom.* 8: 9, 18, 30). Thus begins the career of the one who lives 'according to the Spirit' (Rom. 8: 5).

The distinction between those who live 'according to the flesh' and those who live 'according to the Spirit' is central to Paul's discussion in chapter 8, and likewise to Pelagius's comments. The foil to many of his remarks is the Manichaean view of the body. Pelagius speaks against a simple identification of 'flesh' with the body in a way that suggests that the body alone is responsible for sin (*Rom.* 8: 7–8). He notes that 'flesh' and 'spirit' may be used in two senses, to designate the body and the soul, or to describe a person who is given either to spiritual deeds or to carnal deeds (*Rom.* 8: 5). Though the body, now mortal, may tempt one to sin, sin is not a matter of inclinations but of actions, and the latter are determined, at least initially, by choice (*Rom.* 6: 12–13). Thus Pelagius prefers to speak of the 'carnal mind' (*sensus carnalis*) rather than the 'flesh' (*caro*) to designate the inclination to sin (*Rom.* 8: 7, 10), and he observes that 'the works, not the substance, of the flesh are condemned' (*Rom.* 8: 13; cf. *Rom.* 8: 8). Likewise, lest the expression 'in the Spirit' be misconstrued as an incorporeal form of existence, Pelagius points out that it means being occupied with 'spiritual things'—namely, those virtues which attest the presence of the Spirit (*Rom.* 8: 9–10).

Pelagius continually urges the Christian to grow in these virtues. Paul's remarks on the 'flesh' are, according to Pelagius, intended to encourage his readers to refrain from sin (*Rom.* 8: 7), while those on the 'spirit' exhort them in the pursuit of holiness (*Rom.* 8: 10). To buttress this call to refrain from sin and cultivate holiness, Pelagius appeals chiefly to the Christian's obligation to remain worthy of what God has done in the past and will do in the future. The form of these appeals varies according to the context, but the basic elements are the same in each instance, and recall the comments on the first part of chapter 5 (cf. *Rom.* 5: 1–11). Pelagius, on the one hand, looks back to some divine benefit—forgiveness of sins, the gifts of the Spirit, status as children of God—which he can exhort the Christian to remain worthy of; and, on the other hand, looks ahead to the resurrection as a further incentive to maintain a holy life (*Rom.* 8: 11, 15, 17, 18).

Clearly, Pelagius holds the Christian responsible for his or her progress in holiness. But it would be wrong to conclude that for Pelagius the Christian is the primary actor in the process of salvation. From Pelagius's comments on the sequence of Rom. 8: 28–30 it is evident that the initiative in this process lies with God, who calls, forgives, grants the gifts of the Spirit, and raises from the dead (*Rom.* 8: 29–30). Furthermore, the glory of eternal life, vindicating the fidelity of the Christian in the face of suffering, is far beyond all human merit (*Rom.* 8: 18, 28). Thus, although there is a reciprocal relationship between God and the Christian (as most notably in Pelagius's view of predestination at v. 29), God does not act merely in direct proportion to the Christian's response. The love which binds the Christian to God, though mutual, is begun and fulfilled by God (*Rom.* 8: 35–9).

The Status of the Jews

Chapters 9–11 present a new topic, the question of the status of the Jews. Pelagius organizes Paul's treatment of the question into two parts. Chapters 9 and 10 deal, negatively, with the estrangement of the Jews in the present (*Rom.* 9: 1). Chapter 11, more positive, considers the future of the Jews and the continuing opportunity for their salvation (*Rom.* 11: 1).

The Argument against the Jews (Rom. 9: 1–10: 21)

The comments on chapter 9 begin with Paul's evaluation of the heritage of the Jewish people. According to Pelagius, Paul runs a middle course between two extremes. Paul does not dismiss the Jewish people *en masse* (*Rom.* 9: 6–7), and yet he does not grant them a special status merely on account of their descent from Abraham (*Rom.* 9: 7, 14). Rather, in order to reconcile God's unique relationship with the Jews in the past with God's apparent rejection of them in the present, he turns to the question of who is a child of Abraham and therefore an heir of the promises God made with Abraham (*Rom.* 9: 6). In reviewing the line of descent from Abraham to Jacob, Paul demonstrates, according to Pelagius, that God chooses only one of the children of each generation as heir of the promises, and that God's choice is based on the faith, either present or future, of the persons concerned (*Rom.* 9: 10–11). The Jews are chosen now on the same terms as in the past: their relation to Abraham is a matter of faith.

This explanation of the status of the Jews is common in patristic commentary on Romans. What is interesting in Pelagius's presentation of it is the concern that Paul's view of divine election should not be construed to eliminate human freedom. As he comments on Paul's survey of the descendants of Abraham, Pelagius takes pains to explain, as had Augustine at one time (see the Introduction at n. 138), that

God's election of a person (in this case Jacob) is based on God's foreknowledge of that person's faith, and that God's election in no way rules out the possibility that a sinner may repent and be included among the elect (*Rom.* 9: 10, 12). This question of the relationship between divine election and human freedom becomes the focus of the rest of the chapter, which is construed as a hypothetical debate between the apostle and some Jewish opponents (*Rom.* 9: 14 n. 13).

Although Pelagius's reconstruction of this supposed debate is awkward, it is revealing of the terms on which Pelagius defends his understanding of election. Both Paul and his opponents, as Pelagius portrays them, assume that it would be unjust for God to elect a person without regard for that person's merits, but they disagree on whether God's election of the Gentiles was in fact a violation of that principle (*Rom.* 9: 14). The opponents maintain that the rejection of the Jews and the election of the Gentiles demonstrates that God determines history in a capricious manner without regard for human merits, whereas the apostle holds that the Jews were rejected on account of their unbelief while the Gentiles were accepted because they believed (*Rom.* 9: 16, 19, 26, 30). Both, however, acknowledge that responsibility is a prerequisite for justice, and that a version of divine election which violates human responsibility is unacceptable.

Pelagius believes that the Jews are estranged from God because they rejected the forgiveness offered them in Christ (*Rom.* 9: 27, 30, 32). They were, he says, unwilling to admit that they had not succeeded in keeping the law and were therefore in need of forgiveness (*Rom.* 10: 3). This characterization of the Jews, though not the most vehement in tenor, is common in early Christian writing (*Rom.* 9: 33 n. 32). Pelagius does not, however, wish to denigrate the law or deny that it is an avenue, albeit a difficult one, to salvation (*Rom.* 10: 5). On the contrary, unlike Ambrosiaster and Origen, he holds that before the time of Christ Jews indeed achieved eternal life by keeping the law (*Rom.* 10: 5 n. 4). But now faith in Christ is as necessary for the Jews as for the Gentiles, if only because perfect observance of the law after the coming of Christ requires that one believe in Christ, who has fulfilled the law (*Rom.* 10: 4–5). In short, as Pelagius has asserted time and again, there is no difference in the way to salvation for Jew and Gentile in the Christian era (*Rom.* 10: 10–11).

Chapter 10 concludes with one last argument from Paul's opponents. The Gentiles, they object, could not have been saved by faith because they never heard a message to which they could respond in faith (*Rom.* 10: 14–16). In reply, according to Pelagius, Paul demonstrates from Scripture that the message of the prophets reached the Gentiles, and he challenges the Jews on whether they themselves, ignorant of this fact, were attentive to the prophets (*Rom.* 10: 18–21). The point of this last rebuttal is, as before, the affirmation that faith is the response which determines whether one is chosen of God (*Rom.* 10: 19).

The Argument for the Jews (Rom. 11: 1–36)

Having confronted the Jews in chapters 9 and 10 with their responsibility for their estrangement from God, Paul, according to Pelagius, presents them in chapter 11 with the opportunity to be reconciled to God (*Rom.* 11: 1). Paul's purpose is not only to encourage the Jews to believe, but also to disabuse the Gentiles of any sense of superiority (*Rom.* 11: 2, 20, 25). With regard to the Jews, Paul concedes that few of them believed in Christ (*Rom.* 11: 7), but notes that some of them nevertheless were saved by faith, and that just as some were saved in the past so too some may be saved in the present (*Rom.* 11: 4–5). In no way should the 'spirit of stupefaction' which characterizes the Jews be understood to rob them of the freedom to choose or the ability to repent (*Rom.* 11: 8, 10). There is still hope for the Jews—hope that they will believe and be included among the elect (*Rom.* 11: 5, 11). On the other hand, Paul warns the Gentiles not to assume superiority to the Jews. The knowledge the Gentiles have of Christ is, to begin with, derived from those Jews who believed in Christ (*Rom.* 11: 12, 15). Furthermore, in the analogy of the olive grafts, the Jews were cut off not merely to make room for the Gentiles, but because of their unbelief (*Rom.* 11: 17–20). Should the Jews believe and the Gentiles fall away, their positions would be reversed (*Rom.* 11: 21, 23). As things stand, the histories of the Jews and the Gentiles have transpired to the point that both are in the same position before God, namely, in need of the forgiveness offered in Christ (*Rom.* 11: 25, 32).

Time and again Pelagius indicates, often merely with a phrase, that salvation is conditional upon faith, and that faith, a function of the will, is just as possible for the Jews now as it was in the past (*Rom.* 11: 1, 7, 8, 10, 11, 12, 14, 16, 23, 25, 28, 29). Pelagius takes special care to explain that God has not determined either that the Jews should be rejected or that the Gentiles should be saved. The Jews have received a 'spirit of stupefaction' and have been 'cut off' because of their unbelief; the Gentiles have been elected on account of their faith

(*Rom.* 11: 32). In both cases the response of the people has determined their relationship to God.

Pelagius also emphasizes that salvation, though by faith, is undeserved. It is 'grace', 'freely bestowed' out of God's mercy, not in proportion to merit (*Rom.* 11: 5, 6, 31–3, 35). No one can claim to have received what he or she justly deserves, because the initiative in any relationship to God lies first and last with God, who created the human race, then revealed the law, and finally redeems in Christ (*Rom.* 11: 34–6). All this, according to Pelagius, deprives humankind of any claim to self-sufficiency before God.

Practical Matters

The Mind and Body of Christ (*Rom. 12: 1–21*)

In chapters 12–16 Paul deals with a series of practical matters, beginning with general advice in chapter 12 on the way in which Christians as a whole are to embody Christ. Pelagius's comments on that chapter are as various as Paul's directives. Some themes, however, bear on matters discussed elsewhere in the commentary.

Pelagius's comments on the first two verses of the chapter add to his earlier discussion of the relation between body and soul in the transformation from sin to holiness (see the discussion of Rom. 8 above). Just as the body is governed by the mind, so should the mind be governed by the will of God. To this end, counsels Paul, the Roman believers should renew their minds, which in turn direct their bodies, so that they may know the will of God (*Rom.* 12: 1–2). This would mean an end, however, to public display, that enduring feature of Roman life: a good work done for public notice is done foolishly and does not please God (*Rom.* 12: 1).

The next few verses discuss the various gifts of the Spirit. Pelagius indicates how they enter into the progress of the Christian. The gifts of the Spirit, he explains, are indeed gifts, bestowed by God as God wishes (*Rom.* 12: 3, 6). Nevertheless, in the same comments he adds that they are received only by Christians of sufficient faith or purity, a foretaste for them of the glory which will come to all. Here again, as in Pelagius's discussion of election in chapter 9, human fidelity is not seen to be incompatible with divine grace.

As Paul goes on to describe how Christians should live, there develops in Pelagius's comments an antipathy between the 'world' and 'God' that is akin to Paul's attitude towards 'this age' (*Rom.* 12: 2, 11).

The 'world' represents whatever would sway the Christian from serving God. Thus, what is done out of regard for public opinion is contrasted with what is done for God's sake (*Rom.* 12: 1, 17). The lust for vengeance that predominates in society must be replaced by the readiness to be humiliated (*Rom.* 12: 16–17). Mutual love and support, not competition, should characterize members of Christ (*Rom.* 12: 15). One senses that the 'world' is not far from the Rome of Pelagius's day.

Relations with Authorities (Rom. 13: 1–7)

Pelagius offers two interpretations of the discussion in chapter 13 of the relationship of the Christian to those in authority. 'The authority', he says, can refer to civil authorities or to ecclesiastical authorities (*Rom.* 13: 1). Most patristic interpreters understood Paul to mean civil authorities, and the weight of this tradition is reflected in Pelagius's comments. His remarks about ecclesiastical authorities are inserted among comments that simply assume that the authorities in question are civil authorities (*Rom.* 13: 3, 7).

Pelagius introduces the discussion by setting it in context. Paul raises the issue, he says, because certain Christians had misconstrued their freedom as licence to ignore the authorities (*Rom.* 13: 1). For Pelagius this attitude is dangerous because it reflects badly on Christ: the disdain of these Christians may lead the public to believe that Christ taught his followers to be proud (*Rom.* 13: 6). Though Pelagius acknowledges that civil authority has been instituted by God to maintain order in society (*Rom.* 13: 4), he is concerned more about the misconceptions that an antinomian attitude in Christians will convey about Christ than about disruption to orderly society (*Rom.* 13: 1, 2, 6).

Pelagius is aware that Paul's description of the authorities does not always correspond to reality. It does not escape his notice that not all rulers are just; that generally they do not, as Paul would have it, commend the good; that they can become angry without cause (*Rom.* 13: 1, 3, 7). This awareness of the discrepancy between the ideal and the actual in politics is not unique, and neither is Pelagius's resolution of the dilemma. Like his predecessors, Pelagius distinguishes between the institution and the use of authority. Authority is instituted by God, but may be abused by the ruler—for which abuse the ruler is, of course, accountable (*Rom.* 13: 1 n. 3).

Reservations like these are absent when Pelagius treats ecclesiastical authority. Most of his comments serve to explain how Paul's language can be applied to ecclesiastical authorities, how, for example, priests may be said to bear a sword, to become angry, or to collect taxes (*Rom.* 13: 4–6). In one of these comments there is a hint as to why Pelagius takes pains to apply Paul's exhortations to the relationship between laity and clergy. When he says that 'even the righteous' owe priests respect, he may be alluding to ascetic Christians who disregarded—or were thought to disregard—clergy whom they deemed too worldly (*Rom.* 13: 5 n. 8). It would be characteristic of Pelagius as a moderate among ascetics to temper the scorn of the zealous (see the Introduction at n. 83 above).

Love of Neighbour and Knowledge of God (Rom. 13: 8–14)

The remainder of Pelagius's comments on chapter 13 treat the summary of the law and the analogy between knowledge and light. Pelagius, following Paul, asserts that one keeps the law when one loves one's neighbour as oneself, and, citing a specific example, explains further that to love one's neighbour is not only to refrain from doing harm but also to do good (*Rom.* 13: 9–10). Then, turning to Paul's figurative exhortation to pass from the darkness of night to the light of day, Pelagius likens 'night' to ignorance, 'day' to knowledge of Christ, and the advance of the 'day' as growth in holiness (*Rom.* 13: 11–13). As elsewhere (see the discussion of Rom. 1: 18–3: 20 above), Pelagius posits a direct relationship between knowledge and holiness, and feels none of the sluggishness which Augustine lamented in his *Confessions* (*Rom.* 13: 11 n. 14). According to Pelagius, Christ, who embodies all the virtues (*Rom.* 13: 14), offers greater knowledge of righteousness than ever before (*Rom.* 13: 11), and this knowledge keeps the Christian, who should reflect Christ, from transgressing the law (*Rom.* 13: 13).

Fasting and Abstinence (Rom. 14: 1–23)

The problem which Paul addresses in chapter 14 is a dispute which had arisen among Christians about whether or not they ought to abstain from meat. The occasion for the dispute—probably the fact that the meat had been used in a cultic ritual—is not stated, and patristic commentators were left to supply the details. Unlike some, Pelagius argues that the context is not a Jewish one, since the Jewish dietary laws did not stipulate that one should abstain from meat altogether (*Rom.* 14: 2 n. 4). He ventures no further than this, and instead interprets the chapter in the light of the debate current in his own day about the value of asceticism. Jovinian, the most prominent critic of what seemed to him to be excessive claims for asceticism, had reasoned that to abstain from food and wine was not inherently better than to eat and drink with thanksgiving (see the Introduction at n. 76). Pelagius's response to such views was, compared with Jerome's, moderate. Restraint in the use of food and drink, while not required, is nevertheless preferable, particularly to avoid offending other Christians (*Rom.* 14: 1 n. 1).

Pelagius develops this view by stages. In the first part of the chapter he argues for mutual respect and tolerance between those who abstain and those who do not (*Rom.* 14: 1–12). The issue in these verses, according to Pelagius, is vegetarianism (*Rom.* 14: 2), and since the law is not definitive on this issue those who abstain from meat should not judge those who eat it (*Rom.* 14: 1, 5, 12). Pelagius even mentions several reasons that one may have for eating meat: one may be strong in faith, or in poor health, or elderly (*Rom.* 14: 2). The important thing is, as Paul suggests, not which practice one adopts but why one adopts it. Each party in the dispute should follow its respective practice for God's sake (*Rom.* 14: 4); in other words, they should act in such a way that others will come to believe in the Gospel and be saved (*Rom.* 14: 6). For motives as well as actions will each party be accountable to God, and until such time as these motives are revealed neither party should condemn the other for its practice (*Rom.* 14: 10–11).

Having acknowledged that dietary restraint is not obligatory for the Christian, Pelagius in the second half of the chapter goes on to emphasize that abstinence is nevertheless preferable (*Rom.* 14: 13–23). Following Paul, he argues that it is better to abstain from a particular food than to harm another Christian by eating it (*Rom.* 14: 13, 15, 20–2). But in a number of asides, which extrapolate from the text and are without parallel in his sources, Pelagius also emphasizes that Paul is especially concerned about the adverse effects not of abstinence, but of eating and drinking (*Rom.* 14: 15, 16, 17, 19). If Paul had to decide between Jovinian or his opponents, Pelagius seems to be saying, he would side with the latter. Food and drink are hazardous commodities; their use may degenerate into abuse, and for this reason alone, apart from the offence even prudent use of food may occasion, abstinence is preferable.

Final Exhortations (*Rom. 15: 1–33*)

Paul's final exhortations in chapter 15 are diverse, but some general themes emerge from Pelagius's comments. In the opening verses

Pelagius follows up, as does Paul, the advice of chapter 14 and counsels the 'strong' to bear with the 'weak', even if this is not to one's own advantage (*Rom.* 15: 1–2). This is the Christ-like thing to do (*Rom.* 15: 3, 5, 7). If it entails suffering, there is the consolation that Christ and the saints have likewise suffered (*Rom.* 15: 3–4). Paul is also a model of his own exhortation (*Rom.* 15: 2).

In the next section Pelagius affirms once more that the Gentiles are saved along with the Jews (*Rom.* 15: 8–13). He is especially concerned with exclusive claims on the part of the Jews (*Rom.* 15: 8–9). Paul, he says, cites the prophets to show that the salvation of the Gentiles was indeed foretold and has come to pass as foretold, even though the Jews were unaware of these prophecies or wrongly understood them to refer to proselytes (*Rom.* 15: 9, 12). The burden of Paul's argument, according to Pelagius, is to persuade the Jews to accept the Gentiles so that the two may be united in one faith (*Rom.* 15: 8, 33).

In the final section of the chapter Paul offers an account of his ministry as an apostle, and particularly of his letter to the Romans and of his forthcoming visit. What is distinctive in Pelagius's comments is his depiction of the apostle as a 'good teacher' (*Rom.* 15: 14). Paul is a teacher who encourages his pupils by praising them (*Rom.* 15: 14); who uses argument as a means of instruction (*Rom.* 15: 15); whose example befits his teaching (*Rom.* 15: 16); whose teaching is ratified as apostolic by miracles (*Rom.* 15: 19, 21); whose task is made easy when his students are attentive and his heart is light (*Rom.* 15: 29, 32).

Closing Salutations (*Rom. 16: 1–27*)

Pelagius's comments on this last chapter are few and brief. Frequent reference is made to teaching and instruction. The labours of Priscilla and Aquila are noted (*Rom.* 16: 1, 3–4). There are allusions to converts from Judaism who, arriving in Rome from the east, introduced the Romans to Christianity (*Rom.* 16: 5, 13). The problem of false teachers occasions a description of the marks of true apostolic teaching (*Rom.* 16: 18, 25). And the last comment observes that human beings are good and wise not by nature, as is God, but by instruction (*Rom.* 16: 27). Altogether, these comments convey a sense of a tradition of, the need for, and a confidence in teaching as a means of salvation.

Pelagius's Commentary
on St Paul's
Epistle to the Romans

italic type	the Epistle to the Romans
roman type	the comments of Pelagius
[ ]	variants which are omitted by either the Karlsruhe (Augiensis CXIX) or the Balliol (157) manuscripts
Gen. (etc.)	reference to a book of the Bible
Gen. (etc.)	reference to a commentary on a book of the Bible; unless otherwise noted, *Rom.* refers to Pelagius's commentary on Romans

PROLOGUE[1]

Romans from both Jewish and Gentile backgrounds came to faith. In an arrogant dispute the one group sought to put down the other. For the Jews said, 'We are the people of God, whom he has loved and cherished from the beginning. We, the circumcised, descend from Abraham's line, from holy stock, and in times past "God was known" only "in Judaea". After we had been freed from Egypt by signs and wonders [from God], we crossed the sea on dry ground, while huge waves overwhelmed our enemies. On us the Lord rain[ed] manna in the desert, and for us he provided heavenly food, as if we were his children. Before us he went day and night in the pillar of cloud and fire, to show us a way where there was none. And, not to mention his other immeasurable benefits towards us, we alone were worthy to receive God's law, to hear the voice of God when he spoke, and to know his will. In this law was Christ promised us; in fact, he himself declared that he had come for us, when he said, "I have come only for the lost sheep of the house of Israel", whereas he called you dogs rather than people. Is it then right that, now that you have deserted the idols which you worshipped from the beginning, you should be on equal footing with us, and not rather relegated to the position of proselytes in accordance with the authority and the custom of the law? And even this position you would not have attained had not the abundant mercy of God wished to allow you to imitate us.'

[And] the Gentiles, on the contrary, retorted, 'The greater the benefits of God which you recount to have been shown you, the greater the crime you show yourselves to be guilty of: for you have always been manifestly ungrateful for every one of these benefits. For with the very feet with which you crossed the dry sea you sported before the idols you had made. With the very mouth with which a short while ago you had sung to the Lord on account of the slaughter of the adversary you demanded that images be made for you. With the very eyes with which you used to gaze upon God in the awesome cloud or fire [you looked upon images]. The manna, too, was loathsome [to

---

[1] The prologue summarizes the commentary. It is now thought to have been written by someone other than Pelagius and added to the commentary soon after it was in circulation. See the Introduction, n. 58.

you], and in the desert you were forever grumbling against the Lord, longing to return to Egypt, whence he had thrust you with a mighty hand. Why say more? Thus your fathers vexed the Lord with repeated provocation, so that they all died in the wilderness, and only two of their elders entered the promised land. But why do we repeat ancient history, since, even if you had never done these things, everyone would deem you unworthy of pardon on this ground alone, that you not only refused to receive the Lord Christ, promised you time and again by voice of the prophets, but actually destroyed him in a most ugly death, whereas we believed him as soon as we knew of him, although nothing was proclaimed to us about him beforehand? This goes to show that our submission to idols should be imputed to ignorance, rather than obstinacy of mind: for one who immediately follows what has been recognized would undoubtedly have followed it in the past, if he had recognized it earlier. But you boast of the distinction of your lineage as if physical birth, and not moral imitation, makes us children of the saints. In fact, although Esau and Ishmael were from Abraham's stock, they are [nevertheless] not reckoned among his children.'

Thrusting himself between those who were disputing in this way, the apostle interrupts the questions of the two parties so as to establish that neither of them deserved salvation by their own righteousness; rather, both peoples sinned knowingly and gravely, the Jews inasmuch as they dishonoured God by transgression of the law, the Gentiles in that, although they ought to have worshipped as God the Creator revealed by the creation, they changed his glory into idols fashioned by hand. With [irrefutable] logic the apostle shows, therefore, that they are equal, both having obtained pardon in like manner, especially when in one and the same law it [was] foretold that both Jews and Gentiles were destined to be called to faith in Christ. Wherefore, humbling them in turn, he exhorts them to peace and [to] concord.

1: 1 *Paul*. Do we ask why he writes 'Paul', since he was called 'Saul' before? We should suppose that he did this after the manner of the saints. When they advanced in virtues, they were addressed with a different name so that even in very name they might be new, as, for example, Abraham and Sarah and Cephas (cf. Gen. 17: 5; John 1: 42).[1] *Servant of Jesus Christ*. He begins with 'servant' to give us an example of humility, as an imitator of the one who 'emptied himself, taking the form of a servant, and humbled [himself], having become obedient even unto death: wherefore God also exalted him' (Phil. 2: 7–9).[2] Accordingly, as follows, he merited the office of apostle by faithful and matchless service.[3] *Called an apostle*. [Already in foreknowledge called to be an apostle.][4] *Set apart*. As the Holy Spirit says in the Acts of the Apostles: 'Set Barnabas and Saul apart for me for the work for which I have chosen them' (Acts 13: 2). *For the Gospel of God*. 'Gospel' in Latin means 'good news', the good news, that is, of Christ's birth, passion, resurrection, and ascension into heaven. 2 *Which he had promised beforehand through his prophets*. He indicates that he preaches no other Christ than the Christ whose Gospel the prophets promised would issue from Jerusalem (Isa. 2: 3/Mic. 4: 2).[5] *In the holy Scriptures*. He declares that they are prophets of God, and that the Scriptures which prophesied about Christ beforehand are holy. Indeed, this entire passage contradicts the Manicheans, for in it he states that already beforehand the Gospel was promised both through God's prophets and in the holy Scriptures; and that with regard to the flesh Christ was created from the line of David, that is, of the virgin Mary, just as Isaiah foretold it (Isa. 7: 14).[6] 3 *Concerning his son*. Many are sons by grace,

[1] Cf. Ambstr. *Rom.* 1: 1 (CSEL 81. 1: 9–15); Orig.–Ruf. *Rom.*, praef. (PG 14: 836A 6–838A 9); and see Smith, 'Latin Sources', 20: 148 n. 1; Souter, *Expositions*, i. 70, 108–9.

[2] Cf. Orig.–Ruf. *Rom.* 1. 1 (PG 14: 837B 11–838B 9); Cypr. *Test.* 3. 39 (CCSL 3: 131. 1–132. 17).

[3] Cf., for a greater emphasis on the priority of grace, Anon. *Rom.* 07 (Frede ii. 21).

[4] Cf. Orig.–Ruf. *Rom.* 1. 2 (PG 14: 840A 14–842A 5).

[5] Cf. Just. *Dial.* 24. 1, 34. 1, 43. 1, 109. 2–110. 1 (Archambault i. 110. 2–4, 148. 9, 190. 5, 160. 21–162. 25); Iren. *Haer.* 4. 34 (SC 100: 856. 82–8); Tert. *Marc.* 3. 21. 3 (CCSL 1: 537. 256–60); Cypr. *Test.* 1. 10 (CCSL 3: 13. 2–8); Lact. *Inst.* 4. 17. 3–4 (CSEL 19: 343. 14–344. 7).

[6] Cf. Aug. *Fort.* 19 (CSEL 25: 96. 8–97. 7); *Faust.* 11. 3 (CSEL 25: 316. 8–319. 10); and see Decret, *Aspects du manichéisme*, 123–49, 271–89.

but Christ is a son by nature;[7] even in his physical birth he is shown to be different from the rest [because the holy virgin Mary both conceived and bore him].[8] *Who was made from the seed of David.* Made by the [Holy] Spirit. *As to the flesh.* By adding 'as to the flesh' he has quashed both Photinus and Arius. For if he was made as to the flesh, he assuredly was not made as to the substance of the Word.[9]   4 *Who was predestined Son of God in power.* 'So that he might hold first place over all things' (Col. 1: 18).[10] *As to the spirit of sanctification by the resurrection of the dead.* Predestined as to the spirit of sanctification, so that [by] virtue of his incorruptibility he might rise again before everyone else and open the way of the resurrection for the children of God, about whom he himself says that 'they are children of God, because they are children of the resurrection' (Luke 20: 36).[11] *Of Jesus Christ our Lord.* The form of the resurrection, not of all who rise from the dead, but of all who belong to Christ, is prefigured in Christ.[12]   5 *Through whom we received grace and apostleship.* Grace in baptism;[13] apostleship, when he was directed by the Holy Spirit (cf. Acts 13: 2): for 'apostle' in Greek means 'sent' in Latin. *For the obedience of faith among all the Gentiles.* He received apostleship [among all the Gentiles], so that [now] they might obey not the law, but faith. *For his name's sake.* We discharge our duty in his name, as he says: 'Just as the Father has sent me, I also send you', and again: 'Whoever has received you has received me' (John 20: 21; Matt. 10: 40).   6 *Among whom you also have been called to belong to Jesus Christ.* Among you too, that is among the Romans, we have received the office of apostle.   7 *To all who are in God's love in Rome.* That is, to all believers, whom God loves equally, without partiality for Jew or Greek (cf. Rom. 2: 11).[14] *Called saints.* Saints because of God's

---

[7] A common distinction in the 4th cent., against the Arian notion that the Word participates in divinity by grace.

[8] The clause in brackets is probably not authentic; see the Introduction at n. 212. The belief it asserts, that Mary remained a virgin in conception and delivery, was a matter of debate at the end of the 4th cent.; see the Introduction at n. 72.

[9] The Photinians denied the pre-existence of the Word altogether, while the Arians, accepting the Word's pre-existence, denied that the Word was uncreated. Cf. Pel. *Lib. fid.* 3. 4 (PL 45: 1717).

[10] Cf. Ambstr. *Rom.* 1: 4. 2 (CSEL 81. 1: 17. 16–17).

[11] Cf. ibid. 1: 4. 3 (CSEL 81. 1: 17. 18–19).

[12] On *forma* as 'model' or 'pattern' cf. *Rom.* 5: 12, 5: 16, *2 Cor.* 1: 4, 8: 8, *Gal.* 4: 3, *1 Tim.* 3: 2, 4: 12, 5: 23; as 'standard' cf. *Rom.* 2: 14, *Gal.* 5: 14; as 'archetype' or 'exemplar' cf. *Rom.* 2: 21, 5: 14, *1 Cor.* 15: 22. The latter is the sense of the word here; on its connotations see Greshake, *Gnade,* 83–4, 114–15.

[13] On baptismal justification, or the forgiveness of sins which is freely granted to believers in the sacrament of baptism, see *Rom.* 3: 24, 3: 28, 4: 7–8, 5: 17, 6: 4, 6: 22, 8: 30.

[14] The equality of Jew and Gentile before God is a central theme in Pelagius's inter-

call, not on account of [holiness].[15] *Grace and peace to you from God our Father and the Lord Jesus Christ.* His greeting is everywhere designed both to recall God's benefits and to seek that [they] remain perfect within us, because our sins have been freely pardoned and 'we have been reconciled to God through the death of his Son' (Rom. 5: 10).[16] He also impresses upon them that they ought to live peaceably, since they have obtained one and the same grace. [Here ends the preface.] 8 *First of all, I thank my God through Jesus Christ.* God is God of all by nature, but God of few in merit and will,[17] as in the case of 'the God of Abraham' (Exod. 3: 6). Paul here calls God 'his' in this latter sense. *For you all.* Not for the Jews alone. *Because your faith is being proclaimed throughout the whole world.* He praises them in a prudent fashion, so as to incite them to improve.[18] Or: Because the whole world stood amazed that [the Romans] had believed, [since] they had been engrossed with an extravagant cult of idols, to the degree that they served the gods of all the nations they had conquered. But it is not improbable simply that he praised a faith whose zeal is now evident. 9 *For God is my witness, whom I serve in my spirit in the Gospel of his Son.* That is, I serve with my whole heart and with a ready zeal; 'for if I do this willingly, I have a reward' (1 Cor. 9: 17). Or: Here he has used 'spirit' for 'word', as in the passage: 'The heavens were established by the word of the Lord, and all their strength by the spirit of his mouth' (Ps. 32: 6). *That without ceasing I always remember you* 10 *in my prayers, entreating.* Here he both indicates that he will say everything out of love, so that he may be heard more readily, and presents a model of unceasing prayer (cf. 1 Thess. 5: 17).[19] *If by any means I may now at last by the will of God find the way propitious to come to you.* 11 *For I long to see you.* [If] for any reason I come to you some time by the will of God. For I do not find the way propitious unless the will of God, which knows all

pretation of the first four chapters of Romans; see *Rom.* 2: 11, 2: 13, 3: 9, 3: 19, 3: 29, 5: 1. It is epitomized by Paul's assertion that God does not show favouritism (Rom. 2: 11, Eph. 6: 9, Col. 3: 25); see *Rom.* 2: 2, 2: 10, 9: 26, *1 Cor.* 7: 22, *Col.* 1: 9; cf. Anon. *De indur. cord.* 19–21 (Plinval 157–9).

[15] Pelagius repeatedly asserts that justification is not based on merit but is freely bestowed on the believer; see *Rom.* 3: 24, 4: 4–5. Cf. Aug. *Exp. inch.* 7. 7 (CSEL 84: 155. 3–8).

[16] Cf. Ambstr. *Rom.* 1: 7. 2 (CSEL 81. 1: 21. 4–6); Aug. *Exp. inch.* 8. 4 (CSEL 84: 155. 18–20).

[17] Cf. Ambstr. *Rom.* 1: 8. 3 (CSEL 81. 1: 23. 8). The distinction between 'nature' and 'merit and will' is characteristic of Pelagius's polemic against Manichaean determinism; see Bohlin, *Die Theologie des Pelagius*, 16, 22.

[18] Cf. Ambstr. *Rom.* 1: 8. 3 (CSEL 81. 1: 23. 4–6); see also Pel. *Rom.* 11: 1, 15: 14.

[19] Cf. Ambstr. *Rom.* 1: 9. 3 (CSEL 81. 1: 25. 14–19); see also Pel. *Rom.* 9: 1.

things, has directed me to a place where I may enjoy some fruit. Wherefore we read in the Acts of the Apostles that although they wanted to go to one place, they were destined for another (cf. Acts 16: 7).[20] Or: As James says: 'If the Lord is willing and if we are living, we shall do this or that' (Jas. 4: 15). *In order to impart some spiritual grace to you, to make you strong.* Here he indicates why he praised them earlier on, [because] they need some spiritual grace to strengthen them.[21] 12 *That is, so that I may be comforted among you by the faith that is in turn both yours and mine.* So that we may comfort one another by our common faith. 13 *For I do not suppose you are unaware, brothers, that I often planned to come to you.* For you were able to hear of it through the brothers that were coming and going. *And that I have been prevented until now.* 'Prevented' here means 'busy'[, while he was preaching in other provinces, as he explains at the end of the letter, when he says: 'For this reason, [too,] I was often kept from visiting you' (Rom. 15: 22)].[22] *So that I might enjoy some fruit among you as well.* He calls the reward for his labour 'fruit'. *As among other Gentiles.* 'I enjoy' is understood. 14 *To Greeks and barbarians, wise and foolish.* He calls the Greeks[, who boast a representative of every philosophy,] wise; the barbarians, foolish. *I am under obligation;* 15 *inasmuch as it lies with me, I am ready.* That is, 'prepared'. *To preach the Gospel also to you who are in Rome.* Who are just as wise as the Greeks. 16 *For I am not ashamed of the Gospel.* This is subtly intended to censure the pagans, who, although they do not blush to believe that for the sake of monstrous lust their god Jove turned into irrational animals and inanimate gold, suppose that we should be ashamed to believe that for the salvation of his image our Lord was crucified in the flesh he assumed (cf. Gen. 1: 26), though in the one case the disgrace is shocking, in the other a mark of fidelity and power.[23] At

---

[20] Cf. Ambstr. Rom. 1: 9–10. 4–5, 1: 13. 2–3 (CSEL 81. 1: 25. 22–27. 2, 31. 14–23).

[21] Cf. *Rom.* 1: 8.　　　　　　[22] Cf. Anon. *Rom.* 013 (Frede ii. 23).

[23] For Jove's metamorphoses see Ovid, *Met.* 2. 836–75, 3. 259–61, 4. 611, 6. 103–14; *Amores*, 3. 12. 33. Gibes of the sort Pelagius makes are standard fare in Christian apology; cf. Just. *1 Apol.* 25 (FP 2: 50); Tat. *Orat.* 10. 1 (Whittaker 18, 20); Athenag. *Leg.* 20. 1–22. 12 (Schoedel 40–52); Tert. *Apol.* 11. 10–14 (CCSL 1: 108. 45–109. 67); Lact. *Inst.* 1. 11. 18–23 (CSEL 19: 39. 13–40. 10). It is interesting to note the implied contrast between Jove's incarnation and the Word's incarnation: whereas Jove came in inanimate and irrational forms, the Word came in 'the flesh', i.e. a rational form. The phrase 'in the flesh he assumed' is commonly used in the early 5th cent. to refer to the human nature of Christ and often serves to protect the divine nature from suffering; see Dewart, 'Christology', 1223. Pelagius here specifies the crucifixion. For Pelagius it has propitiatory value as the basis for forgiveness of sins in baptism and exemplary value as the model for the believer's life after baptism; cf. *Rom.* 6: 3–11 and see Rivière, 'Hétérodoxie'; Greshake, *Gnade*, 125–9.

the same time he touches upon those heretics who shrink from the idea [that God should put on a man and give him up to death for the salvation of the human race] as something unbecoming for God, not realizing that nothing is more becoming for the creator than to care for the salvation of his creatures, especially since he could not on account of this suffer loss to his own nature, it being impassible.[24] *For it is the power of God unto salvation.* There is no greater power than that which conquered death and restored to humankind the life it had lost.[25] *For all who believe.* Much as it may seem weakness to the unbelieving (cf. 2 Cor. 13: 4). *First for the Jew, and also for the Greek.* 17 *For the righteousness of God is revealed in it.* Either: Because it was just that the rest of the believers should be saved in the same way that Abraham was, who when he believed was saved from among the Gentiles initially by faith alone.[26] Or: Because the testament which God, who is truthful, promised in the law had to be revealed.[27] *By faith in faith.* Or: Because the Jew is justified by faith and the Gentile in faith; he wrote ['by' and] 'in' to avoid the fault of tautology.[28] *As it is written: the just live by faith.* 'Not by works of the law' (Gal. 2: 16).[29] 18 *For the wrath of God is revealed from heaven.* He begins [to address] the case [of the Gentiles, and he says that the wrath of God is revealed through the Gospel, or else through the testimony of nature]: for people have learnt to expect both benefits and calamities from heaven. *Upon all the impiety and unrighteousness of humankind.* [He said 'against all' because] there seem to be three kinds of impiety. The first and greatest is towards God, which one commits by blasphemy or idolatry. The second is in the form of injury towards or contempt for parents, as it is written in Leviticus: 'If someone sleeps with his father's wife, the two shall be put to death; they have committed impiety and stand condemned'

---

[24] The 'heretics' here probably include the Manichaeans, Marcionites, and gnostic writers; cf. Tert. *Carn.* 3. 4–6 (CCSL 2: 876. 20–877. 38) and *Dial. Adam.* 4. 13 (GCS 4: 171. 23–173. 15).

[25] Cf. Ambstr. *Rom.* 1: 16. 2–3 (CSEL 81. 1: 35. 23–37. 2).

[26] Cf. *Rom.* 4: 5–6.

[27] Cf. Ambstr. *Rom.* 1: 17. 2 (CSEL 81. 1: 37. 22–5).

[28] Pelagius, unlike other writers, does not interpret *ex fide in fidem* to signify the transition from law to Gospel; cf. Tert. *Marc.* 5. 13. 2 (CCSL 1: 702. 5–7); Ambr. *Ep.* 20 (77). 15 (CSEL 82. 3: 153. 167–9); Orig.-Ruf. *Rom.* 1. 15 (PG 14: 861B 9–12); Anon. *Rom.* 15A (Frede ii. 23). The reference to the 'vice of tautology' echoes the judgement of 4th-cent. grammarians; see Charisius, *Ars gramm.* 4 (Keil i. 271. 16–17); Diomedes, *Ars gramm.* 2 (Keil i. 450. 16–18); Donatus, *Ars maior,* 3. 3 (Keil iv. 395. 10). But cf. Anon. *Rom.* 32A (Frede ii. 33), for whom the idiom is not a flaw.

[29] See Hab. 2: 4 at Gal. 3: 10–14; cf. Ambstr. *Rom.* 1: 17. 1a, 4 (CSEL 81. 1: 37.16, 39. 5–9).

(Lev. 20: 11–12). The third is towards someone who is not a relative, as in the example: 'And you have forgiven the impiety of my heart' (Ps. 31: 5); [there are] also many other texts [in addition to this one], but it would take too long to list them. Or: Every sort of impiety must be traced back to the various cults of idols, so that it is clear that impiety refers to injury towards God, but unrighteousness to all sins.[30] *Of those who hold the truth of God in unrighteousness.* They hold the truth of God's name [in] the unrighteousness of the base stuff of which idols are made.[31]   19 *Since what is known about God.* What can be known by nature about God, that he exists and that he is just.[32] *Is plain to them.* To their consciences. For every creature bears witness that it [is] itself [not] God, [and] shows that it was made by another, with whose will it ought to comply.[33] For if God [is] the highest magnitude, invisible, incomprehensible, inestimable, and the one who is over all—that is, the one who has neither superior nor equal in greatness or splendour or might, he obviously cannot correspond to any creature that is seen with the eyes and conceptualized by reason and assessed with judgement.[34] No creature, moreover, is in every way greater than all others, because they all surpass one another, some in size, as heaven and earth; some in splendour, as the sun and the moon or the stars (cf. 1 Cor. 15: 41); some in depth, as the sea. It is evident, therefore, that none of the elements is God.[35] Furthermore, their changeability, which cannot belong to eternity, proves that they were created. Indeed, it is obvious that they did not create themselves, because if they had created themselves, they were already existing before they were created, so as to be able to create themselves—which is an utterly

---

[30] The first of these two comments reflects the several usages of *impietas* in antiquity, but turns to the Scriptures for illustration. The second comment restricts *impietas* to the narrow religious sense it had acquired in the Jewish and Christian traditions; cf. Orig.–Ruf. 1. 16 (PG 14: 863b 6–7) and see Momigliano, 'Impiety', 565–6.

[31] Cf. Aug. *Exp. prop.* 3. 2 (CSEL 84: 4. 2–6); Orig.–Ruf. *Rom.* 1. 16 (PG 14: 863b 14–c 4); and see Schelkle, *Paulus*, 63.

[32] The assertion that 'by nature' one can know that God is just is of particular importance to Pelagius, for it is the basis of his morality; see Pirenne, *La Morale de Pélage*, 29, 33. Later Pelagius explains precisely how one comes by this knowledge; see *Rom.* 1: 32.

[33] The whole point of knowing God is doing God's will; in fact, whoever does not do God's will in a sense does not know God. Cf. *Rom.* 2: 18, 3: 11; and see Pirenne, *La Morale de Pélage*, 29–30; Evans, *Pelagius*, 52.

[34] Cf. Tert. *Apol.* 17. 2 (CCSL 1: 117. 6–12); Min. Fel. *Oct.* 18. 8 (Beaujeu 27); Novat. *Trin.* 31. 1 [182] (CCSL 4: 75. 1–4); Lact. *Epit.* 21 (26). 5 (CSEL 19: 693. 25–8).

[35] Against the Stoics, who were the chief proponents of this view; cf. Diog. Laert. *Vit. phil.* 7. 147 (OCT ii. 360. 14–20); Lact. *Inst.* 2. 5. 25–6. 2 (CSEL 19: 118. 21–119. 24); Aug. *Ciu.* 7. 23 (CCSL 47: 204. 22–30); and see Colish, *Stoic Tradition*, i. 24–5. On the origins of the view see Dillon, *Middle Platonists*, 25.

absurd thing to say. In fact, because they change and vary their courses and give place to one another, they show that they have been created by one Maker and that they perform not their own will but their master's, whose command they cannot disobey.[36] *For God has made it plain to them.* 20 *For since the creation of the world his invisible properties, even his eternal power and divinity, are clearly seen, having been understood through the things that were created, so that they are without excuse.*[37] His hidden qualities are deduced from things that are manifest.[38] For if he made the things which are visible so splendid that some considered them gods and tried to assert that they are eternal, how much the more were these people able to understand that the one who made these things is everlasting and almighty and boundless.[39] As the Book of Wisdom says: 'When the creation is set alongside his greatness, then the creator of these things can be seen', and so on [in what follows] (Wisd. 13: 5). [In fact,] his invisible properties are so plainly understood that they are said to be 'clearly seen'. 21 *Because, although they knew God, they neither glorified him as God.* Either by nature or by considering the creation.[40] *Nor gave him thanks.* For the fact that they had been made in such a way that they could recognize God if they wanted.[41] *But they degenerated in their thinking.* Imagining that they could grasp God's [greatness] with the mind, they degenerated from their natural instinct by worshipping creatures instead of the creator. *And their foolish heart was darkened.* Because it withdrew from the light of truth. 22 *For, declaring themselves to be wise.* As those who had discovered how the invisible God is honoured by means of a visible idol. *They became fools: 23 and they changed the glory of the incorruptible God*

---

[36] Cf. Lact. *Epit.* 21 (26). 1–4 (CSEL 19: 693. 11–25); but see also Cic. *De nat. deo.* 2. 2. 4, 2. 5. 15 (Pease ii. 545–7, 586–9). On the origin and uses of the argument from the uniform motions of the heavens to the existence of God see Pepin, *Théologie cosmique*, 476; Spanneut, *Le Stoïcisme*, 283–5.

[37] The whole of v. 20 is translated here, avoiding the awkward division found in Souter's edition.

[38] Cf. Tert. *Apol.* 17. 2 (CCSL 1: 117. 11–12); Lact. *Epit.* 21 (26). 5 (CSEL 19: 693. 26–8).

[39] Cf. Orig.–Ruf. *Rom.* 1. 17 (PG 14: 864B 3–9).

[40] On the distinction between knowledge of God that is derived from human rationality and a knowledge of God that is acquired by reflection on the created world cf. Cic. *De nat. deo.* 1. 16. 43–4, 2. 2. 4 (Pease i. 293–300, ii. 545–7).

[41] The terms *posse* and *uelle* have come to be trademarks of Pelagius's morality. The former refers to the God-given ability of human beings to know God, recognize God's will, and acknowledge its direction towards good and away from evil. The latter refers to the free choice whereby human beings choose either for good in accordance with God's will or for evil in opposition to it. The emphasis in Pelagius's comment here falls on the responsibility human beings have as a result of their ability. 'If they wanted'— that is the condition on which Pelagius's morality hinges.

into the likeness. Not understanding that there is no likeness between
the mortal and the immortal, the corruptible and the eternal.[42] *Of an
image of a corruptible human being and of birds and animals and serpents*. Not
into the likeness merely of a human being, but [into] the likeness of an
image of a human being, and—what is more—of animals as well.[43]
Here he addresses the worshippers of Jove, who maintain that he was
transformed [into the likes of these because of his most obscene lusts],
and therefore dedicate to him images of the sort in which he satisfied
[his] sexual desire.[44]   24 *Therefore God gave them over to the desires of
their heart*. In the Scriptures God is said 'to give over' when because of
freedom of choice he does not restrain transgressors. As [he says] in
the psalm: 'And I let them go according to the desires of their heart',
and so forth (Ps. 80: 13).[45] *To impurity*. Which occurs in the filthy rites
of the idols. *So that they degrade their bodies with abuses*. When in their
rites they afflict themselves with brands and burns.[46] *Among themselves*.
So that like the insane they avenge their own wrongs on themselves.
25 *Who exchanged the truth of God for a lie and worshipped*. They
exchanged the worship of the true God for the lie of the idols, which
are falsely worshipped as [gods] and somehow lead these fools to
believe that they are what they are not. *And served the creature rather than
the creator*. They not only loved, but also served: indeed, anyone who is
overcome by a desire for some creature serves that creature: 'For one
is the slave of that by which one has been conquered' (2 Pet. 2: 19).[47]

---

[42] Cf. *Rom.* 1: 19.

[43] On the distinction between worshipping human beings (i.e. emperors and other
venerated persons) and worshipping images of human beings (i.e. statues in human
form) cf. Ambstr. *Rom.* 1: 23. 1–2 (CSEL 81. 1: 45. 8–20).

[44] Cf. *Rom.* 1: 16.

[45] All of Pelagius's contemporaries take pains to explain that in handing over sinners
to the desires of their heart God does not violate the freedom of the will; cf. Ambstr.
Rom. 1: 24. 1–2 (CSEL 81. 1: 47. 15–23); Aug. *Exp. prop.* 5 (CSEL 84: 4. 1–2); Anon. *Rom.*
020 (Frede ii. 25–6); Orig.–Ruf. *Rom.* 1. 18 (PG 14: 866c 6–13); and see Schelkle, *Paulus*,
66–9. Of these Augustine alone cites Ps. 80: 13, as does Pelagius, to explain the meaning
of *tradere*. But, unlike Augustine, Pelagius specifies the sort of freedom the sinner
enjoys—*libertas arbitrii*—and in this he echoes Origen–Rufinus; cf. *Rom.* 8: 32. Pelagius
is some distance from the anonymous commentator, who explains that one remains in
sin because of the absence of divine assistance; cf. Anon. *Rom.* 20A (Frede ii. 26).

[46] Pelagius may refer to the cult of Cybele–Attis, in which the initiate was tattooed
with a needle that had been heated in fire; cf. Prud. *Peristeph.* 10. 1076–90 (PL 60: 525–7),
and see Dölger, 'Die religiöse Brandmarkung', 66–70. But Mithraic rituals also
involved the use of fire, and there are suggestions that the initiates were burnt; cf. Greg.
Naz. *Orat.* 4. 70 (SC 309: 180. 6–7), and see Merkelbach, *Mithras*, 101; Burkert, *Ancient
Mystery Cults*, 102–4. For the debate about the evidence see Beskow, 'Branding in the
Mysteries of Mithras'.

[47] Pelagius recognizes that choices, once made, have their consequences; cf. *Rom.* 7:

Who is blessed forever. If they had served him, they too could have been blessed forever: for 'one who does God's will abides in eternity, [even] as God abides in eternity' (1 John 2: 17). 26 *Therefore God gave them over to shameful passions*. Because of the reasons noted above they were abandoned to their monstrous behaviour. *For their women changed their natural relations into relations which are against nature*. Those who turned against God turned everything on its head: for those who forsook the author of nature also could not keep to the order of nature.[48] 'The worship of abominable idols'[, he says,] 'is the cause, the beginning, and the end of every evil' (Wisd. 14: 27). 27 *In the same way men, too, having forsaken natural relations with women, were inflamed with lust for one another, men committing shameful acts with men*. Lust, once unbridled, knows no limit. *And receiving in themselves the due penalty for their errors*. So ran the order of nature, that those who had forgotten God did not understand themselves as well.[49] 28 *And since they did not think it worth while to know God*. Not merely did they not know God, they did not even think it worth while to know God. For one thinks it worth while to know God when, keeping him always in view, one does not dare to sin. *God gave them over to a reprobate disposition*. They were given over to a worthless disposition because they did not think it worth while to know God. *So that they do what is unbecoming*. [So that they do what is unbecoming] for a human being to do. 29 *Filled with every sort of wickedness and malice*. He shows that wickedness and malice are the chief causes of the vices.[50] *Fornication and greed*. He linked fornication with greed because both are on almost the same footing as idolatry.[51] *Villany; full of envy, murder*. How fitting it is for him to associate murder

---

15 ff. 2 Pet. 2: 19, cited here, would later be taken up by Augustine against the Pelagians; see *Vetus Latina*, xxvi. 1. 216–17.

[48] Because they regarded God as the Soul who pervades the world, the Stoics identified the will of nature with the will of God and held that happiness ensues when one bends one's own will to the will of God or nature. Pelagius, holding to a Christian doctrine of creation, does not identify God with nature, but rather asserts that departure from the order of nature is a consequence of abandoning the author of nature. But like the Stoics he regards the laws of nature as a revelation of God's will, and accordingly associates deviation with apostasy. Cf. *Rom.* 1: 31.

[49] The comment is a variation on the classical theme that knowledge of self leads to knowledge of God (and vice versa). This theme courses through Platonic, Stoic, and Neoplatonic writing into the Christian tradition. Cf. e.g. Mar. Vict. *Adu. Arium*, 3. 8 (SC 68: 460. 19–461. 21); Ambr. *Luc.* 7. 220 (CCSL 14: 2900. 2411–13); Aug. *Solil.* 2. 1. 1 (PL 32: 885); *Sent. Sext.* 398, 446 (Chadwick 58–9, 62–3); and see Courcelle, *Connais-toi toi-même*, i. 11–163.

[50] Cf. Ambstr. *Rom.* 1: 29 (CSEL 81. 1: 53. 26–7).

[51] Cf. ibid. 1: 32. 1a (CSEL 81. 1: 55. 20–2); see also Pel. *Rom.* 1: 23, 1: 24, 1: 26.

with envy, since envy is the main cause of this crime. *Strife*. Strife exists where something is defended not by reason [but] with an obstinate spirit; where resolve is wearied [more than] truth is sought. *Deceit*. [Deceit is] secret malice dressed up in flattering speech. *Malignity*. A wish or a work of malice is called malignity.   30 *Murmurers*. [That is,] grumblers. [Or:] Those who speak not to one's face but into one's ear. *Slanderers hateful to God*. Indeed, nothing is so hateful to God as idolatry, and the Scriptures connect slander with idolatry by stipulating the same penalty, that of rooting out. [For he says: 'He who sacrifices to the gods will be rooted out' (Exod. 22: 20), and elsewhere it is written: 'Do not love to slander, lest you be rooted out' (Prov. 20: 13).][52] *Insolent*. Those who are quick with insults. *Proud, haughty, inventors of evil*. One who desires to be more than he is is proud, as was the Devil, [who in this way] ruined what he was. For one who seeks to lord it over others will in so doing end up beneath them. 'Inventors of evil' follows, therefore, because pride is always devising and inventing evils, just as the author of pride in his haughtiness invented evil, which had not existed previously, for himself.[53] And indeed one is called 'haughty' when one is puffed up beyond one's proper limits. *Disobedient to parents*. True parents are those who bring children forth into light and eternal life through the seed of the word.   31 *Foolish, disorderly*. Those who have withdrawn from the fount of wisdom inevitably [also] carry on in a disorderly manner.[54] *Without affection*. Affection is the fulfilment of love. *Without mercy*. How could they who refused to be merciful to themselves be merciful to others? He mentions all these sins, set out one by one, with regard to those who, having abandoned God, have [in turn] been abandoned by him. Let us beware, then, lest we too be likewise abandoned for harbouring one of these evils.   32 *Who, although they had known the righteousness of God, did not realize that those who do such things are worthy of death*. Although they had known the righteousness of God from the fact that they themselves also find evil displeasing, they did not realize that it follows from this that such persons will be punished, if not in the present, then

---

[52] For the association of slander with idolatry by way of their common penalty— *eradicare* in the *uetus latina*—cf. Cypr. *Fort.* 3. 1 (CCSL 3: 189. 3) (citing Exod. 22: 20) and *Test.* 3. 107 (CCSL 3: 173. 1–174. 3) (citing Prov. 20: 13, reading the variant in the MSS DAQM).

[53] On the imitation of the Devil cf. Ambstr. *Rom.* 1: 32. 1a (CSEL 81. 1: 55. 19, 22). On the view, increasingly accepted by the 5th cent., that the sin by which the Devil fell was pride cf. Ambr. *Ps. 118* 7. 8 (CSEL 62: 131. 17–19); Jer. *Ep.* 12. 2 (CSEL 54: 41. 11–12); Aug. *En. in ps.* 58, s. 2. 5 (CCSL 39: 748. 13–22).

[54] Cf. *Rom.* 1: 26.

nevertheless in the future; for if they had realized this, they would have been especially afraid of doing such things.[55] *Not only those who do these things, but also those who agree with those who do.* In case someone should say that he had not done all these things, he added 'those who agree with those who do'. But even someone who [perhaps] does not agree with these doings—because people passed judgement on the sort who do these things—nevertheless seemed to have agreed to them all by agreeing [to] idolatry, which is the source and cause of them all.

2: 1 *Therefore you—every one who passes judgement—are without excuse. For in whatever matter you pass judgement on another person, you condemn yourself: for you who pass judgement do the same things.* Everyone passed judgement on people of this sort, but above all this concerns those who are in a position to pass judgement. Judges and princes are being brought to trial.[1] For by means of natural judgement each person pronounces a sentence which fits the deed, and all know both that uprightness deserves reward and that wickedness meets with punishment. 2 *Now we know that God's judgement is in accordance with the truth against those who do such things.* The judgement by which people of this sort—people who were able to condemn in others what they did not hesitate to commit themselves—are judged is in accordance with the truth. For if you, a sinner, pass judgement upon a sinner like yourself, how much more will God, who is just, judge you to be unjust.[2] Otherwise it would perhaps appear that to him evil is pleasing and good displeasing. In fact, we read that he, showing no favouritism, spared neither his friends nor his angels when they sinned![3] But human judgement is compromised in many ways: the integrity of judges is often violated by love, hatred, fear, and greed, and now and then mercy is inclined against the rule of justice. 3 *But do you— someone who passes judgement on those who do these things and yet do the same things—imagine that you will escape God's judgement? 4 Or do you scorn the riches of his goodness and patience and forbearance, not realizing that God's goodness leads you to repentance?* Or do you delude yourself about your impunity because God does not punish immediately, and, seeing time

---

[54] Cf. *Rom.* 1: 19, 2: 1–4.

[1] See Souter's edition for the variant versions of this comment. Cf. Anon. *Rom.* 21A (Frede ii. 27); Orig.–Ruf. *Rom.* 2. 2 (PG 14: 873C 3–13).

[2] Cf. Anon. *Rom.* 021 (Frede ii. 26); see also Pel. *Rom.* 1: 32.

[3] On the impartiality of divine justice cf. *Rom.* 1: 17. On the 'friends of God', or the patriarchs, see Judith 8: 22, Jas. 2: 23, and cf. Jer. *Ep.* 22. 8 (CSEL 54: 155. 5–156. 8); *Ep.* 47. 2 (CSEL 54: 346. 2–4); *Ep.* 79. 7 (CSEL 55: 95. 18–.21). On the 'sinful angels' see 2 Pet. 2: 4.

wear on and goodness abound, imagine that there is no longer a judgement?[4] [Well then,] listen to the word of Scripture: 'The Lord is not
tardy with his promises, but waits patiently on your account, not wanting anyone to perish, but desiring everyone to turn in repentance'
(2 Pet. 3: 9).[5] [The Lord is] good in so far as he waits, just in so far as he
punishes. Wherefore the prophet warns: 'Do not be slow to turn to the
Lord, nor put it off from one day to the next: for his wrath comes unexpectedly, and at the time of vengeance he will destroy you' (Ecclus.
5: 7).[6] And again: 'You should not say: "I sinned, [and] did any misfor-
tune befall me?" For the Most High is long-suffering in taking vengeance' (Ecclus. 5: 4).[7] People lead themselves far astray on account of
God's patience, [especially] because he does not wish to punish sinners at once: [for] because he delays, they suppose either that he does
not care in the least about human affairs or that he pardons faults.[8]
Many even rail at him, 'Why doesn't he punish right away?', because
they do not realize that, if he had done so, almost no one would have survived, and the righteous would never have come from the unrighteous.[9]
Furthermore, from a human point of view God seems to wait a long time
for sinners, since we consider a hundred years an eternity because our
life-span is so short. But God, 'with whom a thousand years are as one
day', does not equate a hundred years with the space of an hour (Ps.
89: 4). Therefore, it is not enough for God, since even people usually
expect amendment in sinners only after a long time.   5 *But because of
your hardness and your unrepentant heart.* But you, unaware that you are
sick, use the very remedy to sustain greater wounds;[10] in the words of
the blessed Job, you 'waste the opportunity for repentance in pride'
(Job 24: 23). Spurned kindness leads, consequently, to heavier judgement, so that one who refused to be affected by mercy is afflicted with
punishment.[11] *You are storing up wrath for yourself on the day of wrath and of*

---

[4] Cf. Ambstr. *Rom.* 2: 3. 1–2, 2: 4. 2 (CSEL 81. 1: 63. 12–65. 20).

[5] Cf. Anon. *Rom.* 020, 22 (Frede ii. 25–7); Orig.–Ruf. *Rom.* 2. 3 (PG 14: 874ʙ 2–875ᴀ 4).

[6] Cf. Cypr. *Test.* 3. 97 (CCSL 3: 169. 2–170. 4); Orig.–Ruf. *Rom.* 2. 3 (PG 14: 875ᴀ 3).

[7] Cf. Cypr. *Test.* 3. 35 (CCSL 3: 129. 1–130. 9).

[8] Cf. Ambstr. *Rom.* 2: 4 (CSEL 81. 1: 65. 11–12).

[9] The claim that 'almost no one would have survived' if the judgement of God had
been swift implies that some would nevertheless have been found righteous; cf. *Rom.*
5: 12. What is meant by the righteous that come from the unrighteous is unclear.
Pelagius may refer to the conversion of the unrighteous, or to those born of an unrighteous generation.

[10] Cf. Tert. *Paenit.* 10. 1, 10 (CCSL 1: 337. 1–5, 337. 32–338. 36); Cypr. *Ep.* 34. 2 (CSEL
3. 2: 569: 15–570. 2); *Ep.* 59. 13 (CSEL 3. 2: 680. 13–16, 20–2); Ambr. *Paenit.* 1. 7. 31 (SC
179: 80. 14–21).

[11] Cf. Ambstr. *Rom.* 2: 8. 2 (CSEL 81. 1: 69. 18–21); Aug. *Exp. prop.* 8 (9). 1–3 (CSEL

the revelation of God's righteous judgement, **6** *who will render to each one according to his deeds.* You yourself are laying up wrath upon wrath for yourself on the day of judgement, which will be revealed at a time that is fixed and certain [in God's mind]. **7** *To those who with patience in good work.*[12] The reward for good work is awaited with patience because it is not given in this life: 'For we walk by faith, and not by sight' (2 Cor. 5: 7).[13] Or: If a work endures right to the end, it will then be perfect (cf. 1 Cor. 3: 14), because '[one] who perseveres [right] to the end will be saved' (Matt. 24: 13). *Glory and honour and incorruption.* The 'glory' with which 'the saints shall shine as the sun' (Matt. 13: 43). The 'honour' of the children of God: nothing [is] greater than this: on account of it they will judge even the angels (cf. 1 Cor. 6: 3). The 'incorruption' of life without end. *Seek eternal life.* [One who with works of patience seeks eternal life] shall attain all these things, and 'one who has this hope in God, makes himself holy, just as God is holy' (1 John 3: 3).[14] **8** *But to those who live by strife.* Those who often are overcome by enmity and fall into strife should take heed. They should be fearful of persisting in so injurious a habit, lest all the punishments mentioned below be visited upon them. Now it has already been pointed out that one is contentious especially when one tries to defend something against one's conscience.[15] *Who do not accept the truth, but believe what is evil.* They do not believe the truth of the Gospel, and approve of evil, so that, having abandoned the creator, they zealously serve the creature (cf. Rom. 1: 25). *Wrath and displeasure.* These are punishments that judgement brings.[16] **9** *Trouble and distress.* [Of] conscience [and] of fruitless repentance (cf. Matt. 3: 8; Luke 3: 8), as it is written: 'Then they will speak one to another, repenting and groaning in anguish of spirit' (Wisd. 5: 3). *For the soul of every person who does evil, first of the Jew, and also of the Greek.* The apostle threatens the soul with punishment because of heretics who say that only the flesh does

---

84: 5. 21–6. 5); Orig.–Ruf. *Rom.* 2. 4 (PG 14: 877B 5–6); Anon. *De indur. cord.* 42, 44 (Plinval 187. 24–7, 189. 19–24). As Augustine explicitly notes, 'wrath' is explained to mean 'punishment' in order to avoid attributing passion to God. See also Pel. *Rom.* 2: 8.

[12] Pelagius's explanation of v. 7 follows the awkward rendering of the verse in the early Latin versions and subsequent Latin interpreters; cf. Ambstr. *Rom.* 2: 7. 1–2 (CSEL 81. 1: 67. 19–69. 8), and see Schelkle, *Paulus,* 75–6. For the correct Greek interpretation cf. Orig.–Ruf. *Rom.* 2. 5 (PG 14: 880A 7–B 2).

[13] Cf. Orig.–Ruf. *Rom.* 2. 5 (PG 14: 880B 4–13).

[14] Cf. *Rom.* 5: 11, 8: 17–18.

[15] Cf. *Rom.* 1: 26, and see Valero, *Las bases antropológicas,* 103–6.

[16] Cf. *Rom.* 2: 5–6 n. 11.

wrong and deny that the soul can sin.[17] Or: 'Soul' refers to the whole person, as in Genesis it is said that 'Jacob entered Egypt with seventy[-five] souls' (Gen. 46: 27; cf. Acts 7: 14).[18]   10 *But glory and honour and peace for every one who does good.* Glory as opposed to wrath, honour as opposed to displeasure; and what he [called] 'incorruption' above he calls 'peace' here (cf. Rom. 2: 7–8). *First for the Jew, and also for the Greek.* Here he has used the term 'person' to refer to what he described above as 'soul'. Now, he writes 'first' in the sense of 'indeed', for 'God does not show favouritism.' Or: As concerns faith, first in time, not in honour.[19]   11 *For God does not show favouritism.* Therefore the Gentiles should not be smug about their false ignorance, nor the Jews about their privilege in the law and in circumcision.   12 *For whoever sinned without the law will perish without the law, and whoever sinned under the law will be judged by the law.* Without the written law, under the law of nature.[20] He meant the same thing to be understood here by 'will perish' and 'will be judged', for on the one hand one who perishes perishes by God's judgement, and on the other hand one who is judged a sinner perishes, as it is written: 'For sinners will perish' (Ps. 36: 20). He places Jews and Gentiles on a similar footing when he says that doers, rather than hearers, of the law are righteous (cf. Rom. 2: 13); and, a little further on, states that the Gentiles will be judged on the day of the Lord (cf. Rom. 2: 16). For does anyone doubt that those who have been placed under the law will perish just as those who lived without the law, unless they have believed in Christ?[21]   13 *For it is not the hearers of the law who are righteous in God's eyes, but the doers of the law will be justified.* He explains why the Jews are not better than the Gentiles. We too should fear, therefore, lest we, hearing the law but not doing it, perish along with the Gentiles, as he himself says elsewhere: 'Lest we be damned along with this world' (1 Cor. 11: 32).   14 *For when the Gentiles, who do not have the law.* In case someone should perhaps say, 'They do not have the law; by what standard [could] they be

---

[17] Pelagius probably refers here to the Manichaeans; cf. *Rom.* 6: 19, 8: 7, and see Aug. *Fort.* 20 (CSEL 25: 100. 6–8); *Faust.* 22. 22 (CSEL 25: 615. 24–5).

[18] Cf. *Rom.* 6: 19, 8: 5, and see Ambr. *Exam.* 6. 8. 46 (CSEL 32. 1: 236. 23–237. 5); *Ps.* 40. 11 (CSEL 64: 235. 16–18); Aug. *Contin.* 4. 11 (CSEL 41: 154. 5–10); *Dial. Adam.* 5. 20 (GCS 4: 215. 18–21).

[19] Pelagius will not read *primum* in a way which jeopardizes the equality of Jew and Gentile before God. For a different interpretation see Anon. *Rom.* 024 (Frede, ii. 28).

[20] Cf. Orig.–Ruf. *Rom.* 2. 5, 12 (PG 14: 892A 14–D 1, 898C 8–899A 12).

[21] Cf. Ambstr. *Rom.* 2: 12. 2, 2: 25. 2, 2: 26, 2: 27 (CSEL 81. 1: 73. 18–23, 89. 12–17, 91. 3–6, 9–11). But on the possibility of salvation under the law see also Pel. *Rom.* 10: 5.

judged?' *Do by nature what pertains to the law*. Either: He means those
who were by nature righteous in the period before the law. Or: Those
who even now do some good.[22] *They are a law unto themselves, even though
they do not have the written law*. He demonstrates that they do not lack a
law, so as to leave the Gentiles no excuse and to divest the Jews of the
glory owing to the possession of the law. 15 *They show that the work of
the law has been written upon their hearts, inasmuch as their conscience bears
witness to them*. Nature produces a law in [their] heart through the testimony of the conscience.[23] Or: The conscience testifies that it has a
law, because, even if the one who sins fears no one else, the conscience
is apprehensive when one sins and rejoices when sin is overcome. *And
their thoughts in turn accuse or even defend them* 16 *on the day when God will
judge the secrets of humankind*. He asserts that there is a mental debate
when we decide by lengthy deliberation what we ought to do and what
we ought not to do, and that we should be judged according to this on
the day of the Lord, because it proves that we were not ignorant of
good or evil.[24] Or: On the day of judgement our conscience and our
thoughts shall lie before our eyes like lessons of history to be learnt;
they will either accuse us or in fact excuse us, as it is written: 'I shall
accuse you and set these things before your face' (Ps. 49: 21).[25] *According to my Gospel through Jesus Christ*. According to what I preach for
Jesus' sake. Or: God will judge through Jesus Christ.[26] 17 *Now if you
call yourself a Jew*. At this point he turns to the Jews.[27] [He teaches] that
one ought to be a Jew in deed, not only in name, and that one will be

[22] Most interpreters took this passage as evidence of a natural knowledge of God or
of the law of nature; see Tert. *Coron.* 6. 1 (CCSL 2: 1046. 4–6); Ambstr. *Rom.* 2: 14 (CSEL
81. 1: 75. 17–27); Hil. *Ps.* 118, Samech (15) 11 (CSEL 22: 493. 21–494. 5); Ambr. *Ep.* 73. 2
(PL 16: 1305C 10–15); Jer. *Ep.* 121. 8 (CSEL 56: 32. 26–33. 12). Pelagius, however, takes
naturaliter in conjunction with *faciunt* to refer to the natural ability by which one can
become righteous apart from the law of Moses or perform some good works without
knowledge of Christ; cf. Orig.–Ruf. *Rom.* 2. 9 (PG 14: 892B 2–7, C 14–15), and see
Schelkle, *Paulus*, 81–3. Augustine later takes pains to explain that Paul is here speaking
of Gentile Christians whose natural abilities have been restored by the grace of Christ;
see *Spir. et litt.* 27. 47–8 (CSEL 60: 201. 10–202. 11).

[23] Cf. Ambstr. *Rom.* 2: 15. 1–16. 2 (CSEL 81. 1: 75. 28–79. 6).

[24] Though at v. 15 Pelagius speaks particularly of the law of nature among those who
do not have the law of Moses, his comment here addresses Christians as well. For
Pelagius there is no essential change in the role of the conscience throughout human
history; cf. *Rom.* 9: 2.

[25] Cf. Orig.–Ruf. *Rom.* 2. 10 (PG 14: 894A 10–14).

[26] Cf. Ibid. (PG 14: 894B 7–9).

[27] According to Pelagius, Rom. 2: 17–4: 24 is addressed chiefly to the Jews; see *Rom.*
3: 1, 3: 9, 3: 19, 3: 27, 4: 14. On the function of personae in this section see *Rom.* 3: 1, 3: 5;
cf. Orig.–Ruf. *Rom.* 2. 11 (PG 14: 895D 2–895C 3).

deemed a real Jew if what is hidden is good.[28] *And repose in the law*. You are confident and secure. *And glory in God* 18 *and know his will*. You boast that you alone know God and understand his will.[29] *And approve what is superior because you have been taught by the law*. You choose the greater and distinguish among the lesser: for what proves beneficial by nature is made more beneficial by the law.[30]   19 *And are convinced that you are a guide for the blind*. For whom the light [of knowledge] has been darkened. *A light for those who are in darkness*. The darkness of ignorance.   20 *An instructor of the foolish*. Who do not have the wisdom of God. *A teacher of infants*. Of the small, in age or in understanding. *Having the standard of knowledge and truth in the law*. If you would always keep it in view, you could not err.[31]   21 *You then, who teach another, do you not teach yourself?* This is similar to what he said to the Gentiles: 'For you who pass judgement on another condemn yourself' (Rom. 2: 1). [For] if you, O Jew, repose in the law, why do you break the law? If you glory in God, why do you dishonour him? If you know his will, why do you not obey it? If you approve of what is of greater benefit, why do you pursue what is harmful? Why do you, a guide for the blind, not see the right way? For if you saw it, you would surely walk in it. If you are a light for others, why do you not cast off the works of darkness (cf. Rom. 13: 12)? Instructor of the foolish, why have you abandoned the fear of the Lord, which is the beginning of wisdom (cf. Ps. 110: 10)? Teacher of infants, why are you a child in understanding? If you have the standard of knowledge and truth in the law, why do you neither follow it yourself nor, with your wicked example, suffer others to follow it? Why does your life not match your teaching and why does your conduct make a ruin of your faith? As a result it shall come to pass that because you did not keep the law, the law not only does you no good, but even holds you guilty of the greater crime of treating it with contempt.[32]

[28] The first part of this comment summarizes Pelagius's interpretation of Rom. 2: 17–24; the second part, his interpretation of Rom. 2: 25–9.

[29] The comments which follow on vv. 17–21 focus on the theme of knowledge vs. ignorance. On the connection between knowledge of God and knowledge of God's will cf. *Rom.* 1: 19.

[30] It is not clear precisely how something that is beneficial by nature becomes more beneficial by the law. Pelagius may mean that the law improves upon nature by increasing one's knowledge of right and wrong, and particularly of 'lesser sins'; cf. *Rom.* 3: 20.

[31] Cf. *Rom.* 1: 28, 3: 18. On the Platonic notion of contemplating the ideas see Tert. *An.* 18. 3 (CCSL 2: 807. 24–8); Aug., *Diu. quaest.* 46. 2 (CCSL 44A: 71. 21–2). For other intimations of Platonic language see *Rom.* 1: 4, 1: 16, 2: 26.

[32] Some of Pelagius's statements suggest that the Jews did not actually understand the law; if they had, they would certainly have lived by it. Other statements imply that the Jews in fact understood the law but chose to disregard it.

You who preach that one should not steal, steal. Some say: 'You steal from people by hiding Christ from them.'[33] 22 *You who say that one should not commit adultery commit adultery.* There is not just one kind of adultery: for you commit adultery if you yield to anyone other than God all that the soul owes in its entirety to God. *You who abhor idols commit sacrilege.* Sacrilege is something that is committed strictly against God, as a violation of the sacred. 23 *You who glory in the law dishonour God by transgressing the law.* He has explained what he meant by 'sacrilege'. 24 *'For God's name is blasphemed by you among the Gentiles', as it is written.* He reversed the order and cited the passage before he said 'It is written.' For the speaker's words trailed off in such a way that he found what he was saying in his own words written to the same effect in the prophets. [And] indeed, [woe to them] whose unrighteous acts shall cause the Lord's name to be blasphemed. As it is written: 'While they are called the people of the Lord, they have defiled my name among the Gentiles', among whom they sojourned as captives because of their sins (Ezek. 36: 20). 25 *Circumcision is indeed of value, if you keep the law. But if you are a transgressor of the law, your circumcision becomes uncircumcision.* In what way[, then,] is it 'worthless', if it is of value (1 Cor. 7: 19)?[34] [Now,] it is of value in its own day. It is of value as a sign, if righteousness, of which it is a 'seal', accompanies it (Rom. 4: 11); without righteousness the rest will be superfluous.[35] Or: [It is of value because] it enabled the Jew to live and to escape destruction in infancy, before he came to an age of understanding.[36] Or: Because he set it in the law, [where] one discovers, upon close examination, that when the circumcision of the flesh ends the true circumcision of the heart will come. One is then a transgressor of the law when one does not follow what is foretold therein.[37] 26 *If, therefore, the uncircumcision keeps the righteousness of the law, will not their uncircumcision be counted as circumcision?* The visible needs the invisible, but the invisible does not need the visible, because the visible is an image of the invisible, and the invisible is the reality [of the visible]. The circumcision of the

---

[33] Cf. Ambstr. *Rom.* 2: 21. 1 (CSEL 81. 1: 85. 8–11); Orig.–Ruf. *Rom.* 2. 11 (PG 14: 896B 14–C 2, D 2–5, 898A 3–8).

[34] Cf. Ambstr. *Rom.* 2: 25 (CSEL 81. 1: 89. 2–3).

[35] Cf. Just. *Dial.* 23. 4 (Archambault i. 106–8); Tert. *Iud.* 3. 1 (CCSL 2: 1344. 3–4), ps.-Firm. Mat. *Consult.* 2. 8 (FP 39: 63. 29–64. 1).

[36] See Gen. 17: 14; cf. Just. *Dial.* 10. 3 (Archambault i. 48); Tert. *Iud.* 2. 10 (CCSL 2: 1343. 69–71); Zeno, *Tract.* 1. 3. 2. 3 (CCSL 22: 24. 24–9).

[37] Cf. Cypr. *Test.* 1. 8 (CSEL 3: 12. 1–19); Zeno, *Tract.* 1. 3. 6. 13 (CCSL 22: 27. 107–13), on the end of circumcision; Ambstr. *Rom.* 2: 23 (CSEL 81. 1: 87. 7–10) and *passim* on the charge of transgression.

flesh, therefore, needs the circumcision of the heart, but the circumcision of the heart does not need the circumcision of the flesh, because [the reality] does not need the image, [but the image needs] the reality.[38] If circumcision has no value [by itself], one rightly wonders why it was instituted. First, in order to distinguish the people of God in the midst of the Gentiles; accordingly, when they were alone in the desert, they were not circumcised.[39] Or: So that their bodies might be identified in war. Now the reason they were marked in that particular part of the body is, first of all, so that another part which was open to public view might not be disabled or defaced;[40] secondly, on account of the promise of grace, which would render this part acceptable [through] chastity.[41] Or: So that it might be signified that Christ would be born from its seed. He was destined to introduce spiritual circumcision, but until he was born physical circumcision would continue. Thus Joshua, son of Nun, who was a type of Christ, is commanded to circumcise the people a second time (cf. Josh. 5: 2).[42]   27 *Indeed, that which is by nature uncircumcision, but fulfils the law, will judge you, who by the letter of the law and circumcision are a transgressor of the law.* Either: As long as you pursue literal circumcision, you spurn spiritual circumcision.[43] Or: For not following what the law said, namely, that by believing in Christ you might receive true circumcision.[44]   28 *For he is not a Jew who is one outwardly, nor is circumcision something outward in the flesh,* 29 *but he is a Jew who is one inwardly.* He is a real Jew: for everything that previously was performed with regard to the outer person contained a figure of the inner person.[45] *And circumcision is a matter of the heart, in spirit, not according to the letter;* [He has not been circumcised in the

---

[38] Cf. Tert. *An.* 18. 3 (CCSL 2: 807. 24–8).

[39] Cf. Just. *Dial.* 16. 2–3 (Archambault i. 74); Ambr. *Ep.* 72. 11 (PL 16: 1300B 14–C 3); ps.-Firm. Mat. *Consult.* 1. 18, 2. 8 (FP 39: 21. 34–5, 64. 2–8); Orig.–Ruf. *Rom.* 2. 13 (PG 14: 912A 11–15).

[40] Cf. Orig.–Ruf. *Rom.* 2. 13 (PG 14: 912B 1–5).

[41] Cf. Ambr. *Abr.* 1. 4. 27 (CSEL 32. 1: 522. 14–16); *Ep.* 72. 20 (PL 16: 1302–1303B 1); Orig.–Ruf. *Rom.* 2. 13 (PG 14: 909C 1–8, 912B 1–5).

[42] For those who, reading Josh. 5: 2 to say that Joshua circumcised the people of Israel a second time and recognizing this to be physically impossible, gave the verse an allegorical interpretation see Lact. *Inst.* 4. 17. 9–10 (CSEL 19: 346. 5–347. 1); Zeno, *Tract.* 1. 3. 8. 15–16 (CCSL 22: 27. 123–34); Jer. *Iouin.* 1. 21 (PL 23: 239A 7–B 7); Orig.–Ruf. *Rom.* 2. 13 (PG 14: 909C 9–910A 4). However, the verse was also read to say that Joshua received a second command to circumcise the people; see ps.-Firm. Mat. *Consult.* 2. 8 (FP 39: 63. 29–64. 19). Thus Pelagius interprets the words *circumcide secundo* with the words *secundo circumcidere iubetur.*

[43] Cf. Orig.–Ruf. *Rom.* 2. 12 (PG 14: 899A 4–8).

[44] Cf. Ambst. *Rom.* 2: 27 (CSEL 81. 1: 91. 9–11).

[45] Cf. Orig.–Ruf. *Rom.* 2. 13 (PG 14: 912D 2–913A 7).

flesh.] *his praise is not from humankind, but from God.* About this it is written in the law: 'In the last days God will circumcise your heart and the heart of your seed so that you love the Lord your God' (Deut. 30: 6); and again: 'Circumcise yourselves for your God, and circumcise the foreskin of your heart' (Jer. 4: 4),[46] not according to the letter of the law, but according to the new testament, which investigates the inner secrets that God alone sees.[47]

3: 1 *What more is there, therefore, for the Jew, or what is the value of circumcision? 2 Much in every way.* The apostle has explained that the law is useless once it has been treated with contempt, and that the privilege of physical circumcision is worthless unless it is sustained with works. Now, [as though] he asks what advantage a Jew has, he receives a reply in the person of a Jew: 'Much in every way.' For if the expressions 'Much in every way' and 'Everyone is a liar' are Paul's (Rom. 3: 4), in what sense does he later on argue to the contrary by saying: 'But if our wickedness sets off God's righteousness, what shall we say? That God is wicked? Certainly not!' and so on (Rom. 3: 5)? In what sense does he finally assert that the Jews have no advantage, if here he reminds us that they have much (cf. Rom. 3: 9)?[1] *First of all, because the words of God were entrusted to them.* You mean to say this before all else, that the words of God were entrusted to them, while nothing was entrusted to the Gentiles. 3 *And what if some of them did not believe? Will their unbelief cancel God's faithfulness? Certainly not!* The faithfulness of the promises to Abraham, to whom it was said that 'in your seed will all nations be blessed' (Gen. 22: 18). 4 *God is true.* They talk as if God were true just because one is a liar. *Though everyone is a liar.* Here he uses 'all' for the greatest part, as in 'All seek their own', and 'All have abandoned me', 'Luke alone is with me' (Phil. 2: 21; 2 Tim. 4: 16; 2 Tim. 4: 11).[2] *As it is written: So that you may be justified in your words and*

---

[46] Cf. Cypr. *Test.* 1. 8 (CCSL 3: 12. 3–13); Lact., *Inst.* 4. 17. 8–9 (CSEL 19: 345. 10–346. 8); Zeno, *Tract.* 1. 3. 6. 12–13 (CCSL 22: 26. 96–27. 113)); ps.–Firm. Mat. *Consult.* 2. 8 (FP 39: 64. 15–19).

[47] See Jer. 31: 31 ff., and cf. Just. *Dial., passim*; Tert. *Iud.* 3. 7 (CCSL 2: 1345. 43–1346. 51); Cypr. *Test.* 1. 11, 3. 20 (CCSL 3: 13. 3–6, 115. 17–40); Lact. *Inst.* 4. 20. 6 (CSEL 19: 365. 6–10); ps.–Firm. Mat. *Consult.* 2. 7 (FP 39: 61: 14–17).

[1] Unlike other commentators, Pelagius interprets v. 1 as a question posed by the apostle, which an imaginary Jewish opponent answers in vv. 2–4. The resulting commentary, coloured by the interpretation of vv. 5–9, is awkward. See n. 2 below, and cf. Ambstr. *Rom.* 3: 1. 1 (CSEL 81.1: 93. 25–8); Anon. *Rom.* 027 (Frede ii. 30); Orig.–Ruf. *Rom.* 2. 14 (PG 14: 915A 6–B 9).

[2] There is a confusion of voices in Pelagius's representation of vv. 2–4. The abrupt shift at the phrase 'though everyone is a liar', which Pelagius above attributes to Paul's opponents but here treats as Paul's, is telling. If taken literally, the rhetoric of v. 4, like

prevail when you pass judgement. The opposing party has cited this testimony as if David had said, 'For this reason have I sinned, so that you might appear just in judging me.'[3] But the real meaning is this, that God had promised to punish sinners without showing favouritism, and that some judged his patience to be a lie.[4] God prevails when he judges, when he punishes the deeds of those on whom no one had imagined vengeance would be taken. Alternatively: You have shown yourself to be concerned about humankind—you who revealed my secret sins through the prophet[5]—and you have overthrown those who falsely suggest that you are uninterested in human affairs. The objection extended this far: now the apostle begins to answer.   5 *But if our wickedness sets off God's righteousness, what shall we say? That God is unjust?* It is unjust if he punishes those who have sinned merely so that he might appear more righteous.[6] *Who brings wrath*. Just as in the flood and against Sodom, so also in the judgement.[7] (*I am speaking in human terms.*) 6 *Not at all!* As you, who think along these lines. *Otherwise, how will God judge this world?* By what righteousness will he condemn unrighteousness, if according to you he is more righteous by reason of human wickedness?   7 *For if by my falsehood God's truthfulness has redounded to his glory*. That is: has increased. *Why am I still condemned as a sinner?* That is: why am I condemned besides—I, just someone who lies, who ought to be praised, if God's truthfulness is corroborated by my falsehood?   8 *And—as we are maligned, and as some claim we say— why don't we*. Why does he condemn me as a sinner, and why is it not true, as some claim we say, [that] the greater evil we have done, the greater good we receive? *Why don't we do evil, so that good may come?* Perhaps they believed this because they did not understand what he said: 'Where sin abounded, grace abounded all the more' (Rom. 5: 20). *Their condemnation is just*. What could be more just than to experience the very punishment they falsely declared we denied—we who proclaim nothing but the righteous judgement of God?   9 *What*

that of v. 12, contradicts the notion that one can be altogether free of sin. But Pelagius explains that 'everyone' in fact means 'most', citing examples of this usage elsewhere in Paul's letters. That Pelagius cannot let the word 'everyone' stand without qualification even when he has identified the speaker as someone other than the apostle indicates how important it is to him that one should believe that it is possible to avoid sinning.

[3] Cf. Ambstr. *Rom.* 3: 5. 3 (CSEL 81. 1: 101. 18–24).
[4] Cf. *Rom.* 2: 3–4.
[5] Cf. 2 Sam. 12: 1–14.
[6] Cf. Ambstr. *Rom.* 3: 5. 1 (CSEL 81. 1: 101. 6–7); Orig.–Ruf. *Rom.* 3. 1 (PG 14: 923B 3–15).
[7] Cf. Matt. 24: 37–9, Luke 17: 26–30, 2 Pet. 2: 5–6, Jude 7.

advantage, then, do we possess? For we have pleaded that all, Jews and Greeks, are under sin. I find no basis for the idea that we, who are of the Jews, are greater. For reason has discovered that both Jews and Gentiles are under sin—something we deduce not only by reason, but also corroborate with testimony from the Jews.[8]   10 *As it is written: For no one is righteous.* The psalm from which this citation has been taken speaks of the fool (cf. Ps. 13: 1). Paul shows that this testimony was fulfilled especially at the coming of Christ, for at the time he appeared no one, I think, was found righteous.[9]   11 *There is no one who understands, no one who seeks God.* Because one does not understand, one does not seek.[10] Or: One does not understand because one does not seek. Now one seeks God when one enquires after his will. For 'everyone who sins has not seen him, nor known him', because one who sins has not known the will of his master (1 John 3: 6).[11] For one whose will is unknown is even in colloquial speech said to be unknown.   12 *All have fallen away.* One who does not look for support must needs fall away. *And together become useless.* Useless for the work for which they had been begotten. *There is no one who does good, not even one.* If there is no one who does good, in what sense does he later on accuse those who devour his people and ruin the plan of the needy? For they were not God's people, if they did not do good—especially when in the same place they are called a righteous generation (cf. Ps. 13: 4–7). [But] this has to do more with the exposition of the psalm than with the concern of the apostle.[12]   13 *Their throat is an open grave.* Contaminating and killing those who listen with the stench of their teaching and flattery. For this reason is a grave carefully sealed, so that it may not continue to breed disease among the living by its vapour.[13] *They worked craftily with their tongues.* Expressing one thing with the mouth, but contemplating another in the heart.[14] *The venom of asps.*

---

[8] The equality of Gentiles and Jews, a central theme in Pelagius's interpretation of Romans, is such that not only their positions before God, but also the demonstration of their positions, are the same. For both peoples this demonstration proceeds by rational argument, in the one case from presuppositions about nature, in the other from certain Jewish presuppositions. Cf. *Rom.* 5: 1, 6: 19, 15: 15, and see Valero, *Las bases antropológicas*, 102.   [9] Cf. *Rom.* 5: 12, 10: 5.

[10] Cf. Ambstr. *Rom.* 3: 11 (CSEL 81. 1: 107. 8–9). ·   [11] Cf. *Rom.* 1: 8, 1: 19.

[12] In his comments on Ps. 13: 2–3, cited by Paul at Rom. 3: 10–12, Pelagius consistently qualifies the universal character of the statements about human degeneration. The final segment of the psalm is particularly troublesome; cf. Orig.–Ruf. *Rom.* 3. 2 (PG 14: 934A 7–C 2).

[13] Cf. Orig.–Ruf. *Rom.* 3. 3 (PG 14: 934C 14–D 3).

[14] Cf. ibid. (PG 14: 935A 8–10), especially if one reads *uolutantes* (H₁Mᶜᵒʳʳ·Nᶜᵒʳʳ·CV) rather than *uoluentes* (A) in Pelagius's comment.

The venom of these snakes is said to be the most harmful. *Under their lips.* That is: in the heart.   14 *Whose mouth is full of malicious talk.* There is not just one kind of malicious talk: for whatever is said out of malice is without doubt said maliciously.[15] *And bitterness.* Bitterness is the opposite of the sweetness of God's words.   15 *Their feet are swift to shed blood.* Either: He means, simply, murderers. Or: He means those who kill souls by flattery,[16] whence in the Acts of the Apostles Saint Paul says: 'I am innocent of the blood of all: for I did not shrink from preaching to you the whole will of God' (Acts 20: 26–7).   16 *Grief and misery are in their ways.* Souls are worn out and made miserable by their teaching or by the example of their behaviour.[17]   17 *And the way of peace they have not known.* The teaching by which God [was made peaceful] towards humankind; because everything that is similar is at peace, and everything that is contrary is at odds.   18 *There is no fear of God before their eyes.* He has ended with the fear of God, because if they had always kept the fear of God before their eyes, they assuredly would not have transgressed [so seriously]: for a servant dares not sin while the master is present.[18]   19 *But we know that whatever the law says, it says to those who are under the law.* In case they might claim that these verses of the psalm were spoken about the Gentiles, he indicates that what has been said in the law has been said to those who are under the law.[19] Of course, it is a question in what sense the Jews claimed there is no God (cf. Ps. 13: 1).[20] They undoubtedly did not state this in word, but in deed: for 'they avow that they know [God], but they deny it with their deeds' (Titus 1: 6). Here he does not address the Gentiles, because he had already made such statements about them in regard to their own case.[21] *So that every mouth may be stopped up.* Not only of the Gentiles, but also of the Jews, since they have no reason to boast.[22] *And the whole world be made subject to God.* In the confession of sin.   20 *Because all flesh will not be justified in his sight by works of the law.* [Will]

---

[15] A play on the word *maledictio*.

[16] Cf. Orig.–Ruf. *Rom.* 3. 4 (PG 14: 936A 7–11).

[17] The comments on vv. 13–17 refer to various forms of speech—false teaching, flattery, abuse—all of them destructive. They indicate the power of language for Pelagius. For him, as for other Christian teachers of his time, *doctrina* connotes far more than mere statement of doctrine. It is instruction in the truth which yields both right faith and right practice. Cf. *Rom.* 15: 14.

[18] The qualification 'so seriously' (*tam grauiter*) is attested by the Karlsruhe MS alone. See the Introduction at n. 219, and cf. *Rom.* 1: 28, 2: 20. Cf. also Cas. *Rom.* 3 (PL 68: 530B 11–14).

[19] Cf. Ambstr. *Rom.* 3: 19. 1 (CSEL 81. 1: 111. 25–113. 9).

[20] Cf. *Rom.* 3. 10.   [21] Cf. *Rom.* 2: 12–16.   [22] Cf. Rom. 2: 17ff.

be all but justified.[23] Or: By works of the law he means circumcision, the sabbath, and the other ceremonies,[24] which had to do not so much with righteousness as with carnal pleasure.[25] *For through the law comes recognition of sin.* Neither forgiveness, [nor] sin, but recognition.[26] For through the law one realizes what is a sin, either because the natural law had been forgotten,[27] or because prior to the written law the lesser sins—that is, the sins which were not harmful to others, such as concupiscence, drunkenness, and others of this sort—were not recognized to be sins.[28] 21 *But now the righteousness of God has been made plain without the law.* The righteousness which has been given to us freely by God, not acquired by our effort, has been made plain without the written law, and, having lain hidden in the law, has been revealed with greater clarity through the examples of Christ, which are more obvious.[29] *Attested by the law and the prophets.* Either: The law and the prophets foretold that this righteousness would come in the last times.[30] Or: The law and the prophets bore witness to the recognition of sin.[31] 22 *Namely, the righteousness of God through faith in Jesus Christ upon all who believe.* The faith by which one believes in Christ. *For there is no distinction.* Between Jew and Gentile.[32] 23 *For all have sinned and are in need of the glory of God.* Because they do not have their own. 24 *Having been freely justified by his grace.* Without the works of the law, through baptism, whereby he has freely forgiven the sins of all, though they are undeserving.[33] *Through the redemption which is in Christ Jesus.* By

[23] Cf. Ambstr. *Rom.* 3: 20. 1, 4–4a (CSEL 81. 1: 113. 23–115. 4, 117. 1–7); Orig.–Ruf. *Rom.* 3. 6 (PG 14: 937C 9–938C 11, 940C 13–941A 3); Anon. *Rom.* 30A (Frede ii. 32). For Pelagius there was a continuity between the law of nature, the written law, and the teaching of Christ; see *Rom.* 3: 21.

[24] Cf. Ambstr. *Rom.* 3: 20. 4 (CSEL 81. 1: 115. 20–117. 1).

[25] Cf. Iren. *Haer.* 4. 15. 1 (SC 100: 550. 11–20); Tert. *Marc.* 2. 18. 2 (CCSL 1: 495. 24–9); Novat. *Cib. Iud.* 4. 1–5 (CCSL 4: 96. 1–97. 23).

[26] On 'forgiveness' cf. Ambstr. *Rom.* 3: 20. 3 (CSEL 81. 1: 115. 14–15); Aug., *Exp. prop.* 12 (13–18). 5 (CSEL 84: 7. 10–12). On 'sin' cf. Orig.–Ruf. *Rom.* 3. 6 (PG 14: 941A 7–12). But *nec peccatum* is attested by the Karlsruhe MS alone; see the Introduction at n. 219.

[27] Cf. *Rom.* 5: 13, 7: 8–9, and see Valero, *Las bases antropológicas*, 253–5.

[28] Cf. *Rom.* 2: 18. For instances of the 'lesser sins' listed here see Gen. 9: 18–29, 19: 30–8.

[29] The translation follows the variant reading *latebat* (ASC^corr·V). See *Rom.* 3: 28, and cf. Ambstr. *Rom.* 3: 21. 1 (CSEL 81. 1: 117. 12–17).

[30] Cf. Ambstr. *Rom.* 3: 21. 1 (CSEL 81. 1: 117. 17–21); Orig.–Ruf. *Rom.* 3. 7 (PG 14: 943A 13–B 3, 944A 2–9, 944C 5–8).

[31] Cf. *Rom.* 3: 20.

[32] Cf. Ambstr. *Rom.* 3: 23. 1 (CSEL 81. 1: 119. 14); Orig.–Ruf. *Rom.* 3. 7 (PG 14: 945A 7–11).

[33] A classic statement of Pelagius's view of baptismal justification. The phrases 'freely' (*gratis*), 'without the works of the law' (*sine legis operibus*), and 'though

which he has redeemed us with his blood from death. Through sin we had been sold to death—as Isaiah says: 'You were sold by your sins'—but Christ, who did not sin, conquered death (Isa. 50: 1). For we were all condemned to death, to which he handed himself over, though it was not his due, so that he might redeem us with his blood. This is why the prophet prophesied: 'You were sold for nothing, and without money you will be redeemed' (Isa. 52: 3). That is, because you received nothing for yourselves, and have to be redeemed with Christ's blood.[34] At the same time it should be noted that he did not buy us, but bought us back, [because] previously we were his by nature, although we were alienated from him by our transgressions.[35] If we stop sinning, then indeed will our redemption be profitable.[36]   25 *Whom God has presented.* He has set him in public before the eyes of all, so that whoever wishes to be redeemed may draw near. *As a propitiator for faith in his blood to manifest his righteousness.* So that he may be propitious towards those who believe that they need to be freed by his blood.[37] *On account of the plan for the prior transgressions* [which had already been committed long ago].[38] For these Christ died, so that he might stay God's plan, by which he had determined at long last to punish sinners.[39]   26 *By the forbearance of God.* He wants to show that God had in fact waited for transgressors finally to reform themselves, but that they had abused God's patience and gone on to greater sins.[40] Whence Job, that most righteous man of his day, says of the sinner: 'God gave him room for repentance, and he abuses it in pride' (Job

undeserving' (*non merentibus*) echo Ambstr. *Rom.* 3: 24. 1 (CSEL 81. 1: 119. 22–3) and Orig.–Ruf. *Rom.* 3. 7 (PG 14: 945B 7–9).

[34] In the comments on vv. 24–5 Pelagius describes Christ's death as a substitutionary punishment for sin. It is substitutionary inasmuch as Christ undeservedly assumes death; it is penal in that the death Christ bore was a judgement for sins; it is effective because Christ was sinless. This interpretation of Christ's death differs from others which describe it as a ransom to the Devil or the enemy; cf. Chrom. *Serm.* 12. 3 (CCSL 9A: 53. 31–54. 37); Ambstr. *Rom.* 3: 24. 2 (CSEL 81. 1: 119. 25–121. 4); Orig.–Ruf. *Rom.* 3. 7 (PG 14: 945B 12–C 6). See further Rivière, 'Hétérodoxie', 23–6; cf. Studer, *Soteriologie*, 167.

[35] Cf. Chrom. *Serm.* 12. 2 (CCSL 9A: 53: 15–21); Jer. *Gal.* 2 (PL 26: 360A 9–14); and see Evans, *Pelagius*, 108; Greshake, *Gnade*, 126; García-Allen, 'Was Pelagius Influenced by Chromatius of Aquileia?'

[36] On the possibility of not sinning, here addressed to those who live after Christ, cf. *Rom.* 1: 28, 2: 20, 3: 18.

[37] Cf. Ambstr. *Rom.* 3: 25. 1–2 (CSEL 81. 1: 121. 5–7, 9–10).

[38] This comment, attested by the Balliol MS alone, is probably not authentic; see the Introduction at n. 213.

[39] Cf. Orig.–Ruf. *Rom.* 3. 8 (PG 14: 946A 1–952A 12, esp. 946B 15–C 4).

[40] Cf. ibid. (PG 14: 946B 7–15, 951C 13–D 2).

24: 23).[41] *To manifest his righteousness at this time.* So that he might reveal the righteousness which is by faith. *So that he may be just and may justify the one who by faith belongs to Jesus Christ.* Who alone has been found righteous, and also the one whom he has justified, not by works, but by faith. 27 *Where then is your boasting? It is excluded.* He addresses the Jew: [Where is] the ground on which you were boasting that you had merited righteousness by works?[42] *Through which law? The law of deeds? Not.* 'It is' is understood. *But through the law of faith.* He means the law which is the appointed end of faith, namely, the New Testament.[43] 28 *For we deem that a person is justified through faith without the works of the law.* 'We are sure' or 'we judge'. Some misuse this verse to do away with works of righteousness, asserting that faith by itself can suffice [for one who has been baptized],[44] although the same apostle says elsewhere: 'And if I have complete faith, so that I move mountains, but do not have love, it profits me nothing' (1 Cor. 13: 2); and in another place declares that in this love is contained the fullness of the law, when he says: 'The fullness of the law is love' (Rom. 13: 10). Now if these verses seem to contradict the sense of the other verses, what works should one suppose the apostle meant when he said that a person is justified through faith without the works [of the law]? Clearly, the works of circumcision or the sabbath and others of this sort, and not without the works of righteousness, about which the blessed James says: 'Faith without works is dead' (Jas. 2: 26).[45] But in the verse we are treating he is speaking about that person who in coming to Christ is saved, when he first believes, by faith alone. But by adding 'the works of the law' he indicates that there is [also] a [work] of grace [which those who have been baptized ought to perform].[46] 29 *Is God only the God of the Jews? Not of the Gentiles as well?* Did God create the Jews alone, so that he is concerned about them alone? For even if the Gentiles sinned, so did you; and even if you repent, so do they; and if to you Christ came as promised by the law, so [likewise] to them. For often the prophets spoke of their calling too. *Yes, of the Gentiles as well.* His economy of words is admirable. He said 'Yes' so

[41] Cf. *Rom.* 2: 4–5.

[42] On the arrangement of speakers in the exchange of v. 27 cf. Anon. *Rom.* 033, 034, 035 (Frede ii. 34); Orig.–Ruf. *Rom.* 3. 9 (PG 14: 954C 12–D 5).

[43] Cf. Jer. 31: 33; Tert. *Marc.* 4. 1. 4–7 (CCSL 1: 545. 18–546. 26); Cypr. *Test.* 1. 10–11 (CCSL 3: 13); see also *Rom.* 3: 31 below.

[44] Cf. Orig.–Ruf. *Rom.* 3. 9, 2. 4 (PG 14: 953C 1–10, 878C 13–D 2).

[45] Cf. Ambstr. *Rom.* 3: 28 (CSEL 81. 1: 123. 17–20); see also *Rom.* 3: 20 above.

[46] The first reference to baptism is attested by the Karlsruhe MS alone, the second by the Karlsruhe and St Gall MSS. See the introduction at n. 219.

that he might further show the Gentiles that the first saints had not been circumcised, and that Abraham was righteous before circumcision. He reiterated 'as well' so that he might not seem to exclude the Jews. 30 *Because there is in fact one God who justifies.* Both of you have believed in one and the same God and in one and the same Christ. *The circumcision by faith and the uncircumcision through faith.* 'By faith' and 'through faith' undoubtedly mean the same thing, but it is the custom of the Scriptures [in] these instances to prefer to change a word rather than repeat it, as is written in Daniel: 'For the sake of Abraham, your servant, and Isaac, beloved by you, and Israel, your holy one' (Dan. 3: 35).[47] 31 *Do we, then, tear down the law through faith? By no means! Rather, we uphold the law.* Do we, then, deem superfluous the law which enjoined us to be circumcised? Not at all! On the contrary, we enable it to stand firm when we show that what it said is true, namely that law would follow after law, testament after testament, circumcision after circumcision (Jer. 4: 4, 31: 31–4).[48]

4: 1 *What then shall we say that Abraham discovered?* He called them back to the origin of circumcision, so that what it stood for in the beginning might be understood in its entirety. *Our father according to the flesh?* Father according to the circumcision of the flesh; for faith dwells in the mind. 2 *For if Abraham was justified by works, he has glory, but not before God.* If he was justified because he circumcised [himself], then God gave him nothing, but he had glory on account of himself.[1] Alternatively: If he carried out the ordinances, he had glory in his own eyes, but not in God's.[2] 3 *For what does the Scripture say? Abraham believed in God.* Abraham's faith was [in fact] so great that his previous sins were forgiven him and righteousness was reckoned as credit for every one of them by faith alone, and thereafter he burnt with such love that he furnished himself works over and above them all.[3] *And it was credited to him as righteousness.* And therefore he has glory in God's sight, in accordance with what the law deemed satisfactory. 4 *Now to one who works wages are not credited as a gift.* He offers an example. *But as an obligation.* For it is the lot of one who is under obligation to do what he is told, and unless he complies he is condemned. But if he does what he is told he has no glory, because a servant who does nothing more than

[47] Anon. *Rom.* 32A (Frede ii. 33); see also *Rom.* 1: 17 above.
[48] Cf. Ambstr. *Rom.* 3: 31. 3 (CSEL 81. 1: 127. 10–15); see also *Rom.* 2: 29 above.
[1] Cf. Ambstr. *Rom.* 4: 3 (CSEL 81. 1: 129. 12–15).
[2] Cf. Orig.–Ruf. *Rom.* 4. 1 (PG 14: 960C 8–10).
[3] On the idea that good works performed after baptism compensate for sins see *Rom.* 4: 7–8.

[what] he is ordered is still called unprofitable (cf. Luke 17: 10).[4] Alternatively: He is not given righteousness freely, but is paid wages for prior works. 5 *But to one who does not work, but who believes in him who justifies the ungodly, his faith is credited as righteousness.* When an ungodly person converts, God justifies him by faith alone, not for the good works he did not have.[5] Otherwise he should have been punished for works of ungodliness.[6] At the same time one should note that he did not declare the sinner justified by faith, but rather the ungodly, that is, one who has just come to believe.[7] *According to the plan of God's grace.* By which he planned to forgive sins freely by faith alone.[8] 6 *As also David describes the blessedness of the person.* It is great blessedness to obtain [the grace] of the Lord without the labour of the law and of penance, as if one were to receive gratuitously some [public] honour.[9] *To whom God credits righteousness without works.* One's initial faith is credited as righteousness to the end that one may be absolved of the past, justified for the present, and readied for future works of faith.[10] 7 *Blessed are they whose transgressions are forgiven and whose sins covered.* 8 *Blessed is the one against whom the Lord has not reckoned sin.* What is forgiven is not kept in mind, and what is covered does not come to light, and for that reason it is not at all counted against one.[11] Some say that sin is forgiven in baptism, covered by penitential works, and not counted against one through martyrdom.[12] But others say that when sins have been forgiven in baptism, love for God is increased, which covers a multitude of sins [and] finally keeps them from being counted against one as long as daily good works surpass past misdeeds (cf. 1 Pet. 4: 8).[13] 9 *Is this blessedness for the circumcision, or also for the uncircumcision?* He means to assign this blessedness to the three periods

---

[4] Cf. Ambstr. *Rom.* 4: 4 (CSEL 81. 1: 129. 21–3).

[5] Cf. ibid. 4: 5. 2 (CSEL 81. 1: 131. 7–9, 12–13).

[6] Cf. Aug. *Exp. prop.* 15 (21). 3 (CSEL 84: 9. 24–5).

[7] On the distinction between the 'sinner' and the 'ungodly' cf. Orig.–Ruf. *Rom.* 4. 11 (PG 14: 999C 3–10). On the concern, implicit in Pelagius's comment, that the doctrine of justification by faith might be misconstrued to give licence to sin cf. Aug. *Exp. prop.* 16 (22) (CSEL 84: 10. 2–4); Orig.–Ruf. *Rom.* 4. 1 (PG 14: 961B 9–C 5).

[8] Cf. Ambstr. *Rom.* 4: 5. 2 (CSEL 81. 1: 131. 12–16); see also *Rom.* 3: 24 above.

[9] Cf. Ambstr. *Rom.* 4: 6 (CSEL 81. 1: 131. 20–2).

[10] Cf. *Rom.* 4: 5.

[11] Cf. Ambstr. *Rom.* 4: 7–8. 2 (CSEL 81. 1: 133. 11–13).

[12] Cf. Orig.–Ruf. *Rom.* 2. 1 (PG 14: 872C 3–8); see also Ambstr. *Rom.* 4: 7–8. 3 (CSEL 81. 1: 133. 19–28); Anon. *Rom.* 37A (Frede ii. 35). The interpretation dates from a time when martyrdom was less remote than in the 4th cent.; see Tert. *Scorp.* 6. 9–11 (CCSL 2: 1080. 3–1081. 23); *Didasc. apost.* 20 (Connolly 176. 21–7, 178. 10–16).

[13] Cf. Orig.–Ruf. *Rom.* 4. 1 (PG 14: 965C 6–966A 3).

of nature, circumcision, and Christianity.[14] *For we say that faith was credited to Abraham as righteousness*. All, in fact, confess and agree on [this point]; therefore, what reason discovers about Abraham, this will we heed with regard to the rest.[15]	10 *How, then, was it credited? When he was in circumcision, or in uncircumcision?* Let us see whether circumcision is born of righteousness, or righteousness of circumcision. *Not in circumcision, but in uncircumcision*. Because he was righteous before he was circumcised.	11 *And he received the sign of circumcision*. In case they say, 'Therefore he was circumcised unnecessarily,' he says it is the sign of righteousness, not [the beginning or] the increase of righteousness. *The seal of the righteousness of faith, which is in uncircumcision*. He received the seal of the righteousness which the faith he had when he was uncircumcised deserved.[16] For it was so perfect that it deserved a seal: for something that is full is always sealed. Or: So that he might point out how righteous and faithful he was, for he did not hesitate to bring himself grief at God's command, since he did not suppose it irrelevant that he was ordered [by] 'the Lord [of knowledge]' (cf. 1 Sam. 2: 3), just as he did not believe that a parricide enjoined by the fount of fidelity would be an act of infidelity.[17] *So that he is the father of all believers through uncircumcision, in order that righteousness might be credited to them as well*, 12 *and also the father of circumcision, not only among those who are from the circumcision, but also among those who follow the footsteps of faith which our father Abraham had when uncircumcised*. So that all who believe from among the Gentiles are children of Abraham, when faith alone is credited to them as righteousness and they too become circumcised, but in the heart.[18] Or: Because he was righteous in uncircumcision, in order to be the father of uncircumcised [believers], and remained righteous once circumcised, in order to become the father of the righteous who are circumcised.[19]	13 *For not through the law was the promise to Abraham or to his seed*. Here he calls circumcision itself 'the law', because every injunction can be regarded as law. *That he would be heir of the world, but through the righteousness of faith*. Either: That in his seed, namely Christ, all the nations that were

---

[14] Cf. *Rom.* 3: 20, 5: 12.

[15] Cf. *Rom.* 3: 9 on the use of reason, or argument from accepted premisses, towards a general conclusion.

[16] Cf. *Rom.* 4: 3, 4: 22.

[17] On fidelity, or *pietas*, see *Rom.* 1: 18; cf. also Ambr. *Abr.* 1. 8. 66, 73 (CSEL 32: 546. 4–8, 550. 5–11).

[18] Cf. Ambstr. *Rom.* 4: 12. 2 (CSEL 81. 1: 137. 12–15).

[19] Cf. Orig.–Ruf. *Rom.* 4. 2 (PG 14: 977A 3–C 3).

given him as an inheritance by the Father might be blessed (cf. Gal. 3: 16; Gen. 12: 3; Ps. 2: 8).[20] Or: That the nations 'might recline at table with him in the kingdom of heaven' (Matt. 8: 11).   14 *For if those who are of the law are heirs, faith is voided, the promise is annulled*. If, as you desire, only [those] who have been circumcised are heirs, God has not fulfilled the promise to Abraham, that 'he was the father of many nations' (Gen. 17: 4), and, if this is so, it will now seem that they believed God without good reason.[21]   15 *For the law produces wrath*. Because 'it was ordained for the unrighteous' (1 Tim. 1: 9),[22] and weighed down, rather than set free, those who desired to sin in that they were knowingly heaping up sins: for 'if you were blind'[, he says,] 'you would not have sin' (John 9: 41). *For where there is no law, there is also no transgression*. 16 *Therefore, it is by faith, so that by grace the promise to all his seed is sure, not only to one who is of the law, but also to one who is of the faith of Abraham, who is the father of us all*. Because, [then,] faith cannot be voided, nor the promise annulled, heirship is not by the law, but by faith. For the law does not forgive sins, but condemns them, and therefore cannot make all nations children of Abraham, since all must finally be punished, inasmuch as all are found under sin. But faith makes all believers children of Abraham, their sins having been forgiven by grace. *For where there is no law, there is also no transgression*. Either: There is nothing to be transgressed, where there is no law.[23] Or: There is nothing to be punished, where the law is not necessary. 17 *As it is written: 'Because I have established you a father of many nations'*. Not of the one nation of Israel. *Before God whom he believed*. Before God, [who] is the father of all believers. *Who gives life to the dead*. Here he means 'dead for the purpose of bearing children', so as to fit in with the present discussion.[24] *And calls things that are not as things that are*. Although in the beginning he [also] called things that did not exist (cf. Gen. 1: 1), and immediately they began to exist, nevertheless here he means that they were past the time of bearing children.[25]   18 *Who, against hope, believed in hope*. It was against the hope of nature for a man a hundred years old to believe that from a wife now as feeble as he was, who even in her youth had been barren, his seed would become as the

---

[20] Cf. Ambstr. *Rom.* 4: 13 (CSEL 81. 1: 137. 22); Orig.–Ruf. *Rom.* 4. 3 (PG 14: 970B 9–15).

[21] Cf. Ambstr. *Rom.* 4: 14 (CSEL 81. 1: 139. 6–10).

[22] Cf. Orig.–Ruf. *Rom.* 4. 4 (PG 14: 973B 6–12).

[23] Cf. ibid. (PG 14: 973A 9–14).

[24] Cf. Ambstr. *Rom.* 4: 17. 3 (CSEL 81. 1: 143. 21–145. 4).

[25] Cf. ibid. (CSEL 81. 1: 145. 2–4); Orig.–Ruf. *Rom.* 4. 5 (PG 14: 978D 2–979A 6).

stars of the sky (cf. Gen. 15: 5).[26] *So that he became the father of many nations, as it was said: 'So shall your seed be.'* Now by himself he had not been able to become the father of even one son; one wonders[, therefore,] how Abraham, with a body as good as dead, produced sons by Keturah, when before he could not produce one by Sarah (cf. Gen. 25: 1–2). He did not beget by Sarah because she was old and barren: but with Keturah, as with a young woman, he was able easily to beget in the course of nature.[27] 19 *And he was not weak in faith. He did not take into account that his body* was *dead, since it was almost a hundred years old, and that Sarah's womb was dead.* Faith takes no aspect of nature into account, because it knows that the one who spoke is almighty.[28] 20 *And he did not waver in unbelief about the promise of God, but was strengthened in faith.* He doubted neither the impossibility of old age nor the enormity of the promise. *Giving glory to God,* 21 *knowing full well that whatever he has promised he is able also to do.* Giving thanks as for a thing received. 22 *Therefore it was credited to him as righteousness.* Because he believed so completely and so steadfastly.[29] 23 *Yet not only for him was it written that it was credited to him,* 24 *but also for us, to whom it will be credited.* Not so that we only know of his faith, but [also] so that we imitate his example as the example of a father, just as we imitate all the examples of the saints, by which they have pleased the Lord;[30] they were, in fact, tempted so that they might know themselves and so that we might follow [their steps].[31] *Who believe in him who raised Jesus our Lord from the dead.* If we believe as completely that he has raised Christ from the dead as Abraham believed that his body, which was as good as dead, could be made alive in order to produce offspring. 25 *Who was handed over for our transgressions and raised for our justification.* Who wiped out our sins by his death and, of necessity rising again in the same state in which he had died, appeared in order to confirm the righteousness of believers.[32]

[26] Cf. Ambstr. *Rom.* 4: 18. 2 (CSEL 81. 1: 145. 19–25); Orig.–Ruf. *Rom.* 4. 6 (PG 14: 981A 3–5).

[27] Cf., for a different explanation, Orig.–Ruf. *Rom.* 4. 6 (PG 14: 982B 15–983A 7).

[28] Cf. Ambstr. *Rom.* 4: 18. 2, 4: 19–22. 1, 1a (CSEL 81. 1: 145. 21, 147. 12, 15, 16).

[29] On the notion of meritorious faith cf. Ambstr. *Rom.* 4: 19–22. 1–3 (CSEL 81. 1: 147. 13–15, 17–21, 24–6, 27–149. 2). See also *Rom.* 4: 3, 4: 11 above.

[30] Cf. Ambstr. *Rom.* 4: 19–22. 2, 4: 23–5. 1 (CSEL 81. 1: 147. 21–6, 149. 16–18); Orig.–Ruf. *Rom.* 4. 7 (PG 14: 988A 1–14) on the exemplary role of Abraham. See also *Rom.* 12: 13 below.

[31] Cf. Orig.–Ruf. *Gen.* 8. 8 (GCS 29: 82. 29–83. 10); Aug. *Serm. dom.* 2. 9. 31 (CCSL 35: 120. 655–61); *En. in ps.* 55. 2 (CCSL 39: 678. 38–43); *Quaest. Gen.* 58 (CCSL 33: 22. 718–19). See also *Rom.* 8: 27 below.

[32] Pelagius seems to be saying that Christ, by appearing in his raised body, shows that the faith of those who believe in him is justified, i.e. that they are right in believing him to be raised; cf. *Lib. fid.* 5 (PL 45: 1717).

5: 1 *Therefore, since we have been justified by faith, let us have peace with God through our Lord Jesus Christ.* He has discussed the point that none of them is justified by works, but all by faith, and he proves this with the example of Abraham, of whom the Jews think they alone are children. He has also explained why neither race nor circumcision but faith makes people children of Abraham, who was justified initially by faith alone. Now, having finished this argument, he urges them to be at peace, because none is saved by his own merit, but all are saved in the same way by God's grace.[1] ['Let us have peace with God.'] Either, let us both submit to God; or, let us have the peace of God, not merely of the world. 2 *Through whom we also have access through faith to that grace.* Through whom we have drawn near, [because] we were far away (cf. Eph. 2: 13). *In which we stand.* Who were previously prostrate.[2] *And glory in the hope of glory for the children of God.* We glory in the fact that we hope to possess the glory of God's children. What we hope for is so great that no one would venture it on his own, lest it be regarded not as hope but as blasphemy, and as something that many consider incredible on account of its greatness. 3 *What is more, we also glory in sufferings, knowing that suffering produces patience,* 4 *and patience endurance, and endurance hope.* We glory not only in the hope of glory, but also in sufferings which are most salutary, being mindful of the greatness of the reward, as James says: 'Count it all joy, brothers', and so on (Jas. 1: 2). This is why we should also desire to suffer something for the Lord's name (cf. Acts 5: 41), so that after the sufferings come to an end we may obtain an endless reward for them. For when we consider the reward, we cannot possibly regard the effort to be worthy of the reward. For indeed we know that people willingly consent to fight with beasts for the sake of gold, though they will not be able to keep it for ever.[3] How much the more [ought we] according to the example [of the apostles to rejoice in sufferings] (cf. 2 Cor. 7: 4), which indeed, although they are temporal, obtain eternal salvation and set one free from everlasting torment. For many[, in fact,] undergo terrific pains in the hope of a little health and out of concern for the body, but still cannot attain complete health. And, even if their health were to make good progress, when death intervenes a little later it will be undone! We know, therefore, on what grounds we may properly and safely glory. For it is a

[1] A summary of the argument of *Rom.* 1: 8–4: 24.
[2] Cf. Ambstr. *Rom.* 5: 2 (CSEL 81. 1: 153. 3–6).
[3] Pelagius probably refers to the fee received by those entering into a gladiatorial contract. He may also refer to the rewards showered upon a victorious combatant. See Ville, *La Gladiature en occident*, 251, 426.

considerable glory to rise from the lowest to the highest and to arrive at the greatest from nothing. We are called from the mire to heaven and from slavery to kingship—if, that is, we disdain every glory and delight of the world and glory only in that which has been promised us. And even if you did this, it is as if someone scorned a lead penny and acquired a crown jewel.[4] Yet even this is not a very fitting analogy, because here, although there is a difference in value, corruption [still] awaits both: but there the corruptible is changed into the incorruptible [and] the perishable into the eternal (cf. 1 Cor. 15: 53).[5] 5 *And hope does not dismay*. The hope of things to come casts out all confusion. This is why one who is dismayed by Christ's injunctions is shown to lack hope. *Because the love of God is poured out into our hearts*. Greatness of benefits arouses in one greatness of love,[6] which, being perfect, does not know what it is to be dismayed and afraid (cf. 1 John 4: 18). *Through the Holy Spirit, who has been given to us*. From this we learn how [God] loves us, because he has not only forgiven us our sins through the death of his Son, but has also given us the Holy Spirit, who already shows us the glory of things to come. 6 *For why did Christ, while we were still weak*. Why did he without any obligation die for us, except to manifest his love at a time when we were still weighed down with the lassitude of sins and vices? *At that time*. At that time, when righteousness had already almost disappeared, we were weak.[7] Or: Because Christ died in the last [time].[8] Or: He was dead for the time of three days, as had been foretold (cf. Matt. 26: 61; Mark 8: 31; 1 Cor. 15: 4).[9] *Die for the ungodly?* He wants to point out that Christ died for the ungodly, in order to commend the grace of Christ by a consideration of his benefits, and to show how much we, who have been undeservedly

---

[4] *Nummus plumbeus*—here 'lead penny'—is a figurative expression for a worthless coin.

[5] On the difference between corruptible and incorruptible existence see *Rom.* 1: 19.

[6] Pelagius interprets *caritas dei* as the believer's love for God, which, as he explains in the next comment, is in turn a response to the love God has shown in the death of Christ and the gift of the Spirit. Cf. Ambstr. *Rom.* 5: 5. 1 (CSEL 81. 1: 155. 9–18); Orig.–Ruf. *Rom.* 4. 9 (PG 14: 997A 15–C 11); Aug. *Exp. prop.* 20 (26) (CSEL 84: 10. 14–19); and Aug. *Ad Simpl.* 1. 2. 21 (CCSL 44: 53. 740–54. 758). The difference between Augustine and Pelagius is telling. Whereas Pelagius attributes the believer's love for God only indirectly to God's prompting, Augustine attributes it directly to God's action. In the first decade of the Pelagian controversy this difference would be magnified many times over; see la Bonnardière, 'Le verset paulinien', 659–65.

[7] Cf. Orig.–Ruf. *Rom.* 4. 10 (PG 14: 998C 9–12). On the difference between the 'weak' and the 'ungodly' see ibid. 4. 11 (PG 14: 999C 3–8).

[8] Cf. ibid. 4. 10 (PG 14: 998A 12–14).

[9] Cf. Ambstr. *Rom.* 5: 6–7. 1 (CSEL 81. 1: 157. 5–6).

loved, ought to love him, [and] so that we might see whether anything should be valued more highly than one so generous and holy, since he neither valued his life above us ungodly people nor withheld the death that was indispensable for us.[10] 7 *For one scarcely dies for a righteous person*. It is hard to die for a righteous person, because a righteous person is not destined to die:[11] for one who is to die another may perhaps die. *Now for a good person perhaps one may dare to die*. A good person is one who is also righteous: for elsewhere he says 'a righteous and holy and good commandment' (Rom. 7: 12). [But] perhaps this is the reason [one] so easily dares to die, [namely,] so that no harm may come to him.[12] 8 *But God demonstrates his love for us*. He becomes the object of love, when he conveys how much he loves us.[13] For when one does something while under no obligation, then especially one demonstrates love. And what would be less of an obligation than that a master who is without sin should die for his faithless servants, and that the creator of the universe should be hanged on behalf of his own creatures?[14] *Because, while we were still sinners*. One should note that the apostle, by saying that many who now believe in Christ were sinners, means that now they are not sinners, so that they may recall how they ought to behave. *Christ died for us:* 9 *how much more, therefore, shall we, who have now been justified*. If he loved sinners so much, how much more will he now preserve the righteous![15] *In his blood, be saved from wrath through him*. Not [by the blood] of animals, as in the law (cf. Heb. 9: 11–14). Let us take care, then, that we do not render him unclean by sinning, as the apostle himself tells the Hebrews (cf. Heb. 10: 29). 10 *For if, while we were enemies, we were reconciled to God through the death of his Son*. Sinners are enemies because they show contempt, as the apostle says: 'Do you know that friendship with this world is inimical to God?[16] Whoever, [then], wishes to become a friend of this age, becomes an enemy of God' (Jas. 4: 4). We were enemies, then, in our

[10] Cf. Cypr. *Fort.*, praef. 5. 6 (CCSL 3: 186. 90–8); Koch, 'Cyprian in den *Quaestiones Veteris et Novi Testamenti*', 551–2. See also *Rom.* 5: 8–10 below.

[11] The comment could be read to suggest that the righteous will be spared physical death as well as spiritual death. However, Pelagius may mean merely that a righteous person, not being guilty of a serious crime, is not liable to a death penalty and therefore is in no need of a substitute.

[12] 'Harm' here may mean death at the hands of enemies or as a result of dangerous circumstances, which may undeservedly befall a good person.

[13] Cf. Orig.–Ruf. *Rom.* 4. 11 (PG 14: 1000A 9–11); see also *Rom.* 5: 5 above.

[14] Cf. *Rom.* 1: 16, 3: 24.

[15] Cf. Ambstr. *Rom.* 5: 8–9. 1 (CSEL 81. 1: 161. 6–10). For the kind of life expected of the 'righteous' see *Rom.* 5: 10 below.

[16] Cf. Orig.–Ruf. *Rom.* 4. 11 (PG 14: 999C 8–10).

actions, not by nature: we have been reunited in peace, because by nature we had been united in peace.[17] *How much more, having been reconciled, shall we be saved in his life.* If we have been saved by Christ's death, how much more shall we glory in his life, if we imitate it![18] 11 *What is more, we also glory in God through our Lord Jesus Christ.* Not only shall we be [granted] eternal life, but we are promised a certain likeness through Christ to divine glory as well. As the apostle John says: 'It has not yet become manifest what we shall be; we know that [when] he appears, we shall be like him' (1 John 3: 2). *Through whom we have now received reconciliation.* Thus he means to show that Christ suffered so that we who had forsaken God by following Adam might be reconciled to God through Christ. 12 *Therefore, just as through one person sin came into the world, and through sin death.* By example or by pattern.[19] Just as through Adam sin came at a time when it did not yet exist, so in the same way through Christ righteousness was recovered at a time when it survived in almost no one.[20] And just as through the former's sin death came in, so also through the latter's righteousness life was regained.[21] *And so death passed on to all people, in that all sinned.*[22] As long as they sin the same way, they likewise die.[23] For death did not pass on to Abraham and Isaac [and Jacob], [concerning whom the Lord says: 'Truly they are all living' [Luke 20: 38].[24] But here he says

---

[17] Orig.–Ruf. *Rom.* 4. 12 (PG 14: 1002A 3–8).   [18] Cf. *Rom.* 2: 7, 8: 29.

[19] The idea that sin is passed on from Adam 'by example or by pattern', emphasized by Pelagius in reaction to traducianist interpretations of the fall, came to be regarded as a trademark of his thought. Cf. *Rom.* 5: 15 and see pp. 18–24 above.

[20] Cf. *Rom.* 3: 20.

[21] 'Death' in the sense of 'spiritual death'; see the remainder of Pelagius's comment on this verse.

[22] The phrase *in quo*, a peculiar rendering of the Greek ἐφ' ᾧ, appeared in the *uetus latina* and was thence imported into the Vulgate. Whereas the Greek construction has a causal or conditional sense, the Latin construction is most readily understood in a relative sense, though it was also given a causal or conditional interpretation. The latter was probably the understanding of the Latin translator; cf. the Vulgate rendering of ἐφ' ᾧ at Rom. 8: 3, 2 Cor. 5: 4, Phil. 3: 12, and see Freundorfer, *Erbsünde*, 130; Beatrice, *Tradux peccati*, 274 n. 59.

[23] Pelagius gives the phrase *in quo* a conditional force, explaining that Adam's descendants die if they sin as Adam did. Inasmuch as he refers here to spiritual death, his view is finally not unlike that of Ambrosiaster, the first Latin commentator to comment explicitly on the phrase; see Ambstr. *Rom.* 5: 12 (CSEL 81. 1: 163. 12–13), and cf. Aug. *Duas ep.* 4. 4. 7 (CSEL 60: 528. 9–16). Though Ambrosiaster took *in quo* to mean that all sinned in Adam 'as in a lump', he explained further that only physical death is the result of sinning *in* Adam, whereas spiritual death is the result of sinning *like* Adam; see Ambstr. *Rom.* 5: 12. 2a–4 (CSEL 81. 1: 165. 9–19), and cf. *Rom.* 5: 14 below.

[24] Pelagius refers here to spiritual death. He would hardly have been ignorant of the accounts of the physical death of Abraham, Isaac, and Jacob (Gen. 25: 7–11, 35: 27–9, 49: 28–50: 30), and the saying of Jesus which he cites was commonly understood to mean

all are dead because in a multitude of sinners no exception is made for a few righteous. So also, elsewhere: 'There is not one who does good, not even one' (Ps. 13: 1; cf. Rom. 3: 12), [and 'every] one a liar' (Rom. 3: 4).[25] Or: Death passed on to all who lived in a human, [and] not a heavenly, fashion. 13 *For before the law sin was in the world.* [The law] came as a punisher of sin. Before its coming sinners enjoyed the length of at least this present life with less restraint. There was indeed sin before the law, but it was not reckoned to be sin because [natural] knowledge had already been almost wiped out.[26] *But sin is not counted against one when the law does not exist.* How did death reign, if sin [was] not counted against one? Unless you understand: it was not counted against one 'for the present time'. 14 *But death reigned from Adam to Moses, even over those who did not sin after the manner of Adam's transgression.* Either: As long as there was no one who distinguished beforehand between the righteous and the unrighteous, death imagined that it was lord over all.[27] Or: Death reigned not only over those who, like Adam, transgressed a commandment—such as the sons of Noah, who were ordered not to eat the life in the blood (cf. Gen. 9: 4), [and] the sons of Abraham, for whom circumcision was enjoined (cf. Gen. 17: 10)—but also over those who, lacking the commandment, showed contempt for the law of nature.[28] *Who is a type of the one to come.* Either: He was a type of Christ because, just as Adam was made by God without sexual intercourse, so Christ issued from a virgin by the work of the Holy Spirit.[29] [Or, as] some say: An antithetical type: that is, as Adam is the source of sin, so too Christ is the source of

that the patriarchs are alive in spirit with God: Iren. *Haer.* 4. 5. 2 (SC 100: 428. 30); Novat. *Trin.* 25. 11 [144] (CCSL 4: 61. 50–62. 61); Aug. *En. in ps.* 77. 11 (CCSL 39: 1077. 20–2).

[25] For others who understand 'all' to mean 'many' cf. Ambstr. *Rom.* 5: 19. 1–1a (CSEL 81. 1: 185. 2–6); Orig.–Ruf. *Rom.* 5. 2, 5 (PG 14: 1023A 6–B 13, 1030A 2–D 10); and see Schelkle, *Paulus*, 190–2. On the possibility of sinlessness after the fall cf. Ruf. Syr. *Lib. fid.* 39 (Miller 112. 6–114. 8); contrast Anon. *Rom.* 40A (Frede ii. 38).

[26] Cf. *Rom.* 3: 20.

[27] For the premiss that only those who sin deliberately are the legitimate subjects of death's reign see Ambstr. *Rom.* 5: 14. 2 (CSEL 81. 1: 171. 9–15); Orig.–Ruf. *Rom.* 5. 1 (PG 14: 1017B 8–C 7, 1018B 7–C 1, 1019A 9–B 6). Contrast Anon. *Rom.* 43A, 44A (Frede ii. 39).

[28] There were two versions of v. 14 in Latin, one reading *in eos qui peccauerunt in similitudinem praeuaricationis Adae*, the other reading *in eos qui non peccauerunt in similitudinem praeuaricationis Adae*. Ambstr. *Rom.* 5: 14. 4e–5 (CSEL 81. 1: 177. 10–26) and Orig.–Ruf. *Rom.* 5. 1 (PG 14: 1019A 9–B 6) are aware of the latter but prefer the former; cf. Bammel, *Römerbrieftext*, 219. Pelagius comments on *qui non peccauerunt*, as does Aug., *Exp. prop.* 22 (29). 1–2 (CSEL 84: 11. 5–15).

[29] See Tert. *Carn.* 16. 5, 17. 3–4, 18. 3 (CCSL 2: 903. 32–8, 904. 15–29, 905. 12–14); cf. Iren. *Haer.* 3. 21. 10 (SC 211: 428. 220–8).

righteousness.[30]　15 *But the gift is not like the trespass.* In case one grants equal value to the type.[31] *For if many died by the trespass of the one, how much more has God's grace and the gift in the grace of the one person Jesus Christ overflowed to more.* Righteousness had more power in bringing to life than sin in putting to death, because Adam killed only himself and his own descendants, but Christ freed both those who at that time were in the body and the following generations.[32] But those who oppose the transmission of sin try to assail it as follows:[33] 'If Adam's sin', they say, 'harmed even those who were not sinners, then Christ's righteousness helps even those who are not believers. For he says that in like manner, or rather to an even greater degree are people saved through the one than had previously perished through the other.'[34] Secondly, they say: 'If baptism washes away that ancient sin, those who have been born of two baptized parents should not have this sin, for they could not have passed on to their children what they themselves in no wise possessed.[35] Besides, if the soul does not exist by transmission, but the flesh alone, then only the flesh carries the transmission of sin and it alone deserves punishment.'[36] [Thus,] declaring it to be unjust that a soul which is born today, not from the lump of Adam, bears so ancient a sin belonging to another, they say that on no account should it be granted that God, who forgives [a person] his own sins, imputes to him another's.[37]　16 *Again, the effect of the gift is not the same as that of the one sinner.* Rather, it is greater. *For the judgement from the one person is to condemnation.* From one [righteous] person who sinned has proceeded a judgement of death. *But grace is from many transgressions to justification.* Because Adam did not come by as much righteousness as

---

[30] Cf. Aug. *Exp. prop.* 22 (29). 3 (CSEL 11: 17–19); Orig.–Ruf. *Rom.* 5. 1, 2 (PG 14: 1020A 1–11, 1022A 3–9).

[31] In fact, as Pelagius goes on to explain, the type, Christ, is greater than the antetype, Adam; cf. Ambstr. *Rom.* 5: 15 (CSEL 18. 1: 179. 11–15).

[32] Cf. Orig.–Ruf. *Rom.* 5. 2 (PG 14: 1022C 1–7, 1023C 3–14).

[33] See pp. 18–19 above.

[34] 'Those who were not sinners' recalls Rufinus of Syria's distinction between adults and children in regard to personal sin; see Ruf. Syr. *Lib. fid.* 41 (Miller 116. 5–13, 118. 8–13); cf. Caelestius as quoted in Aug. *De gest. Pel.* 11. 23 (CSEL 42: 76. 18–19, 21–2). Contrast Anon. *Rom.* 43A, 44A (Frede ii. 39).

[35] See Ruf. Syr. *Lib. fid.* 40 (Miller 114. 13–17); cf. Jer. *Ep.* 85. 2 (CSEL 55: 136. 11–13); Aug. *Pecc. merit.* 3. 4. 7 (CSEL 60: 133. 24–134. 3).

[36] On the discussion at the beginning of the 5th cent. about the origin of the soul see the Introduction at n. 118. The notion that the body alone bears the taint of sin could seem dangerously close to Manichaeism; see *Rom.* 6: 19, 7: 17, 7: 18, 8: 7, 8: 8.

[37] Cf. Cypr. *Ep.* 64. 5 (CSEL 3. 2: 720. 19–721. 2); Aug. *Pecc. merit.* 3. 5. 10 (CSEL 60: 135. 14–137. 7); and see Pelikan, *Development of Christian Doctrine*, 73–94; Beatrice, *Tradux peccati*, 185–9, 260–78; Scheffczyk, *Urstand, Fall und Erbsünde*, 89–103.

he destroyed [by his example], but Christ by his grace discharged the sins of many; and because Adam became only the model for transgression, but Christ [both] forgave sins freely and gave an example of righteousness.[38]   17 *For if by the sin of one person death reigned through one person, how much more shall those who have received an abundance of grace and of the gift and of righteousness reign in life through the one person Jesus Christ.* By which he has forgiven many sins; and an abundance of the gift of the Holy Spirit, because there are many gifts (cf. 1 Cor. 12: 4); and also righteousness is given through baptism, and is not gained by merit.[39]   18 *Therefore, just as through one person's transgression in all people to condemnation, so also through one person's righteousness in all people to justification of life.* Death reigned, is understood; 'so also grace reigned through justification'.[40]   19 *For just as through one person's disobedience many were made sinners, so also through one person's obedience many will be made righteous.* Just as by the example of Adam's disobedience many sinned, so also many are justified by Christ's obedience.[41] Great, therefore, is the crime of disobedience that kills so many.   20 *For the law stole in so that transgression abounded.* In case they say, 'But the law forgave us our sins', he says, 'It did not come to forgive transgressions, but to point them out, and when it is transgressed knowingly, transgression begins to abound.' It is as [if] he were saying, as I see it, that the law did not take away sins, but added to them, and not because of its own fault, but because of theirs.[42] Now it 'stole in'—that is, it entered unexpectedly—and so it turned out that transgression abounded.[43] *But where transgression abounded, grace abounded all the more.* Just as the Saviour says: 'One who is forgiven more loves more' (Luke 7: 47). For the amount of sin has been revealed so that the greatness of grace might be known and so that we might pay back a corresponding debt of love.[44]   21 *So that, just as sin reigned in death, so also grace reigns through righteousness in eternal life, through Jesus Christ our Lord.* [So that,]

[38] The phrase 'by his example' (*suo exemplo*) is omitted by the Karlsruhe MS. It may have been interpolated by a Pelagian to sharpen Pelagius's insistence on example as the medium of Adam's influence. See the Introduction at n. 219.

[39] This comment is concise to the point of obscurity. The three clauses refer respectively to the three terms of the lemma in the Vulgate: grace, gift, and righteousness.

[40] The comment supplies the ellipses in the two clauses of the lemma. The punctuation after *subauditur* follows the MSS BAGV rather than Souter.

[41] Cf. Orig.–Ruf. *Rom.* 5. 5 (PG 14: 1032A 6–14).

[42] Pelagius, like other patristic commentators, reads *ut abundaret delictum* as a result clause rather than a final clause in order to avoid making the law responsible for sin; see Schelkle, *Paulus*, 192–5, and cf. Ambrst. *Rom.* 5: 20. 2a, c (CSEL 185. 8–12, 21–9).

[43] A play on the word *subintrauit*.

[44] Cf. *Rom.* 5: 5.

just as the reign of sin was abundantly established through contempt for the law, so also the reign of grace is established through the forgiveness of many sinners and thereafter through the doing of righteousness without cease.[45]

6: 1 *What then shall we say? Shall we remain in sin, so that grace may abound? 2 Certainly not!* Lest those who do not understand say: 'If grace increases in accordance with the number of transgressions, we should sin, so that more and more grace can abound.' Certainly not! I speak of those whom faith found in sin, not of us who have already died to sin so that we might live for grace. *For how shall we who have died to sin still live in it?* He wants one who has been baptized to be as steadfast and as perfect [as one who in a way cannot sin].[1]   3 *Or are you unaware?* Or do you not know about this sacrament, baptism? *That whoever of us was baptized into Christ Jesus.* Baptism is received in the Scriptures in three ways: with water; with the Holy Spirit, who is also called fire; and with blood in martyrdom, concerning which [our] Saviour said: 'I am to be baptized with a baptism' (Luke 12: 50).[2] *Was baptized into his death.* So that we died with him in baptism.   4 *For we were buried with him through baptism into death, so that, just as Christ arose from the dead by the glory of the Father, so we too might walk in newness of life.* He shows that we were baptized in this manner so that through the mystery we are buried with Christ, dying to our offences and renouncing our former life, so that just as [the Father] is glorified in the resurrection of the Son, so too on account of the newness of our way of life he is glorified by all, provided that not even the signs of the old self are recognizable in us (cf. Rom. 6: 6).[3] For we ought not to want or desire anything that those who are not yet baptized, and all those who

---

[45] Cf. *Rom.* 5: 14 on deliberate transgression.

[1] The MSS vary in their witness to the clause *quasi qui quodam modo peccare non possit.* The entire clause is found in the Karlsruhe MS (A) alone; the St Gall (G), Paris (V), and one of the pseudo-Jerome MSS (C) read *quasi qui peccare non possit*; the remainder of the MSS omit the clause. The phrase *quodam modo*, which is added in the Karlsruhe MS, tempers the assertion that the baptized should live as one who cannot sin. On its authenticity see the Introduction at n. 219; cf. also *Rom.* 6: 7. For the significance of the high standard Pelagius set for the baptized see Brown, 'Pelagius and his Supporters', 105–7, and now Markus, *The End of Ancient Christianity*, 40–3, 63–5. On the later controversy surrounding Pelagius's assertion of the possibility of sinlessness see Evans, *Pelagius*, 21–5.

[2] On baptism with water cf. Matt. 3: 11, Mark 1: 8, Luke 3: 16, John 1: 26, Acts 1: 5, 11: 16. On baptism with the Holy Spirit and with fire cf. Matt. 3: 11, Luke 3: 16. On baptism with blood cf. Luke 12: 50, 1 John 5: 6–7, and also Tert. *Bapt.* 16. 1 (CCSL 1: 290. 1–6); Cypr. *Ep.* 73. 22 (CSEL 3. 2: 795. 24–796. 3); Orig. *Martyr.* 30 (GCS 2: 26. 24–7).

[3] Cf. Orig.–Ruf. *Rom.* 5. 8 (PG 14: 1041C 10–15)

are still entangled in the errors of the old life, want or desire. 5 *For if, having been planted with him, we have been made in the likeness of his death, we shall at the same time also be made in the likeness of his resurrection.* If we are buried with him now, we can also be participants in his resurrection then; and if we have become new and been changed [in] our way of life, we shall be likewise new and changed in glory.[4] 6 *Knowing this, that our old self.*·Who used to sin by imitating the old earthly man, Adam (cf. 1 Cor. 15: 47). *Was at the same time crucified.* Understand that through baptism you, who have been made a member of his body, were crucified with Christ (cf. Eph. 5: 30). And he, in fact, hangs his innocent body so that [you] may restrain your guilty body from vices.[5] In accordance with this mystery Moses suspended the bronze serpent in the desert (cf. Num. 21: 9; John 3: 14). *So that the body of sin might be torn down, so that we are no longer slaves to sin.* That is, so that all the vices might be torn down, because one vice constitutes a member of sin, all vices the body; for Christ was crucified not in part, but altogether. Or: So that our body might be torn away from slavery to sin, and what used to be the property of transgression become the property of righteousness: for 'everyone who commits sin is a slave of sin' (John 8: 34).[6] 7 *For one who has died is justified from sin.* That is, alienated from sin: for the dead do not sin in any way.[7] So also, 'one who is born of God does not sin' (1 John 3: 9): for because he has been crucified, and all his members are filled with sorrow, he will hardly be able to sin.[8] 8 *For if we have died with Christ, we believe that at the same time we shall also live with him.* If we have not died with him, we shall also not live with him, because we are not his members. 9 *Because we know that since Christ arose from the dead he is no longer dead: death shall no longer have dominion over him.* So we too shall not fear the second death, if here we have died willingly (cf. Rev. 2: 11). Or: No longer can you be baptized a second time, because Christ cannot be crucified for you a second time, as he writes to the Hebrews: 'It is impossible that those who have once been enlightened', and so on (Heb. 6: 4). He does not

---

[4] Cf. Ambstr. *Rom.* 6: 5 (CSEL 81. 1: 193. 22–195. 5); Orig.–Ruf. *Rom.* 5. 9 (PG 14: 1044C 5–8); and see Schelkle, *Paulus*, 204–5.

[5] The play on words in the comment—*adpendere, suspendere, innoxium, noxium*—is not easily conveyed in English.

[6] Cf. Orig.–Ruf. *Rom.* 5. 9 (PG 14: 1045C 11–1046C 13).

[7] Cf. Orig.–Ruf. *Rom.* 5. 10 (PG 14: 1054C 4–D 3).

[8] On the assertion that the baptized should hardly be able to sin see *Rom.* 6: 3 n. 1. On the use of 1 John 3: 9 in support of this assertion cf. Jer. *Iovin.* 2. 1 (PL 23: 281D 7–282D 11); Aug. *Pecc. merit.* 2. 7. 9 (CSEL 60: 79. 16–19).

refuse these people penance, but denies them a repetition of baptism.[9]
10 *For in that he died to sin, he died once for all*. Because 'he carried our sins'
and suffered for us, so that in future we might not sin. *But in that he lives, he
lives to God*. He lives in the glory of divinity.   11 *So also you should consider yourselves to be in fact dead to sin, but alive to God in Christ Jesus*. As members of him, you should understand that, having died with him once for
all, you ought now always to live for God in Christ; in him our life is hidden with God, and since we have been clothed with him, we should
follow his example.   12 *Therefore do not let sin reign in your mortal body,
so that you obey its desires*. You should live in your mortal body as if you
were immortal: he [also] explained how sin reigns in the body, namely,
by obedience and consent.[10]   13 *Also, do not present your members to sin as
instruments of wickedness*. Every single member is made a weapon of
wickedness to defeat righteousness, if it turns its function to bad use. At
the same time it should be noted that it is through freedom of choice that
a person offers his members for whatever side he wishes.[11] *But present
yourselves to God, as those who are alive from the dead*. As if you have already
been raised from the dead, because then people neither live carnally nor
sin. *And your members to God as instruments of righteousness*. So that the eye
which in times past looked over the naked with lust [now looks to clothe
them]. In the same way take heed of the rest of the members [as well].[12]
14 *For sin shall not have dominion over you: for you are not under the law*. Sin
shall not vanquish you: for you are not children, but adults (cf. Gal.
3: 23–6). It is as if a teacher [says] to a young man, 'Avoid errors of style;
you are no longer learning from a grammarian, but from an orator'.[13] Or
'[Shall] not [have dominion' for] 'should [not] have dominion'. *But
under grace*. He offered, by way of grace to overcome sin, teaching [and]
example[, and in addition power through the Holy Spirit].[14]   15 *What*

---

[9] In recommending public penance, rather than second baptism, as the remedy for
serious sin, Pelagius reflects the consensus of the church at the end of the 4th cent.; see
García-Allen, 'Pelagius and Christian Initiation', 132–56; Neunheuser, *Baptism and Confirmation*, 108; Poschmann, *Penance*, 84. On the reference to Hebrews cf. Anon. *Heb.* 011
(Frede ii. 311–12).

[10] According to Pelagius, the resurrected body, unlike the present body, will present
no occasion for sin. However, Pelagius is quick to assert that the present body is not
inherently sinful. Cf. Aug. *Exp. prop.* 12 (13–18). 1–13 (CSEL 84: 6. 17–9. 4).

[11] Cf. Orig.–Ruf. *Rom.* 6. 3 (PG 14: 1059C 12–1060A 1).

[12] Cf. ibid. (PG 14: 1063B 9–11).

[13] On the social distinction between the grammarian and the rhetorician see Marrou,
History of Education, 274–84; cf. Kaster, *Guardians of Language*, 15–31.

[14] The last phrase—*insuper et uirtutem per spiritum sanctum*—is attested by the Karlsruhe and St Gall MSS alone. For evidence in favour of its authenticity see the Introduction at n. 223.

then? Shall we sin, because we are not under the law, but under grace? In case
they say: 'Then, because the punishment of the law has come to an
end, we shall sin with impunity.' *By no means!* If you sin, you will not be
under grace.   16 *Do you not know that when you present yourselves to obey
someone as slaves, you are the slaves of the one whom you obey, whether of sin or of
obedience to righteousness?* If you wish to be in the service of sins, you
[will] begin to subject yourself to the judgement of the law, which
exacts punishment against sinners: but if you obey righteousness, you
are not under the law, but under grace.   17 *But thanks be to God that you
were slaves of sin.* 'Were', he says, not 'are'. *But have obeyed from the heart.*
That is, faithfully. *According to the form of teaching to which you were
delivered:* 18 *and, having been set free from sin, have been made slaves of
righteousness.* According to the teaching and example of Christ, who
taught one to eliminate not only sins, but also occasions for sins.
19 *I speak in human terms on account of the weakness of your flesh. For just as
you presented your members to serve impurity and wickedness upon wickedness,
so now present your members to serve righteousness unto sanctification.* I speak
in human terms because you are not yet able to listen entirely 'in
divine terms'. For although you ought to serve righteousness much
more than you previously served sin, I nevertheless make allowance
for your weakness, so that you may serve righteousness merely as
much as you served sin.[15] Or: I speak in terms befitting human reason
so that everyone can agree with me and no one dissent.[16] [He says,
'You presented your members', because] whatever the soul does in a
carnal fashion is held against the flesh; but if the flesh performs a
spiritual deed, the whole person is made spiritual: or, as the saying
goes: 'The body that is corrupted weighs down the soul' (Wisd.
9: 15).[17] [The fact is,] we presented our members to serve sin; it is not
the case, as the Manichaeans say, that it was the nature of the body to
have sin mixed in.[18]   20 *For although you were slaves of sin, you have
become free for righteousness.* That is, since you are in no way slaves to sin
inwardly, so now also become free from every sin.   21 *What benefit,
then, did you have at that time in the things of which you are now ashamed? For
the end of those things is death:* 22 *but now that you have been set free from sin,
and have become slaves to God.* Without doubt there is no benefit in a

---

[15] Cf. Ambstr. *Rom.* 6: 19. 1–2 (CSEL 81. 1: 207. 9–11, 15–22); Orig.–Ruf. *Rom.* 6. 4
(PG 14: 1063A 14–B 3); and see Schelkle, *Paulus*, 222.
[16] On the universal validity of reason cf. *Rom.* 3: 9, 15: 15, and see Schelkle, *Paulus*,
222.
[17] Cf. *Rom.* 8: 5.
[18] See the Introduction at nn. 96 and 102.

thing for which one feels shame in repentance. For everyone who comes to know goodness is ashamed of former actions: but whoever is ashamed of righteousness is not aware of its fruit (cf. Heb. 12: 11). Therefore, those who sin do not even have any benefit in the present, and in the future reap death without end: but those who serve God both have a benefit in the present—the gift of the Holy Spirit—and eternal life in the future.[19] Alternatively: What sort of benefit have you had in doing those things of which even the recollection brings a feeling of shame? *You have your benefit in sanctification, and have life eternal as the end.* This itself is already a benefit, that, having been sanctified by baptism, you are alive.   23 *For the wages of sin is death.* One who does military service for sin receives death as remuneration.[20] *But the grace of God is life eternal.* He did not say in a similar manner: 'the wages of righteousness', because there was no righteousness in us beforehand for him to repay: for it is not procured by our effort, but is presented as a gift of God.[21] *In Christ Jesus our Lord.* [In Christ] is grace or life.[22]

    7: 1 *Or do you not know, brothers—for I speak to those who know the law—that the law has dominion over a person as long as he lives?* From here on he begins to demonstrate the difficulty of the law, in order to urge them to pass over to grace without the fear which belongs to the law. ['As long as he lives':] the person or the law that is for him.[1]   2 *For a woman who is subject to a husband is bound to him by law as long as he lives: but if the husband dies, she is released from the law of her husband.* By way of analogy he calls the commandment of the law a husband, [and the people or the soul a wife,] to show that without the power to punish the law, as it were dead, cannot hinder us, who have already been mortified, from passing over unimpaired to Christ, who has risen from the dead. For the law would legitimately go on living in us if it found something it could punish in us.   3 *Therefore, as long as her husband is alive, she will be called an adulteress if she is with another man: but if her husband dies she is freed*

---

[19] Cf. Ambst. *Rom.* 6: 20. 1, 6: 22 (CSEL 81. 1: 209. 6–7, 18–22); Orig.–Ruf. *Rom.* 6. 5 (PG 14: 1064c 12–1065a 13).

[20] Cf. Orig.–Ruf. *Rom.* 6. 6 (PG 14: 1067b 12–d 1).

[21] Cf. ibid. (PG 14: 1067c 1–4).

[22] That is, the phrase 'in Christ Jesus' can refer to 'grace' or 'life'.

[1] Either 'person' (*homo*) or 'law' (*lex*) can serve as the implied subject of the clause 'as long as he (or it) lives' in the Latin (*quanto tempore uiuit*). Orig.–Ruf. *Rom.* 6. 7 (PG 14: 1071c 6–8) understands *uiuit* to refer to *lex*. There is a question as to whether Pelagius's comment reads *lex hominis* or *lex homini*. The translation follows the majority of the MSS and reads the latter, taking the phrase to be an allusion to the verse, which reads *lex dominatur homini*.

from the law, so that she is not an adulteress if she is with another man. As long
as her husband is alive, she must live according to his will alone: but
when, after he has died, the wife is married to another man, she should
no longer live according to the custom of [her] former husband.
4 *Now then, my brothers, you also have become dead to the law.* He was
reluctant to tell them, according to the analogy, that the law is dead,
but what he dared not say among the Jews he leaves to be understood.
Through the body of Christ. By dying with Christ, who 'condemned sin in
the flesh' (Rom. 8: 3). *So that you belong to another.* ['Man' is understood.] *Who has risen from the dead, so that we may bear fruit for God.* One
bears fruit for God when in works of righteousness one, after the
manner of fruit, first [breaks out] in blossom, then [grows] into fruit,
and finally becomes fully ripe: for no fruit is forever in blossom. [One
who is led by the pleasure of the flesh and is kept from obeying the law
of God is in the flesh, because it is not possible to serve two masters
(cf. Matt. 6: 24). But now we who have been taught by the grace of the
Holy Spirit to overcome the passions are not in the flesh, because we
are dead to the law, which does not contain the teaching of grace.]
[The new form of service is not to love the world, nor the things that
are in the world (cf. 1 John 2: 15), and not to devote the attention of the
flesh to evil desires (Rom. 13: 14). For when the law promised the good
things of the earth, it knew how to nourish the desires of the lovers of
the flesh. But the disciples of Jesus, who have renounced the world,
have with good reason died to the law.][2] 5 *For when we were in the flesh,*
the passions for sins, which were through the law, worked in our members.
When we were in a way of life that was carnal, the passion of concupiscence[, for instance,] worked in the eyes, and the rest of the
passions in the rest of the members (cf. Matt. 5: 28); these passions
were shown to be sins by the law.[3] *So that they bore fruit unto death.* So
that the severity of the law killed us.   6 *But now we have been released*
from the law, dying to that by which we were held prisoner. Because we die to
the sin for which we were held by the law. *So that we serve in the newness*
of the spirit, not in the oldness of the letter. According to the biddings of
spiritual grace, not of the written law.   7 *What shall we say then? Is the*
law sin? Because he had said that he was released from the law through
death. *Certainly not!* [This contradicts] the Manichaeans. Because [if]

---

[2] The comments enclosed in brackets, omitted by the Karlsruhe and Paris MSS, are
pseudo-Jerome interpolations; see the Introduction at n. 213 and ps.-Hi. *Rom.* 51*II* and
52 (Frede ii. 44–5).
    [3] Cf. Ambstr. *Rom.* 7: 5. 3–4 (CSEL 81. 1: 219. 6–11, 13–16).

they say: 'He is afraid of giving offence', [one should reply: 'If, therefore,] he was always afraid and never spoke against the law, [then] on
what basis do you venture to say that he did not keep it?'[4] *But I did not
recognize sin except through the law.* From here on he speaks in the person
of one who accepts the law, that is, who first comes to know God's
commandments while he is still in the habit of breaking them.[5] *For I
would not have known covetousness if the law had not said: 'You shall not covet.'*
He did not say: 'I would not have been in the habit' or 'I would not have
done it', but 'I would not have known', that is, I would not have
known that covetousness is a sin.[6]　　8 *Then sin, once it received the opportunity through the commandment.* Here he seems to call the Devil sin, as
he is [also] called in the Apocalypse, namely, as the author of sin.[7] He
is saying, then, that because the opportune arrival of the commandment took away the excuse of ignorance, it made him sin more
vehemently than before, just as every hateful person does. One especially seizes the opportunity for doing harm when one entrusts something to a person for whom one is setting a trap. *Worked in me every sort
of covetousness.* [Every sort] which has been forbidden [by] the law. *For
without the law sin was dead.* The natural law, which had [first] brought
to mind what was sin, had almost been forgotten. Therefore the
written law was added to remind those who had forgotten.[8]　　9 *Now I
lived without the law once.* I imagined I lived as one righteous and free.[9]
Or: [Meanwhile] I was alive at least for this present life. *Yet when the
commandment came.* When the commandment arrived to put an end to
forgetfulness, sin was once again recognized, so that everyone who
commits it knows that he is dead.[10] *Sin came back to life.* Because sin had
lived by natural knowledge and died through forgetfulness, it is

[4] On the Manichaean view of the law cf. Aug. *Faust.* 19. 1, 9. 1 (CSEL 25: 496. 21–497.
16, 307. 18–28).

[5] Cf. Orig.-Ruf. *Rom.* 6. 9 (PG 14: 1089C 6–1090C 9); Jer. *Ep.* 121. 8 (CSEL 56: 34. 14–
22, 36. 20–37. 35); and see Bammel, 'Philocalia IX'. Cf. also Aug. *Diu. quaest.* 66. 3, 5
(CCSL 44A: 154. 86–155. 105, 155. 121–158. 178); *Exp. prop.* 12 (13–18). 1–13, 37 (44). 2
(CSEL 84: 6. 17–9. 4, 19. 15–18); *Ad Simpl.* 1. 1. 1, 4 (CCSL 44: 8. 20–1, 10. 69–71); and see
Berrouard, 'L'exégèse augustinienne', 120–6, 140–4, 176–82, 189.

[6] Cf. Orig.-Ruf. *Rom.* 6. 8 (PG 14: 1081A 10–12); Aug. *Ad Simpl.* 1. 1. 2 (CCSL 44: 9.
38–41).

[7] Cf. Ambstr. *Rom.* 7: 4. 2–3, 7: 8. 3, 7: 11. 1, 7: 17, 7: 20 (CSEL 81. 1: 215. 23–6, 225. 16–
19, 229. 2–3, 237. 14–15, 241. 1); Orig.-Ruf. *Rom.* 6. 8 (PG 14: 1083C 11–13). The Apocalypse in fact nowhere addresses the Devil as 'the author of sin', but the term 'the
serpent', to which Origen alludes, is used often; cf. Rev. 12: 9, 20: 2, 20: 9.

[8] Cf. *Rom.* 3: 20, 5: 13, 11: 24.

[9] Cf. Aug. *Ad Simpl.* 1. 1. 4 (CCSL 44: 10. 54–6).

[10] Cf. ibid. (CCSL 44: 10. 57–9).

said to have come back to life through the law.   10 *But I died.* Because now I transgressed knowingly.[11] *And I found that the commandment that was intended for life actually resulted in death.* The commandment that would have progressed to life, if it had been kept, led to death, because it was disregarded.[12]   11 *For, once it received the opportunity through the commandment, sin led me astray and killed me through the commandment.* 12 *Thus the law is indeed holy, and the commandment holy and just and good.* Against those who attack the law and against those who separate justice from goodness, the law is called a good and holy grace [on the one hand], and a just grace on the other: 'For unless your righteousness abounds' (Matt. 5: 20). Moreover, God is regularly called good in the Old Testament (cf. Ps. 72: 1) and just in the New: 'O righteous Father', says the Lord (John 17: 25). This contradicts the Marcionites.[13]   13 *Then that which is good becomes death for me? By no means!* The law does not become for me the actual cause of death, but I do, when by sinning I encounter death.[14] *But in order that sin might be manifest as sin, it worked death for me through what is good.* Sin was revealed through the law, which is good, and was punished by it. *So that sin becomes a transgressor beyond measure through the commandment.* Before the law sin had limits because of ignorance: it is beyond limits when it is committed knowingly.   14 *Now we know that the law is spiritual.* Which enjoins spiritual things. [Now the argument proceeds in the person of one who is of legal age. For one who says that the law is spiritual condemns himself when he sins of his own will. This is why he added: 'But I am carnal, sold as a slave under sin.' He indicates that while he was free he sold himself as a slave to sin. For what, again, does he say?][15] *But I am carnal.* I, someone who accepts the law and is in the habit of living carnally. *Sold to sin.* 15 *For I do not understand what I do: for I do not do what I want to do, but what I hate to do I do.* [Sold as if] I were resolved upon sin, so that, should I accept its advice, I make myself its slave, I of my own accord subjecting myself to it (cf. John 8: 34);[16] and

[11] See also *Rom.* 7: 13 and 7: 15; cf. Aug. *Ad Simpl.* 1. 1. 4 (CCSL 44: 11. 77–8).

[12] Cf. Ambstr. *Rom.* 7: 10. 2 (CSEL 81. 1: 227. 21–5).

[13] Cf. Tert. *Marc.* 1. 19. 4, 5. 13. 14 (CCSL 1: 460. 22–9, 704. 6–7).

[14] Cf. Ambstr. *Rom.* 7: 13. 2 (CSEL 81. 1: 231. 1–4).

[15] The comment in brackets, omitted by the Karlsruhe and Paris MSS and by the Vatican fragment, is a pseudo-Hieronymian interpolation; see the Introduction at n. 213 and ps.-Hi. *Rom.* 62*II* (Frede ii. 49). For the analogy of the child coming of age cf. Anon. *Rom.* 054, 059, 062, 067 (Frede ii. 45–8); Orig.–Ruf. *Rom.* 6. 8 (PG 14: 1082A 4–B 3); Jer. *Ep.* 121. 8 (CSEL 56: 33. 19–26); and see Bammel, 'Philocalia IX', 65–6. For Pelagius's interpretation of the persona of Rom. 7: 7–25 see *Rom.* 7: 7.

[16] Cf. Orig.–Ruf. *Rom.* 6. 9 (PG 14: 1087B 3–1089A 9). The initial consent whereby the will becomes enslaved to sin is, however, highlighted by Pelagius; see also *Rom.* 7: 17, 7: 20.

now, as if drunk with the habit of sins, I do not know what I do: 'For I do not understand what I do.'[17] Or: It should be read this way: I do not understand[, therefore,] that what I accept [in a way] against my will is evil.[18]   16 *If then I do what I do not want to do, I agree with the law that it is good*. If I do not want to do the particular evil I commit, at least I agree with the law, which does not desire evil and prohibits it. But it can also be understood thus: If I sin, I myself subject myself to the severity of the law.[19]   17 *However, now I no longer do it*. Before it became a habit, therefore, I myself did it willingly.[20] *But sin that lives in me*. It lives as a guest and as one thing in another, not as one single thing; in other words, as an accidental quality, not a natural one.[21]   18 *For I know that what is good does not live in me, that is, in my flesh*. He did not say: 'My flesh is not good.'[22] *For it is near to me to wish*. The will is there, but not the deed, because carnal habit opposes the will.[23] *But I do not find it in myself to carry out what is good*. I do not see myself doing it.   19 *For I do not do the good that I want, but the evil that I do not want I do*. Just as if, for instance, someone who has been swearing regularly now for a long time swears even when he does not wish to.[24]   20 *But if I do what I do not want to do, it is not I that does it, but sin that lives in me*. Not I, because I do it [as it were] against my will, but the habit of sin, though I myself have provided myself with this compulsion.[25]   21 *So then I find a law for me when I wish to do good, that evil is there with me*. If I want, I find that I have a law to do good against the evil that lies near [me].[26]   22 *For I delight in the law of God with the inner self*. [The inner self is the rational and intelligible soul, which is in harmony with God's law, for its law is to live

---

[17] Cf. Aug. *Fort.* 22 (CSEL 25: 103. 26–104. 12); *Lib. arb.* 3. 18. 52–19. 53 (CCSL 29: 305. 41–306. 22); and see the Introduction at nn. 136–7.

[18] The phrase 'in a way' (*quodam modo*) is attested only by the Karlsruhe and St Gall MSS. Cf. *Rom.* 7: 20 and see the Introduction at n. 219.

[19] Doignon, '"J'acquiesce à la loi"', 133–4, erroneously reads *ueritati legis* in place of *seueritati legis*. The latter reading, attested by the Karlsruhe MS with the support of all others except the Balliol MS, is to be preferred.

[20] Cf. *Rom.* 7: 15, 7: 20.

[21] On the meaning of *unum* see Schelkle, *Paulus*, 249; Greshake, *Gnade*, 90; Jonas, *Augustin und das paulinische Freiheitsproblem*, 92; Valero, *Las bases antropólogicas*, 208.

[22] Cf. Ambstr. *Rom.* 7: 18. 1 (CSEL 81. 1: 237. 19–21).

[23] Cf. Orig.–Ruf. *Rom.* 6. 9 (PG 14: 1087B 7–10); Aug. *Lib. arb.* 3. 18. 52 (CCSL 29: 305. 43–5).

[24] Cf. Aug. *Fort.* 22 (CSEL 25: 104. 12–15).

[25] Cf. Ambstr. *Rom.* 7: 20 (CSEL 81. 1: 241. 3–11); Aug. *Fort.* 22 (CSEL 25: 106. 2–5). The phrase 'as it were' (*uelut*) is attested by the Karlsruhe and St Gall MSS alone. Cf. *Rom.* 7: 15 and see the Introduction at n. 219.

[26] Cf. Ambstr. *Rom.* 7: 21 (CSEL 81. 1: 241. 13–16). For a different rendering of *legem bonum facere* see Schelkle, *Paulus*, 256.

rationally and not to be led by the passions of the irrational animals. The outer self, on the other hand, is our body. Now its law is the wisdom of the flesh, which instructs one to eat and to drink and to enjoy other sensual pleasures. These fight against reason, and if they gain the upper hand subject it to the law of sin. For if it is the case, as some suppose, that we do what we do not want to do, he would not have said: 'I see another law in my members, fighting against the law of my mind.']²⁷ I agree to the law with the mind.   23 *But I see another law in my members, fighting against.* Habitual desires, or the persuading of the enemy.²⁸ *The law of my mind.* Namely, of natural conscience, or of the divine law, which resides in the mind.²⁹ *And taking me prisoner for the law of sin that is in my members.* In the habit of transgressions.   24 *What a wretched person I am! Who will set me free from the body of this death?* I who am held prisoner in this way—who will set me free from this fatal, corporeal habit?³⁰   25 *The grace of God through Jesus Christ our Lord.* [Grace sets free] the one whom the law could not have set free.³¹ Was Paul then not yet set free by the grace of God? This shows that [the apostle] is speaking in the person of someone else, [not in his own person].³² *Therefore I serve the law of God with my mind.* He reviews the main points in order to bring the discussion to an end. *But the law of sin with my flesh.* The carnal person is, in a sense, made up of two persons and is divided within himself.³³

8: 1 *There is therefore no condemnation for those who are in Christ Jesus, who walk not according to the flesh.* There is nothing deserving of condemnation in those [who] have been crucified to the works of the flesh. 2 *For the law of the spirit of life in Christ Jesus.* Observe that he calls the law grace.¹ *Has set you free from the law of sin and death.* Which [was given to sinners and] puts them to death (cf. 1 Tim. 1: 9). [Or: From the law which above he had said was in the members (cf. Rom. 7: 4).]²   3 *For*

²⁷ This comment, omitted by the Karlsruhe MS, is a pseudo-Hieronymian interpolation; see the Introduction at n. 213 and ps.-Hi. *Rom.* 70II (Frede ii. 51–2).

²⁸ i.e. the Devil; cf. Ambstr. *Rom.* 7: 14. 4–5 (CSEL 81. 1: 235. 9–26).

²⁹ Cf. ibid. 7: 23. 2 (CSEL 81. 1: 243. 12–23).

³⁰ Cf. ibid. 7: 22 (CSEL 81. 1: 241. 19–26); Orig.-Ruf. *Rom.* 6. 9 (PG 14: 1089B 10–11).

³¹ Cf. Aug. *Diu. quaest.* 66. 1, 5 (CCSL 44A: 151. 26–30, 158. 169–78); *Exp. prop.* 38 (45–6). 4 (CSEL 84: 20. 6–11); *Ad Simpl.* 1. 1. 14 (CSEL 44: 18. 247–50); and see Babcock, 'Augustine's Interpretation of Romans', 60–1; Burns, *Development*, 34–6.

³² Cf. *Rom.* 7: 7.

³³ Cf. Ambstr. *Rom.* 7: 24–5. 5 (CSEL 81. 1: 247. 15–22).

¹ The comment is directed against the Marcionites and the Manichaeans; cf. *Rom.* 7: 7, 7: 12.

² Cf. Ambstr. *Rom.* 8: 2 (CSEL 81. 1: 251. 19–21). The second comment is found in the Karlsruhe MS alone; see the Introduction at n. 219.

because it was impossible for the law. To make carnal people preserve
righteousness, since neither example [nor grace] was given for morti-
fying the flesh (cf. Rom. 8: 4, 13).[3] *Inasmuch as it was weakened by the flesh.*
It was weakened in the flesh, not in itself. *God sent his Son.* Against
Photinus, who denies the existence of the Son before the flesh.[4] *In the
likeness of the flesh of sin.* Here 'the likeness [of the flesh]' possesses
reality, just as 'Adam begat according to his likeness' (Gen. 5: 3). He
therefore took flesh like the flesh of the rest of humanity[, as far as the
nature is concerned].[5] *And by sin he condemned sin in the flesh.*[6] As if you
were to say: 'By like he overcame like.'[7] Just as the sacrificial victims
that they offered for sin under the law were given the name of sin,
although these victims were unacquainted with transgressions—as it is
written: '[And] he shall place his hand on its head for its sin' (Lev.
4: 29)—so also Christ's flesh, which was offered for our sins, took the
name of sin.[8] Some, in fact, say that by means of the sin of the Jews,
whereby they killed the Lord, he condemned through humankind the
sin of the Devil, whereby the Devil had deceived humankind; as he
says to the Hebrews: 'So that through death he destroyed him who
held the power of death' (Heb. 2: 14).[9] Or: Through the substance of

---

[3] Only the Karlsruhe MS mentions 'grace' in addition to 'example' (*nec exemplo . . . nec
gratia*) as the way in which, it is implied, Christ remedies the deficiency of the law. On
the authenticity of the reading see the Introduction at nn. 219 and 223. 'Grace' may refer
here to the action of God in Christ to free sinners from the power of sin and the Devil,
which Pelagius discusses in the remaining comments on this verse. But see further
Greshake, *Gnade*, 112–23.

[4] Cf. *Rom.* 1: 3.

[5] Cf. Tert. *Marc.* 5. 14. 2 (CCSL 1: 705. 23–4); Hil. *Trin.* 10. 25 (CCSL 62A: 481. 29–33);
Ambr. *Ps.* 37. 5 (CSEL 64: 140. 4–9); Orig.–Ruf. *Rom.* 6. 12 (PG 14: 1095A 2–7). The
phrase 'as far as the nature is concerned' (*quantum ad naturam*) is found in the Karlsruhe
MS alone; see the Introduction at n. 219.

[6] Patristic commentators were divided as to whether to read *de peccato* with *misit* or
damnauit; see Schelkle, *Paulus*, 274–5. Pelagius, following a tradition at least as old as
Tertullian, takes the latter course; cf. Tert. *Pud.* 17. 11 (CCSL 2: 1316. 40–8); Hil. *Trin.*
9. 55 (CCSL 62A: 434. 8); Ambst. *Rom.* 8: 3. 3 (CSEL 81. 1: 255. 21–2); Ambr. *Ps.* 37. 5
(CSEL 64: 140. 9–10); Aug. *Diu. quaest.* 66. 6 (CCSL 44A: 159. 196–7); Orig.–Ruf. *Rom.* 6.
12 (PG 14: 1094C 4–8).

[7] The expression is translated as found in Souter's edition. It is attested by the Karlsruhe MS alone; all the other MSS read *hostis* ('enemy') in place of *gens* (here rendered
'like', as in species or kind, rather than 'people' or 'race').

[8] Cf. Orig.–Ruf. *Rom.* 6. 12 (PG 14: 1094C 6–8, 1095A 9–B 12); and see Bammel, *Römerbrieftext*, 223. On Origen's contribution to the substitutionary understanding of atonement see Rivière, *Doctrine of Atonement*, i. 166–7.

[9] Cf. Ambst. *Rom.* 8: 3. 3–4 (CSEL 81. 1: 255. 22–257. 7). On the view that the Jews
were confederates with the Devil in killing Christ see Simon, *Verus Israel*, 246–7, 255–6;
Ruether, *Faith and Fratricide*, 128–31; Gager, *The Origins of Anti-Semitism*, 13–34, 265–9.
Cf. also *Rom.* 11: 10.

that flesh which previously was slave to sin, he conquered sin by never sinning, and in that same flesh he condemned sin, to show that the will was arraigned, not the nature, which God created in such a way that it [was able] not to sin[, if it so wished].[10]   4 *So that the righteousness of the law might be fulfilled in us, who walk not according to the flesh, but according to the Spirit.* So that, since it could not have been fulfilled in those in whom carnal habit fights back, it at least may be fulfilled in us, who have mortified the flesh according to Christ's example.[11]   5 *For those who live according to the flesh occupy their minds with the things that are of the flesh: but those who live according to the Spirit set their minds on the things that are of the Spirit.* A person is composed of spirit and flesh. When, then, a person performs carnal deeds, the whole person is called 'flesh'; but when spiritual deeds, the whole person is called 'spirit'. For when one of these substances brings the other under its sway, this other substance in a way loses its own power and name. For individual, separate [substances] desire things that are related to them and close to them.[12]
6 *For the prudence of the flesh is death, but the prudence of the Spirit is life and peace.* He says elsewhere that it is human prudence to repay evil for evil (cf. Rom. 12: 16–18). Such prudence, then, procures death by transgressing the precept (cf. Matt. 5: 38–48): but the prudence of the Spirit enjoys peace now because it does not repay in kind, and will obtain life in the future. Indeed, 'prudence' is derived from 'providence'.[13]   7 *Because the wisdom of the flesh is hostile to God: for it is not subjected to the law of God.* The flesh itself is not hostile to God, as the Manichaeans say, but the carnal mind is. For everything that is not subject is hostile, and anyone who wishes to clear himself sometimes even goes beyond the limit of the old law.[14] *Nor can it be.* He said it is

[10] On the mastery Christ exercised over the flesh cf. Ambstr. *Rom.* 8: 4. 3 (CSEL 81. 1: 259. 4–5); Ambr. *Ps.* 37. 6 (CSEL 64: 141. 6–11); Aug. *Diu. quaest.* 66. 6 (CCSL 44A: 159. 196–200). On the potential for the will to refrain from sin cf. *Rom.* 1: 28, 2: 20, 3: 18, 6: 2, 6: 7. Where the Karlsruhe MS reads that the nature 'was able not to sin, if it so wished' (*ut posset non peccare si uellet*), the Vatican fragment reads that it 'is able not to sin if it so wishes' (*ut possit non peccare si uelit*). (Souter's data: posset AG: possit 𝕽BHV | si uellet *om.* B | uellet A: uelit 𝕽E^{corr.}C^{corr.}V: uellit E*MNG.) On the authenticity of the Karlsruhe reading see the Introduction at n. 219.

[11] On the resistance of carnal habit cf. *Rom.* 7: 14–22. On the example of Christ cf. *Rom.* 8: 3 at n. 3.

[12] Cf. *Rom.* 6: 19, and see Valero, *Las bases antropológicas*, 33–6. The third reference to 'substance' is attested by the Karlsruhe and St Gall MSS alone, and is omitted by the Vatican fragment; on its authenticity see the Introduction at n. 219.

[13] Cf. Cic. *Inu.* 2. 53. 160 (LCL 386: 326); *Re pub.* 6. 1 (LCL 213: 256).

[14] Cf. Ambstr. *Rom.* 8: 7. 1 (CSEL 81. 1: 261: 24–263. 1); Anon. *Rom.* 076 (a) (Frede ii. 54). On Pelagius's anti-Manichaean polemic see the Introduction at n. 102.

impossible so that at least by this means he might call them back from the desires of the flesh.			8 *Indeed, those who are in the flesh*. This proves that above he found fault not with the flesh, but with the works of the flesh, because those to whom he says this were no doubt living in the flesh. *Cannot please God*. For it is impossible that one does not sin some time or other once one has given oneself over to the flesh.			9 *You, however, are not in the flesh, but in the Spirit*. That is, busy [with] spiritual things.[15] *If indeed the Spirit of God dwells in you*. The Spirit of God dwells in those in whom his fruit is manifest, as he says to the Galatians: 'Now the fruit of the Spirit is love, joy', and so on (Gal. 5: 22).[16] *But anyone who does not have the Spirit of Christ does not belong to him*. The Spirit of Christ, who loved his enemies and prayed for them, is the Spirit of humility, patience, and all the virtues (cf. Matt. 5: 44; Luke 23: 34; Ecclus. 2: 4).			10 *But if Christ is in you, your body is in fact dead because of sin*. If you imitate Christ, the carnal mind, as if dead offers no resistance. This is why David also said: 'But like the deaf I did not hear, and like the mute who does not open his mouth', and so on (Ps. 37: 14). *But the spirit lives because of righteousness*. The spirit lives in order to produce righteousness: for the object is not just that we leave off carnal things, but also that we do spiritual things.			11 *Because if the Spirit of him who raised Jesus from the dead dwells in you, he who raised Jesus Christ from the dead will also give life to your mortal bodies through the indwelling of his Spirit in you*. If you are so pure that the Holy Spirit deigns to dwell in you, God will not allow the temple of his Spirit to perish (cf. 1 Cor. 6: 19), but in the same way he raised Jesus from the dead so also will he restore your body.[17]			12 *Therefore, brothers, we are under obligation, not to the flesh, to live according to the flesh*. The force of this whole argument is to show that the law, which was given for the carnal-minded, is not necessary for them.			13 *For if you live according to the flesh, you shall die*. Because, as has been explained, carnal people cannot preserve righteousness.[18] *But if by the Spirit you have put to death the deeds of the flesh, you will live*. [If] you have substituted the works of the flesh with spiritual deeds. One should note that the works, not the substance, of the flesh are

---

[15] Pelagius often transposes Paul's references to the Spirit into language about spiritual deeds; see *Rom.* 8: 5, 8: 10, 8: 13, and Valero, *Las bases antropológicas*, 136–40. Cf. Ambstr. *Rom.* 8: 5. 2, 8: 6. 1, 8: 7. 1, 8: 9. 3 (CSEL 81. 1: 261. 2–4, 7–11, 261. 24–263. 1, 267. 2–4).

[16] Cf. Orig.–Ruf. *Rom.* 6. 12 (PG 14: 1096C 1–8). See also *Rom.* 8: 11 below and García-Allen, 'Pelagius and Christian Initiation', 245–6.

[17] Cf. Orig.–Ruf. *Rom.* 6. 13 (PG 14: 1099C 10–13, 1100A 14–B 4). See also *Rom.* 6: 22.

[18] Cf. *Rom.* 8: 3, 8: 8.

condemned.[19]   14 *For all who are moved by the Spirit of God are children of God*. All who are worthy to be governed by the Holy Spirit; just as, on the contrary, those who sin are moved by the spirit of the Devil, a sinner from the beginning (cf. 1 John 3: 8).[20]   15 *For you have not received again a spirit of slavery in fear, but you have received the Spirit of adoption as children*. The Jews received a spirit which constrained them into service by means of fear. For it is in the nature of slaves to fear, of sons to love, as it is written: 'The slave shall fear his master, and the son shall love his father' (Mal. 1: 6). Therefore, those who were not willing to labour out of the desire of love are compelled by the constraint of fear: but let us perform all things willingly, so that we may show that we are sons.[21] *By which we cry out: Abba, Father*. He who calls to his father declares himself a son: he ought, therefore, to be found to resemble his father in character, lest he be subject to a greater penalty because he in fact assumed the name of his father in vain (cf. Exod. 20: 7; Deut. 5: 11).[22]   16 *That Spirit testifies to our spirit that we are children of God*. The evidence of our adoption is the fact that we have the Spirit, through whom we pray in the manner mentioned above; [for] such a pledge only sons could receive (cf. 2 Cor. 1: 22, 5: 5; Eph. 1: 14).   17 *But if children, then also heirs, heirs in fact of God, and co-heirs with Christ*. He who is worthy to be a son is worthy to be made an heir of the Father and a co-heir with the true Son.[23] *If indeed we suffer with him*. If, when it becomes necessary, we suffer for his name's sake such things as he endured for us (cf. Acts 5: 41). *So that we may also be glorified with him*. As John says: 'We know that, when he appears, we shall be like him' (1 John 3: 2).[24]   18 *For I consider that the sufferings of this age are not worth comparing*. He desires to commend future glory so that we may more easily bear present afflictions. And indeed, no human being could suffer anything that equals heavenly glory, even if that glory were comparable to this present life. For whatever he will suffer in dying is no more than what in fact he previously deserved for his sins; now, however, his sins are forgiven, and in the future he will be granted life eternal, fellowship with the angels, the splendour of the

---

[19] Cf. ibid. 8: 7–8.

[20] Cf. ibid. 1: 30, 7: 8.

[21] Cf. Aug. *Exp. prop.* 44 (52). 1 (CSEL 84: 24. 12–14).

[22] Cf. Ambstr. *Rom.* 8: 15. 2a (CSEL 81. 1: 273. 26–275. 1); see also Cypr. *Domin. orat.* 11 (CCSL 3A: 96. 181–4), and Koch, 'Cyprian in den *Quaestiones Veteris et Novi Testamenti*', 552.

[23] Cf. Orig.–Ruf. *Rom.* 7. 3 (PG 14: 1106B 4–6, B 13–C 5).

[24] Cf. Ambstr. *Rom.* 8: 17. 2 (CSEL 81. 1: 277. 2–3); Aug. *Exp. prop.* 45 (53). 6–7 (CSEL 84: 26. 18–23); Orig.–Ruf. *Rom.* 7. 4 (PG 14: 1109B 4).

sun, and the other things which we read have been promised for the saints (cf. Dan. 12: 2–3; Matt. 13: 41–3; Rev. 7: 9–17).[25] *With the future glory which will be revealed to us.* For at the moment 'it is hidden with Christ in God' (Col. 3: 3), and 'it has not yet become manifest what we shall be' (1 John 3: 2).[26] **19** *For the expectation of creation awaits the revelation of the children of God.* Different interpreters explain this passage in different ways. Either: The whole creation awaits the time of the resurrection, because then it will be changed into something better.[27] Or: Angelic, rational creation: for Peter says that [even] the angels long for the glory of the saints (cf. 1 Pet. 1: 12).[28] Some even say that 'creation' is Adam and Eve, because they did not sin by themselves, but at the instigation of the serpent, who long ago, when they were exposed to deception in the hope of divine existence, made them subject to corruption. 'And they', say these interpreters, 'will be set free, so that they are no longer subject to corruption.'[29] But 'the whole creation', they say, is those who were righteous up to the coming of Christ, because they too, not yet having received, [wait, 'while God] provides something better for us' (Heb. 11: 39).[30] Not only they, how-ever, but we, in whom these things have been fulfilled, do not yet hold it in our grasp, but bear up in hope, although we have seen things which many righteous longed to see (cf. Matt. 13: 17; Luke 10: 24). **20** *For to vanity creation.* Vanity is everything that some day comes to an end.[31] *Was subjected.* As the angels, who wait upon humankind. *Not of its own will, but on account of him who has subjected it in hope,* **21** *because even creation will be set free from the slavery of corruption into the freedom of the glory of the children of God.* It shall no longer serve those who have corrupted the image of God [in themselves] (cf. Gen. 1: 26). **22** *Now we know that the whole creation groans and is in labour right up to the present time.* Just as 'the angels rejoice over those who repent' (Luke 15: 10), so they grieve for those who are unwilling to repent.[32] **23** *Not only creation, however, but we too, who have the first-fruits of the Spirit, we too groan within ourselves for adoption as children.* Not only do the angels, who are kinder

---

[25] Cf. *Rom.* 5: 3–4.
[26] Cf. Aug. *Exp. prop.* 45 (53). 6–7 (CSEL 84: 26. 18–23).
[27] Cf. Ambr. *Ep.* 22 (35). 1–2, 13 (CSEL 82: 159. 3–160. 25, 165. 123–35).
[28] Cf. Orig.–Ruf. *Rom.* 7. 4 (PG 14: 1111C 1–1113A 12), and see Lebeau, 'L'interpréta-tion origénienne de Rm. 8: 19–22'. Cf. also Ambr. *Ep.* 21 (34). 4–10 (CSEL 82: 155. 36–158. 113).
[29] Cf. Anon. *Rom.* 85A, 86A (Frede ii. 58), and see Frede, *Ein neuer Paulustext*, i. 200–1.
[30] Cf. Anon. *Rom.* 87A (Frede ii. 59).
[31] Cf. Ambstr. *Rom.* 8: 20. 1 (CSEL 81. 1: 279. 21–6).
[32] Cf. *Rom.* 8: 19.

than we are, [grieve] over these unrepentant people, but we too, who already [have] the Holy Spirit, groan for such people, as also Jeremiah groaned: 'Alas, my soul, for the God-fearer has vanished from the face of the earth!', and so on (Mic. 7: 1–2).[33] *Awaiting the redemption of our body: 24 therefore we were saved in hope.* We have not yet beheld the very things that were promised, but we hope, as he says to the Corinthians: 'For we walk by faith, and not by sight' (2 Cor. 5: 7). *Now hope that is seen is not hope: for who sees what he hopes for?* What is seen is not hoped for, but, if it belongs to one, is owned. Christians, therefore, have no hope in the things that can be seen, for we have been promised not things present, but things future. 25 *But if we hope for what we do not see, we await it with patience.* The reward for faith with patience is great, because one believes what one does not see (cf. John 20: 29), and is as sure of what has not yet been received as if one has already received it. As he says to the Hebrews: 'You must have patience, so that by doing the will [of God] you obtain the promise' (Heb. 10: 36). For hope does not know how to exist without patience. 26 *And in the same way the Spirit also helps our weakness.* He helps in accordance with this hope, so that we request not earthly but heavenly things. For our ability is weak, unless it is helped by [the illumination] of the Holy Spirit.[34] *For we do not know what to pray for as we ought.* Because we still [see] through a glass (cf. 1 Cor. 13: 12), [and] often the things we judge to be helpful are harmful. Therefore the things we requested are not granted by divine providence, as also he himself says elsewhere: 'Therefore three times I asked the Lord that it might leave me', and so on (2 Cor. 12: 8).[35] [Alternatively: We are scarcely able to put into words the intractable longing of our prayer as we have conceived it in our heart. That is why this statement follows directly:][36] *But that very Spirit makes requests for us with groans that words cannot describe.* [God, then, who searches hearts, knows to what extent we desire to believe, even if we

---

[33] The passage Pelagius attributes to Jeremiah is in fact from Micah.

[34] Where the Karlsruhe MS speaks of the 'illumination of the Holy Spirit' (*illuminatio* in the original hand; *illuminatione* as corrected), the other MSS speak of the 'instruction of the Holy Spirit' (*doctrina*). On the authenticity of the former see the Introduction at nn. 219 and 223. Illumination here refers, as it does at *Eph.* 3: 16, to the revelation of the glory of eternal life, whereby the believer is encouraged and guided. The term may have been replaced in the other MSS on account of its Augustinian connotations. But see also Orig.–Ruf. *Rom.* 7. 6 (PG 14: 1118c 1–4, 1119b 10–1120a 7), where the Spirit is said to remedy ignorance by instruction.

[35] Cf. Ambstr. *Rom.* 8: 26. 2 (CSEL 81. 1: 287. 18–19); Aug. *Exp. prop.* 46 (54). 2 (CSEL 84: 29. 10–11); Orig.–Ruf. *Rom.* 7. 6 (PG 14: 1118c 1–9).

[36] This comment and the next two are pseudo-Hieronymian interpolations; see the Introduction at n. 213 and ps.-Hi. *Rom.* 88*ii*, 90 (Frede ii. 61–2).

are unable to express it in words. He knows, furthermore, that in accordance with his will we make requests for holy things, not worldly things.]   27 *And he who searches hearts knows what the Spirit desires.* [As if a high priest.] *Because in accordance with God he makes requests for the saints.* Here he has called a gift of the Spirit 'the Spirit', as where he says: 'If I pray in a tongue, my spirit prays' (1 Cor. 14: 14), and [elsewhere]: 'You are emulators of the spirits' (1 Cor. 14: 12).[37] Now 'he makes requests' because he makes us request with groans which cannot be described, just as God is said to tempt us in order to know, that is, to make us know what sort of people we are (Deut. 13: 3).[38] Even according to popular usage is the master himself said to accomplish what he commands to be done, as in the statement 'he built a house', or 'he wrote a book', though he neither wrote nor built.   28 *Now we know that all things work together for good for those who love God.* Whatever we do or suffer out of love for God, it all grows into a reward for us. [For] whatever the righteous do will be prospered (cf. Ps. 1: 3). *For those who have been called according to his purpose.* 29 *For those he foreknew.* The purpose according to which he planned to save by faith alone those whom he had foreknown would believe, and those whom he freely called to salvation he will all the more glorify as they work [towards salvation].[39] *He also predestined to be conformed to the image of his Son.* To predestine is the same as to foreknow. Therefore, those he foresaw would be conformed in life he intended to be conformed in glory, because 'he will transform the body of our humility into the likeness of the body of his splendour' (Phil. 3: 21).[40] So that he might be the first-born among many brothers. [Here] 'first-born from the dead' into glory (Col. 1: 18). 30 *And those he predestined he also called, and those he called he also justified, and those he justified he also exalted.* Those he foreknew would believe he called. Now a call gathers together those who are willing, not those who are unwilling;[41] or at any rate the discrimination is not

[37] Cf. Anon. *Rom.* 89A (Frede ii. 61); Orig.–Ruf. *Rom.* 7. 5–6 (PG 14: 1114B 15–C4, 1120A 4–11). See also Ambr. *Spir.* 3. 11. 70 (CSEL 79: 179. 9–13).

[38] Cf. Aug. *Exp. prop.* 46 (54). 7 (CSEL 84: 30. 1–4).

[39] On the relationship between initial faith and subsequent works cf. *Rom.* 4: 5–6. On predestination based on foreknowledge of faith cf. Ambstr. *Rom.* 8: 28–29. 1 (CSEL 81. 1: 289. 28–291. 7); Aug. *Exp. prop.* 47 (55). 4–5 (CSEL 84: 30. 15–21); Orig.–Ruf. *Rom.* 7. 8 (PG 14: 1125B 13–C 11, 1126B 5–C 2). For subsequent changes in Augustine's view see the Introduction at n. 132 and ff.

[40] Cf. *Rom.* 5: 10–11.

[41] Cf. Aug. *Exp. prop.* 47 (55). 4 (CSEL 84: 30. 15–19); Orig.–Ruf. *Rom.* 7. 8 (PG 14: 1126B 14–D 4).

against persons, but rather in time.[42] He says this on account of the enemies of the faith, so that they may not judge God's grace to be fortuitous. Therefore, they are called to believe through the preaching, and are justified through baptism when they believe, and are glorified in charismatic powers or in the resurrection to come.[43] 31 *What then shall we say of these things? If God is for us, who is against us?* He wants to show that no one can keep those who love God and are loved by God from attaining the glory that has been promised, because the perfect love [that] is in them casts out every reason for mortal fear (cf. 1 John 4: 18).[44]   32 *He who did not spare even his Son.* He allowed him to be handed over, so that the freedom of choice of those who handed him over might be left intact and so that he might set us an example of patience.[45] *But handed him over for us all.* Not for some.[46] *How has he not also bestowed on us all things with him?* What dearer thing can he have to deny us, who did not deny his Son?   33 *Who will bring a charge against God's elect? It is God who justifies.* 34 *Who is there to utter condemnation?* Who will dare to charge for previous sins or for disregard of the commandments of the law the believers whom God chose and shows to be righteous by signs and wonders (cf. Acts 2: 22)? *It is Christ Jesus who died, I should rather say, who also rose again, who also is at the right hand of God.* He speaks with regard to the form of the man he assumed, who died and rose again (cf. Phil. 2: 7).[47] *Who in fact intercedes for us.* So that we may be with him where he is (cf. John 14: 3). The Arians, obviously, are wont to stir up false accusation on the basis of his intercession, claiming that the one to whom intercession is made is greater than the one who intercedes.[48] To these one must answer that God does not forget so as to need always to be reminded of those whom he himself chose, but that Christ intercedes when as a true and eternal high priest he constantly presents and offers as our guarantee to the Father the man whom he received (cf. Heb. 6: 20).[49]   35 *Who, then, will separate us*

[42] Pelagius's remark reflects perhaps the same question which moved Augustine to speak of a 'congruent' call; cf. Aug. *Ad Simpl.* 1. 2. 13 (CCSL 44: 38. 360–71), and see Babcock, 'Augustine's Interpretation of Romans', 66; Burns, *Development*, 39–41.

[43] On the *uirtutes gratiarum*, here rendered 'charismatic powers', cf. *Rom.* 12: 3, 12: 6, and see Valero, *Las bases antropológicas*, 134–6.

[44] Cf. Orig.–Ruf. *Rom.* 7. 7 (PG 14: 1121C 2–7). See also *Rom.* 5: 5 above.

[45] For this interpretation of *tradere* see *Rom.* 1: 24. On the exemplary function of the crucifixion cf. Orig.–Ruf. *Rom.* 7. 9 (PG 14: 1129A 4–12).

[46] Cf. Orig.–Ruf. *Rom.* 7. 9 (PG 14: 1129A 13–B 1).

[47] Cf. *Rom.* 1: 16.

[48] Cf. Aug. *Maxim. Arian.* 1. 12 (PL 42: 716. 22–37).

[49] Pelagius appears to echo the liturgy of the Eucharist here. The Roman liturgy of his day is not extant, but cf. *Liber sacramentorum Romanae aeclesiae*, § 949 (Mohlberg

from the love of Christ? Will trouble, or hardship, or persecution, or famine, or nakedness, or peril, or sword? **36** *As it is written.* After so many and such splendid benefits or promises, what affliction could be so heavy that it tears us away from love for Christ?[50] And in saying 'us' he is saying that all should be the sort of Christians that even perils cannot separate from Christ. At the time of writing, however, the Jews wanted to separate them from Christ in order to recall them to the observance of the law. *Because of you we face death all day long.* Not because of some crime, but because of you, who said: 'Blessed are you, when they persecute you', and so on (cf. Matt. 5: 11). *We are reckoned as sheep for the slaughter.* This is especially fulfilled in us Christians, for we are not permitted to defend ourselves, but are to bear all attacks with the greatest patience, according to the example of our Lord and Teacher, who 'was led as a sheep for sacrifice' (Isa. 53: 7; cf. Acts 8: 32).[51] **37** *But in all these things we overcome because of him who loved us.* All these troubles we count as nothing because of him who loved us so much that he even died for us. And we especially triumph when we die for his name, particularly since it is a light thing to suffer oneself what the [Lord] first deigned [to suffer] for others.[52] **38** *For I am sure that neither death, nor life, nor angels, nor principalities, nor things present, nor things to come, nor powers,* **39** *nor height, nor depth.* I am sure without a doubt that even if [someone] threatens me with death, or promises life, or says he is an angel sent from the Lord, or feigns to be the prince of the angels, or bestows honour in this present life, or holds out the glory of things to come, or works wonders, or promises heaven and staves off hell, or tries to persuade with depth of learning—I am sure that he will never be able to sever us from the love of Christ.[53] *Nor will any other creature be able to separate us from the love of God.* He named almost every creature, and was not satisfied with this list unless he added that even if there were another creature, it too could not separate us. *Which is in Christ Jesus our Lord.* He loved God in Christ. Love for Christ consists in keeping his commandments; as Christ himself says: 'If you love me, keep my commandments' (John 14: 15). He established that brotherly love is the imitation of his own love,

---

[50] Cf. *Rom.* 8: 38–9.

[51] Cf. ibid. 8: 32.

[52] Cf. Ambstr. *Rom.* 8: 37. 1–2 (CSEL 81. 1: 299. 1–4); see also Cypr. *Fort.* 5 (CCSL 3: 192. 23–31), and Koch, 'Cyprian in den *Quaestiones Veteris et Novi Testamenti*', 552.

[53] Cf. Ambstr. *Rom.* 8: 39. 1–4 (CSEL 81. 1: 299. 12–301. 27).

when he said: 'By this will all know that you are my disciples, if you love one another' (John 13: 35). [For this reason] John also [says: 'If] you do not love a brother whom you see, how can you love God, whom you do not see?' (1 John 4: 20).[54]

9: 1 *I speak the truth in Christ, I do not lie, for my conscience bears witness to me in the Holy Spirit, 2 that my sorrow is great and the anguish in my heart is unceasing.* Because he intends to proceed against the Jews, he first assures them that he does not say these things out of hatred for them, but out of love, for it pains him that they do not believe in Christ, who had come to save them as soon as possible.[1] Moreover, because he says that he speaks the truth in Christ, he indicates that a person who has been baptized is one who through communion with the body and blood of Christ abides in Christ, and Christ in him (cf. 1 Cor. 10: 16; John 6: 56); that whatever he says or does in Christ, Christ, of whom he is a member, says or does, and that whatever insults are hurled [against him] are likewise inflicted upon Christ.[2] Furthermore, because he says that on this point his conscience bears him witness, he shows that he tells the truth, which the conscience corroborates in all people, and establishes that he is not charged with lying by an accusation from within.[3]   3 *For I wished that I myself were cursed by Christ for the sake of my brothers, who are my kindred according to the flesh, 4 who are Israelites.* At one time I wished. Had I been a follower of Christ, I would not have wished. Indeed, I knew that all these things were for them, but after I recognized the truth I forsook those I used to love in this way, and they do not repent.[4] *Theirs is the adoption as children.* For of them it was said: 'Israel, my first-born son' (Exod. 4: 22). *And the glory and the covenants and the giving of the law.* The giving of the old law and the promise of the new law.[5] *And the service and the promises.* That is, the ministry of the angels and the prophets.   5 *Theirs are the fathers.* Abraham [and] Isaac and Jacob (cf. Gen. 50: 24). *And from them is Christ according to the flesh, who is over all, God blessed for ever.* Against the Manichaean, Photinus, and Arius, because he [is] from the Jews,[6] [and] according to the flesh [alone from them],[7] [and] God blessed for ever.[8] So also Thomas worships 'and says: My God and my Lord!',

[54] Cf. Cypr. *Test.* 3. 18 (CCSL 3: 112. 7–113. 12); Ambstr. *Rom.* 8: 35. 1–2 (CSEL 81. 1: 297. 9–15); Jer. *Ep.* 121. 9 (PL 22: 1028. 16–17).
[1] Cf. *Rom.* 5: 12.   [2] Cf. ibid. 6: 4.
[3] Cf. ibid. 2: 15, 7: 23.   [4] Cf. Anon. *Rom.* 92A (Frede ii. 63–4).
[5] The comment is a play on *legislatio*. Cf. Orig.–Ruf. *Rom.* 7. 13 (PG 14: 1139C 7–13).
[6] Cf. Aug. *Faust.* 2. 1, 23. 1–4 (CSEL 25: 253. 18–23, 707. 1–710. 9).
[7] Cf. Ambstr. *Quaest.* 91. 8 (CSEL 50: 157. 5–14).
[8] Cf. Mar. Vict. *Adu. Arium*, 1. 18 (SC 68: 228. 4–6).

which Christ confirms when he says: 'Because you have seen, you have believed' (John 20: 28–9).   6 *The word of God, however, did not fail.* Since he had said above that it pained him that the people of Israel were shut out of the kingdom by their own fault, for all these things had belonged to them (cf. Rom. 9: 1–5), he shows here that those who do not believe are not sons of Abraham, lest one suppose that he was prejudicial to all Jews and upbraid him with the question: 'Did God then lie to Abraham?' *For not all those who are from Israel are Israelites,* 7 *nor are all children because they are offspring of Abraham.* If not all, then still some; and, if not all Israelites are from Israel, then some '[true Israelites] in whom there is no guile' are [also] from the Gentiles (cf. John 1: 47). *But in Isaac will your offspring be named.* Even then the sons of Abraham were named [in] Isaac alone, and not in Ishmael as well, though he too descended from Abraham's line.   8 *That is, those who are children of the flesh are not children of God, but those who are children of the promise are counted among the offspring.* For Ishmael was born of a maid-servant by sexual intercourse (cf. Gal. 4: 23), but Isaac was begotten beyond natural means from old people by the promise of God.[9] So [too] the promise now makes Christians sons of Abraham—the promise which [his] faith merited[10]—so that he is indeed the father of many nations (cf. Rom. 4: 17–18).   9 *For this is the wording of the promise: 'After this time I shall come, and Sarah will have a son.'* Here he shows that the people who came afterwards belonged to the promise after the manner of Isaac.   10 *Not only her, but also Rebecca.* Not only are Ishmael and Isaac, who were begotten [of different mothers], though of one father, not equal in the sight of God; Jacob and Esau too, who were born of Rebecca as a result of a single conception, were separated in God's sight before they were born on account of their [subsequent] faith, so that God's purpose for choosing the good and resisting the evil existed already in foreknowledge. So too, then, he has now chosen those whom he foreknew would believe from among the Gentiles, and has rejected those whom he foreknew would be un-believing out of Israel.[11] *Who bore children by Isaac our father as a result of a single conception.* Rebecca is thought to be the first woman to have begotten twins; because this unheard-of thing has befallen [her], she, panic-stricken, enquires of God (cf. Gen. 25: 22–3).   11 *For although they had not yet been born or done anything good or evil, so that according to election the plan of God might stand.* Or: So that it might be shown that even from a set of twins the one who does not believe is given up.

<hr/>

[9] Cf. *Rom.* 4: 18.   [10] Cf. ibid. 4: 11.   [11] Cf. ibid. 8: 29.

12 *Not because of works, but because of the one who calls, was it said, 'The elder shall serve the younger.'* God's foreknowledge does [not] prejudge the sinner, if he is willing to repent. For he says through Ezekiel: 'If I say to a sinner: "You shall surely die", and he, having repented, does what is right, he shall surely live and shall not die' (Ezek. 33: 14–15).[12] 13 *As it is written: 'Jacob I loved, but Esau I hated.'* Through the prophet the apostle shows that what had been told [first] to Rebecca was fulfilled in later descendants.　　14 *What then shall we say? That there is injustice on God's part? Certainly not!* He was afraid that because he had argued to show that racial prerogative is of no consequence in the sight of God, or in case they did not understand that already at that time it was signified that the later people would be a better people, they supposed him to say that God makes some good, others evil. [And] [because] in their judgement it was unjust to punish those who had not sinned of [their] own free will, he also calls to mind the contrary texts with which they usually supported this view, and, replying to these examples with brief objections, [shows] that they should not be understood as they understand them.[13]　　15 *For Moses says: 'I will have mercy on whom I have mercy, and I will show compassion to whom I will have mercy.'* This is correctly understood as follows: I will have mercy on him whom I have foreknown will be able to deserve compassion, so that already then I have had mercy on him.[14] 16 *Then, it does not depend on the one who wills or the one who runs, but on God, who has mercy.* [The argument of the Jew, on the contrary, is: 'Then it does not depend on the one who wills or the one who runs', and again: '[Therefore] he has mercy on whom he wills and he hardens whom he wills.' The apostle, in fact, does not [take away] what we possess in our own will, since he says above: 'Not realizing that God's goodness leads you to repentance?' (Rom. 2: 4), and also writes to Timothy: 'In every great house there are not only vessels of

---

[12] Cf. Ambstr. *Rom.* 9: 11–13. 5 (CSEL 81. 1: 313. 24–6, 317. 4–11); Anon. *De indur. cord.* 31 (Plinval 171. 7–11).

[13] Pelagius appears to divide vv. 14–33 into two parts. Verses 14–19 express the view of Paul's opponents; cf. Orig.-Ruf. *Rom.* 7. 16 (PG 14: 1144B 8–1145A 1), and see Schelkle, *Paulus*, 342–3. Paul represents his opponents by alternating a passage from Scripture (vv. 15, 17) with a remark which is intended to be a rebuttal (vv. 16, 18–19). Verses 20–33 are read in two different ways. According to the one, the opponents continue their argument until v. 29, after which Paul offers a brief reply; see *Rom.* 9: 30. According to the other, Paul begins his response at v. 20; see *Rom.* 9: 20. The latter seems to be Pelagius's view. His comments often assume that Paul is the speaker, adding the alternative interpretation as something of an afterthought; see *Rom.* 9: 26, 9: 29, 9: 30. The opponents are once represented as Jews, twice as 'those who object'.

[14] Cf. Ambstr. *Rom.* 9: 15. 1 (CSEL 81. 1: 319. 13–16).

gold and silver, but also of wood and clay, [and indeed] some for noble use, others for ignoble. Now if someone cleanses himself from the latter, he will be a vessel for noble use, made holy' (2 Tim. 2: 20–1).][15] If, as some suppose, it does not depend on the one who wills or on the one who runs, why does he himself also run, as he says: 'I have finished the race' (2 Tim. 4: 7), and why has he urged others to run, saying: 'Run so as to take all' (1 Cor. 9: 24)? For this reason it is understood that here he takes on the voice of one who questions [and refutes], rather than of one who denies.[16] [Or: Thus it does not only depend on the one who wills or the one who runs, but also on the Lord, who assists.][17]   17 *For concerning Pharaoh the Scripture says: 'I have raised you up for this very purpose, to show my power in you, and to proclaim my name in the whole earth.'* They present this passage in the wrong way as well. Now it is explained by different interpreters in two ways. Either: Since each one will be punished when the measure and limit of his sins is complete, as in the case of the inhabitants of Sodom and Gomorrah (cf. Gen. 19: 24–5), Pharaoh accordingly had already exceeded his limit, [and] God wished to make an example of him for the others, as of one already doomed to die, so that the people of God might come to know God's justice and power, and neither dare to sin nor fear their enemies.[18] The same sort of thing that happened to Pharaoh happens when a doctor, seeking the causes of sickness, discovers a remedy in the course of torturing someone already condemned to death for many crimes;[19] or when a judge, though he could punish a guilty man immediately, afflicts him with various torments to rouse the fear of all.[20] Or:

---

[15] Cf. Aug. *Exp. prop.* 54 (62). 1 (CSEL 84: 36. 15–17); Anon. *Rom.* 098 (c) (Frede ii. 68); Orig.–Ruf. *Rom.* 7. 17 (PG 14: 1148c 1–1149b 15). The comment is omitted by the Karlsruhe and the Paris MSS (Souter does not note the latter in his apparatus); see the Introduction at n. 212.

[16] Pelagius probably has Augustine's letter to Simplician in view; cf. Aug. *Ad Simpl.* 1. 2. 3, 10–16 (CCSL 44: 27. 92–28. 107, 34. 273–42. 491)—especially his use of 2 Tim. 4: 7–8 and 1 Cor. 9: 24—and see the Introduction at n. 132 and ff. For a similar reaction to Augustine's position see Anon. *De indur. cord.* 18, 36 (Plinval 155. 32–157. 7, 179. 2–3).

[17] Cf. Aug. *Exp. prop.* 54 (62). 1 (CSEL 84: 36. 14–19). The comment is found only in the Karlsruhe MS and in Cassiodorus's revision of the commentary. On its authenticity see the Introduction at nn. 219 and 223. It is noteworthy that at *Col.* 1: 10, where Pelagius acknowledges the need for God's assistance, he takes care to construe it in ways which do not eliminate freedom of choice—the teaching of wisdom and the granting of understanding.

[18] Cf. Ambstr. *Rom.* 9: 17. 2 (CSEL 81. 1: 325. 8–15); Aug. *Exp. prop.* 54 (62). 7–8 (CSEL 84: 37. 10–16); Orig.–Ruf. *Rom.* 7. 16 (PG 14: 1146b 4–6).

[19] Cf. Ambstr. *Rom.* 9: 17. 2 (CSEL 81. 1: 325. 15–19); see also Celsus, *Med.* proem. 23–6 (LCL 292: 14); Tert. *An.* 10. 4, 25. 5 (CCSL 2. 794. 16–22, 820. 52–5).

[20] Cf. Orig.–Ruf. *Rom.* 7. 16 (PG 14: 1146a 7–b 11).

He was hardened by God's patience, for after a plague from God ended Pharaoh became harder, and although God knew that Pharaoh had not repented, he wished nevertheless to show his forbearance even towards him.[21] 18 *Therefore God has mercy on whom he wills and he hardens whom he wills.* 19 *Then you say to me: 'What is he still looking for? For who can resist his will?'* If, then, this too is understood as follows: 'He has mercy on whom he wills [and] he hardens whom he wills' because there is enough wickedness, then your argument also will be lost—the argument that not you, but the will of the Lord, to which there can be no opposition, is the cause of your wickedness. The very nature of God's justice opposes this reasoning of yours. 20 *Who are you, a mere human being, to talk back to God? Does what is formed say to the one who formed it: 'Why did you make me like this?'* To some it seems that thus far he is still speaking in the person of those who object, because to say that no one can oppose the will of God, who has mercy on one and hardens another, and to add that no one [should] talk back to God [for doing whatever he wishes] amounts to the same thing.[22] But some say that now from here on the apostle replies that even if there were cause for them to make accusation, they ought not to talk back to their Maker, for in comparison to God we are as a piece of pottery is to its artisan.[23] 21 *Or does not the potter have the right to make from the same lump of clay one vessel for noble use and another for ignoble use?* According to those who say that these [are] the words of the apostle, he says that the lump of clay is all those who sojourned in Egypt, because Israel too had served idols there. [This is why Ezekiel says that her virginity was defiled in Egypt (cf. Ezek. 23: 8).] 22 *But if God, choosing to show his wrath and make known his power, bore with great patience.* Because he bore with Pharaoh for a long time, while Pharaoh blasphemed and oppressed his people with hard labours and, in addition, had ruthlessly ordered that little children of an innocent age be put to death (cf. Exod. 1: 8–16). *The vessels of wrath, prepared for destruction.* By filling up the quota of their sins they became vessels worthy of wrath, and by their own doing they became vessels prepared for destruction.[24] 23 *And in order to show the riches of his glory to the vessels of mercy, which he prepared for glory.* They were worthy of mercy, because they had committed lesser sins and had been

---

[21] Cf. ibid. (PG 14: 1146C 7–1147A 9).

[22] See *Rom.* 9: 14 n. 13.

[23] Cf. Ambstr. *Rom.* 9: 20. 1–2 (CSEL 81. 1: 327. 9–18); Aug., *Exp. prop.* 54 (62). 19 (CSEL 84: 39. 3–6); Orig.–Ruf. *Rom.* 7. 17 (PG 14: 1147B 11–C 1); Anon. *De indur. cord.* 18 (Plinval 157. 15–19); Jer. *Ep.* 120. 9 (CSEL 55: 503. 5–8).

[24] Cf. *Rom.* 9: 17.

severely oppressed.   24 *Even us, whom he also called, not only from the Jews, but also from the Gentiles,* 25 *as he says in Hosea: 'I will call those who are not my people "my people", and she who has not received mercy "she who has received mercy",* 26 *and it will come to pass in the place where it was said to them, "You are not my people", there they will be called "children of the living God".'* Since even then some of the Egyptians had left with the children of Israel—for if God showed favouritism, Israel alone ought to receive salvation—so too now he has called not only Jews but also Gentiles to faith. But those who think that this is said not in the person of the apostle, but in the person of the Jews, say, 'He saved as many as he wished, so that he chose even idol-worshipping Gentiles, who had never served God, [and] called few from Israel, as Isaiah testifies'.[25] 27 *And Isaiah cries out concerning Israel.* The warning is shown to be for them. *'If the number of the children of Israel is as the sand of the sea, only a remnant will be saved.'* Showing that few of them will believe.   28 *'For he will finish his word and cut it short in equity, because the Lord will make a shortened word upon the earth.'* The historical sense is this: just as I shorten and quickly finish off a word, so God will accomplish [this] with all speed. But in prophecy the 'shortened word' is taken to mean the New Testament, because everything is briefly comprehended [and contained] in it.[26]   29 *And also Isaiah foretold.* 'Foretold' is a good choice of words, because it is written earlier.[27] *'If the Lord of Hosts had not left us offspring, we would have become like Sodom and we would have been like Gomorrah.'* Because he did not suffer a few righteous individuals to perish with a multitude of godless people (cf. Gen. 18: 20–33). Or: [Unless] Christ, Abraham's offspring, had been sent to set the people free.[28] The interpretation of those who are bringing objections, however, is this: unless he had wished to call at least a few from the Jews.   30 *What then shall we say? That the Gentiles, who did not pursue righteousness, have obtained righteousness?* If the above is spoken in the person of the apostle, he here once more imagines that they could say: 'If it is not the case, as we say, that it does not depend on the one who wills or on the one who runs (cf. Rom. 9: 16), why have the Gentiles found righteousness, which they never sought before, while Israel could not find it, although they have always sought it?' But if the whole

---

[25] See *Rom.* 9: 14 n. 13.

[26] Cf. Ambstr. *Rom.* 9: 28. 1 (CSEL 81. 1: 333. 17–25); *Quaest.* 44. 5 (CSEL 50: 73. 27–74. 24).

[27] That is, Isa. 1: 9, cited here, precedes Isa. 10: 22–3, cited at vv. 27–8.

[28] Cf. Ambstr. *Rom.* 9: 29. 1 (CSEL 81. 1: 335. 6–12); Orig.–Ruf. *Rom.* 7. 19 (PG 14: 1154A 9–B 3).

of the above thought is attributed to those who are bringing objections, the apostle here replies and briefly reviews the question by saying:[29] 'What shall I say to these objections that are presented to us, except that the Gentiles believed as soon as they were called, and that the Jews refused to believe?'[30] *The righteousness which is by faith.* Because righteousness is by faith, and they refused to believe.   31 *Israel, on the other hand, pursuing the law of righteousness, did not attain to the law.* 32 *Why? Because they pursued it not by faith, but as if it were by works.* He explains once again why they did not find righteousness: because, having wrongly gloried in works, they refused to believe and, as if they were righteous, spurned grace.[31] *For they stumbled over the stumbling-stone,* 33 *as it is written: 'Behold, I am laying in Sion a stumbling-stone and a rock of offence.'* One who sees a stone does not stumble, but one who is blind dashes himself against it, as befell the Jews, who were blinded by their malice and crucified Christ because they did not recognize him.[32] Now it was foretold that Christ would be the stumbling-stone and the rock of offence precisely because many take offence at his birth and death, just as it is written that 'they were offended by him' (Matt. 13: 57; Mark 6: 3). The apostle himself speaks of 'Christ crucified, a stumbling-block to the Jews, foolishness to the Gentiles, but to those who have been called, Christ the power of God and the wisdom of God' (1 Cor. 1: 23–4). Therefore the above passage continues: 'Who believes in him will not be put to shame' (Rom. 9: 33; cf. Isa. 28: 16). Peter too says that 'for those who believe, the chosen stone' is 'the cornerstone, but for those who do not believe a stone for stumbling' (1 Pet. 2: 6–8). '*And everyone who believes in him will not be put to shame.*' Not the Jew alone, but everyone who believes will not be put to shame by former transgressions.

10: 1 *Brothers, truly my heart's desire and prayer to God is for their salvation.* Here he shows that he prays for his enemies not only with the tongue, but also with the heart (cf. Matt. 5: 44; Isa. 29: 13/Matt. 15: 8).   2 *For I bear witness to them that they are zealous for God, but not in accordance with knowledge.* They are zealous in pursuing the law, but they do not understand that Christ came according to the law, and that they cannot be justified by the law.[1] Indeed, it is risky to do

---

[29] The tenses of *respondit* and *recapitulat* do not agree. Souter suggests *respondet*; cf. a similar construction at *Rom.* 9: 14.

[30] On the question of persona see *Rom.* 9: 14 n. 13.   [31] Cf. ibid. 5: 1.

[32] On such general statements about the Jews see Simon, *Verus Israel,* 246–7; Blumenkranz, *Juifs et chrétiens,* 269; Ruether, *Faith and Fratricide,* 129–31.

[1] Cf. *Rom.* 2: 12 at n. 21.

[something] without knowledge, because it often turns out contrary to expectation.   3 *For since they did not know of God's righteousness and sought to establish their own, they did not submit to God's righteousness.* Because they did not know that God justifies by faith alone, and because they thought that they were righteous by the works of a law they did not keep, they refused to submit themselves to the forgiveness of sins, to prevent the appearance of their having been sinners, as it is written: 'But the Pharisees, rejecting the purpose of God for themselves, refused to be baptized with John's baptism' (Luke 7: 30).[2]   4 *For the end of the law is Christ, for the righteousness of all who believe.* On the day one believes in Christ, it is as if one has fulfilled the whole law (cf. Gal. 5: 3).[3]   5 *For Moses wrote of the righteousness which is by the law.* Moses himself distinguished between the two kinds of righteousness, namely the righteousness of faith and the righteousness of deeds, because the one justifies the suppliant by works, but the other by belief alone. *That the person who does these things will live by them.* Therefore, none of them will live, because in this age no one keeps the law perfectly without Christ, since it is also part of the law to believe in him. On account of this passage some think that the Jews have merited only this present life by the works of the law,[4] but the words of the Lord show that this is not true. When he was asked about eternal life, he stipulated the commandments of the law, saying: 'If you wish to enter into life, keep the commandments' (Matt. 19: 17). From this we understand that one who kept the law in his own time had everlasting life.   6 *But the righteousness that is by faith says this: 'Do not say in your heart: "Who ascends into heaven?"'—that is, to bring Christ down. 7 '"Or who descends into the abyss?"'—that is, to call Christ back from the dead. 8 But what does the Scripture say? 'The word is near, in your mouth and in your heart.'* According to the historical sense, Moses in fact said this about the law (cf. Deut. 30: 14), but the apostle applies it to Christ, because the law was [neither] in heaven nor in the abyss.[5] Or: He orders them always to meditate upon the law, so that there they may be able to find Christ (cf. Ps. 1: 2). *That is, the word of faith, which we preach.* Namely, of the New Testament.   9 *Because if you confess the Lord Jesus with your mouth, and*

    [2] Cf. Anon. *Rom.* 107A, 108 (Frede ii. 71–2).
    [3] Cf. Ambrstr. *Rom.* 10: 4 (CSEL 81. 1: 345. 10–11); Orig.–Ruf. *Rom.* 8. 2 (PG 14: 1160B 12–C 2).
    [4] Cf. Ambrstr. *Rom.* 10: 5, 10: 6–7. 2 (CSEL 81. 1: 345. 18–20, 347. 11–14); Orig.–Ruf. *Rom.* 8. 2 (PG 14: 1161A 4–11).
    [5] Cf. Ambrstr. *Rom.* 10: 6–7 (CSEL 81. 1: 345. 23–4, 347. 1); Orig.–Ruf. *Rom.* 8. 2 (PG 14: 1161B 8–C 12); and see Schelkle, *Paulus*, 371.

believe with your heart that God raised him from the dead. The testimony of
the heart is the confession of the mouth (cf. Rom. 10: 10). *You will be
saved.* From past transgressions, not future.[6]   10 *For one believes with
the heart unto righteousness, but confession is made with the mouth unto
salvation.* If, then, faith avails for righteousness, and confession for
salvation, there is no distinction between the Jew who believes and the
Gentile who believes.   11 *For the Scripture says: 'Everyone who believes in
him'.* Not the Jew alone. *'Will not be put to shame.'* Do not put them to
shame, therefore, on account of their former actions, since the
Scripture says that they cannot be put to shame.   12 *For there is no
distinction between Jew and Greek. For the same Lord is Lord of all, generous
towards all who call on him.* 13 *And 'everyone who calls on the name of the Lord
will be saved.'* There is one Lord of all, who abounds in mercy and
possesses salvation, with which he is generous [to all] (cf. Deut. 5: 10,
6: 4).   14 *How then are they to call on one in whom they have not believed?*
[This is an objection raised by the Jews about the Gentiles,] that they
could not call upon God.[7] *Or how are they to believe in one of whom they
have not heard? And how are they to hear without a preacher?* 15 *Or how are
they to preach unless they are sent?* Because the prophets were never sent
to them. *As it is written: 'How beautiful are the feet of those who preach the
Gospel of peace, the Gospel of good things!'* Beautiful are the feet of those
who proclaim peace, but the feet of those who run after the vain things
of this age are ugly and misshapen.   16 *But not all obeyed the Gospel.* If,
then, not all those to whom the prophets were sent obeyed, how much
less those to whom no one was sent! *For Isaiah says: 'Lord, who has
believed our report?'* Who has believed what he hears from us,[8] or what
we have heard from you to proclaim to others?[9]   17 *Faith, therefore,
comes from hearing, and hearing through the word.* From here on the
apostle's response.   18 *But I say: Have they not heard?* He confirms that
they had in fact heard before. *'Their sound has gone out into all the land, and
their words to the ends of the earth.'* He intends this passage to be
understood allegorically to refer to the cries of the prophets.   19 *But I
say: Has Israel not known?* That the Gentiles were to be called to faith [is
understood]. *First, Moses says.* Moses is first because [almost] all the
prophets after him spoke of the salvation of the Gentiles. *'I will make
you jealous of those who are not a people; with a people that has no understanding*

[6] Cf. *Rom.* 9: 33, 10: 11.
[7] Pelagius reads vv. 14–16 as the objections of Jewish opponents and vv. 17–21 as
Paul's response; cf. *Rom.* 9: 14 n. 13.
[8] Cf. Orig.–Ruf. *Rom.* 8. 6 (PG 14: 1171A 7–14).
[9] Cf. Ambstr. *Rom.* 10: 16. 2 (CSEL 81. 1: 355. 17–18).

I will make you angry.' Before they believed in God, they were not the people of God. Therefore, it is as if he says: 'I shall call those who are not my people, and they will believe in me in order to provoke you, so that, though you should have been their betters, you may be glad to be their equals.' Just as [if] someone has a disobedient son and in order to reform him gives half of his patrimony to his slave, so that when at last he has repented he may be glad—if, at least, he deserves to receive that much. Or: We were not a people, because 'we were dead in sins' (Eph. 2: 1, 5).   20 *And Isaiah is bold to say: 'I have been found by those who did not seek me.'* To the Gentiles, who did not enquire after God in the law, but after idols in ignorance. *'I have been revealed to those who did not ask of me.'* [Who] asked not of God, but of demons, through the augurs [and] astrologers and haruspices of the idols.   21 *But what does he say to Israel?* The very prophet who made promises of this sort to the Gentiles issues warnings here of a similar sort to the Jews, so that you may know that both were foretold![10] *'The whole day I have held out my hands.'* The whole time I showed wonders or plagues,[11] [and] even so they have not believed. *'To an unbelieving and contrary people.'* The holding out of the hands means allegorically the cross.[12]

11: 1 *I say, then, has God rejected his people? By no means!* Because Paul had sufficiently humbled them, he encourages them in the way a good teacher would, lest he seem to provoke them unduly. God has not rejected everyone, he says, and not for ever, but only [those who do not believe, and] as long as they do not believe.[1] *For I too am an Israelite.* If he had rejected everyone, he also certainly would not have accepted me. *Of the seed of Abraham, of the tribe of Benjamin.* Not from the class of proselytes.   2 *God has not rejected his people, whom he foreknew.* He has not rejected the people that he foreknew would believe.[2] *Do you not know what the Scripture says of Elijah?* In the Book of Kings, where it is written about Elijah (cf. 1 Kgs. 19: 9–18). *How he appeals to God against*

---

[10] On the separation of promise from judgement in prophecies originally addressed to the Jews alone, such that promise is referred to the Gentiles while judgement is referred to the Jews, see Schelkle, *Paulus*, 377; Simon, *Verus Israel*, 253–4; Ruether, *Faith and Fratricide*, 131–2.

[11] Cf. Isa. 65: 1–2 and Ps. 87: 10–11 (LXX); see also Cypr. *Test*. 2. 20 (CCSL 3: 57. 2–4).

[12] Cf. *Barn*. 12. 1, 4 (FP 1: 54–5); Just. *1 Apol*. 35. 6 (FP 2: 68); Just., *Dial*. 97. 2 (Archambault ii. 110); Iren. *Demon*. 79 (SC 62: 146); Tert. *Iud*. 13. 10–11 (CCSL 2: 1386. 49–58); Novat. *Trin*. 28. 10 [156] (CCSL 4: 66. 31–3); Cypr. *Test*. 2. 20 (CCSL 3: 57. 2–4); Ambstr. *Rom*. 10: 21. 1 (CSEL 81. 1: 361. 10–12); Orig.–Ruf. *Rom*. 8. 6 (PG 14: 1174D 1–4).

[1] Cf. Orig.–Ruf. *Rom*. 8. 7 (PG 14: 1175B 9–C 5).

[2] Cf. Ambstr. *Rom*. 11: 1. 2, 11: 2 (CSEL 81. 1: 363. 2–4, 9–11).

Israel. He eliminates opportunity for pride among the Gentiles, in case they become boastful because so few of the Jews believed.   3 *'Lord, they have killed your prophets, overthrown your altars, and I alone am left, and they seek my life.'* All the prophets knew only the things that had been revealed to them by the Lord. This is why the king, uncertain of mind, asked Jeremiah if in the hour in which he spoke with [him] a word of the Lord had come to him (cf. Jer. 37: 17).[3] And even Elisha says: 'Why has the Lord hidden these things from me?' (2 Kgs. 4: 27).[4] So too[, then], in this passage Elijah was unaware that there were others beside him who worshipped God (cf. 1 Kgs. 19: 18).   4 *But what does the divine answer tell him? 'I have left for myself seven thousand men'.* If so many men were hidden from the prophet, how much more are you unaware of how many Jews have been saved and are to be saved! *'Who have not bowed the knee before Baal.'* One serves idols not only by offering sacrifice, but also by transgressing. For if one denies God by one's actions, then surely one is at the same time honouring the demons. 5 *So too, then, at the present time.* Therefore, just as all did not perish then, so too some are saved now. *A remnant has been saved according to the election of grace.* The election of grace is faith, just as works are the election of the law. Otherwise, what sort of election is it, where there is no difference in merits?[5]   6 *But if by grace, then not by works.* In case they replied to him about those concerning whom the word comes to Elijah: 'They were righteous; why were these sinners elected?', he added that they too are saved freely, just as the Gentiles. *Otherwise, grace is no longer grace.* Because to bestow gratuitously is called 'grace'. 7 *Then, Israel has not obtained what it sought.* Israel as a whole has not obtained righteousness, because it did not seek it by faith, but thought that it was justified solely by works of the law, though it disregarded the greatest commandments of the law.[6] This is why the Saviour censures those who strain a gnat and swallow a camel (cf. Matt. 23: 24). *The election has obtained it.* Those who are elected through faith.[7] *But the rest have been blinded,* 8 *as it is written.* The rest have been blinded through unfaithfulness, as it is written: 'Unless you believe, you will also not understand' (Isa. 7: 9). *'God gave them a spirit of stupefaction, eyes so that they should not see, and ears so that they should not hear'.* [The

---

[3] See 2 Kgs. 24: 18–25: 7.
[4] See ibid. 4: 8–37.
[5] Cf. Aug. *Exp. prop.* 52 (60). 8–9 (CSEL 84: 34. 16–22). For subsequent developments in Augustine's thought on this point see the Introduction at n. 132 and ff.
[6] Cf. *Rom.* 10: 3.
[7] Cf. ibid. 11: 5.

Scripture says:] 'Before man are life and death; what pleases him will be given to him' (Ecclus. 15: 18)—clearly, so as not to eliminate freedom of choice.[8] It is therefore God's prerogative to give, to allow—to give, however, the spirit of stupefaction that they desired, for they have always disbelieved the words of God. Indeed, if they had wanted to have a spirit of faith, they would have received it. But [even] today Christians who doubt the resurrection [and] reward or Gehenna have sought a similar spirit for themselves:[9] for in this passage the prophet was addressing both unbelievers and sinners. *'To this very day.'* Until they repent, as he says to the Corinthians with regard to the veil of the heart (cf. 2 Cor. 3: 15). 9 *And David says: 'Let their table become a snare and a trap and a stumbling-block and a recompense for them.* 10 *Let their eyes be darkened so that they cannot see, and may you bend their back for ever.'* [Alternatively: May you bend them for ever with the weight of their sins, so that they are not forgiven unless they believe.][10] [The table] where they rejoiced at the death of Christ, while they ate the passover.[11] This prophecy speaks of those who gave the Saviour vinegar and gall to drink.[12] Nevertheless Peter says to them: 'Now I know that you did this out of ignorance. . . . Repent, therefore, and be baptized, every one of you' (Acts 3: 17, 2: 38). And Paul himself says a little later: 'Even these are ingrafted, if they do not abide in unbelief' (Rom. 11: 23), so that we may know that the spirit of stupefaction has not taken away from them the ability to repent. For immediately afterwards [the apostle] himself releases them. 11 *I say, then: Have they stumbled.* Once again he explains the position of the Jews. *So as to fall? Not at all!* They have not fallen away completely and beyond hope. *But out of love for them there is salvation for the Gentiles, so that they may be jealous of them.*[13] He loved them

---

[8] Cf. Orig.-Ruf. *Rom.* 1. 18 (PG 14: 886c 10–13).

[9] This is an oblique reference to the supporters of Origen in the Origenist controversy at the end of the 4th cent. Cf. Jer. *Ep.* 51. 4, 5 (CSEL 54: 402. 2–3, 403. 4–9) and *Ioan.* 23–6 (PL 23: 375c 12–389b 2); Ruf. *Apol.* 1. 25. 37 (CCSL 20: 58. 6–10, 72. 35–45), and *Ad Anast.* 4–5 (CCSL 20: 26–7). See also the Introduction at n. 108.

[10] This comment is a pseudo-Hieronymian interpolation; see the Introduction at n. 213 and ps.-Hi. *Rom.* 113*ll* (Frede ii. 75).

[11] Cf. *Rom.* 8: 3 at n. 9.   [12] Cf. Ps. 68: 22–4 (LXX).

[13] The lemma reads *delicto* in all the MSS, but on account of Pelagius's comment Souter emended it to read *dilecto*. The latter is unusual; other Latin writers read *delictum* or *delicto*: Ambstr. *Rom.* 11. 11 (CSEL 81. 1: 371. 16); Ambr. *Luc.* 6. 57 (CCSL 14: 194. 572); *Ps.* 36. 4 (CSEL 64: 72. 25); Orig.–Ruf. *Rom.* 8. 9 (PG 14: 1184a 9); Jer. *Esaiam*, 3. 6. 9. 10 (CCSL 73: 93. 83); Aug. *Ciu.* 18. 46 (CCSL 48: 644. 42). The reading suggested by Souter has no equivalent in the Greek MSS of the epistles. If Pelagius indeed followed it, it adds to the evidence that he had little Greek when he wrote the commentary; see Chapman, 'Pélage et le texte de s. Paul', 18: 472–3.

so much that the Gentiles were called for their salvation, so that when they saw that the Gentiles were allowed into the kingdom of God, they might perhaps repent more readily.   12 *But if their transgression is riches for the world, and their loss is riches for the Gentiles, how much more their fullness!* If their transgression benefited you to the extent that without the works of the law you were made co-heirs with them, and if the few Jews who believed called all of you to salvation, how much more could they benefit you with instruction, if they all believed!   13 *For I say to you Gentiles.* He wants to show that he is especially anxious to save the Jews. *As long as I am an apostle to the Gentiles, I shall honour my ministry.* As long as I reside in the body, I shall honour my ministry, striving to save many of them by my example (cf. 2 Cor. 5: 6–8).   14 *If in any way I am zealous for my flesh.* So that in every way I present myself to them in such a manner that they desire to imitate me. *So that I may save some of them.* At least some, if not all are willing.[14]   15 *But if the loss of them means the reconciliation of the world.* He has repeated what he had said above (cf. Rom. 11: 12). *What is their reception, if not life from the dead?* What was the occasion for the reception of the Gentiles, but that they came to life as a result of the death of the Jews?[15] [Or:] From among the Jews that were dead, Christ and the apostles have become life to the Gentiles. Or: If those whom I set free from death contribute to your life.[16] 16 *But if the first-fruit is holy, so is the whole lump.* If the few who believed are holy, so will they all be holy, if they believe. *And if the root is holy, so are the branches.* The root of the patriarchs. That is, both the first and the last saints come from the patriarchs.[17]   17 *But if some of the branches were broken off.* They were not broken off for your sake, but you were grafted in because of the fact that they were broken off.[18] *And you, although you were a wild olive-tree.* An olive-tree, to be sure, but uncultivated and wild. *Were grafted into them, and were made to share in the root and the fatness of the olive-tree.* In the root of the fathers; in the fatness of Christ.   18 *Do not boast over against the branches: for though you boast, you do not support the root, but the root supports you.* Do not rejoice in their perdition, or else you will hear that they do not abide through you, but

---

[14] Cf. Orig.–Ruf. *Rom.* 8. 10 (PG 14: 1190A 12–13).

[15] Cf. Ambstr. *Rom.* 11: 15 (CSEL 81. 1: 373. 23–4); Orig.–Ruf. *Rom.* 8. 10 (PG 14: 1190C 1–7). See also *Rom.* 11: 17 below.

[16] Cf. *Rom.* 11: 12.

[17] That is, the righteous of both the Old Testament and the New Testament are derived from Abraham, Isaac, and Jacob; cf. *Rom.* 4: 12, 9: 6–13.

[18] Cf. Ambstr. *Rom.* 11: 18. 1 (CSEL 81. 1: 375. 24–377. 2); Aug. *Exp. prop.* 62 (70). 2 (CSEL 84: 43. 10–13).

you through them, and that you do not supply them with life, but they supply you.[19]   19 *Then you say: 'The branches were broken off so that I might be grafted in;* 20 *it is a good thing that they were broken off on account of unbelief.'* You say that they have been broken off so that you may be grafted in. Let us see if they perished for this reason, and not rather because of their unbelief.[20] *But you stand by faith.* It is not that God was partial towards you and rejected them without cause (cf. Rom. 2: 11; Gal. 2: 6). *Do not be high-minded, but be afraid.* Some interpreters, who do not understand this passage and do not consider the reason for which or the people to whom the apostle speaks, think that here [the pursuit] of wisdom is forbidden.[21] But if this is so, he will in their view seem to contradict himself, since here he forbids what elsewhere he asks of the Lord [with great supplications], that the Ephesians and others may receive.[22] 'Do not be high-minded', therefore, means this: do not be proud towards them.[23]   21 *For if God did not spare the natural branches, perhaps he will also not spare you.* If on account of their unbelief he did not spare those who sprang from the holy root, how much less will he spare you, if you sin![24]   22 *Behold, then, the kindness and the severity of God.* Against those who assert that there is one righteous God and another good God; and against those who deny that God punishes sinners.[25] *Severity towards those who have fallen away, but kindness towards you.* Because they were justly broken off and you were mercifully grafted in. *If you continue in his kindness.* In the faith which has been bestowed upon you by the kindness of God. *Otherwise you too will be cut off.* 23 *But even they, if they do not continue in unbelief, will be grafted in.* If, however, [each of you change,] you will experience severity and they kindness. *For God is able to graft them in again.* It is in fact humanly impossible to restore withered cuttings, but with God all things are possible and are indeed easy (cf. Matt. 19: 26).[26]   24 *For if you were cut*

---

[19] Cf. Ambstr. *Rom.* 11: 18. 1–2 (CSEL 81. 1: 375. 23, 377. 6).

[20] Cf. ibid. 11: 19 (CSEL 81. 1: 377. 10–13).

[21] Pelagius may refer here to ascetics who thought love of letters incompatible with love for Christ. On this conflict see Kelly, *Jerome*, 41–4; Chadwick, *Poetry and Letters*, 65–7, 115–16; and now Markus, *The End of Ancient Christianity*, 34–8.

[22] Cf. Eph. 3: 14–21, Phil. 1: 9–11, Col. 1: 9–15.

[23] Cf. Ambstr. *Rom.* 11: 20. 3 (CSEL 81. 1: 379. 4–5); Orig.–Ruf. *Rom.* 8. 11 (PG 14: 1194A 13–14).

[24] Cf. Ambstr. *Rom.* 11: 21 (CSEL 81. 1: 379. 7–12); Orig.–Ruf. *Rom.* 8. 11 (PG 14: 1194B 4–14).

[25] Pelagius refers in the first instance to the Marcionites, in the second instance to the Manichaeans. But heresiologists tended to conflate the two views; cf. Iren. *Haer.* 3. 25. 3 (SC 211: 482. 26–31); Aug. *Ep. fund.* 39 (CSEL 25: 244. 27–245. 22); *Nat. bon.* 31 (PL 42: 561. 3–25).   [26] Cf. Orig.–Ruf. *Rom.* 8. 11 (PG 14: 1194C 3–7).

from what is by nature a wild olive-tree. For [long ago] their fathers had fallen away from nature because they had forgotten the law of nature, and, when habit had become fixed through repeated sinning, they came to be bitter and unproductive as it were by nature.[27] *And, contrary to nature, were grafted into a good olive-tree, how much more will they in accordance with nature be grafted into their own olive-tree!* It is against nature to graft a wild olive-tree into a cultivated olive-tree, because the branch usually alters the efficacy of the root, rather than that the root changes the efficacy of the branches to conform to its character.[28] 25 *For I do not want you to be ignorant, brothers.* All of what follows is likewise to prevent the Gentiles from being filled with pride towards the Jews. *Of this mystery.* A secret which is unknown to humankind, why the Gentiles were saved, because Israel's blindness in fact furnished the occasion for their salvation. *So that you be not wise in yourselves.* Lest in accordance with human wisdom you say: 'God chose us and rejected them.'[29] *That blindness has taken hold of a part of Israel.* Both transgressions and faithlessness seized Israel to such an extent that the time came when all the Gentiles were given access to life. All of Israel, thus, was being saved in the same way as the full number of Gentiles—by faith alone—so that, because they had been equals in transgression, they were equals in Christ.[30] *Until the full number of the Gentiles has come in,* 26 *and so all Israel has been saved.* The blindness continued until they saw that the Gentiles were being saved, since all were called to salvation. Or: From Judah and Israel, namely from the law. *As it is written: 'There will come from Sion one who seizes and drives away the godless from Jacob.'* Some interpreters regard all these as future events.[31] To these one must reply: 'Then this prophecy—"He who delivers" Israel "will come from Sion" (Isa. 59: 20)—must still take place, and Christ will come again to set them free;[32] and, [if] they have been blinded temporarily by God, and not by themselves, what [will come] of those

---

[27] Cf. *Rom.* 3: 20, 7: 14–25.

[28] Cf. Ambstr. *Rom.* 11: 17. 2 (recens αβ) (CSEL 81. 1: 374. 16–20); Aug. *Faust.* 26. 3 (PL 42: 480. 34–42) and *En. in ps.* 72. 2 (CCSL 39: 987. 12–17); Orig.–Ruf. *Rom.* 8. 11 (PG 14: 1195A 5–12).

[29] Cf. Orig.–Ruf. *Rom.* 8. 12 (PG 14: 1195B 12–C 1).

[30] Cf. *Rom.* 11: 31–2.

[31] This was a common view in the 4th cent., but opinion was shifting away from a millennial interpretation. Cf. Ambstr. *Rom.* 11: 25–6. 1–2 (CSEL 81. 1: 381. 22–383. 11); Hil. *Ps.* 121. 4 (CSEL 22: 573. 4–5); Ambr. *Ps.* 40. 33 (CSEL 64: 252. 9–11); Aug. *Quaest. euang.* 2. 33 . 5 (CCSL 44B: 79. 130–80. 134); and see Judant, *Judaïsme et christianisme,* 177–218.

[32] Cf. Jer. *Esaiam,* 17. 60. 1–3, 4. 11. 11–14 (CCSL 73A: 692. 15–695. 103, 73: 154. 13–33).

who perish now as unbelievers?'   27 *'And this is the covenant from me
with them, when I shall take away their sins.'* The new covenant that
Jeremiah promised, which only those who are new, whose sins have
been wiped away, will receive (cf. Jer. 31: 31).[33]   28 *According to the
Gospel they are indeed enemies on your account.* They are my enemies
because I preach Christ to you (cf. 1 Cor. 1: 23), [as he himself says
elsewhere]: 'They keep us [from speaking to the Gentiles so that they
may be saved' (1 Thess. 2: 16).[34] *But according to election they are beloved on
account of their forefathers.* And if they believe, they are beloved, twice
blessed.[35]   29 *For the gifts and calling of God are without repentance.* If they
believe, their sins will not be able to be counted against them,]
because God does not repent that he made a promise with Abraham's
descendants.[36] Or: If they believe, they will be saved without the
anguish of penance.[37]   30 *For just as you too at one time did not believe
God.* When the Jews still believed. *But now have received mercy on account
of their unbelief.* Not because you deserved it.[38]   31 *So too now they have
not believed in your mercy.* Christ is the mercy of the Gentiles. *So that they
too may receive mercy.* They have been such unbelievers that they too
are justified not by their works, but in mercy, as you are.[39]   32 *For
God has confined all things in unbelief.* He has not imprisoned them by
force, but with cause has confined those whom he found in unbelief:
that is, all Jews and Gentiles. He confined the Jews because previously
they were only sinners, not also faithless. But since they have not
believed Christ, they are equal to the Gentiles, and all receive mercy
in the same way. *So that he may have mercy on all.* He does it for this
reason, so that he may have mercy on all.   33 *Oh, the depth of the riches
of the wisdom and knowledge of God!* He praises the wisdom of God, who
according to his foreknowledge waited until all were in need of mercy,
so as to take from everyone the glory that derives from unfounded
boasting in works. *How incomprehensible are his judgements.* 'The judgements' of God 'are a great deep' (Ps. 35: 7): for they cannot be clearly
grasped. *And how unsearchable his ways.* That is, the knowledge of his
plans.   34 *For who has known the mind of the Lord?* [Previously no one

---

[33] The lemma is in fact a conflation of Jer. 31: 31 and Isa. 27: 9. Identification of the
latter portion eluded Origen as well; cf. Orig.–Ruf. *Rom.* 8. 12 (PG 14: 1197A 5–8).

[34] Cf. Orig.–Ruf. *Rom.* 8. 13 (PG 14: 1199B 4–7).

[35] Cf. Ambstr. *Rom.* 11: 28. 2 (CSEL 81. 1: 385. 16–20); Orig.–Ruf. *Rom.* 8. 13 (PG 14:
1199B 8–13).

[36] Cf. Orig.–Ruf. *Rom.* 8. 13 (PG 14: 1199A 7–13).

[37] Cf. Ambstr. *Rom.* 11: 29 (CSEL 81. 1: 385. 21–387. 3).

[38] Cf. ibid. 11: 30–1 (CSEL 81. 1: 387. 11–14).

[39] The translation follows the MSS AH₂GV and renders only two instances of *non*.

knew it; but at the time of writing Paul himself assuredly knew it, as he indicated to others when he said: 'But we have the mind of the Lord' (1 Cor. 2: 16; cf. Wisd. 9: 134). Or: No one has known it by himself without God's law and grace, and even one who had been furnished with a special word from God needs his teaching.][40] *Or who has been his counsellor?* So as to know his hidden secrets.   35 *Or who has first given to him, and is to be repaid?* Who has done something beforehand, so that he does not magnify God's mercy, but boasts that [he has received] his just deserts?   36 *For from him and through him and in him are all things.* From him all creation received its beginning, through him it is governed, and in him are all things contained, whereas he is not con-tained by anything [that is created] (cf. Wisd. 1: 7).[41] *To him be glory for ever. Amen.* He alone should receive glory, for it is from him, in fact, that we are and live and move (cf. Acts. 17: 28). At the same time this passage also contradicts the Arians, when it is said that it is one and the same God from whom and through whom all things are revealed to have been made, since the evangelist indicated that in the beginning everything that was made was through the Word (cf. John 1: 1–3), and the apostle here teaches that what the evangelist testifies concerning the Son should be understood and believed of the Father through the mystery of the unity.

12: 1 *Therefore, I beseech you, brothers.* Because he had mentioned the mind [of the Lord] (cf. Rom. 11: 34), he now instructs them how they ought to conduct themselves so that they are worthy to have the mind of the Lord. *By the mercy of God.* They possessed nothing greater than this, for they had been set free by it. *To present your bodies.* [How much more the soul!][1] Not the bodies of animals, as under the law, which, in spite of the fact that they were a symbolic offering, were nevertheless offered up healthy and unblemished.[2] *As a living sacrifice, holy.* That is, pure and free from the total death of sin.[3] *Pleasing to God.* You should only please God, not people. Or: A sacrifice of the sort that pleases him. *Let your service be reasonable.* Every good work pleases God if it is done in a reasonable manner.[4] For one is deprived of one's reward if,

---

[40] Pelagius may refer here to the Montanists; cf. Jer., *Ep.* 41. 2 (CSEL 54: 313. 1–4); Aug. *Agone chr.* 28. 30 (CSEL 41: 130. 16–18, 131. 6–11); and see de Labriolle, *La Crise montaniste*, 472–9.

[41] Cf. *Rom.* 1: 19. On creation as the primary act of divine grace see Bohlin, *Die Theol-ogie des Pelagius*, 15–22; Evans, *Pelagius*, 92–6; Greshake, *Gnade*, 54–81.

[1] This remark, omitted by the Karlsruhe and Paris MSS, is probably a pseudo-Hier-onymian interpolation; see the Introduction at n. 212.

[2] Cf. Orig.-Ruf. *Rom.* 9. 1 (PG 14: 1203B 12–C 1, 1205A 12–B 15).

[3] Cf. *Rom.* 6: 12–14.   [4] Cf. ibid. 16: 19–20.

for example, one fasts for public notice (cf. Matt. 6: 1, 16); one performs a good [service] foolishly. And the same should be applied to all the vices that border on the virtues.[5]   2 *Do not be conformed to this age, but be transformed in the newness of your mind, so that you may prove what is the will of God.* Do not be like the children of the world, you who have been made children of God, but renew your mind, by which the body is governed and all the members are directed, so that even the movements of the body become new, that thereby you may be able to recognize the will of God and his mind: for these are revealed only to a new mind. *What is good and pleasing and perfect.* That is, what is good and better and best.   3 *For by the grace given to me I say.* Since he is about to disallow human wisdom that goes beyond the law, he declares that he speaks not his own mind, but by the authority of a spiritual gift.[6] *To all who are among you.* Who are priests or teachers, whose example the rest follow.[7] *Not to be wiser than one ought, but to be wise with sober judgement.* One who searches into matters of which the law does not speak seeks to be 'wiser'. This is why Solomon says: 'Do not enquire after things higher than yourself and do not search after things greater than yourself, but think always on the things that God has commanded you' (Ecclus. 3: 21 (22)). *And to each one, as God has apportioned.* Observe that he calls the Holy Spirit God, for he declares to the Corinthians that the Holy Spirit apportions gifts to each person as he wishes (cf. 1 Cor. 12: 11, 28). *A measure of faith.* A charismatic power, which none but the faithful receive, is to be considered a measure [of faith].[8]   4 *For as in one body we have many members.* He exhorts them to live in harmony by comparing them with the body, in case they are not roused at least by the fact that they have received different gifts. For they could not as individuals each have all the gifts, lest they became proud because they lacked none. Nor could they all have the same gift, in order that the likeness of the body of Christ may be evident among us. *But all the members do not have the same function.* For the eye cannot hear and the ear

---

[5] Cf. Aug. *Ep.* 167. 6 (CSEL 44: 593. 7–10); *Iul.* 4. 20 (PL 44: 748. 35–8).

[6] Cf. Orig.–Ruf. *Rom.* 9. 2 (PG 14: 1208B 10–C 15); see also Pel. *1 Cor.* 2: 13 (Souter, *Expositions*, ii. 139. 15–17).

[7] *Sacerdos* (here 'priest') originally had a narrower meaning than *doctor* (here 'teacher'), but by the middle of the 4th cent. the terms were interchangeable, usually referring to the bishop. In some areas, however, *doctor* was reserved as a distinct title, perhaps for priests especially assigned to catechetics; see Gaudemet, *L'Église dans l'empire romain*, 102.

[8] On the phrase *gratia uirtutum*—here rendered 'charismatic power'—cf. Valero, *Las bases antropológicas*, 134–6. On faith as a necessary but not sufficient condition for the receipt of a spiritual gift see *Rom.* 12: 6.

cannot see, and likewise for the other members (cf. 1 Cor. 12: 17). 5 *So we who are many are one body in Christ, and as individuals are members one of another.* So that as we offer to one another what we have, love may grow stronger and stronger. 6 *But having different gifts according to the grace given to us.* The gift depends not upon us, but upon the decision of the one who gives it. To all who believe there is promised the glory to come, but the person who has a heart so pure that he deserves it receives even in this present life the charismatic power [which God has chosen to give to him].[9] *Whether prophecy, in proportion to faith.* To faith, not to the law. Or: Because faith deserves it. For each one receives as much as he believes. 7 *Or service, in serving.* The service of the office of priest or deacon.[10] *Or one who teaches, in teaching,* 8 *one who exhorts, in exhorting.* One who teaches is greater than one who exhorts: for those with less skill can still exhort according to their abilities. It should be noted, in fact, that he listed the person who exhorts only in third place. Or: Whatever the reason why he made this distinction, the spiritual reader should acknowledge it. *One who gives, without reserve.* [So that] he is generous to all without reserve, trusting that all who make requests are honest and in need. *One who is in charge, with solicitude.* One who is in charge of the church or of the brothers should be solicitous.[11] *One who shows mercy, with cheerfulness.* Mercy must be shown especially towards [all] the distressed. Or: A general ascription of mercy is: to present oneself towards all in a gentle manner. 'For God loves a cheerful giver' (2 Cor. 9: 7), and doubtless hates a cheerless one, because 'a good word' is 'better than a gift' (Ecclus. 18: 16–17). 9 *Let love be genuine, detesting what is evil, holding to what is good.* Complete purity should dwell in the Christian, just as God is pure light (cf. 1 John 1: 5): for it is typical of slaves to dissemble (cf. 1 Tim. 1: 5; 2 Cor. 6: 6). And let us love not only in word, but in deed and in truth (cf. 1 John 3: 18), so that, if it were necessary, we would even die

---

[9] Cf. Ambstr. *Rom.* 12: 6. 1 (CSEL 81. 1: 397. 21–2); Orig.–Ruf. *Rom.* 9. 2–3 (PG 14: 1211A 7–B 2, 1213C 1–12). Contrast Anon. *Rom.* 0123 (Frede ii. 80). The clause 'which God has chosen to give him' (*quam deus ei donare uoluerit*) is attested by the Karlsruhe and St Gall MSS alone; see the Introduction at n. 219.

[10] Pelagius appears to regard the office of deacon as complementary, rather than subordinate, to the office of priest. On the late-4th-cent. dispute in Rome over the relationship between the two cf. Ambstr. *Quaest.* 101. 1–10 (CSEL 50: 193. 20–198. 22); Jer. *Ep.* 146. 1–2 (CSEL 56: 308. 1–312. 5); and see Pietri, *Roma Christiana*, i. 693–6; Domagalski, 'Römische Diakone'.

[11] Cf. Orig.–Ruf. *Rom.* 9. 3 (PG 14: 1217B 15–C 10), where 'brothers' is a synonym for 'church' to designate a congregation under the direction of a bishop. For other meanings of the term see Schelkle, 'Brüder', 639–40.

[for each other].[12]   10 *Loving one another with brotherly love*. You should love one another as if you had been born of the same mother. *Outdoing one another in mutual esteem*. If we always observe this injunction, we would [unfailingly] maintain love and patience, as he says elsewhere: 'Counting the other greater' (Phil. 2: 3). For if we considered ourselves less than everyone else, we would neither insult anyone gratuitously, nor be deeply hurt if someone insulted us. 11 *Not slow in concern*. Do not become slow and lazy in God's work through concern for the world. *Glowing with the Spirit*. Because the Lord does not love those who are cold and is nauseated by those who are lukewarm (cf. Rev. 3: 15–16).[13] If we are cold to the world, we then manifestly glow with the Spirit. *Serving the Lord*. Doing all things not for the world, nor for the vices, but for the Lord.[14]   12 *Rejoicing in hope*. [In hope, not in something at hand: for 'hope which is seen is not hope' (Rom. 8: 24). *Patient in trouble*.] Bear all things on account of the joy of the hope to come, as [the blessed James] says: 'Count it all joy,' [and so on] (Jas. 1: 2). *Urgent in prayer*. Urgency in prayer affords us [counsel in good times and] help in bad times.   13 *Sharing in the needs of the saints*. Provide for those who need the services of others for a while because they neglect their own affairs on account of Christ. Some codices read: *Sharing in remembrances of the saints*. This should be understood in such a way that they remember in what manner and with what works the saints won favour with God, and become partners with them by imitating their examples.[15] And then there follows, *Eager in hospitality*, because the saints did this too—Abraham, for example, and Lot, who detained even [guests] that were reluctant to stay (cf. Gen. 18: 1–5, 19: 1–3).[16] On this subject it is said: 'For by this some were unaware, while angels received hospitality' (Heb. 13: 2).   14 [*Bless those who persecute you*,] *bless and do not curse*. Let us not suppose [that we are obliged] to curse as well as bless, for the blessed Peter also says: 'Nor curse for curse, but on the contrary

[12] Cf. Orig.–Ruf. *Rom.* 9. 4 (PG 14: 1218B 10–11); Pel. *2 Cor.* 6: 6 (Souter, *Expositions*, ii. 264. 13–15).

[13] Cf. Ambstr. *Rom.* 12: 11. 1a (CSEL 81. 1: 403. 17–20); Orig.–Ruf. *Rom.* 9. 9 (PG 14: 1219C 6–9).

[14] Cf. Orig.–Ruf. *Rom.* 9. 10 (PG 14: 1219C 11–1220A 1).

[15] Cf. Ambstr. *Rom.* 12: 13. 1–1a (CSEL 81. 1: 407. 4–10); Orig.–Ruf. *Rom.* 9. 12 (PG 14: 1220B 4–14). See also *Rom.* 4: 24 above.

[16] Cf. Ambstr. *Rom.* 12: 13. 2 (CSEL 81. 1: 407. 11–13); Orig.–Ruf. *Rom.* 9. 13 (PG 14: 1220C 7–9). According to Gen. 19: 3, only the guests of Lot were, as Pelagius puts it, 'reluctant to stay'. Origen–Rufinus discusses Lot alone. Similarly, the Balliol and Paris MSS read *detinebat* instead of *detinebant*.

bless' (1 Pet. 3: 9).[17]   15 *Rejoice with those who rejoice, weep with those who weep*. So that 'if one member suffers something, all the members suffer it together' (1 Cor. 12: 26).[18] As Job [also] says: 'Did I not groan and did I not weep, when I saw people in need?' (Job 30: 25). The Lord too was brought to tears by the tears of Mary, to give us an example (cf. John 11: 33–5). For one should not suppose that he wept for Lazarus, whom he would bring back to life (cf. John 11: 4, 14–15, 40), nor because of the unbelief of those who again and again did not believe him when he performed wonders (cf. John 11: 45–53). But we now contrariwise weep with those who rejoice, and rejoice with those who weep. For if someone has been praised, we are made unhappy: if someone has fallen, we leap for joy. When we behave in this way, we show that we do not belong to the body of Christ (cf. Eph. 4: 1–16)[19]—we who do not grieve for a member that has been cut off, but are enemies of our own side and friends of the opposing side; who do not grieve when the strongest men of our battle-line fall, and do not rejoice if we see them fighting bravely, though we ourselves are not [as] mighty in battle. 16 *Having the same opinion, one of another*. So that you regard the other as you regard yourself.[20] *Not being high-minded, but agreeing with the humble*. That person thinks proud thoughts who desires to avenge [his] wrongs by himself, and does not agree to things humble, that is, to humiliation.[21] *Do not be wise in your own eyes*. Do not boast [of] human wisdom, but be fools to the world, so that you may be wise in the Lord.[22] As it is written: 'Blessed is [the man] whom you instruct, Lord, and from your law you teach him' (Ps. 93: 12).   17 *Repaying no one evil for evil*. It is human wisdom if you seek to repay your enemies in turn: for it is foolishness in this world if, having been struck, [you wish to offer the other cheek as well (cf. Matt. 5: 39). But if you have such great patience and humility, you will be found praiseworthy not only in the Lord's eyes, but also in the eyes of all people. *Seeing to what is good not only in the sight of God, but also in the sight of people*. Take care not to act so that you seek to please not God, but people alone.   18 *If it is possible, inasmuch as it depends on you, being at peace with all people*. Inasmuch as it concerns you, be at peace with all, and say with the prophet: 'With those who

---

[17] Cf. Orig.–Ruf. *Rom.* 9. 14 (PG 14: 1221A 12–15).

[18] Cf. Ambstr. *Rom.* 12: 15. 1 (CSEL 81. 1: 407. 20–409. 1).

[19] Cf. *Rom.* 9: 1–2.

[20] Cf. Orig.–Ruf. *Rom.* 9. 16 (PG 14: 1222A 12–14).

[21] Cf. Ambstr. *Rom.* 12: 16. 2 (CSEL 81. 1: 409. 7); Orig.–Ruf. *Rom.* 9. 17 (PG 14: 1222B 3–4).

[22] Cf. Orig.–Ruf. *Rom.* 9. 18 (PG 14: 1222B 13–C 1).

hated peace, I was peaceable' (Ps. 119: 6–7), desiring, that is, their conversion and salvation.[23] Or: It is in your power for it to be possible. 19 *Not defending yourselves, beloved, but giving place to wrath.* By fleeing, or by letting yourself be injured. *For it is written: '"Vengeance is mine: I will repay." says the Lord.'* I will avenge the wrong, says the Lord, as my own, not as yours; for the prophet says: 'Whoever touches you is as one who touches the pupil of his eye' (Zech. 2: 8 (12)).[24] 20 *'But if your enemy is hungry, feed him; if he is thirsty, give him drink'.* Do not deny him what God denies no one, though he be a godless blasphemer (cf. Matt. 5: 45/ Luke 6: 35).[25] *'For in doing this, you will heap coals of fire upon his head.'* So that when he has realized that the coals have been amassed upon him through your undeserved mercy, he may shake them off, that is, repent, and may love you, whom at one time he had detested.[26] Otherwise, it is not mercy, but cruelty, if you show mercy so that something worse may befall him, for whom you are bidden to intercede to the Lord (cf. Matt. 5: 44). 21 *Do not be overcome by evil, but overcome evil with good.* That person is said to have overcome who brings another over to his side, such as the heretic or the pagan. If, then, he makes you repay him in turn, he has conquered you by making you like himself: but if by your patience you make him abandon wrongdoing, you have conquered.

13: 1 *Let every person be subject to the higher authorities.* This is an argument against those who thought that they were obliged to use their Christian freedom in such a way that they rendered honour or paid taxes to no one.[1] Paul wishes, therefore, to humble them in whatever way possible, lest perchance they suffer reproach on account of pride rather than on account of God. Thus, he teaches them to redeem the time with humility (cf. Eph. 5: 16; Col. 4: 5). Alternatively: 'Higher authorities' can mean ecclesiastical authorities.[2] *For there is no authority except from God.* And in what sense does God say through the prophet about some authorities: 'They have reigned, and not by me'

---

[23] Cf. Ambstr. *Rom.* 12: 18. 1–2 (CSEL 81. 1: 413. 1–25); Orig.–Ruf. *Rom.* 9. 21 (PG 14: 1223B 2–10).

[24] Cf. *Rom.* 9: 1–2 at n. 2, 15: 3.

[25] Cf. Orig.–Ruf. *Rom.* 9. 23 (PG 14: 1224B 14–15).

[26] Cf. Ambstr. *Rom.* 12: 20. 1, 12: 21. 1 (CSEL 81. 1: 415. 27–417. 3, 417. 14–17); Anon. *Rom.* 0125 (Frede ii. 81); Orig.–Ruf. *Rom.* 9. 25 (PG 14: 1225A 2–10).

[1] Cf. Aug. *Exp. prop.* 64 (72). 1, 4 (CSEL 84: 44. 14–19), and see Affeldt, *Die weltliche Gewalt in der Paulus-Exegese*, 86–91.

[2] Cf. Cypr. *Ep.* 59. 5, 67. 4 (CSEL 3. 2: 672. 22–3, 739. 5–6); Aug. *Parm.* 1. 10. 16 (CSEL 51: 37. 21–6); and see Schelkle, *Wort und Schrift*, 233; Affeldt, *Die weltliche Gewalt in der Paulus-Exegese*, 96–7.

(Hos. 8: 4)? *And those which exist have been instituted by God.* If it seems he speaks of secular authorities: they will not all be just, even if they received their beginning from God.[3] In fact, the authorities are given over each one to their own desire, for Solomon says: 'because authority is given to you by God. But although you were servants of his kingdom, you did not judge rightly. Soon he will appear before you in dreadful array', and so on (Wisd. 6: 3–5). For the ruler is established by God to judge with righteousness, and so that sinners may have reason to be afraid, should they sin. 2 *Therefore, one who resists the authority resists the institution of God, and those who resist bring condemnation upon themselves.* As it is said to Rahab: 'Whoever goes outside will be responsible for himself' (Josh. 2: 19). 3 *For rulers are not a terror to good work, but to evil.* The wicked should be afraid of the authority, whereas the good have no reason to fear, for if they are unjustly killed they come into glory.[4] *Do you wish to have no fear of authority?* Take my advice and you will never be afraid. *Do what is good, and you will be commended by it.* Condemnation of the wicked is itself commendation of the good (cf. 1 Pet. 2: 14).[5] 4 *For it is a servant of God for your good.* Because it is concerned about your security. *But if you do wrong, be afraid: for not without reason does it bear the sword.* It also has the responsibility towards you that, if you sin, it does not accrue to your profit. Or: Priests bear a spiritual sword, as when Peter struck down Ananias and Paul, the sorcerer (cf. Acts. 5: 1–6, 13: 4–12).[6] *For it is God's servant, an avenger to execute wrath upon one who does wrong.* Because God does not love the wicked, and 'hates all who work iniquity' (cf. Ps. 5: 6). 5 *Therefore, you must be subject, not only because of wrath, but also because of conscience.* Not only because the authorities can become angry even without cause, but also so that you may not be condemned for the consciousness of some sin.[7] Or: Not only so that the priests may not become angry, but also because you know that even the righteous owe them respect.[8] 6 *For this reason you also pay taxes: for they are God's servants, serving in this very thing.* 'Taxes' can also mean taxes for the priests, which were

---

[3] Cf. Ambr. *Luc.* 4. 29 (CCSL 14: 116. 335–9); Ambrst. *Quaest.* 35 (CSEL 50: 63. 13–19); Orig.–Ruf. *Rom.* 9. 26 (PG 14: 1226c 11–1227a 7); and see Affeldt, *Die weltliche Gewalt in der Paulus-Exegese*, 105–9.

[4] Cf. Cypr. *Ep.* 66. 2 (CSEL 3. 2: 727. 20–1); Aug. *Exp. prop.* 65 (73). 3 (CSEL 84: 46. 4–7).

[5] Cf. Orig.–Ruf. *Rom.* 9. 28 (PG 14: 1228b 10–15).

[6] Cf. Cypr. *Ep.* 4. 4 (CSEL 3. 2: 476. 18–477. 3).

[7] Cf. Ambrst. *Rom.* 13: 5 (CSEL 81. 1: 421. 10–14).

[8] The remark alludes to the censorious view some ascetics took of the clergy; see Stancliffe, *St. Martin*, 265–73; Wiesen, *St. Jerome as a Satirist*, 65–90.

established for them by God (cf. Exod. 30: 11–16; Lev. 7; Num. 31: 25–54).[9] Or: You pay taxes to those who rule because in possessing the world you were willing to be subject to them.[10] He calls them God's servants, so that people might at least render to them what they owe (cf. Matt. 22: 21), lest it seem that Christ taught pride.[11]   7 *Therefore, pay them all their dues.* Even alms can be called a due, as the Scriptures say: 'Incline your ear to the poor and pay your due' (Ecclus. 4: 8). *Taxes to whom taxes are due, revenue to whom revenue is due.* Revenue is ours to give to those who are passing by, or to give to those who are seated by the road while we pass by, and thus to bestow upon those who are alive.[12] *Fear to whom fear is due.* Why, then, is it written elsewhere: 'No one is to be feared besides the Lord' (Prov. 7: 2)? He is saying, however: 'Behave in such a way that you are afraid of no one.' For the fear of God casts out human fear (cf. 1 John 4: 18). But because you still have reason to be afraid, it is inevitable that you are afraid. *Honour to whom honour is due.* Fear, in addition to honour, for those who are your superiors, but honour alone for those who are your equals. 8 *Owe no one anything.* Do not fail to repay a debt to anyone (cf. Ecclus. 4: 8). *Except to love one another.* This debt alone should always remain, because it can never be paid in full. *For one who loves his neighbour.* According to the parable of the Lord, who bids us show mercy to all without distinction, we must consider every person our neighbour (cf. Luke 10: 29–37). *Has fulfilled the law.* He mentioned love first because he was writing to the faithful and dealing with behaviour proper to righteousness.   9 *For 'You shall not commit adultery', 'You shall not kill', 'You shall not steal', 'You shall not covet', and every other commandment is restated in these words: 'You shall love your neighbour as yourself.'* The whole of righteousness is summed up in the love of one's neighbour, and unrighteousness is born when we love ourselves more than others. For one who loves his neighbour as himself not only does him no wrong, but also does him good, because he also wishes both to be performed with regard to himself.   10 *Love of one's neighbour does no wrong.* Even not to do good is wrong. For if one sees that one's neighbour is in danger of starvation, does one not kill him if, while one has an

[9] Cf. Pel. *Gal.* 2: 24 (Souter, *Expositions*, ii. 329. 16–18).

[10] Cf. Orig.–Ruf. *Rom.* 9. 30 (PG 14: 1230A 3–6, B 4–C 9).

[11] Cf. ibid. (PG 14: 1230B 4–C 9), and see Grant, *Early Christianity and Society*, 11–36.

[12] Taxation in the Roman empire took two general forms: direct (*tributum*; here 'taxes') and indirect (*uectigal*; here 'revenue'). The latter included death duties. Pelagius could be alluding to a legitimate way for wealthy Romans to avoid such duties, namely, by giving their wealth away before they died. See Brown, 'Late Antiquity', 277–82.

abundance, one does not give him food, though one has not used up one's own provisions (cf. Jas. 2: 15–16)? For anyone who is able to help someone close to death in whatever situation of need kills that person if he does not come to his aid. *Therefore love is the fullness of the law.* That is, the fulfilment.[13]   11 *And knowing this is the time, that now it is the hour for us.* It is the hour for you to strive for that which is more perfect and complete: for you should not always be children and infants, as he likewise says in another place: 'For you ought to have been teachers by this time', and so on (Heb. 5: 12). *To rise up from sleep.* Let us together arise from the sleep of idleness and ignorance, for now the knowledge of Christ shines forth. *Now our salvation is nearer to us than when we believed.* With the increase of knowledge our salvation is nearer than when we believed.   12 *The night has gone; the day will draw near.* He likens knowledge to the day and ignorance to the night, in accordance with what Hosea says: 'I have likened your mother to the night; my people have become as those who have no knowledge' (Hos. 4: 5–6).[14] *Let us therefore cast off the works of darkness and put on the armour of light.* Together with ignorance let us cast off] also the works of ignorance, and let us put on the armour of light, that is, works of light. For 'one who acts wickedly hates the light; but one who does the truth comes to the light' (John 3: 20–1).   13 *Let us conduct ourselves becomingly as in the day.* Just as the light of day keeps everyone from doing what he freely committed at night, so too knowledge keeps us from spurning the commandments of the law.[15] Or: Because we know that we are always watched by God. *Not in revelling and drunkenness, not in sexual indulgence and impurity.* A revel is a luxurious banquet: but we have a spiritual feast, as [the apostle] says: 'When you gather together, each one [of you] has a psalm', and so on (1 Cor. 14: 26). Moreover, that drunkenness is ruinous and an occasion for debauchery is further proved by the fact that he has appended 'impurity'. He also says elsewhere: 'Do not become drunk with wine, for therein lies debauchery' (Eph. 5: 18).[16] *Not in quarrelling and jealousy.* That quarrelling and jealousy too are objects of reproach is demonstrated [both] here and by [many] other examples, as James says: 'For if you have a bitter spirit of

[13] Cf. Ambstr. *Rom.* 13: 10. 1 (CSEL 81. 1: 425. 16).

[14] Cf. ibid. 13: 11. 1, 13: 12. 1 (CSEL 81. 1: 427. 10–17, 429. 5–11); Orig.–Ruf. *Rom.* 9. 32 (PG 14: 1233B 13–C 3); see also Schelkle, *Wort und Schrift*, 239–50.

[15] Cf. Ambstr. *Rom.* 13: 13. 1 (CSEL 81. 1: 431. 3–5); contrast Aug. *Conf.* 8. 5. 12 (CCSL 27: 120. 33–121. 54).

[16] Cf. Ambstr. *Rom.* 13: 13. 4 (CSEL 81. 1: 431. 15–18); Orig.–Ruf. *Rom.* 9. 33 (PG 14: 1233C 11–14).

jealousy', and so on (Jas. 3: 14).   14 *But put on the Lord Jesus Christ.*
Christ alone should be seen in us, not the old self (cf. Rom. 6: 6):[17] for
'one who says he abides in Christ should himself walk as he walked'
(1 John 2: 6), in whom are all of the virtues [and none of the vices].[18]
And make no provision for the flesh, for its desires. As Solomon also says: 'Do
not follow after your desires' (Ecclus. 18: 30); and again: 'If you grant
the desire of your heart, it will [also] make you an occasion for
rejoicing among your enemies' (Ecclus. 18: 31).

14: 1 *Accept the weak in faith.* From here on he begins indirectly to
upbraid those who considered themselves strong and therefore ate
meat without restraint.[1] *Not for disputes about opinions.* Do not judge
according to your opinions one whom the law does not judge.
2 *Someone believes he may eat everything.* Who has such faith that he is
not disturbed, or who is worn out by abstinence or is older.[2] *But let him
who is weak.* Weak on account of [youthful] age or the heat of the body.[3]
Eat vegetables. This proves that he is speaking not of the Jews, as some
suppose,[4] but of those who abstain: for they did not eat even meats that
are clean according to the law, but ate vegetables alone.[5] [Alternat-
ively: If you become faint of heart because you happen to know
another person who has resolved to eat vegetables alone and you
shudder to eat meat on account of his faith, do not be the judge of the
other's decision or demand of him what has been left to each person's
discretion. But if, on the other hand, you take offence and do not wish
to eat meat, set a limit for yourself and, doing the better thing, eat only
vegetables, so that everyone may be incited to abstinence by your
agreeableness rather than annoyed in this matter [and] offended by
you [and] strengthened instead in the resolve to eat meat. For you
cannot censure another as [reprehensible], if someone ventures it in

---

[17] Cf. Ambstr. *Rom.* 13: 14. 2 (CSEL 81. 1: 433. 8–10).

[18] Cf. Orig.–Ruf. *Rom.* 9. 34 (PG 14: 1234B 1–6).

[1] In his comments on Rom. 14: 1–12 Pelagius allows that fasting is not obligatory
and may in some circumstances be detrimental. But his preference, indicated in the
comment here and further in the comments on Rom. 14: 13–23, is for restraint in the use
of food and wine. See esp. *Rom.* 14: 15–17, 19; cf. also *Rom.* 16: 18.

[2] Cf. Cassian, *Coll.* 2. 22 (CSEL 13: 61. 22–5); Caes. Arel. *Reg. mon.* 24 (PL 67: 1103A
7–8); Bened. *Reg.* 36. 9, 37. 2, 39. 11 (CSEL 75: 96, 97, 100); and see Arbesmann, 'Fasten',
478–9.

[3] On the notion that food fuelled lust cf. Jer. *Iouin.* 2. 10, 11 (PL 23: 299C 6–11, 301B
14–C 1), and *Ep.* 54. 9 (CSEL 54: 474. 17–476. 9); Cassian, *Coll.* 2. 22–3, 5. 11. 5 (CSEL 13:
62. 3–16, 131. 9–10), and *Inst.* 5. 11. 1 (SC 109: 206. 8–9).

[4] Cf. Ambstr. *Rom.* 14: 1 (CSEL 81. 1: 433. 12–24); Jer. *Iouin.* 2. 16 (PL 23: 310C 2–6,
but cf. 310B 1–9); Orig.–Ruf. *Rom.* 9. 35 (PG 14: 1234C 9–1235A 4).

[5] Cf. Orig.–Ruf. *Rom.* 9. 36 (PG 14: 1235B 4–7).

faith or perhaps does it because it is necessary for health or required in old age.]⁶ 3 *He who eats should not despise him who does not eat, and he who does not eat should not pass judgement on him who eats.* They took offence at one another. Those who did not eat judged those who ate to be carnal, and those who ate ridiculed those who did not eat as fools and considered them superstitious. *For God has accepted him.* [God] called him just as he called you. 4 *Who are you to judge someone else's servant?* What authority do you have to judge him whom the law does not judge?⁷ This is why James says: 'One who judges a brother judges the law' (Jas. 4: 11); in other words, judges himself to be wiser than the law. Nevertheless, Paul himself judged those who broke a commandment, and ascribed to others the power to judge (cf. 1 Cor. 5: 3–5, 6: 2–3).⁸ *By his own master he stands or falls.* He either lives or dies; for the one abstains for God's sake, and the other in following God does not abstain. *But he will stand: for God is able to make him stand.* God, who made three young men who had been fed on beans look better than those who had eaten from the table of the king, can also enable them to remain in the body for a long while yet (cf. Dan. 1: 8–16). 5 *For one distinguishes one day from another, another distinguishes every day. Let each one abound in his own understanding.* With regard to food, the Jews could not judge between one day and the next. Therefore he is speaking about fasting and abstinence, which are not treated under a fixed limitation of the law.⁹ Each one should do as much as he can, [and] as much as he desires to share in the reward. Thus it follows that in such a matter each one should do simply what he has judged to be better. 6 *One who observes a day observes it for the Lord.* One who fasts on account of God, [and] not on account of people, observes the day for the Lord (cf. Matt. 6: 18). *And one who eats, eats for the Lord: he gives thanks to God.* Because he eats for God's sake, so that he may have the strength to preach the Gospel, for which those who have been converted should return thanks to God; he is devoted not to his own belly, but to the salvation of others (cf. 1 Cor. 10: 31–2). *And one who does not eat, does not*

---

⁶ This comment, omitted by the Karlsruhe and Paris MSS, is a pseudo-Hieronymian interpolation; see the Introduction at n. 213 and ps.-Hi. *Rom.* 1300*II* (Frede ii. 85).

⁷ See *Rom.* 14: 1, and cf. Ambstr. *Rom.* 14: 10 (CSEL 81. 1: 439. 22–3).

⁸ See *Rom.* 14: 12, and cf. Aug. *Exp. prop.* 71 (79). 1–3 (CSEL 84: 49. 3–19).

⁹ It seems that Pelagius believed that the Jews did not observe fast-days or abstain from meat and wine because he did not find these practices stipulated in the law of Moses. In fact there was a tradition of fasting and abstinence among the Jews, which was regularized in the post-exilic period. But in the regulations for the Day of Atonement, the only fast-day ordained in the Pentateuch, there is no explicit mention of fasting and abstinence (cf. Lev. 16: 29–34, 23: 26–32; Num. 29: 7–11).

eat for the Lord, and gives thanks to God. Because by the example of this person [as well] many are saved and return thanks to God. For one who gives thanks with the voice gives thanks alone: but one who gives thanks in deed as well gives thanks with many.   7 *For none of us lives for himself, and none dies for himself.* 8 *For if we live, we live for the Lord: or if we die, we die for the Lord. Therefore, whether we live or die, we are the Lord's.* None of the faithful lives for himself and none dies for himself because Christ 'has died for all, so that those who live no longer live for themselves, but for him' (2 Cor. 5: 15). Take care[, then], that we, on the contrary, do not live for ourselves in eating, or die on account of people in fasting.   9 *For to this end Christ both died and rose from the dead, so that he might be Lord of both the dead and the living.* The coming of Christ will find people alive and will bring those who are dead back to life. It is of no importance whether he brings you back to life or finds you [alive], as long as you appear righteous before him.[10]   10 *But why do you judge your brother?* By what authority do you condemn him as a voracious glutton? *Or for what reason do you despise your brother?* For what reason do you look down on him [as though] he were weak or his fast were needless (cf. Rom. 14: 3)? *For we shall all stand before the judgement-seat of God.* Then the Lord will judge our consciences to see with what sort of desire and intention we did what we did.   11 *For it is written: '"As I live," says the Lord, "every knee shall bow before me, and every tongue shall confess to God."'* This testimony shows that all of us must give an account of our actions to the Lord alone.   12 *So let each one of us give an account of himself to God.* Concerning those things about which the law is silent. But on the other hand, if one does not reprimand someone when one sees him sin, one will also give an account to the Lord for him as well.[11]   13 *Therefore, let us no longer judge one another.* What you have done up to now is enough. *But decide instead not to put a stumbling-block or an obstacle in your brother's way.* From here on he subtly begins [to] recommend abstinence, and he says that, although those who eat are strong, they ought to abstain lest the weak are subjected to a stumbling-block by their example.[12]   14 *I know and am convinced in the Lord Jesus that nothing is common in itself.* I do not hereby assert that I consider anything to be [common: for I know that all things have been made clean by Christ] (cf. Acts 10: 28).[13] For whatever is called

[10] Cf. Pel. *1 Cor.* 15: 51 (Souter, *Expositions*, ii. 225. 4–7).
[11] Cf. *Rom.* 14: 4.
[12] Cf. ibid. 14: 1.
[13] Cf. Ambstr. *Rom.* 14: 14. 1 (CSEL 81. 1: 441. 19–22).

common is regarded as unclean among the food of the Jews.[14] *Except for someone who considers something to be common, to him it is common.* To him it becomes common because of conscience, for in such matters, after coming to faith in Christ, he still deems something unclean according to Jewish custom.[15] 15 *For if your brother is distressed because of food.* He did not say 'because of fasting', but that you should not by your example incite or constrain one [who is weak or abstemious]. *You are no longer walking in love.* Because against his will he eats something that is not good for him, and you no longer love your neighbour as yourself if you do not think of his good as you do your own (cf. Rom. 13: 8–10). *Do not by your food ruin him for whom Christ died.* He did not say 'By [your] abstinence', as some wish.[16] 16 *So, do not let our good be spoken of as evil.* [Our] freedom, which we have in the Lord, so that all things are clean to us.[17] We should not use it in such a way that we appear to live for the belly and for feasts. Or: It is spoken of as evil, if we argue about such things. 17 *For the kingdom of God is not food and drink.* We are not justified by food.[18] However, one should also note that he did not say, 'Fasting and temperance are not the kingdom of God', but 'food and drink'. *But righteousness and peace and joy in the Holy Spirit.* Which are more easily maintained through abstinence: for where there is righteousness, by loving one's neighbour as oneself (cf. Rom. 13: 10), there is also peace; and where there is peace, there is also spiritual joy, because distress and trouble always arise out of discord. 18 *For one who serves Christ in this pleases God and is approved by people.* Concerning such a person, no one can doubt that he is holy. 19 *So, let us pursue what makes for peace.* So that [we] do not judge one another in matters of this sort. *And preserve what makes for mutual edification.* Abstinence is edification: food, on the other hand, even if it does not ruin anyone, edifies no one. 20 *Do not destroy the work of God for the sake of food.* Namely, a human being, created by God.[19] *For all things are indeed clean.* He repeats what he had said above (cf. Rom. 14: 14), lest he seem to

---

[14] Cf. Orig.–Ruf. *Rom.* 9. 42 (PG 14: 1245B 11–14).

[15] Cf. *Rom.* 14: 2. Pelagius appears to distinguish between those who abstain from meat altogether, which is not necessarily a Jewish practice, and those who abstain from meats deemed unclean, which was an aspect of Jewish discipline.

[16] i.e. Jovinian or those sympathetic to his views; cf. Pel. *Phil.* 3: 18 (Souter, *Expositions*, ii. 409. 10–12). See also Jer. *Iouin.* 1. 3 (PL 23: 214B 6–8), and the Introduction at n. 76 and ff.

[17] Cf. Ambstr. *Rom.* 14: 14. 1 (CSEL 81. 1: 441. 19–22); Orig.–Ruf. *Rom.* 9. 42 (PG 14: 1247A 14–B 3).

[18] Cf. Ambstr. *Rom.* 14: 15. 1 (CSEL 81. 1: 443. 13–14).

[19] Cf. ibid. 14: 20. 1 (CSEL 81. 1: 447. 23–5).

condemn creation.[20] *But it is wrong for the person who eats while giving offence.* What is clean becomes wrong for him if another takes offence on account of him. 21 *It is good not to eat meat and not to drink wine.* He explains on what account he said the weak took offence. *Nor anything at which your brother takes offence or is made to stumble.* Nor any food or drink at which another takes offence. *Or is weakened.* Is weakened from virtue, for 'wine and women lead [even] the wise astray' (Ecclus. 19: 2). 22 *Do you have faith? Keep it to yourself before God.* If you consider yourself faithful in this matter, eat in such a way that no one is weakened by your example. *Blessed is the one who does not judge himself on account of what he approves.* Who in demonstrating his own strength does not think of himself, but of the salvation of the other, who is weak. 23 *But one who discriminates is condemned if he eats.* [If anyone discriminates concerning someone else and says: 'That person, if he eats, is clearly damned', he does not have faith, and therefore the following ensues:] *Because it is not of faith.* [For it is not of faith if you condemn another because he eats while you fast. Alternatively:][21] Who thereby judges himself: [for] discrimination and judgement are the same thing, [because judgement] comes about by discriminating and discrimination by judging. *And all that is not of faith is sin.* Not of faith, which works through love. Whatever, then, destroys another is not of faith and is therefore sin.

15: 1 *We who are stronger should bear with the failings of the weak.* If you really are strong, do as I did, I who 'became weak [to the weak], in order to gain the weak' (1 Cor. 9: 22).[1] *And not please ourselves.* 2 *Let each one of you please his neighbour.* Let us be commended not by ourselves, but by our neighbours (cf. Prov. 27: 2), just as also elsewhere he sets his example before us, when he says: 'As I [too] please everyone in everything, not seeking what is to my advantage, but what is to the advantage of many, so that they may be saved' (1 Cor. 10: 33).[2] For no one can build up another if he has [not] pleased that person beforehand by his good life. But those who do their own will because they are seeking their own advantage are in fact self-pleasers. *To build him up in a good way.* He indicates the way and the reason to please, so that we do

---

[20] Cf. Tert. *Ieiun.* 15. 1 (CCSL 2: 1273. 12–17); Aug. *De mor.* 2. 14. 31–15. 37 (PL 32: 1358–61).

[21] The first two comments on v. 23, omitted by the Karlsruhe and Paris MSS, are pseudo-Hieronymian interpolations; see the Introduction at n. 213 and ps.-Hi. *Rom.* 134*11* (Frede ii. 87).

[1] Cf. Orig.–Ruf. *Rom.* 10. 6 (PG 14: 1257B 1–3).

[2] Cf. ibid. (PG 14: 1258C 11–1259A 7).

not please for worthless glory. When he says 'to build up in a good way', he at the same time indicates that there is also a bad way, as, for example: 'Will he not be encouraged to eat [what has been sacrificed to idols]?' (1 Cor. 8: 10).³ **3** *For even Christ did not please himself.* An imitator and disciple of Christ does not seek his own advantage.⁴ In fact, Christ even died for the salvation of others, and bore the most bitter [insults] from those who said: 'Hah, he who destroys the temple', and so on (Mark 15: 29).⁵ *But as it is written: 'The insults of those who insult you have fallen upon me.'* Whatever insults are cast upon not only Christ but also the saints for God's sake are said to be cast upon God, as, for example: 'Where is your God?'⁶ **4** *For whatever was written, was written for our instruction.* Nothing, therefore, is written without reason; for the merits and temptations of the righteous contribute to our edification, because they so very clearly lived for God. *So that through patience and the encouragement of the Scriptures we may have hope.* Through the encouragement of the Scriptures, we await with great patience the hope to come. As it is written: 'Those who love your law have great peace, and nothing can cause them to stumble' (Ps. 118: 165). That is, those who enjoy the encouragement of the law cannot be moved by any temptation. [Thus,] so that by the examples of patience [and] encouragement, which have been written down, we may hope for encouragement both in present temptations and, as Lazarus, [in the time to come] (cf. Luke 16: 25). For it is great cause for encouragement if we know that our Lord and his saints have previously borne the things which we suffer. **5** *And may the God of patience and encouragement.* [In this passage he indicates that 'the God of patience' is the Holy Spirit, who grants that with one mind in accordance with Christ we glorify the God and Father of our Lord Jesus Christ.]⁷ His patience, which is meant to lead to repentance (cf. 2 Pet. 3: 9): encouragement, for those who have already repented.⁸ Or: Of patience and encouragement, not of wrath and discord, so as to refer to those [who practice such virtues].⁹ *Grant that you be of one mind with one another in accordance with Jesus Christ.* So that each one seeks the

---

³ The link between Rom. 15: 2 and 1 Cor. 8: 10 is the verb *aedificare*, which is here rendered 'to build up' or 'to encourage'.

⁴ Cf. Orig.–Ruf. *Rom.* 10. 6 (PG 14: 1257C 8–1258A 9, 1259C 8–1260A 13).

⁵ Cf. *Rom.* 15: 5, 15: 7.

⁶ Cf. Orig.–Ruf. *Rom.* 10. 6 (PG 14: 1260A 13–B 4).

⁷ This comment, omitted by the Karlsruhe and Paris MSS, is an interpolation; see the Introduction at n. 212 and Anon. *Rom.* 134A (Frede ii. 88).

⁸ Cf. *Rom.* 2: 3–4.

⁹ Cf. Orig.–Ruf. *Rom.* 10. 7 (PG 14: 1261B 9–15).

salvation of the other as his own, in the same way that Christ saved everyone from death by his own death.[10]   6 *So that with one mind and one voice you may glorify the God and Father of our Lord Jesus Christ*. God is truly glorified [by us when] he is praised [with one] mind and one voice. For 'if two agree on earth about anything, whatever they ask shall be done for them' (Matt. 18: 19).[11]   7 *For this reason bear one another up*. For the sake of God's honour, 'bear one another's burdens and [thereby] you will fulfil the law of Christ' (Gal. 6: 2). He took us upon himself while we were ungodly (cf. Rom. 5: 6); how much more[, then,] should we, who are like one another, support each other![12] *As also Christ bore you up to the honour of God*. Either into divine glory, or for the sake of God's honour.   8 *For I declare that Jesus Christ was a servant of the circumcision because of the truth of God*. [Here he shows that with regard to the flesh Christ was born from the circumcision according to the promise to the forefathers and fulfilled the precepts of the law.][13] Once again he urges each of the two peoples to unity. 'I agree with you, O Jews,' he says, 'that Christ, who was promised to you, came to you first, and that the Gentiles were called because of God's mercy; nevertheless, you have been made into one body.' [The word 'servant' is used] 'because he had come not to be served, but to serve, and to give his life as a ransom for many' (Matt. 20: 28). *To confirm the promises made to the forefathers*. Because Christ had been promised to them, as he himself [also] says: '[For] I have come only to the lost sheep of the house of Israel' (Matt. 15: 24).[14]   9 *And that the Gentiles glorify God for his mercy*. For 'one who is forgiven more loves more' (Luke 7: 47). *As it is written: 'Therefore I will acknowledge you among the Gentiles and sing to your name.'* He deprives the Jews of presumption when he teaches that it was foretold [about] the salvation of the Gentiles, although it was not announced to them. Christ [therefore] acknowledges those who have received mercy among the Gentiles, because they too belong to his body.   10 *And again he says: 'Rejoice, O Gentiles, with his people.'* [Who have been brought to salvation with them.][15]   11 *And again he says:*

---

[10] Cf. *Rom*. 15: 3, 15: 7.   [11] Cf. Orig.–Ruf. *Rom*. 10. 7 (PG 14: 1261C 9–1262A 2).
[12] Cf. *Rom*. 15: 3, 15: 5.
[13] This comment, omitted by the Karlsruhe MS and designated *aliter* in the Paris MS, is an interpolation; see the Introduction at n. 212 and Anon. *Rom*. 0135 (Frede ii. 89).
[14] Cf. Aug. *Exp. prop*. 74 (82). 3 (CSEL 84: 51: 11–14).
[15] The wording and placement of this comment vary in the MSS. One version follows v. 10, where Souter follows the wording of the Balliol MS. However, the wording of the other MSS—'Because with them you have been brought to salvation' (*quia cum ipsis* instead of *qui cum ipsis*)—is probably the better reading, on account of its affinity to the other version of the comment, attested by the Karlsruhe MS and placed after v. 11.

'Praise the Lord, all you nations, and magnify him, all you peoples.' [Because with the Jews you have been brought to salvation.] 12 *And again Isaiah says: 'There will be a root of Jesse'.* Jesse was the father of David, of whose seed, that is Mary, Christ was born (cf. Rom. 1: 3).[16] *'And he who will rise up to rule the Gentiles, in him the Gentiles will hope.'* So that they might not allege [that this was said] about proselytes; in fact, it is like the following passage: 'A ruler will not be wanting from Judah, nor a leader from his loins', [and so on] (Gen. 49: 10). It is thus proved to the Jews that Christ has indeed already come, since it is plain that all the Gentiles hope in him.[17] 13 *Now may the God of hope.* In whom we [all] hope. *Fill you with all joy and peace in believing.* All the joy of the faithful should be in the hope to come. Where there is peace, all is joy. There is no joy, however, in discord, but widespread sorrow. *So that you abound in hope in the power of the Holy Spirit.* Abundance of hope rests in the wonders and signs [of the Spirit].[18] 14 *Now I, my brothers, I too am confident of you.* A good teacher, he rouses them to further advancement by praising them, so that they might blush for not being the sort of people they were believed to be by the apostle.[19] *That you are full of love.* He takes care that it should not seem as if he has sternly rebuked the quarrelsome, the dissident, or the foolish. *Filled with all knowledge.* That is, of the New and Old Testaments. *So that you are able to admonish one another.* [And at the same time] he shows that Christians should always admonish one another. 15 *I have written to you quite boldly, brothers, partly.* Indeed, I had greater confidence to write because I knew that you, being sensible people, readily accept a reasonable argument. As it is written: 'Reprove a wise man, and he will love you' (Prov. 9: 8).[20] *Calling you as it were to mind again.* Recollecting that you are sensible. Or: I do not teach you [as] those who are ignorant, but I remind you as those who are knowledgeable. *On account of the grace that was given me by God.* Not on account of earthly obligations or of praise, but in order to discharge the task I received. 16 *To be a servant for Christ Jesus among the Gentiles.* A servant of the Gospel; that is, calling slaves who were once runaways back to him. *Sanctifying the Gospel of God.* Showing by my example that what I perform with so much fear is holy. For some slight as human what they proclaim as divine, with the result that something holy seems to be unholy, since it is not

---

[16] Cf. Ambstr. *Rom.* 15: 12. 2 (CSEL 81. 1: 463. 18–23).
[17] Cf. Cypr. *Test.* 1. 21 (CCSL 3: 22. 25–7, 23. 42–5).
[18] Cf. *Rom.* 15: 19.
[19] Cf. Ambstr. *Rom.* 15: 13–14 (CSEL 81. 1: 465. 4–7); see also *Rom.* 15: 29 below.
[20] Cf. *Rom.* 3: 9, 6: 19.

performed in a holy way.[21] [For this reason it is said: 'Sanctify the fast' (Joel 1: 14); that is,] make it, or show that it is, [holy]. *So that the offering of the Gentiles may be made acceptable, sanctified in the Holy Spirit.* So that by my example [and my speech] the Gentiles may be made an acceptable sacrifice to God, sanctified and borne up not by fire, but by the Holy Spirit, just as it is written that it 'settled on' the apostles 'and diverse tongues as of fire appeared to them' (Acts 2: 3).   17 *I have glory, therefore, in Christ Jesus towards God.* 'Let him who glories glory in the Lord' (1 Cor. 1: 31). [Alternatively:] I have glory in the sight of God, though I am defamed and bespattered in the public eye.   18 *For I do not venture to say anything about those things which Christ does not accomplish through me for the obedience of the Gentiles.* I have not ventured to claim that [at least] as far as these things are concerned I have done anything in my own strength, and that God did not work all these things through me. *In word and deed,* 19 *in the power of signs and wonders, in the power of the Holy Spirit.* That is: By teaching and signs; he was not talking about works [here], but about miracles.[22] *So that from Jerusalem round about to Illyricum I have disseminated the Gospel of Christ.* The Gospel is fully disseminated when the Gentiles also believe.   20 *And thus I preached this Gospel, not where Christ was named, lest I build on another's foundation.* One who builds on another's foundation does not do wrong so long as he builds with gold and so on (cf. 1 Cor. 3: 12). Here he refers to the false apostles who always went to those who had already come to believe, and never to the Gentiles,[23] because they could not work miracles (cf. Gal. 3: 5).[24] He also shows that he had done a complete job, for he both laid the foundation and also built the building on top of it (cf. 1 Cor. 3: 12).   21 *But as it is written.* He shows that his work was foretold [beforehand]. *'Those who were not told about him shall see, and those who have not heard shall understand.'* Christ is manifest in the apostles through the miracles which they performed in his name (cf. Acts 4: 7–10).   22 *This is why I was often hindered from coming to you.* He has explained what he had said at the outset: 'And I have been prevented until now' (Rom. 1: 13).[25]   23 *But now that I do not have any more opportunity in these parts.* Where all the people are already established, he says that he does not have any reason for laying a

---

[21] Cf. Orig.–Ruf. *Rom.* 10. 11 (PG 14: 1268B 8–C 5).

[22] Cf. *Rom.* 15: 20–1.

[23] Cf. Ambstr. *Rom.* 15: 20. 1–2 (CSEL 81. 1: 467. 22–469. 10).

[24] For a recent reconsideration of the role of miracle (whether witnessed or credited) in conversion see MacMullen, *Christianizing the Roman Empire*, 108–9, 165 n. 8.

[25] Cf. Ambstr. *Rom.* 15: 22–24. 1 (CSEL 81. 1: 469. 22–471. 5).

foundation (cf. 1 Cor. 3: 10).[26] *And have a desire to come to you.* Observe that there is in fact a desire that is good, as: 'I long to be set free and to be with Christ' (Phil. 1: 23), and: 'My soul has longed to desire your just ordinances' (Ps. 118: 20). *After the many years that have now passed.* He indicates what necessity it was that detained him for many years. 24 *When I begin to make my way to Spain.* It is not certain whether he ever was in Spain. *I hope to see you in passing, and to be brought on my way there by you, as soon as I have enjoyed your company for a while.* Because you conduct yourselves in such a way that there is neither cause nor need for me to stay with you longer. The reason he says he will enjoy their company 'for a while' is that they did not need to come to faith, but only to be strengthened in faith. Or: The reason he says 'for a while' is that no amount of time satisfies love.[27] 25 *Now, then, I shall go to Jerusalem.* [This task remains for me. *To serve the saints.* In Jerusalem there were saints] who, having sold all their possessions and laid them at the feet of the apostles (cf. Acts 4: 34–5), devoted themselves to prayer, reading, and teaching (cf. 1 Tim. 4: 13). It is apparent from this passage that they were of such character that the apostle himself journeys to attend them in person and desires that his offering be received by them—that is, that they deign to receive it—therefore showing that giving benefits those who give more than it benefits those who receive (cf. Acts 20: 35). He does this to contradict those who attack the glory of perfection.[28] 26 *For Macedonia and Achaea thought it right to collect something.* They thought that it would be good for them, if they made some collection for expenses [among] the saints (cf. 2 Cor. 9: 1–15). *For the poor among the saints who are in Jerusalem.*[29] Because they wished to be poor for the edification of the saints. Or: One is to understand simply saints who are poor. 27 *For it seemed good to them: for they are indebted to them.* By their example he incites the Romans to a similar effort, indicating

---

[26] Cf. Orig.-Ruf. *Rom.* 10. 13 (PG 14: 1271A 6–B 6).

[27] Cf. ibid. (PG 14: 1271C 6–B 8).

[28] Among Pelagians Christian perfection was often identified with redistribution of wealth; see Brown, 'Pelagius and his Supporters', 101–2. For one description of the animosity which aristocratic Christians aroused in Roman society when they renounced their wealth see Jer. *Ep.* 45. 4 (CSEL 54: 325. 21–326. 13); cf. also Markus, *The End of Ancient Christianity*, 35–8. On the debate about perfectionism, particularly about the meaning of sinlessness, which later engaged Pelagius and Jerome, see Evans, *Pelagius*, 22–3, 54–6.

[29] The phrase *in pauperes sanctorum* can be rendered either 'among the poor for the saints' or 'for the poor among the saints'. Pelagius comments on both alternatives, but the English of the lemma is capable only of one.

that not without cause did it seem good to them.[30] *For if the Gentiles have been made partakers of their spiritual things, they should also attend to them in material things.* Because they obtained teachers from them and 'were made to share in the root and the fatness of the olive-tree' (Rom. 11: 17), each one should share with the other whatever he has in abundance (cf. 2 Cor. 8: 14).[31] 28 *So when I have accomplished this, and have delivered this fruit to them, I shall go on to Spain by way of you.* 29 *For I know that I when I come to you, I shall come in the fullness of Christ's blessing.* If you conduct yourselves well, good teaching will abound in us for you, for the teacher is incited to teach to the extent that the student shows progress.[32] As he says elsewhere: 'Our mouth is open towards you, O Corinthians' (2 Cor. 6: 11). Or: Christ will be more fully praised when I come among you.   30 *Therefore, I appeal to you, brothers, by our Lord Jesus Christ, and by the love of the Spirit, that you assist me with prayers on my behalf to God.* He asks that the whole church earnestly pray for him, because he knows that the prayers of many people together have great effect.[33] For when James was killed, Peter was freed from prison [by the prayers] of the brothers, who offered prayers not so much for his good as for their own, [namely] that they could be strengthened by his teaching (cf. Acts 12: 2–10). [Truly,] spiritual love makes us pray for one another.   31 *So that I may be delivered from the unbelievers who are in Judaea.* Either: So that they may all believe. Or: That while I am serving the believers I may not fall into the hands of unbelievers so that it would be impossible for me to come to you. *And that the offering of my service may be accepted by the saints in Jerusalem,* 32 *so that by the will of God I may come to you with joy, and be refreshed with you.* I shall come in joy if my offering has been accepted by them, and with peace of mind I shall speak the word of God in great measure. For heaviness of heart greatly hinders teaching.   33 *May the God of peace be with you all. Amen.* The God of peace dwells only in those who are peaceable. And it is good that he has concluded with peace, because the two peoples are called back to peaceful concord.[34]

16: 1 *I commend to you Phoebe, your sister.* Although the text of the letter is, as it were, already finished, he has attached this material below for the purpose of commendation and greeting, as is his custom.

[30] Cf. Ambstr. *Rom.* 15: 25–6 (CSEL 81. 1: 471. 19–22); Orig.–Ruf. *Rom.* 10. 14 (PG 14: 1273B 2–7).
[31] Cf. *Rom.* 11: 12, 11: 15.
[32] Cf. ibid. 15: 14.
[33] Cf. Ambstr. *Rom.* 15: 30–1 (CSEL 81. 1: 475. 7–12).
[34] Cf. ibid. 15: 33 (CSEL 81. 1: 477. 6–9); see also *Rom.* 1: 7 above.

Who is in the service of the church which is in Cenchrea. As even today women deaconesses [who live] in the east are known to minister to their own sex in baptism.[1] Or: In the ministry of the word (cf. Acts 6: 4), for we find that women taught privately, as for example Priscilla, whose husband was called Aquila (cf. Acts 18: 1–3, 24–6).[2] 2 *That you receive her in the Lord, as is fitting for the saints, and assist her in whatever matter she requires of you: for she has stood by many others and me as well.* That you help her with expenses or support, because she also has helped many people as long as she had the means.[3] 3 *Greet Priscilla and Aquila, my helpers in Christ Jesus.* Who are said to have established Apollo in the faith (cf. Acts 18: 24–6), [and] whom he calls 'helpers' because they also helped in the work of instruction in which he himself laboured (cf. Acts 18: 19).[4] 4 *Who risked their necks for my life, to whom not only I but also all the churches of the Gentiles give thanks.* By approving of my teaching, they exposed themselves to danger.[5] Therefore all the churches thank them, for I was kept from harm by them. 5 *And the church in their house.* He shows that a gathering of believers is called a church.[6] *Greet my beloved Epenetus, who is the first-born of Asia for Christ.* He [was] the first-born of the church in Asia. We understand from the names that all those he greets were foreigners, and it is not unreasonable for us to suppose that the Romans came to faith [through] their example and teaching. 6 *Greet Mary, who has worked hard among you.* 7 *Greet Andronicus and Junias, my relatives and fellow prisoners, who are esteemed among the apostles, and who were in Christ even before me.* 8 *Greet Ampliatus, especially beloved to me in the Lord.* 9 *Greet Urbanus, my helper in Christ, and my beloved Stachys.* 10 *Greet Apelles, approved in Christ. Greet those who belong to Aristobulus.* 11 *Greet my relative Herodion. Greet those who belong to Narcissus who are in the Lord.* 12 *Greet Tryphena and Tryphosa, who labour in the Lord. Greet my dearest*

---

[1] Cf. Pel. *1 Tim.* 3: 11, 5: 9, 5: 11 (Souter, *Expositions*, ii. 487. 6–8, 494. 15–18, 495. 7–9), and see Gryson, *Le Ministère des femmes*, 160–1; Martimort, *Les Diaconesses*, 192.

[2] In stating that Priscilla taught privately, Pelagius reflects the custom of his day, when aristocratic women both sought and gave instruction in the privacy of their homes; see Jer. *Ep.* 50. 1, 3, 5 (CSEL 54: 388. 15–16, 390. 19–20, 394. 10–12); Aug. *De mor.* 1. 33. 70 (PL 32: 1340. 11–16); and cf. Witherington, *Women in the Earliest Churches*, 154.

[3] The meaning of the term applied to Phoebe (προστάτις) has occasioned considerable discussion in recent years; see Meeks, *The First Urban Christians*, 60; Witherington, *Women in the Earliest Churches*, 114. Pelagius understands Phoebe to have been one who assisted others out of her means; his reading, though four centuries after the fact, agrees with that of Witherington.

[4] Cf. Ambstr. *Rom.* 16: 3–5. 1 (CSEL 81. 1: 479. 2–8).

[5] Cf. ibid. 16: 3–5. 2 (CSEL 81. 1: 479. 15–22).

[6] Cf. ibid. 16: 3–5. 3 (CSEL 81. 1: 479. 22–4).

Persis, who has laboured much in the Lord. 13 *Greet Rufus, chosen in the Lord.* These came from the Jews and, because together with Paul they had suffered tribulation but had not been intimidated, they are here deservedly held in esteem. They, among others, had been sent to further the progress of the Romans, and according to the testimony of Paul himself are reported to have believed before him. *And his mother and mine.* In age, [and] not by birth.   14 *Greet Asyncritus, Phlegon, Hermes, Patrobas, Hermas, and the brothers who are with them.* 15 *Greet Philologus and Julia, Nereas and his sister Olympiades, and all the saints who are with them.* By his example he teaches us what sort of friends we should greet in our letters, not those who are[, for instance,] rich in worldly goods, or honoured with positions of rank, but well supplied in grace and faith.   16 *Greet one another with a holy kiss: all the churches of Christ greet you.* Not with a feigned and treacherous [kiss], of the sort with which Judas betrayed the Saviour (cf. Luke 22: 48). For in the church the peace is proclaimed first, so that one may show oneself to be at peace with all who are about to partake of the body of Christ (cf. 1 Cor. 10: 16).[7]   17 *I appeal to you, brothers, to watch out for those who create disagreements and obstacles contrary to the teaching which you have learnt, and to avoid them.* 18 *For these sort do not serve Christ our Lord, but their own belly.* He is speaking of those who in his day came from among the circumcised and did away with fasts and abstinence. Disagreeing with apostolic teaching and setting obstacles before the brothers, they preached new moons and sabbaths and other feast-days for the sake of the belly.[8] *And with sweet-sounding speeches and words of praise they lead astray the hearts of the innocent.* With blandishments and flatteries framed in polished speech.   19 *For your obedience has been noised abroad everywhere.* If you obeyed those you should not have obeyed, how much more should you obey us! For this is why these persons came to you, because they knew that you could readily be led astray by unsuspecting obedience. *Therefore I rejoice in you, but I want you to be wise in what is good, and guileless in what is evil:* 20 *and the God of peace will crush Satan under your feet quickly.* [I rejoice with you] because obedience is good only if it is reasonable,[9] and therefore I want you to be wise in what is good, so that by being ignorant of evil you bring the enemy down under the feet of innocence. For accordingly the Lord

---

[7] Cf. Orig.-Ruf. *Rom.* 10. 33 (PG 14: 1282C 13–1283A 8). In the Roman mass of the 4th cent. the kiss of peace stood between the *pax domini* and communion; see Jungmann, *Roman Rite*, ii. 321–3.

[8] Cf. Aug. *Exp. prop.* 76 (84). 3–4 (CSEL 84: 52. 11–18).

[9] Cf. *Rom.* 12: 1 at n. 4.

'has given' us 'power to tread upon scorpions and snakes and every power of the enemy' (Luke 10: 19):[10] that is, so that he may not prevail over us, and [so that] we can walk over him with all members free and unfettered.   21 *Timothy, my helper, greets you, and Lucius and Jason and Sosipater, my relatives.* 22 *I, Tertius, who wrote this letter, greet you in the Lord.* 23 *Gaius, my host, and the whole church greets you. Erastus, the treasurer of the city, greets you, and also brother Quartus.* Here he calls the former treasurer 'treasurer', just as he has often called the believers who were formerly Gentiles 'Gentiles', [after] the manner [of the law], which still calls Abigail 'the wife of Nabal' though she had passed over in marriage to David once Nabal had died (1 Sam. 30: 5).[11]   24 *The grace of our Lord Jesus Christ be with you all. Amen.*[12] This is the closing formula written in his own hand in all his letters (cf. 2 Thess. 3: 17), by which he means to call to mind Christ's benefits.   25 *To him who is able to strengthen you.* With signs and teachings.[13] *According to my Gospel and the proclamation of Jesus Christ.* So that you live in the way that I have preached by the example and authority of Christ.[14] *According to the revelation of the mystery which was kept secret from time eternal,* 26 *but which has now been disclosed through the writings of the prophets.* The mystery of the calling of all the Gentiles, which through Paul's Gospel, using the testimonies of the prophets, had now been plainly disclosed in Christ (cf. Eph. 3: 1–13), had been hidden in the law [for a long time]. Although the prophets had previously said many things about the Gentiles, none had recognized as clearly as Paul how the Gentiles and the Jews became one in Christ. For they had been able to determine that some should be admitted to the faith as proselytes. *Made known among all the Gentiles according to the command of the eternal God for the obedience of faith,* 27 *to the only wise God, through Jesus Christ, to whom be honour and glory for ever and ever. Amen.* God commanded that all the

---

[10] Cf. Orig.–Ruf. *Rom.* 10. 37 (PG 14: 1286B 7–13, 1287B 9–12).

[11] On the person and status of Erastus, much disputed, cf. Acts 19: 22 and 2 Tim. 4: 20, and see Theissen, *The Social Setting of Pauline Christianity*, 75–83. The office named in Pelagius's text, *arcarius ciuitatis*, was a low position of financial administration, often occupied by a slave. Cadbury, 'Erastus of Corinth', 57, suggests that Pelagius speaks of Erastus as being a *former* treasurer because, since Acts 19: 22 reports that Erastus travelled, Pelagius concluded that he must have resigned his office, which restricted opportunity for travel.

[12] This verse, a repetition of v. 20, is omitted in the best Greek MSS of Romans. It appears at both v. 20 and v. 24 in all the MSS of Pelagius's commentary except the Balliol and Paris MSS, which include it only at v. 24. Ambstr. *Rom.* 16: 20 (CSEL 81.1: 491. 9) and Orig.–Ruf. *Rom.* 10. 38 (PG 14: 1287B 13–15) treat it as v. 20.

[13] Cf. *Rom.* 15: 20.

[14] Cf. ibid. 1: 1, 15: 14.

Gentiles obey and acknowledge God. He alone knew that this would happen at some time, for he alone [is] naturally wise, just as he is naturally good. Humankind, it is true, is also called good, but we have the ability to be good or wise as a result of instruction, whereas God is good and wise by nature.[15] To him be glory [and] honour through Jesus Christ for ever. Amen.

---

[15] Cf. Orig.–Ruf. *Rom.* 10. 43 (PG 14: 1292A 9–B 6).

Appendix

PELAGIUS'S BIBLICAL TEXT

When Hermann Frede established the text of Ephesians for Pelagius's commentary, the method he used was the following.[1] He noted, first of all, that when the Karlsruhe (A) and Balliol (B) manuscripts agree on a reading, the reading is most often from the Vulgate. Secondly, he observed that the pseudo-Jerome manuscripts H_1 and the Paris manuscript V almost always support the Karlsruhe and Balliol manuscripts when the latter agree, whether for the Vulgate or for the *uetus latina*. He accordingly concluded that when the Karlsruhe and Balliol manuscripts disagree with each other, the manuscript group H_1V can be used to decide between the variants. Thirdly, he noted that the Paris manuscript is heavily corrupted by the *uetus latina*, and surmised that the Paris manuscript probably preserves an authentic reading when it attests the Vulgate. If, then, the Karlsruhe and Balliol manuscripts disagree and the manuscript group H_1V is divided in its witness, a Vulgate reading in the Paris manuscript and either the Karlsruhe or the Balliol manuscript is to be preferred. In short, to ascertain Pelagius's biblical text, the order of priority among the witnesses is as follows: (1) AB; (2) AH_1V or BH_1V; (3) AV = Vulgate or BV = Vulgate.

Similar studies of the text of other epistles in Pelagius's commentary have confirmed Frede's conclusions.[2] Those conclusions are also corroborated by internal evidence from the commentary on Romans, which is presented below in two tables: Table I consists of instances in which the comments on Romans support a Vulgate reading; Table II consists of instances in which the comments support a variant to the Vulgate. In the tables the text is listed in the third column, the manuscripts which attest that text follow in the fourth, and the evidence from the comment follows in the fifth. The sigla and the data of the manuscripts are taken from Souter's edition (for a list of the sigla see p. 167 below). When there is a lacuna in a manuscript, the manuscript is listed in

---

[1] *Pelagius*, 16–29. For a summary of the debate about Pelagius's biblical text see the Introduction at nn. 42–51. For a discussion of the MSS see the Introduction at nn. 193–201.

[2] Tinnefeld, *Untersuchungen*, 78–82; Nellessen, *Untersuchungen*, 223–35. Borse, *Der Kolosserbrieftext des Pelagius*, and Wolfgarten, 'Der dem Pelagiuskommentar zugrundliegende Text des Titusbriefes', were not available to me. See also *Vetus Latina*, xxiv. 2, for a recension of Pelagius's text for Philippians.

square brackets. When a manuscript varies slightly from the others in its company, it is listed in parentheses. In the fifth column the reference in parentheses after the citation from the commentary is to Souter's edition by page and line. If the citation is not from the comment on that verse, but from elsewhere in the commentary, it is marked by a dot ($\bullet$). Doubtful evidence is marked by a question mark (?). In Table II the reading judged to be Pelagius's is presented first, and the Vulgate is presented second. When a variant to the Vulgate appears in the major manuscripts of the Vulgate, this is noted with a square ($\blacksquare$).[3]

The evidence from the comments confirms that the Karlsruhe manuscript, which departs from the Vulgate less often than the Balliol one, is generally more reliable than the Balliol manuscript as a witness to Pelagius's biblical text. In Table I, A attests the Vulgate without B ninety-two times, whereas B attests it without A four times; they agree on the Vulgate together with other manuscripts nineteen times. In Table II, which is a third of Table I in length, AB agree on the *uetus latina* fourteen times, B attests the *uetus latina* against A nineteen times, and A attests the *uetus latina* against B three times. Clearly, when A and B agree they are a reliable witness to Pelagius's biblical text, even if the reading is *uetus latina*.

The evidence further suggests, as Frede concluded, that when A and B disagree the Paris manuscript can help to decide between them. In Table I, when AB or A attest the Vulgate, the Paris manuscript attests the *uetus latina* more often than the other remaining manuscripts: ten times by itself, twice with HG, and once with H_1, H_2, and H_2G. Since in these instances the Paris manuscript tends to support the *uetus latina* against the evidence of the commentary, it would seem reasonable to assume that when, contrary to this pattern, it attests the Vulgate in conjunction with A or B, it is a reliable witness to Pelagius's text.

However, there is reason for caution in regard to the second of Frede's guidelines, namely, that when A and B disagree and the manuscripts H_1V agree with one or the other, the reading attested by H_1V is authentic. Table II suggests that it is possible that the *uetus latina* attested by B or BG is authentic even though the Vulgate is attested by AH_1V. If one decided simply for AH_1V or BH_1V in a number of instances, one would have accepted a reading which is not supported by Pelagius's comment (see Nos. 6, 7, 13, 14, 19, 20, 29, 30, 37). One must bear in mind, however, that the weight of evidence in favour of the Vulgate (Table I) is far greater than the weight of evidence in favour of the *uetus latina* (Table II), and that it is always possible that Pelagius recalled a familiar *uetus latina* reading in a comment even though the Vulgate was before him in the lemma.

---

[3] These are drawn from the Stuttgart edition of the Vulgate, *Biblia Sacra iuxta Vulgatam Versionem*, 3rd rev. edn. (1983). Cf. *Biblia Sacra*, pp. xxii–xxiii, and Fischer, 'Das Neue Testament in lateinischer Sprache', 67, on the method and apparatus of the edition.

A new recension of the text of Romans for Pelagius's commentary follows below. It has been prepared according to Frede's method from the data of Souter's edition.[4] The witness of Cassiodorus (Cas, Cas^ed, Cas^cod) has not been included in the apparatus. Souter's data for Cassiodorus, when compared with reprints of the *editio princeps* at Cologne (1538) and Paris (1547), as well as with the reprint in Migne (PL 68), do not inspire confidence.[5] When Pelagius's comment suggests a reading other than that indicated by Frede's method, the text suggested by the comment has been followed. Because, as Table II indicates, H_1V is not an infallible guide for deciding between A and B, and AV = Vulgate is not necessarily authentic when H_1 and V disagree, the reader is advised to consult the apparatus when undertaking a detailed study of Pelagius's biblical text of Romans.

[4] The witnesses which were discovered after Souter completed his edition have not been collated (see p. 29, nn. 200–1). The fragments do not pertain to Romans, and the Göttweig and Ivrea MSS, with their affinity to the longer pseudo-Jerome group, are unlikely to contribute much to establishing Pelagius's biblical text. It is expected, of course, that if and when a new edition of Pelagius's commentary appears, its recension will supersede the one here offered.

[5] See Souter, *Expositions*, i. 318–26; ii, p. viii. Regrettably, the edition Souter was preparing of Cassiodorus did not come to light. No doubt it would have allowed for a surer comparison of Pelagius's lemmata with Cassiodorus's.

TABLE I. Comments that support the Vulgate

No.	Verse	Vulgate	Manuscripts	Evidence
1.	1:5	ad oboediendum	AHGV	ut … oboedirent (9. 19)
2.	1:24	in semet ipsis	AHGV	in se (15. 21)
3.	1:28	probauerunt	AHGV	probauerunt (16. 21)
4.	1:29	homicidio	AHG	homicidium (-o HG) (17. 6)
5.	1:31	insipientes	AHGV	qui … recesserunt (18. 8)
6.	2:7	deum om.	BHGV	boni … expectatur (21. 7–8)
7.	2:8	et incred. sunt om.	AHGV	audiant … defensare (21. 18–22)
8.	2:11	acceptio apud deum	BHGV	'acc. apud deum' (22. 14–15; ●165. 19)
9.	2:12	in lege	AHGV	in lege naturae (22. 20–1)
10.	2:15	cogitationum … defendentium	AH(−N^corr.)JGV	altercationes cogitationum (23. 22)
11.	2:18	nosti	AHGV	nosse, agnoscere (24. 10, 11)
12.	3:4	sit om.	AH[G]V	'omnis homo mendax' (●28. 1; ●45. 22)
13.	3:5	iustitiam dei	AH[G]V	'iustitiam dei' (●28. 2)
14.	3:21	a lege et prophetis	AHGV	a lege et prophetis (32. 16, 17–18)
15.	3:27	fidei	AHGV	fidei (34. 6)
16.	4:2	legis om.	ABV	ex operibus (●41. 12)
17.	4:4	sed secundum	ABEH₂GV	debitoris … damnatur (36. 8–9)
18.	4:11	ut … iustitiam	[A]JHGV	ut … reputatur (38. 11–12)
19.	4:14	exinanita	AHGV	fides exinaniri (39. 8)
20.	4:16	est Abrahae	[A]JHGV	lex … Abrahae (39. 9–14)
21.	4:17	deum	AHGV	ante deum (39. 18)
22.	4:17	uiuificat	AHGV	mortuos ad generandum (39. 20)

23.	4:17	ea *om.*	AH₂V	uocauerit quae non erant (39. 22)
24.	4:18	contra	AHGV	contra spem (39. 24)
25.	5:2	habemus	AESH₂G	accessimus (41. 21)
26.	5:2	filiorum	AHV	filiorum (41. 23)
27.	5:5	confundit	ABEH₂GV	confunditur (43. 4)
28.	5:12	intrauit	AHGV	intrauit (45. 14)
29.	5:12	pertransiit	ABSRCFGV	pertransiit (45. 18, 22)
30.	5:14	etiam	AHGV	etiam (46. 13)
31.	5:14	non	AHGV	sive . . . naturae (46. 10–14)
32.	5:16	peccantem	AHGV	imo . . . peccante (47. 15)
33.	5:17	mors . . . unum	AHGV	mors regnauit (48. 2)
34.	5:17	donationis et	AHGV	abundantiam donationis (47. 24)
35.	5:19	peccatores	AHGV	peccauerunt (48. 6)
36.	5:19	multi	AHGV	multi (48. 6)
37.	5:21	sicut	AH,[H₂]GV	sicut (48. 21)
38.	6:3	sumus	ABH₂GV	sumus (●220. 2)
39.	6:4	quo modo	AHGV	quo modo (49. 20)
40.	6:8	uiuemus	ABECFGV	conuiuemus (50. 23)
41.	6:9	ultra	AHGV	iterum (51. 1)
42.	6:15	non	ABHV	cessante (52. 9)
43.	6:19	sicut	AHGV	tantum (53. 5)
44.	6:19	iustitiae	AHV	iustitiae (53. 5)
45.	7:6	morientes	AV	morientes (56. 4)
46.	7:10	ad uitam	AHGV	ad uitam (57. 14)
47.	7:10	ad mortem	AHGV	ad mortem (57. 14)
48.	7:16	si	AHGV	si (58. 21)
49.	7:16	nolo	AHGV	nolo facere (58. 22)

No.	Verse	Vulgate	Manuscripts	Evidence
50.	7: 21	uolenti	ABCGV	si ego uolo (59. 15)
51.	7: 21	malum adiacet	AHGV	adiacens (59. 15)
52.	7: 22	uoluntate *om.*	AHGV	consentio legi (60. 2)
53.	7: 24	liberabit	ABCG	liberabit ABH₂GV (60. 9)
54.	8: 3	impossibile	ABH₁Nᶜᵒʳʳ·CFGᶜᵒʳʳ·V	'impossibile' (●322. 8)
55.	8: 3	infirmabatur	AHVGᶜᵒʳʳ·	infirmabatur (61. 2; ●322. 8)
56.	8: 9	in carne non estis	ABESH₂GV	'in carne non estis' (●224. 21)
57.	8: 9	Christi	AHGV	Christi AH,GV (63. 7)
58.	8: 13	spiritu	AHGV	spiritalibus actibus (64. 3–4)
59.	8: 18	non sunt condignae	AHGV	condignum (65. 7); 'condignae' (●255. 12)
60.	8: 28	deum	AHGV	dilectione dei (68. 16)
61.	8: 30	iustificauit	AHGV	iustificantur (69. 11)
62.	8: 33	accusabit	ABSEᶜᵒʳʳ·H₂Gᶜᵒʳʳ·	audebit accusare (70. 3)
63.	8: 35	caritate	AHGV	caritate (70. 19)
64.	8: 38	principatus	AHGV	angelorum principium (71. 15–16)
65.	8: 38	neque futura	AHGV	gloriam futurorum (71. 17)
66.	8: 38	fortitudines	A	uirtutes (71. 1)
67.	9: 1	Iesu *om.*	AHGV	in Christo (72. 13)
68.	9: 4	et promissa	AHGV	ministerium … prophetarum (73. 4–5)
69.	9: 6	Israhelitae	ABHG	Israhelitae (73. 19; ●342. 17)
70.	9: 15	cuius[1]	ASR	illius (75. 21, 22)
71.	9: 15	cuius[2]	AEG	illius (75. 21, 22)

72.	9: 15	miserebor	AHV	miserebor (75. 21)
73.	9: 18	deus *om.*	AHGV	deus *om.* (76. 3; 77. 12)
74.	9: 22	sustinuit	AHG	sustinuit (78. 7)
75.	9: 22	uasa	AHGV	uasa (78. 11)
76.	9: 33	credit	ABV	credit (80. 24)
77.	10: 16	obaudierunt	A	obaudierunt ABHG (83. 17)
78.	10: 19	primus Moses	AH,MN*CFG^corr.(V)	primus Moses (84. 5)
79.	11: 11	illorum	ABHV	illorum ABSH₂GV (88. 9)
80.	11: 13	honorificabo	AHGV	honorificabo (88. 16)
81.	11: 17	radicis et pinguedinis	BHGV	radicis … pinguedinis … (89. 11)
82.	11: 19	si *om.*	AHGV	ideo factus ut (89. 17)
83.	11: 19	inserar	AHGV	inseraris (89. 17)
84.	11: 20	propter incredulitatem	AHGV	propter incredulitatem (89. 18)
85.	11: 28	fratres *om.*	AHGV	inimici … Christum (92. 4–5)
				secundum … uos (●357. 7)
86.	11: 33	incomprehensibilia (——ebilia A)	ABHV	conprehendi non possunt (93. 7)
87.	12: 2	sensus uestri	AHGV	sensum uestrum (95. 1)
88.	12: 3	dei *om.*	ABS	spiritalis ABV (95. 9)
89.	12: 10	diligentes	AHGV	diligite (97. 8)
90.	12: 17	dicit dominus	A[B]HG	dicit dominus (100. 12)
91.	13: 4	malum	A[B]H,GV	malum ABMNFGV (●508. 3)
92.	13: 5	sed et	A[B]H₂GV	sed et (102. 15)
93.	13: 8	proximum	A[B]RH,V	proximum (●202. 16)
94.	14: 2	infirmus est	AHGV	infirmus (106. 5)
95.	14: 12	reddet	AH,NCFGV	reddet (109. 8)
96.	14: 14	cibum *om.*	AHGV	aliquit (109. 16); quitquit (109. 17)
97.	14: 14	ille commune est	AHGV	ille … commune (109. 19–20)

No.	Verse	Vulgate	Manuscripts	Evidence
98.	14: 23	non est ex fide	AHGV	ex fide non est (112. 2)
99	15: 4	scripturarum spem	AHGV	per ... expectamus (113. 7–8)
100.	15: 5	Iesum Christum	AHGV	Christus (114. 3)
101.	15: 13	in³	ABV	abundantia ... signis (116. 4)
102.	15: 16	accepta	AH₁GV	accepta (117. 8)
103.	15: 19	repleuerim	AH₁NCFGV	repletur (117. 22)
104.	15: 23	cupiditatem ... ueniendi	AHG(V)	cupiditatem (118. 17)
105.	15: 24	si uobis	AHG	illis (119. 6)
106.	15: 24	fruitus	BHGV	frui (119. 6)
107.	15: 26	sanctorum	AHGV	sanctorum (119. 21)
108.	15: 30	ac sollicit. *om.*	AHG	spiritalis ... exormus (121. 1)
109.	15: 30	ut	AHG	ut (120. 19; cf. 121. 2)
110.	15: 30	pro me	AH₁V	pro eo (120. 19); pro inuicem (121. 2)
111.	15: 31	obsequii ... sanctis	AH₁GV	oblatio mea (121. 8); fuerit accepta (121. 9)
112.	15: 32	ueniam ... gaudio	AH₂Gcorr.V	in gaudio (121. 8)
113.	16: 18	et benedictiones	AHGV	adulationes (124. 17)
114.	16: 19	bono	AH₁Gcorr.	bono ABH₂Gcorr.V (125. 4)
115.	16: 19	malo	AHG	bono ABH₂Gcorr.V (125. 4)
116.	16: 20	pedibus uestris	Acorr.BHG	pedibus (125. 5)
117.	16: 27	est *om.*	AH₁GV	cui ... Christum (126. 18)

TABLE II. Comments that support a variant to the Vulgate

No.	Verse	Variant	Manuscripts	Evidence
■ 1.	1:18	dei²	BH₂G	?ueritatem . . . dei (13. 13)ᵃ
	Vg	—	AH₂V	
2.	1:13	non enim	AB(V)	per . . . potuistis (11. 13–14)
	Vg	nolo autem	HG	
3.	1:18	in omnem	BV	?in omnem' A (13. 2–3)ᵇ
	Vg	super omnem	AHG	
■ 4.	1:18	iniustitia	ABERCFGV	iniustitia (13. 14)
	Vg	iniustitiam	SMN	
■ 5.	1:25	mendacium	AHG	in mendacium (15. 23)
	Vg	mendacio	BV	
6.	1:29	et¹	BRH₂G	et (17. 2)
	Vg	—	AESV	
7.	1:29	et²	BH₂G	et (17. 4)
	Vg	—	AH₁V	
8.	1:31	—	AB	[no comment]ᶜ
	Vg	absque foedere	HGV	
9.	3:25	propitiatorem	ABGV	?ut propitietur (33. 15–16)ᵈ
	Vg	propitiationem	H	

ᵃ Because the comment specifies *ueritatem nominis dei*, one could argue that *dei* is absent from Pelagius's lemma.
ᵇ The clause which supports the *uetus latina*, *ideo dixit 'in omnem' quia*, is found in A alone.
ᶜ There is no comment on *absque foedere*. The absence of a comment suggests the absence of the phrase from Pelagius's text because at this point in the commentary there is a series of brief comments following the text word by word or phrase by phrase.
ᵈ The lemma at No. 10 is a continuation of the lemma at No. 9, and there the comment clearly supports the *uetus latina*.

No.	Verse	Variant	Manuscripts	Evidence
10.	3. 25	propositum	ABG	propositum (33. 18)
	Vg	remissionem	HG	
■ 11.	3. 27	tua	BHGV	gloriabaris ABH$_2$V (34. 4)
	Vg	—	A	
■ 12.	4. 5	secundum . . . dei	(A)BHGV	gratis . . . dimittere (36. 19)
	Vg	—	B	
13.	4. 11	in praeputio	AHGV	?in praeputio (38. 12)[e]
	Vg	per praeputium	BG	
14.	4. 19	iam emortuum	AHV	iam emortuo corpore (40. 6)
	Vg	emortuum	AB	
15.	4. 25	surrexit	HGV	surrexisse ABH$_1$V (41. 4)
	Vg	resurrexit	BESG	
■ 16.	5. 19	oboedientiam	ARH$_2$V	oboedientia (48. 6–7)
	Vg	oboeditionem	ABV	
17.	6. 16	iustitiae	HG	?si . . . oboedieritis (52. 15)[f]
	Vg	ad iustitiam	BV	
■ 18.	8. 7	est subiecta	AHG	?non subiectum (62. 18)[g]
	Vg	subicitur	BG	
19.	8. 10	uiuit	AHV	uiuit (63. 14)
	Vg	uita	B	
20.	8. 10	iustitiam	AHGV	iustitiam (63. 14)
	Vg	iustificationem		

■21.		et[1]	AH₁N^corr.CFGV	atque A^corr.V; et HG (70. 7)
	Vg	—	BMN*	
■22.		cui	BHGV	cui (77. 12)
	Vg	cuius	A	
■23.		ad salutem	BH₁N*CFG	ad salutem (82. 23–4)
	Vg	in salutem	AMN^corr.V	
24.		quidem om.	ABH₁V	?quam diu fuero (88. 14)[h]
	Vg	quidem	H₂G	
■25.		incredulitate	BHGV	incredulitate (-m M) (92. 20)
	Vg	incredulitatem	A	
26.		omnibus	ABGV	omnibus ABV (93. 2)[i]
	Vg	omnium	H	
27.		quod bonum ... perfectum est	AB(V)	quod bonum ... optimum (95. 5–6)
	Vg	bona et beneplacens et perfecta	HG	
■28.		sicut	A[B]HG	sicut (103. 22)
	Vg	tamquam	V	
29.		concupiscentiis	B	'concupiscentias'; 'concupiscentiam' (105. 20–1)[j]
	Vg	desideriis	AHGV	

e There are two difficulties with the evidence from the commentary. First, it conflicts with the evidence for the remainder of the verse (see Table I, No. 18). Secondly, the presence in the comment of the phrase *in praeputio* could be derived from its occurrence at vv. 9–11.

f The comment is not conclusive; it is merely suggestive of righteousness as the object of obedience (*oboeditio iustitiae*) rather than the purpose or outcome of obedience (*oboeditio ad iustitiam*).

g The use of *subiectum* in the comment may be stylistic rather than allusive.

h The comment is not conclusive; it would not be unusual for an adverb like *quidem* to be omitted from a paraphrase of the text.

i The evidence from the comment is not weakened by the fact that only ABV attest *omnibus*. HG do not attest an alternative, but rather omit the entire clause *ut omnibus misereatur*.

j It is possible that the verbal associations with Ecclus. 18: 30–1 issue from a recollection of the *uetus latina*.

No.	Verse	Variant	Manuscripts	Evidence
■ 30.	14: 2	holera	BG	holera (106. 9)
	Vg	holus	AHV	
■ 31.	14: 5	diem inter diem	AH,GV	diem inter diem (107. 16)
	Vg	diem plus inter diem	H_2	
32.	15: 2	ad bonam aedif.	ABV	ad . . . placeamus (112. 14)
	Vg	in bonam aedif.	HG	
33.	15: 16	seruiens	ABV	seruiens (116. 21)
	Vg	minister	H,MCFG	
34.	16: 3	Priscillam	ABV	Priscillam (121. 20)
	Vg	Priscam	HG*	
35.	16: 20	gratia . . . uobiscum *om.*	BV	haec . . . Christi (125. 19–21)
	Vg	gratia . . . vobiscum	AHG	
36.	16: 26	omnes gentes cognitum	BV	praecepit . . . agnoscat (126. 13–14)
	Vg	cunctis gentibus	AHG	
37.	16: 27	et gloria	B(G)	gloria [et] honor (126. 18)
	Vg	—	AHV	

LIST OF MANUSCRIPTS

See Souter, *Expositions*, ii. 2; cf. Frede, *Ein neuer Paulustext*, ii. 14, and the Introduction above at nn. 193–201.

𝕽   Rome, Biblioteca Apostolica Vaticana lat. 10800, saec. vii
A   Karlsruhe, Badische Landesbibliothek Augiensis CXIX, saec. ix
B   Oxford, Balliol College 157, saec. xv
K   Freiburg-im-Breisgau, Stadtarchiv s.n., saec. viii–ix
H   Pseudo-Hieronymus (saec. v)
H₁ archetypus Pseudo-Hieronymi classis breuioris
        E   Paris, Bibliothèque Nationale lat. 9525, saec. ix
        S   Salisbury, Cathedral Library 5, saec. xii
        R   Munich, Bayerische Staatsbibliothek 13038, saec. ix in.
H₂ archetypus Pseudo-Hieronymi classis prolixioris
        M   Paris, Bibliothèque Nationale lat. 1853, saec. ix in.
        N   Épinal, Bibliothèque Municipale 6, saec. ix
        C   Troyes, Bibliothèque Municipale 486, saec. xii
        F   Florence, Biblioteca Mediceo-Laurenziana Plut. xv dext. cod. 1, saec. xii
       R$^{corr.}$ uide R supra; corrector saec. ix
G   St Gall, Stiftsbibliothek 73, saec. ix
V   Paris, Bibliothèque Nationale lat. 653, saec. ix in.

Other conventions used in the apparatus, following Souter:

* (e.g. A*)	text prior to a correction
corr. (e.g. A$^{corr.}$)	text after a correction
eras. (*erasum*)	an erased portion of text
exp. (*expunctum*)	the deletion of a character by a point
in ras. (*in rasura*)	text written over an erasure
⁎ (e.g. *so⁎⁎⁎rorem*)	erased letters
ms (*manus secunda*; e.g. A^{ms})	text of a second hand
om. (*omissum*)	text omitted
praem. (*praemissum*)	the word in the text preceded by the word in the apparatus
1/2 (e.g. H 1/2)	the manuscript attests two versions of the lemma
– (e.g. H(−N))	except for the manuscript(s) following the minus sign, the family of manuscripts attests the variant

1: 1 Paulus · seruus Iesu Christi · uocatus apostolus · segregatus · in euangelium dei · 2 quod ante promiserat per prophetas · suos in scripturis sanctis · 3 de filio suo · qui factus est ex semine Dauid · secundum carnem · 4 qui praedestinatus est filius dei in uirtute · secundum spiritum sanctificationis ex resurrectione mortuorum · Iesu Christi domini nostri · 5 per quem accepimus gratiam et apostolatum · ad oboediendum fidei in omnibus gentibus · pro nomine eius · 6 in quibus estis et uos uocati Iesu Christi · 7 omnibus qui sunt Romae in caritate dei · uocatis sanctis · gratia uobis et pax a deo patre nostro et domino Iesu Christo · 8 primum quidem gratias ago deo meo per Iesum Christum · pro omnibus uobis · quia fides uestra adnuntiatur in uniuerso mundo · 9 testis enim mihi est deus cui seruio in spiritu meo in euangelio filii eius · quod sine intermissione memoriam uestri facio 10 semper in orationibus meis obsecrans · si quo modo tandem aliquando prosperum iter habeam in uoluntate dei ueniendi ad uos 11 desidero enim uidere uos · ut aliquid inpertiar gratiae uobis spiritalis ad confirmandos uos · 12 id est simul consolari in uobis per eam quae inuicem est fidem uestram atque meam · 13 non enim arbitror uos ignorare fratres quia saepe proposui uenire ad uos · et prohibitus sum usque adhuc · ut aliquem fructum habeam et in uobis · sicut et in ceteris gentibus · 14 Graecis ac barbaris sapientibus et insipientibus · debitor sum 15 ita quod in me promptum est · et uobis qui Romae estis euangelizare · 16 non enim erubesco euangelium · uirtus enim dei est in salutem · omni credenti · Iudaeo primum et Graeco 17 iustitia enim dei in eo reuelatur · ex fide in fidem · sicut scriptum est iustus autem ex fide uiuit · 18 reuelatur enim ira dei de caelo · super omnem impietatem et iniustitiam

1: 1 Chr. Iesu G = Vg   2 antea A   3 est] + ei BHG   secundum] sanctum B   5 ad oboediendum] per oboedientiam B   7 in caritate] dilectis HG = Vg   nostro et domino] a domino H₂   8 adnuntiatur] praedicatur B 10 semper *om.* BGV   quo modo *om.* B   tandem] tamen B   11 uidere] uenire ad R   inpertiar] inpertiam SH₂   uob. grat. BH₂G   12 in uobis] uobiscum B fides uestra atque mea E   13 non enim] non autem V: nolo enim HG: *cf.* Vg ign. uos B   aliquem] aliquid B   et² *om.* HV   15 quod in me *om.* H₁ promptum est] est promptus sum B: *om.* H₁   et] in H₁   16 erubesco] + super B salute EN   credenti] + in eo B   17 enim] autem G   fidem] fide V 18 enim *om.* B   super] in BV   et *om.* G hominum · eorum qui ueritatem dei in iniustitia detinent · 19 quia quod notum est dei · manifestum est in illis · deus enim illis manifestauit 20 inuisibilia enim ipsius a creatura mundi per ea quae facta sunt · intellecta conspiciuntur sempiterna quoque eius uirtus et diuinitas ita ut sint inexcusabiles · 21 quia cum cognouissent deum non sicut deum glorificauerunt · aut gratias egerunt · sed euanuerunt in cogitationibus suis · et obscuratum est insipiens cor eorum · 22 dicentes enim se esse sapientes · stulti facti sunt 23 et mutauerunt gloriam incorruptibilis dei in similitudinem · imaginis corruptibilis hominis et uolucrum et quadrupedum et serpentium · 24 propter quod tradidit illos deus in desideria cordis eorum · in immunditiam · ut contumeliis adficiant corpora sua · in semet ipsis · 25 qui conmutauerunt ueritatem dei in mendacium et coluerunt · et seruierunt creaturae potius quam creatori · qui est benedictus in saecula · 26 propter ea tradidit illos deus in passiones ignominiae · nam feminae eorum immutauerunt naturalem usum in eum usum qui est contra naturam · 27 similiter autem et masculi relicto naturali usu feminae exarserunt in desideriis suis inuicem masculi in masculos turpitudinem operantes · et mercedem quam oportuit erroris sui in semet ipsos recipientes · 28 et sicut non probauerunt deum habere in notitiam · tradidit eos deus in reprobum sensum · ut faciant quae non conueniunt · 29 repletos omni iniquitate et malitia · fornicatione et auaritia · nequitia plenos inuidia homicidio · contentione · dolo · malignitate · 30 susurrones · detractores deo odibiles · contumeliosos · superbos elatos inuentores malorum · parentibus non oboedientes · 31 insipientes incompositos · sine affectione · sine misericordia · 32 qui cum iustitiam dei cognouissent non

qui] quae B   dei *om.* AH₂V = Vg   iniustitiam SMN = Vg   19 in *om.* H₂ illis²] illi B   20 ipsius] eius BV   sempiterna quoque] et sempiterna V   ita *om.* HV = Vg   ut sint *om.* H₁   inexcusabilis H₁   21 cognouerunt AG1/2V magnificauerunt BG1/2V   23 incorruptibilis *om.* G   similitudine BH₂ imaginis] in imaginis B   et quadrupedum *om.* B   24 inmunditia H   adficiant] efficiant G   in semet ipsis] inter semet ipsos B   25 dei *om.* ES   mendacio BV   est] + deus R   saecula] + amen H₂V = Vg   26 nam] + et B usum² *om.* B   27 et¹ *om.* BH₁   femineo V   in inuicem HV = Vg   operantes] exercentes B   ipsos] ipsis HG = Vg   28 probauerunt] existimauerunt B notitia A = Vg   eos] illos BRG   faciunt SH₂   et quae HG   29 repletus H₁: + enim G   iniquitate *om.* ES   et¹ *om.* AESV = Vg   fornicationem H   et² *om.* AH₁V = Vg   auaritiam H   nequitia plenos] pl. neq. BSRH₂G: pl. nequitiae E homicidio] homicidiis BV   malignitate] malitia B   30 susurrones] susurratores B   obaudientes V   31 insipientes incompositos] inc. ins. G^corr.: insensatos inc. B   affectione] + absque foedere HGV = Vg

intellexerunt quoniam qui talia agunt digni sunt morte · non solum qui
ea faciunt sed et qui consentiunt facientibus.

2: 1 propter quod inexcusabilis es o homo omnis qui iudicas in quo
enim iudicas alterum te ipsum condemnas eadem enim agis qui
iudicas · 2 scimus enim quoniam iudicium dei est secundum ueritatem in eos qui talia agunt · 3 existimas autem hoc o homo qui
iudicas eos qui talia agunt et facis ea quia tu effugies iudicium dei
4 an diuitias bonitatis eius et patientiae et longanimitatis contemnis
ignorans quoniam benignitas dei ad paenitentiam te adducit ·
5 secundum duritiam autem tuam et inpaenitens cor · thesaurizas tibi
iram in die irae et reuelationis iusti iudicii dei · 6 qui reddet unicuique
secundum opera eius · 7 his quidem qui secundum patientiam boni
operis · gloriam et honorem et incorruptionem · quarentibus uitam
aeternam · 8 his autem qui ex contentione · qui non adquiescunt
ueritati credunt autem iniquitati · ira et indignatio · 9 tribulatio et
angustia · in omnem animam hominis operantis malum Iudaei
primum et Graeci · 10 gloria autem et honor et pax omni operanti
bonum · Iudaeo primum et Graeco · 11 non est enim personarum
acceptio aput deum · 12 quicumque enim sine lege peccauerunt sine
lege peribunt et quicumque in lege peccauerunt per legem iudic-
abuntur · 13 non enim auditores legis iusti sunt aput deum sed
factores legis iustificabuntur · 14 cum enim gentes quae legem non
habent · naturaliter quae legis sunt faciunt · eius modi legem non
habentes ipsi sibi sunt lex · 15 qui ostendunt opus legis scriptum in
cordibus suis testimonium reddente illis conscientia · ipsorum et inter
se inuicem cogitationum accusantium aut etiam defendentium 16 in
die cum iudicabit deus occulta hominum · secundum euangelium
meum per Iesum Christum · 17 si autem tu Iudaeus cognominaris ·

32 faciunt ea B: faciunt illa V   facientibus] + ea H₂
2: 1 propter quod] propterea B   iudicas alterum] alterum iud. V: alium iud. B
qui] quae AHG   2 enim] autem BV   quoniam] quod G   aui talia agunt *om.*
B   3 autem *om.* G   homo] + omnis BH₁G   eos] de his B   et . . . dei *om.*
H₂   quia] quoniam AH₂   4 ignoras HG   benignitas] bonitas B   5 aut.
dur. B   cor inp. B: cor sine penitentia V   iusti iudicii] iudicis G   6 reddit
BRMNF   eius] sua BG   7 secundum] + deum A   incorr.] corruptionem B
8 contentione] + et incredulitate sunt B   qui²] et qui BH   non adquiescunt] diffi-
dunt AV   ueritate[m] H₁   autem] enim H₂   iniquitatem SR   9 Greco G
10 omni] + homini BE   11 est enim] enim est EᵐˢV: est H: enim EG   aput
deum acc. A   12 lege²] + et AMCF = Vg   lege³] legem B   13 sed *om.* A*
iustificabuntur] + apud deum B   15 ipsorum *om.* A   inter *om.* B   inu.
se BH₂   cogitationibus accusantibus aut et defendentibus B: cogitationum (-ibus
Nᶜᵒʳʳ·) inuicem accusantium (-ibus Nᶜᵒʳʳ·) aut etiam defendentium (-ibus Nᶜᵒʳʳ·) H₂
16 iudicauerit HG   Christum] + dominum nostrum BV   17 tu *om.* H₁

et requiescis in lege · et gloriaris in deo 18 et nosti uoluntatem · et
probas utiliora instructus per legem · 19 confidis te ipsum ducem esse
caecorum · lumen eorum qui in tenebris sunt · 20 eruditorem
insipientium · magistrum infantium · habentem formam scientiae et
ueritatis in lege · 21 qui ergo alium doces te ipsum non doces · qui
praedicas non furandum furaris · 22 qui dicis non moechandum
moecharis · qui abominaris idola sacrilegium facis · 23 qui in lege
gloriaris per praeuaricationem legis deum inhonoras · 24 nomen enim
dei per uos blasphematur inter gentes sicut scriptum est ·
25 circumcisio quidem prodest si legem obserues si autem
praeuaricator legis sis circumcisio tua praeputium facta est · 26 si
igitur praeputium iustitias legis custodiat nonne praeputium illius in
circumcisione reputabitur · 27 et iudicabit quod ex natura est praeputium legem consummans te qui per litteram et circumcisionem
praeuaricator legis es · 28 non enim qui in manifesto Iudaeus est
neque quae in manifesto in carne circumcisio 29 sed qui in abs-
condito Iudaeus est · et circumcisio cordis in spiritu non littera cuius
laus non ex hominibus sed ex deo est.

3: 1 quid ergo amplius est Iudaeo aut quae utilitas circumcisionis
2 multum per omnem modum · primum quidem quia credita sunt illis
eloquia dei · 3 quid enim si quidam illorum non crediderunt numquid
incredulitas illorum fidem dei euacuabit absit · 4 est autem deus
uerax · omnis autem homo mendax · sicut scriptum est ut iustificeris
in sermonibus tuis et uincas cum iudicaris · 5 si autem iniquitas
nostra iustitiam dei commendat quid dicemus numquid iniquus deus ·
qui infert iram · secundum hominem dico 6 absit · alioquin quo modo
iudicabit deus hunc mundum · 7 si enim ueritas dei in meo mendacio
abundauit in gloriam ipsius · quid adhuc et ego tamquam peccator
iudicor · 8 et non sicut blasphemamur et sicut aiunt nos quidam

18 nosti] scis B   uoluntatem] + eius HG   20 eruditorum MN   infantum
H₂ abentem A   21 praedicas] dicis A   22 dicis] doces BR   abominaris]
exsecraris B   24 enim *om.* A   sicut *om.* V   est] enim V   25 obserues]
obseruas G: custodias BV   26 iustitias . . . praeputium *om.* B   iustitias *om.* H₁
custodit G   illius] eius B   circumcisionem A = Vg   reputabitur] putatur B*:
reputatur G   27 2: 27–3: 9 *om.* G   praeputio ES   consummans] perficiens B
circumcisione ES   es legis B   legis sis H₂   28 in *om.* BSM   quae] qui
S*R   in manifesto] manifesta MN: manifeste C: palam B   carne *om.* B
29 abscondito] absconso V: occulto B   est *om.* ESH₂V = Vg   circumcisio] in circumcisione V   in] qui AV   est *om.* BMN

3: 1 utilitatis B   2 multum . . . modum *om.* B   multum] + quidem E
3 si *om.* B   quidam] quidem EMN   illorum¹] eorum B   illorum²] eorum H
euacuauit ECV   4 homo] + sit B   iudicaueris V   5 dei iust. B
dicimus H₁V   6 absit sec. hom. dico A   7 gloria HV   et *om.* V

dicere · faciamus mala ut ueniant bona · quorum damnatio iusta est ·
9 quid ergo tenemus amplius causati enim sumus Iudaeos et Grecos
omnes sub peccato esse · 10 sicut scriptum est quia non est iustus
quisquam · 11 non est intellegens non est requirens deum · 12 omnes
declinauerunt · simul inutiles facti sunt · non est qui faciat bonum non
est usque ad unum · 13 sepulcrum patens est guttur eorum · linguis
suis dolose agebant · venenum aspidum · sub labiis eorum · 14 quorum
os maledictione · et amaritudine plenum est · 15 ueloces pedes eorum
ad effundendum sanguinem · 16 contritio et infelicitas in uiis eorum ·
17 et uiam pacis non cognouerunt · 18 non est timor dei ante oculos
eorum · 19 scimus autem quoniam quaecumque lex loquitur his qui in
lege sunt loquitur · ut omne os obstruatur · et subditus fiat omnis
mundus deo · 20 quia non iustificabitur ex operibus legis omnis caro
coram illo · per legem enim cognitio peccati · 21 nunc autem sine lege
iustitia dei manifestata est · testificata a lege et prophetis · 22 iustitia
autem dei per fidem Iesu Christi super omnes qui credunt · non enim
est distinctio · 23 omnes enim peccauerunt et egent gloria dei · 24 iustificati gratis per gratiam ipsius · per redemptionem quae est in
Christo Iesu · 25 quem proposuit deus · propitiatorem fidei in
sanguine ipsius ad ostensionem iustitiae suae · propter propositum
praecedentium delictorum · 26 in sustentione dei · ad ostensionem
iustitiae eius in hoc tempore · ut sit ipse iustus et iustificans eum qui
ex fide est Iesu Christi · 27 ubi est ergo gloriatio tua exclusa est · per
quam legem factorum non · sed per legem fidei · 28 arbitramur enim
iustificari hominem per fidem sine operibus legis · 29 an Iudaeorum
deus tantum nonne et gentium · immo et gentium · 30 quoniam
quidem unus deus qui iustificat · circumcisionem ex fide et praeputium per fidem · 31 legem ergo destruimus per fidem absit sed legem
statuimus.

    4: 1 quid ergo dicemus inuenisse Abraham · patrem nostrum

8 ueniant] + nobis H₂   9 igitur H = Vg   tenemus amplius] praecellimus eos
nequaquam H = Vg   17 agnouerunt A   20 quoniam B   ex op. leg. non
iust. om. caro HG = Vg: non iustificatur om. caro ex. op. leg. B   pecc. cogn. G
21 sine . . . manif. *om.* V   per legem et prophetas B   22 Chr. Iesu B   super]
in omnes et super V: nominis et super B   credunt] + in eum B   23 enim *om.*
ES   gloriam HGV = Vg   24 redemptorem B   25 propitiationem H =
Vg   fidei] per fidem H = Vg: + per fidem V   sanguinem ER   ad . . . suae *om.* A
ad] in V   suae] eius V   propositum] remissionem HG = Vg   26 sustenta-
tionem ERG   eius] suae B   et *om.* BV   est *om.* B   Christi *om.* H₁MNCFV =
Vg   27 ergo *om.* B   tua *om.* A = Vg   fidei] dei B   29 tant. deus G
30 quoniam] si B   iustificauit ASRH₂   31 ergo] + et (*exp.*) B   destruemus G
    4. 1 dicimus ESH₂GV

secundum carnem · 2 si enim Abraham ex operibus iustificatus est
habet gloriam sed non aput deum · 3 quid enim scriptura dicit
credidit Abraham deo · et reputatum est illi ad iustitiam · 4 ei autem
qui operatur merces non imputatur secundum gratiam · sed secundum debitum · 5 ei uero qui non operatur credenti autem in eum qui
iustificat impium reputatur fides eius ad iustitiam · secundum
propositum gratiae dei · 6 sicut et Dauid dicit beatitudinem hominis ·
cui deus accepto fert iustitiam sine operibus · 7 beati quorum
remissae sunt iniquitates et quorum tecta sunt peccata 8 beatus uir
cui non inputauit dominus peccatum · 9 beatitudo ergo haec in
circumcisione an etiam et in praeputio · dicimus enim quia reputata
est Abrahae fides ad iustitiam · 10 quo modo ergo reputata est in
circumcisione cum esset an in praeputio · non in circumcisione sed in
praeputio · 11 et signum accepit circumcisionis · signaculum iustitiae
fidei quae est in praeputio · ut sit pater omnium credentium per
praeputium ut reputetur et illi ad iustitiam 12 et sit pater circumcisionis non his tantum qui sunt ex circumcisione sed et his qui
sectantur uestigia quae est in praeputio fidei patris nostri Abrahae ·
13 non enim per legem promissio Abrahae aut semini eius · ut heres
esset mundi sed per iustitiam fidei · 14 si enim qui ex lege heredes
sunt exinanita est fides abolita est promissio · 15 lex enim iram
operatur · ubi enim non est lex nec praeuaricatio 16 ideo ex fide ut
secundum gratiam firma sit promissio omni semini non ei qui ex lege
est solum sed et ei qui ex fide est Abrahae qui est pater omnium
nostrum · 17 sicut scriptum est quia patrem multarum gentium posui
te · ante deum cui credidit · qui uiuificat mortuos · et uocat quae non

---

2 operibus] + legis HG   3 enim] ergo HG   illi] ei G   illi ad] illud A*
4 mercis S*MN*GV   imputatur] reputatur E: inputabitur V   sed sec. deb. *om.* SR
5 uero] autem B   credenti autem] credentes G   eum] eo B   impium] + per
fidem B   reputatur] deputatur B   gratiae *om.* A   dei gr. G   7 sunt[2] *om.*
A*   9 ergo *om.* G   circumcisione] + tantum dicta est B: + tantum manet EG:
+ manet SRH₂   etiam et] etiam HGV = Vg: *om.* B   praeputium H₁MNF   fid.
Abr. G   10 reputata] deputata B   est] ei E   cum esset *om.* HV = Vg   esse
B   11 circumcisionem V   per praeputium] in praeputio B   ut[2] ... Abrahae
om. A   ut[2] ... iustitiam] ut illi accepto feratur iustitia B   et *om.* E   illis H₂ = Vg
·12 et] ut V   non his tantum] qui non solum B   non] + in G   ex] in G   his[2]]
eorum B   sectantur] secuntur B   uestigia] + eius H₁G   quae est in praep. fid.
om. B   13 promissio] + facta est B   14 lege] + hi[i] H₂G[corr.]   exinanita]
euacuata B   15 ubi ... nostrum *om.* A   lex non est G   neque E
16 gratiam] + ut V = Vg   semini] semine MN: + eius B   non] + et E   et *om.*
GV   est Abrahae] Abraham B   nostrorum ES   17 quia *om.* G   deum]
eum B   credidit] credidisti deo B: credidisti H₁G   uiuificat] iustificat B   uocat]
ea BH₁G

sunt tamquam ea quae sunt · 18 qui contra spem in spem credidit · ut
fieret pater multarum gentium secundum quod dictum est sic erit
semen tuum · 19 et non est infirmatus in fide non considerauit corpus
suum emortuum cum fere centum annorum esset et emortuam
uuluam Sarrae · 20 in repromissione etiam dei non haesitauit diffi-
dentia sed confortatus est fide · dans gloriam deo 21 plenissime sciens
quia quaecumque promisit potens est et facere · 22 ideo et reputatum
est illi ad iustitiam · 23 non est autem scriptum tantum propter ipsum
quia reputatum est illi 24 sed et propter nos quibus reputabitur ·
credentibus in eum qui suscitauit Iesum dominum nostrum a mortuis · 25 qui traditus est propter delicta nostra et surrexit propter
iustificationem nostram.

5: 1 iustificati igitur ex fide pacem habeamus ad deum per dominum nostrum Iesum Christum · 2 per quem et accessum habemus per
fidem in gratia ista · in qua stamus · et gloriamur in spe gloriae
filiorum dei · 3 non solum autem sed et gloriamur in tribulationibus
scientes quod tribulatio patientiam operatur · 4 patientia autem
probationem probatio uero spem · 5 spes autem non confundit · quia
caritas dei diffusa est in cordibus nostris · per spiritum sanctum qui
datus est nobis · 6 ut quid enim Christus cum adhuc infirmi essemus ·
secundum tempus · pro impiis mortuus est · 7 uix enim pro iusto quis
moritur · nam pro bono forsitan quis audeat mori · 8 commendat
autem suam caritatem deus in nobis · quoniam cum adhuc peccatores
essemus · Christus pro nobis mortuus est 9 multo igitur magis iustificati nunc · in sanguine ipsius salui erimus ab ira per ipsum · 10 si
enim cum inimici essemus reconciliati sumus deo per mortem filii

tamquam . . . sunt *om.* B   ea *om.* V   18 contra] praeter B   spem²] spe
BH₁MNFG   est] + ei H₁G   tuum] + sicut stellae et arena V   19 et . . . fide
om. G   est *om.* HV = Vg   inf. est G   in *om.* H₁C = Vg   considerabat V
suum] + iam BG   fere cent. ess. ann. H₁G: esse. fere cent. ann. V: ess. cent. fere ann.
B   emorturam B   20 etiam] autem B   deffidentia BMN*   est *om.* H₁
fide] in fide G   21 quoniam BV   promisit] + deus EH₁   et *om.* B
22 ideo et reputatum] propter quod deputatum B   et *om.* ES   23 prop. ips.
tant. B   ipsum] illum A   reputatum] deputatum B   illi] + ad iustitiam BEC
24 et *om.* G   dom. nost. Ies. V   dominum nostrum *om.* B   nostrum] + Christum
BSG   25 surrexit] resurrexit HGV = Vg   propter *om.* B
5: 1 Ies. Chr. dom. nost. R   2 per quem] pacem B   habeamus BRV   per
fidem] fidei A: fide V = Vg   gratia ista] gratiam istam H₂V: gloriam istam B   gloria
H₂   filiorum *om.* BV   3 autem] + hoc BG   tribulationibus] + nostris B
scientes . . . probationem *om.* G   4 uero] autem BSRH₂   spem] spetie B
5 confundet SR   6 quid enim] quidem B   7 audeat] + etiam EH₂G
8 deus su. car. B   nos A* = Vg   quoniam] + si BV   9 igitur *om.* BV
iustificati *om.* G

eius · multo magis reconciliati salui erimus in uita ipsius · 11 non
solum autem sed et gloriamur in deo per dominum nostrum Iesum
Christum · per quem nunc reconciliationem accepimus · 12 propter
ea sicut per unum hominem in hunc mundum peccatum intrauit et per
peccatum mors · et ita in omnes homines mors pertransiit in quo
omnes peccauerunt · 13 usque ad legem enim peccatum erat in
mundo · peccatum autem non imputatur cum lex non est · 14 sed
regnauit mors ab Adam usque ad Mosen etiam in eos qui non peccauerunt in similitudinem praeuaricationis Adae · qui est forma
futuri · 15 sed non sicut delictum ita et donum · si enim unius delicto
multi mortui sunt multo magis gratia dei et donum in gratia unius
hominis Iesu Christi in plures abundauit · 16 et non sicut per unum
peccantem ita et donum · nam iudicium ex uno in condemnationem ·
gratia autem ex multis delictis in iustificationem · 17 si enim unius
delicto mors regnauit per unum multo magis abundantiam gratiae et
donationis et iustitiae accipientes in uita regnabunt per unum Iesum
Christum · 18 igitur sicut per unius delictum in omnes homines in
condemnationem sic et per unius iustitiam in omnes homines in
iustificationem uitae · 19 sicut enim per inoboedientiam unius
hominis peccatores constituti sunt multi ita et per unius oboedientiam
iusti constituentur multi · 20 lex autem subintrauit ut abundaret
delictum · ubi autem abundauit delictum superabundauit gratia ·
21 ut sicut regnauit peccatum in mortem ita et gratia regnet per
iustitiam in uitam aeternam per Iesum Christum dominum nostrum.

6: 1 quid ergo dicemus permanebimus in peccata ut gratia abundet
2 absit · qui enim mortui sumus peccato quo modo adhuc uiuemus in
illo · 3 an ignoratis · quia quicumque baptizati sumus in Christo Iesu ·
in morte ipsius baptizati sumus · 4 consepulti enim sumus cum illo

---

11 autem] + hoc B   gloriemur G   12 intrauit] introit B   mors[2] *om.* BRV
pertransiuit E: pertransiet MN   13 erat *om.* B   in] + hoc BGV   imputa-
batur RN*   14 etiam] et B: + et S   non *om.* B   similitudine B   futura E
15 sed] nam ESH₂   donum¹] gratia B   enim] + in S   16 unum] + hominem
ES   peccantem] delictum B   iudicium] + quidem BG   iustificatione BES
17 unius] in unius H₂V = Vg: omnibus B   mors . . . unum] regnat mors ut ab Adam
usque ad Moysen B   unum] + hominem V   donationis et] donum B   uitam
AG   regnabimus B   18 in¹ *om.* ESG   et *om.* G   in³ *om.* G   iustificatione B   uitae *om.* G   19 peccatoris B   multi] plurimi B   oboedientiam]
oboeditionem ARH₂ = Vg: obauditionem V   constituuntur H: constituiuntur G
20 superhabundabit G   21 ut . . . nostrum *om.* H₂   sicut] quem ad modum B
morte GV = Vg   et *om.* G
6: 1 permaneamus B   2 qui enim] nam qui B   adhuc] iterum B   uiuimus
SRMNG   3 ignoratis] + fratres BR   quoniam BV   sumus¹] estis H₁
4 per bap. cum illo B   cum illo *om.* ES

per baptismum in mortem ut quo modo Christus surrexit a mortuis per gloriam patris ita et nos in nouitate uitae ambulemus · 5 si enim complantati facti sumus similitudini mortis eius simul et resurrectionis erimus · 6 hoc scientes quia uetus homo noster · simul crucifixus est · ut destruatur corpus peccati ut ultra non seruiamus peccato · 7 qui enim mortuus est iustificatus est a peccato · 8 si autem mortui sumus cum Christo credimus quia simul etiam uiuemus cum illo · 9 scientes quod Christus surgens ex mortuis iam non moritur mors illi ultra non dominabitur · 10 quod enim mortuus est peccato mortuus est semel · quod autem uiuit uiuit deo · 11 ita et uos existimate uos mortuos quidem esse peccato uiuentes autem deo in Christo Iesu · 12 non ergo regnet peccatum in uestro mortali corpore ut oboediatis concupiscentiis eius · 13 sed neque exhibeatis membra uestra arma iniquitatis peccato · sed exhibete uos deo tamquam ex mortuis uiuentes · et membra uestra arma iustitiae deo · 14 peccatum enim in uobis non dominabitur non enim sub lege estis · sed sub gratia · 15 quid ergo peccabimus quoniam non sumus sub lege sed sub gratia · absit · 16 nescitis quoniam cui exhibetis uos seruos ad oboediendum serui estis eius cui oboeditis siue peccati siue oboeditionis iustitiae · 17 gratias autem deo quod fuistis serui peccati · oboedistis autem ex corde · in eam formam doctrinae in qua traditi estis 18 liberati autem a peccato serui facti estis iustitiae · 19 humanum dico propter infirmitatem carnis uestrae sicut enim exhibuistis membra uestra seruire inmunditiae et iniquitati ad iniquitatem ita nunc exhibete membra uestra seruire iustitiae in sanctificationem · 20 cum enim serui essetis peccati liberi eratis iustitiae · 21 quem ergo fructum habuistis tunc in quibus nunc erubescitis nam finis illorum mors est 22 nunc uero liberati a peccato serui autem facti deo · habetis fructum uestrum in sanctificatione

morte SMN*V   quo modo] quem ad modum B   sur. Chr. A = Vg
5 facti *om.* B   6 crucifixus est] confixus est cruci B   8 autem] enim BES
simul *om.* B   uiuimus SRMN   illo] Christo HV = Vg   9 ex] a G   illi] in
eum B   ultra] iam B   10 uiuit² *om.* B   11 mort. uos B   quidem *om.* V
esse *om.* B   12 non ergo] non enim H₁: igitur non B   ut . . . eius] ad oboediendum illi B   14 enim] inquit B   non dom. in uob. B   in *om.* R = Vg   dominetur ESH₂   estis sub lege BHG   15 peccauimus H₁MNFGV = Vg   non
om. G   16 exhibuistis BG   oboedistis BSNCFGV   peccati] + in mortem B:
+ ad mortem R   oboeditionis] + eius E   iustitiae] ad iustitiam HG = Vg
17 autem] enim H₂   peccatis B   oboedistis autem] sed oboed. B   ea forma
ERMNF   quam A   18 liberati autem] nunc uero lib. B   a *om.* A*   facti]
fac A   19 sicut] si B   inmunditiae] iniustitiae G   uestra² *om.* B   iustitiae
om. B: iustificatione G   20 ess. ser. B   eratis] fuistis A = Vg   21 tunc]
aliquando in his B: + in his S   22 facti *om.* B   sanctificationem ER*N = Vg

finem uero uitam aeternam · 23 stipendia enim peccati mors · gratia
autem dei uita aeterna · in Christo Iesu domino nostro.

7: 1 an ignoratis fratres scientibus enim legem loquor quia lex in
homine dominatur quanto tempore uiuit · 2 nam quae sub uiro est
mulier uiuente uiro alligata est legi si autem mortuus fuerit uir soluta
est a lege uiri · 3 igitur uiuente uiro uocabitur adultera si fuerit cum
alio uiro si autem mortuus fuerit uir eius liberata est a lege ut non sit
adultera si fuerit cum alio uiro · 4 itaque fratres mei et uos mortificati
estis legi · per corpus Christi · ut sitis alterius · qui ex mortuis resurrexit ut fructificaremus deo · 5 cum enim essemus in carne passiones
peccatorum quae per legem erant operabantur in membris nostris · ut
fructificarent morti · 6 nunc autem soluti sumus a lege morientes in
quo detinebamur · ita ut seruiamus in nouitate spiritus et non in
uetustate litterae · 7 quid ergo dicemus lex peccatum est · absit · sed
peccatum non cognoui nisi per legem · nam concupiscentiam nescie-
bam nisi lex diceret non concupisces · 8 occasione autem accepta
peccatum per mandatum · operatum est in me omnem concupiscentiam · sine lege enim peccatum mortuum erat · 9 ego autem uiuebam
sine lege aliquando · sed cum uenisset mandatum · peccatum reuixit ·
10 ego autem mortuus sum · et inuentum est mihi mandatum quod
erat ad uitam hoc esse ad mortem · 11 nam peccatum occasione
accepta per mandatum seduxit me et per illut occidit 12 itaque lex
quidem sancta et mandatum sanctum et iustum et bonum · 13 quod
ergo bonum est mihi factum est mors absit · sed peccatum ut appareat
peccatum per bonum mihi operatum est mortem · ut fiat supra
modum peccans peccatum per mandatum · 14 scimus enim quod lex
spiritalis est · ego autem carnalis sum · uenundatus sub peccato
15 quod enim operor non intellego non enim quod uolo hoc ago sed
quod odi illud facio · 16 si autem quod nolo illut facio consentio legi

23 stipendium B   mors] + est A*   dei *om.* H₂   uitam eternam B(E)SMN*
7: 1 enim *om.* A*   dom. hom. in B   2 alligata est] ligata est *bis* B   fu. mort.
B   uir] + eius BHG   3 cum alio] iuncta alteri B   lege] + uiri HG: + uiri ita
B   4 ex] a F   resurrexit] + uiri B   fructificemus A   5 peccatores G*
6 morientes] mortis BHG   quo] qua BHG   ut *om.* ES   7 dicimus ESMN
sed] nam V: + ego B   dic. lex G   concupiscis V   8 occa[n]sionem H
autem] ergo B   acceptam H   9 aliq. sine lege B   sed cum uenisset] at ubi
uenit B   uenisset] uenit V   10 ad¹] in B   uita ℟   ad²] in B   morte ℟
11 occa(n)sionem SR*N*   occidit] + me B   12 quidem *om.* H₂   13 factum est mors] mors est B: factum mors V   operatus B*   supra] super ℟
modum] + ipsum B   peccans peccatum] peccatum delinquens B: peccant pecc. A*
mandatum] + legis B   14 enim] autem B   quod] quia BR: quoniam ℟MNC
15 hoc *om.* B   odii MN*: odio G   16 si] sed B   autem] ergo B   nolo]
odi B

quoniam bona · 17 nunc autem iam non ego operor illut · sed quod
habitat in me peccatum · 18 scio enim quia non habitat in me hoc est
in carne mea bonum · nam uelle adiacet mihi · perficere autem bonum
non inuenio · 19 non enim quod uolo bonum hoc facio sed quod nolo
malum hoc ago · 20 si autem quod nolo illut facio non ego operor illut
sed quod habitat in me peccatum · 21 inuenio igitur legem uolenti
mihi facere bonum quoniam mihi malum adiacet · 22 condelector
enim legi dei secundum interiorem hominem · 23 uideo autem aliam
legem in membris meis repugnantem · legi mentis meae · et captiuantem me in lege peccati quae est in membris meis · 24 infelix ego homo
quis me liberabit de corpore mortis huius · 25 gratia dei per Iesum
Christum dominum nostrum · igitur ego ipse mente seruio legi dei ·
carne autem legi peccati.

8: 1 nihil ergo nunc damnationis est his qui sunt in Christo Iesu qui
non secundum carnem ambulant · 2 lex enim spiritus uitae in Christo
Iesu · liberauit te a lege peccati et mortis · 3 nam quod impossibile
erat legis · in quo infirmabatur per carnem · deus filium suum mit-
tens · in similitudine carnis peccati · et de peccato damnauit peccatum
in carne · 4 ut iustificatio legis impleretur in nobis qui non secundum
carnem ambulamus sed secundum spiritum · 5 qui enim secundum
carnem sunt quae carnis sunt sapiunt qui uero secundum spiritum
quae sunt spiritus sentiunt · 6 nam prudentia carnis mors est prudentia autem spiritus uita et pax · 7 quoniam sapientia carnis inimica est
deo legi enim dei non subicitur · nec enim potest · 8 qui autem in
carne sunt · deo placere non possunt · 9 uos autem in carne non estis
sed in spiritu · si tamen spiritus dei habitat in uobis · si quis autem
spiritum Christi non habet hic non est eius · 10 si autem Christus in
uobis est corpus quidem mortuum est propter peccatum · spiritus

quoniam bona] *om.* B: + est HG   17 ill. op. B   18 scio enim] nam scio B
quoniam B: quod V   inhabitat AH₂   adiecit ESMN*   19 bonum hoc
om. B   20 illut facio] hoc ago B   ill. op. B   inhabitat V   21 uolentem
H₁MNFG   bon. fac. B   quia B   malum adiacet] inest malum B
22 enim] + uoluntate B   23 autem *om.* H   leg. al. H₂1/2   meis¹] + et H₂
legi] legem ES   captiuantem me] captiuum me ducentem B   quae] quod A
24 liberauit H₁MNFV   25 ser. men. G   legi²] lege V
    8: 1 ambulant] + sed secundum spiritum BV1/2   2 Iesu] + et B   liberabit
MN   te] me HG = Vg   3 inpossibili MN*G*   legi R^corr·N^corr·C   infirma-
batur] confirmabatur B: infirmabamur G*   misit B   similitudinem BH₁MNFG =
Vg   5 quae¹] qui B   spir. sunt H₂G   7 sapientia] prudentia HG   est
om. A*   deo] in deum RH₂   enim] autem HG   subicitur] est subiecta BV
8 autem] enim HG   9 non est. in car. R   tamen] autem H₂   Christi] dei B
10 si] sic MN   mortuus MN*

uero uiuit propter iustitiam · 11 quod si spiritus eius qui suscitauit
Iesum a mortuis habitat in uobis qui suscitauit Iesum Christum a
mortuis uiuificabit et mortalia corpora uestra propter inhabitantem
spiritum eius in uobis · 12 ergo fratres debitores sumus non carni ut
secundum carnem uiuamus · 13 si enim secundum carnem uixeritis
moriemini · si autem spiritu facta carnis mortificaueritis uiuetis ·
14 quicumque enim spiritu dei aguntur hii filii sunt dei · 15 non
enim accepistis spiritum seruitutis iterum in timore sed accepistis
spiritum adoptionis filiorum · in quo clamamus abba pater · 16 ipse
spiritus testimonium reddit spiritui nostro quod sumus filii dei ·
17 si autem filii et heredes heredes quidem dei coheredes autem
Christi · si tamen compatiamur · ut et simul glorificemur · 18 exis-
timo enim quod non sunt condignae passiones huius temporis · ad
futuram gloriam quae reuelabitur in nobis · 19 nam expectatio
creaturae reuelationem filiorum dei expectat · 20 uanitati enim creatura · subiecta est · non uolens sed propter eum qui subiecit in
spem 21 quia et ipsa creatura liberabitur a seruitute corruptionis in
libertatem gloriae filiorum dei · 22 scimus enim quod omnis creatura congemescit et parturit usque athuc · 23 non solum autem illa
sed et nos ipsi primitias spiritus habentes et ipsi intra nos gemimus
adoptionem filiorum · expectantes redemptionem corporis nostri
24 spe enim salui facti sumus · spes autem quae uidetur non est spes
nam quod uidet quis quid sperat · 25 si autem quod non uidemus
speramus per patientiam expectamus · 26 similiter autem et spiritus
adiuuat infirmitatem nostram · nam quid oremus sicut oportet nesci-
mus · sed ipse spiritus postulat pro nobis gemitibus inenarrabilibus ·
27 qui autem scrutatur corda scit quod desideret spiritus · quia
secundum deum postulat pro sanctis · 28 scimus autem quoniam

---

uero] autem ESG   uiuit] uita AHV = Vg: uita uiuit R   iustitiam] iustificationem
AHGV = Vg   11 Chr. Ies. V   Iesum *om.* B   Christum *om.* R   uiuificauit
H,V   et *om.* R   12 simus B   13 spiritu] per spiritum B   mortificatis
A = Vg   14 enim] autem ESG   dei[1] *om.* G   hi BC   dei sunt G
15 filiorum] filiorum dei R: dei filiorum G   16 ipse] + enim B   reddet H,
17 compatimur E^corr.R^corr.N*   et *om.* A   simul *om.* HG   18 non sunt condig-
nae] indignae sunt B   nobis] uobis G   19 filiorum *om.* V   20 uolens]
sponte B   subiecit] + eam B   spe BRN^corr.C^corr.GV   21 quia] quoniam B
libertate BESMNC^corr.F   22 enim] autem BV   ingemescit V = Vg   et] +
aeque A   23 ipsi] qui B   primitias] receptaculum B   habemus B   et[2] *om.*
A: nos B   nos[2] *om.* B   adoptionem filiorum] *om.* BV: + dei RH,G   24 enim]
ergo B   uidet] uidit MNV   speret G*   25 si autem] sed si B   26 et
om. HG   spiritus] deus G*   infirmitati B   nostram] nostrae orationis BV
pro nobis *om.* B1/2   innarrabilis MN*   27 corda *om.* B   28 autem] *om.* R

diligentibus deum omnia cooperantur in bonum · his qui secundum propositum uocati sunt · 29 nam quos praesciuit · et praedestinauit conformes fieri imaginis filii eius · ut sit ipse primogenitus in multis fratribus · 30 quos autem praedestinauit hos et uocauit et quos uocauit hos et iustificauit quos autem iustificauit illos et magnificauit · 31 quid ergo dicemus ad haec si deus pro nobis quis contra nos · 32 qui etiam filio suo non pepercit · sed pro nobis omnibus tradidit illum · quo modo non etiam cum illo omnia nobis donauit · 33 quis accusabit aduersus electos dei deus qui iustificat 34 quis est qui condemnet · Christus Iesus qui mortuus est immo qui et resurrexit qui et est ad dexteram dei · qui etiam interpellat pro nobis · 35 quis ergo nos separabit a caritate Christi tribulatio an angustia an persecutio an fames an nuditas an periculum an gladius 36 sicut scriptum est · quia propter te morte adficimur tota die · aestimati sumus ut oues occisionis · 37 sed in his omnibus superamus propter eum qui dilexit nos · 38 certus sum enim quia neque mors neque uita neque angeli neque principatus neque instantia neque futura neque fortitudines 39 neque altitudo neque profundum · neque creatura alia poterit nos separare a caritate dei · quae est in Christo Iesu domino nostro.

9: 1 ueritatem dico in Christo non mentior testimonium mihi perhibente conscientia mea in spiritu sancto 2 quoniam tristitia est mihi magna et continuus dolor cordi meo · 3 optabam enim ipse ego anathema esse a Christo pro fratribus meis qui sunt cognati mei secundum carnem 4 qui sunt Istrahelitae · quorum adoptio est filiorum · et gloria et testamenta et legis latio · et obsequium et promissa · 5 quorum patres · et ex quibus Christus secundum carnem qui est

deum] bonum B   omnia cooperantur] concurrunt om. B: om. procedunt V
sunt] + sancti BHG = Vg   29 nam *om.* BV   praesciit B   imaginis] + gloriae
B   eius] sui B   primog. ipse B   30 et quos uocauit *om.* B   iustificauit]
sanctificauit B   quos autem iustificauit *om.* B   illos et] hos autem B   magnifi-
cauit] honorificauit B   31 dicimus H_1MN*FG   ad] aduersus V   32 qui]
si deus V   etiam *om.* BV   filio suo] + proprio B   omn. nob. cum illo V
omnes G*   donabit A = Vg   33 quis] quid B   accus[s]auit E*RG*V
aduersus *om.* A   deus] + est G   34 condemnet] contemnet G*: + simul autem
B   Iesus *om.* B   et[1] *om.* BMN* = Vg   et[2] *om.* BHG   est[3]] etiam sedet H_2
35 ergo *om.* H = Vg   separauit H_1GV   caritate] dilectione B   famis SRMNFV
36 morte adficimur] morti aff. B: mortificamur ESH$_2$G = Vg: mortificabimur R
occisiones R*M*   37 nos dil. B   38 certus sum] confido B   angelus V
principatus] initia B   neque futura *om.* B   fortitudines] uirtus B: fortitudo HGV
39 alia creat. B   a *om.* B   dei *om.* V1/2

9. 1 Christo] + Iesu B   2 mihi magna est H   3 an. esse ego ipse B: an.
esse ipse ego V   mei *om.* B   4 Israelitae A   est *om.* BH$_2$ et[1] *om.* B
testamentum HG   et promissa *om.* B   5 et *om.* B   quibus] + est R

super omnia deus benedictus in saecula · 6 non autem excidit uerbum
dei · non enim omnes qui ex Istrahel hii sunt Istrahelitae 7 neque quia
semen sunt Abrahae omnes filii · sed in Isaac uocabitur tibi semen ·
8 id est non qui filii carnis hii filii dei sed qui filii sunt promissionis
aestimantur in semine · 9 promissionis enim uerbum hoc est secundum hoc tempus ueniam et erit Sarrae filius · 10 non solum autem sed
et Rebecca · ex uno concubitu habens Isaac patre nostro · 11 cum
enim nondum nati fuissent aut aliquit egissent bonum aut malum ut
secundum electionem propositum dei maneret · 12 non ex operibus
sed ex uocante dictum est quia maior seruiet minori · 13 sicut scriptum est Iacob dilexi Esau autem odio habui · 14 quid ergo dicemus
numquit iniquitas aput deum absit · 15 Mosi enim dicit miserebor
cuius misereor et misericordiam praestabo cuius miserebor · 16 igitur
non uolentis neque currentis sed miserentis dei · 17 dicit enim
scriptura Pharaoni quia in hoc ipsum excitaui te ut ostendam in te
uirtutem meam et ut adnuntietur nomen meum in uniuersa terra ·
18 ergo cui uult miseretur et quem uult indurat 19 dicis itaque mihi
quid athuc quaeritur uoluntati enim eius quis resistit · 20 o homo tu
quis es qui respondeas deo numquit dicit figmentum ei qui se finxit ut
quid me fecisti sic · 21 aut non habet potestatem figulus luti ex eadem
massa facere aliut quidem uas in honorem aliut uero in contumeliam ·
22 quod si uolens deus ostendere iram et notam facere potentiam
suam sustinuit in multa patientia · uasa irae apta in interitum · 23 et ut

omnes B   saecula] + amen H₂GV = Vg   6 autem] enim H₁G*: + quod HG =
Vg   exciderat E*R*: exciderit SCE^corr·G(?) = Vg: excederit MN: excideret R^corr·
hi BRH₂   Istrahelitae] Israhel V = Vg   7 nec B   quia] qui SG   sunt
semen B   semine E^corr·MN   filii] + dei H₁   8 qui¹ *om.* B   hi BRC
filii¹] + sunt V   prom. sunt BH₁G   promissionis] repromissionis H₂   semen A
10 autem] + illi B   Rebeccae B   concubito V   habent A*   patrem nostrum
H₁MNF: patris nostri BCV   11 cum enim] nam cum B: qui cum V   egissent]
elegissent G   boni C   aut] uel B   mali C   electionem . . . maneret] propositum quod per electionem dei factum est permanerit B   12 uocante] uocatione
BESMNC*F   est] *om.* G: + ei HGV = Vg   min. seru. B   13 autem *om.* R
14 dicimus HG^corr·   15 Moses B   cuius¹] cui BEH₂GV   miserebor] misertus
ero B   cuius²] cui BSRH₂V   miserebor] misericordiam praestitero B: misertus ero
G   16 non] + est B   uolentes E*M   currentis E*M   miserantis
BMNFG*: + est BHG   17 ipso B   te exc. B   ut² *om.* HG   uniuersam
terram G   18 cui] cuius A = Vg   uult¹] + deus B   19 quid] quod MN: +
agitur B: + igitur V   queritur ESH₂G = Vg   uol. enim] nam uol. G   resistit]
resistere poterit G   20 ut *om.* HV = Vg   ut quid] quare V   21 aut] an
AC = Vg   habit MN*   potestatem *om.* V   figulis MN*   honore BESG
uero] autem B: *om.* H₂   contumelia BEG   22 deus *om.* B   iram] + suam V
notam facere] manifestare B   sustinuit *om.* BV   uasa] in uasis B: in uasa V
apta] praeparatis B: aptata V = Vg   23 et *om.* HG = Vg

ostenderet diuitias gloriae suae in uasa misericordiae quae praepara-
uit in gloriam · 24 quos et uocauit nos non solum ex Iudaeis sed etiam
ex gentibus 25 sicut in Osee dicit uocabo non plebem meam plebem
meam et non misericordiam consecutam misericordiam consecutam
26 et erit in loco ubi dictum est eis non plebs mea uos ibi uocabuntur
filii dei uiui · 27 Esaias autem clamat pro Istrahel · si fuerit numerus
filiorum Istrahel tamquam harena maris reliquiae saluae fient ·
28 uerbum enim consummans et breuians in aequitate quia uerbum
breuiatum faciet dominus super terram · 29 et sicut praedixit Esaias ·
nisi dominus sabaoth reliquisset nobis semen sicut Sodoma facti
essemus et sicut Gomorra similes fuissemus · 30 quid ergo dicemus
quod gentes quae non sectabantur iustitiam adprehenderunt iustitiam · iustitiam autem quae ex fide est · 31 Istrahel uero sectans legem
iustitiae in legem non peruenit 32 quare quia non ex fide sed quasi ex
operibus · offenderunt enim in lapidem offensionis 33 sicut scriptum
est ecce pono in Sion lapidem offensionis et petram scandali · et
omnis qui credit in eum non confundetur.

10: 1 fratres uoluntas quidem cordis mei et obsecratio ad deum fit
pro illis in salutem · 2 testimonium enim perhibeo illis quod aemulationem dei habent sed non secundum scientiam · 3 ignorantes enim
dei iustitiam et suam quaerentes statuere iustitiae dei non sunt
subiecta · 4 finis enim legis Christus ad iustitiam omni credenti ·
5 Moses enim scripsit iustitiam quae ex lege est · quoniam qui fecerit
ea homo uiuet in eis · 6 quae autem ex fide est iustitia sic dicit ne
dixeris in corde tuo quis ascendit in caelum id est Christum deducere
7 aut quis descendit in abyssum hoc est Christum ex mortuis reuocare
8 sed quid dicit scriptura prope est uerbum in ore tuo et in corde
tuo · hoc est uerbum fidei quod praedicamus · 9 quia si confitearis

uasis B   gloria B   24 nos *om.* H₁   25 dicit] + et B   mis. con. mis.
om. B   consecutam²] dilectam B   26 et erit] erit enim B   dictum est eis]
uocabuntur B   uos *om.* B   27 salui H₁G   fierit A*: fiant ER   28 quoniam BG   breu. uerb. H*₂   29 sicut²] quasi H₂   30 dicimus ESH₂G
quae¹ *om.* B   iustitiam³] iustitia ASRH₂G   31 Ist. uero] nam Ist. B   sec-
tando BRV   legem²] + iustitiae HGV = Vg   32 quasi] + non (*exp.*) B
operibus] + legis H₁H₂1/2   offendunt G: offendit V   enim *om.* BV   33 cre-
diderit H₁NCF   eo H₁NCF
10: 1 quidem *om.* G   deum] dominum B   sit pro illis R: pro illis sit B
2 enim *om.* B   secundum] + dei A   3 suam] + iustitiam B   iustitiae] +
enim G   4 Christus] + est B   credendi V   5 Moses *in ras.* A   scripsit]
+ quoniam HG = Vg   iustitia H₁   quoniam *om.* HGV = Vg   ea *om.* HG = Vg
uiuit H₁MNF   eis] ea HG = Vg   6 quis] qui F   ascendet A^corr.   id] hoc B
7 descendet A   ex] a A   reuocare] reducere B   8 quit A*   scriptura *om.*
ESH₁GV = Vg   9 quia] quod H₂

in ore tuo dominum Iesum et in corde tuo credideris quod deus illum
excitauit a mortuis · saluus eris · 10 corde enim creditur ad iustitiam
ore autem confessio fit in salutem · 11 dicit enim scriptura omnis qui
credit in illum · non confundetur · 12 non enim est distinctio Iudaei et
Graeci nam idem dominus omnium diues in omnibus qui inuocant
illum 13 omnis enim quicumque inuocauerit nomen domini saluus
erit · 14 quo modo ergo inuocabunt in quem non crediderunt · aut
quo modo credent ei quem non audierunt quo modo autem audient
sine praedicante 15 quo modo uero praedicabunt nisi mittantur ·
sicut scriptum est quam speciosi pedes euangelizantium pacem
euangelizantium bona · 16 sed non omnes obaudierunt euangelio ·
Esaias enim dicit domine quis credidit auditui nostro · 17 ergo fides
ex auditu auditus autem per uerbum · 18 sed dico numquit non
audierunt · in omnem terram exiit sonus eorum et in fines orbis terrae
uerba eorum · 19 sed dico numquid Istrahel non cognouit · primus
Moses dicit · ego ad aemulationem uos adducam in non gentem in
gentem insipientem in iram uos mittam · 20 Esaias autem audet et
dicit inuentus sum non quaerentibus me · palam apparui his qui
me non interrogabant · 21 ad Istrahel autem quid dicit · tota die
expandi manus meas · ad populum non credentem et contradicentem.

11: 1 dico ergo numquit reppulit deus populum suum absit · nam et
ego Istrahelita sum · ex semine Abraham de tribu Beniamin · 2 non
reppulit deus plebem suam quam praesciit · an nescitis in Helia quid
dicit scriptura · quem ad modum interpellat deum aduersus Istrahel ·
3 domine prophetas tuos occiderunt altaria tua suffoderunt et ego
relictus sum solus et quaerunt animam meam · 4 sed quid dicit illi
responsum diuinum reliqui mihi septem milia uirorum · qui non

in *om.* B   dom. Ies. ore tuo B   cred. in cor. tuo B   illum excitauit] suscitauit
illum B   a] ex V = Vg   10 in] ad BH₁N*CFG   11 omnis] + enim B
illo H₁MNFG   confunditur MN   12 non enim] nam non ESG   Graeci]
gentis G   in omnibus] *om.* E: in omnes SH₂GV = Vg   13 enim] autem B
14 ergo] enim (*eras.*) ergo A: *om.* G   inuocabunt] + eum B   credent] credunt RM
15 quo modo uero] aut quo modo B   uero *om.* V   mittantur] missi fuerint B
16 oboediunt BHGV   enim] autem G   credit A*   17 uerbum] + Christi
H₁MNCG = Vg: + dei FV   18 audierunt] + et quidem HGV = Vg   exiuit
BHG   in . . . eorum] reliqua H₂   19 primus Moses] Moses primum B: primum
Moses Nᶜᵒʳʳ: Moses primus V   non in E   in gentem *om.* EG*   20 autem *om.*
BV   audit MN   inuentus sum] palam factus sum B: apparui V   sum] + a H₂
palam apparui] inuentus sum BV   his] ab his B: inter eos V   21 quid] quia B
populum] plebem B   contradicentem] + mihi BHG

11: 1 ergo] igitur B   populum suum] hereditatem suam BV   absit *om.* G
Abrahae C   de *om.* V = Vg   Benialnin A: Beniabin G*   2 suam] meam G
praesciuit HG   quem ad modum] quo modo B   interpellat] postulat B   aduer-
sus] contra B   3 animam *partim in ras.* A   4 quid] qui SM

curuauerunt genu ante Bahal · 5 sic ergo et in hoc tempore · reliquiae secundum electionem gratiae saluae factae sunt · 6 si autem gratia non ex operibus · alioquin gratia iam non est gratia · 7 quid ergo quod quaerebat Istrahel hoc non est consecutus · electio autem consecuta est · ceteri uero excaecati sunt 8 sicut scriptum est · dedit illis deus spiritum compunctionis oculos ut non uideant et aures ut non audiant · usque in hodiernum diem · 9 et Dauid dicit fiat mensa eorum in laqueum et in captionem et in scandalum et in retributionem illis 10 obscurentur oculi eorum ne uideant et dorsum illorum semper incurua · 11 dico ergo numquit sic offenderunt · ut caderent absit · sed illorum dilecto salus gentibus ut illos aemulentur · 12 quod si delictum illorum diuitiae sunt mundi et diminutio eorum diuitiae gentium quanto magis plenitudo eorum · 13 uobis enim dico gentibus · quamdiu ego sum gentium apostolus ministerium meum honorificabo · 14 si quo modo aemuler carnem meam · ut saluos faciam aliquos ex illis · 15 si enim amissio eorum reconciliatio est mundi · quae adsumptio nisi uita ex mortuis · 16 quod si delibatio sancta est et massa · et si radix sancta et rami · 17 quod si aliqui ex ramis fracti sunt · tu autem cum oleaster esses · insertus es in illis et socius radicis et pinguedinis oliuae factus es · 18 noli gloriari aduersus ramos quod si gloriaris non tu radicem portas sed radix te · 19 dicis ergo fracti sunt rami ut ego inserar 20 bene propter incredulitatem fracti sunt · tu autem fide stas · noli altum sapere sed time · 21 si enim deus naturalibus ramis non pepercit ne forte nec tibi parcat · 22 uide ergo bonitatem et seueritatem dei · in eos quidem qui ceciderunt seueritatem in te autem bonitatem · si permanseris in bonitate · alioquin et tu exci-

curuata sunt G   genua HG: genua sua B   ante *om.* H$_1$ = Vg   5 ergo] igitur B   **reliquiae A: reliqui ES   saluae] salui ES: *om.* V = Vg   facti H$_1$
6 autem] enim H$_2$ gratia] + iam BHG   7 quid] quod B   quod *om.* B
quaerebant A*   8 illis] eis H$_2$ compunctionis] computationis B   9 et]
praem. sicut B   eorum] ipsorum G: + coram ipsis H$_1$G   in^3 *om.* SRNC
10 eorum] Iudeorum B*   ne] ut non B   illorum] eorum BRH$_2$ 11 ergo] igitur B   dilecto] *Souter:* delicto ABH$_2$GV = Vg: delicti A^{ms}: delictum H$_1$ gentium
AH$_2$G   12 illorum] eorum G   sunt *om.* G   mundo V   diuitiae^2] + sunt G
13 quamdiu] + quidem H$_2$G = Vg   meum] me enim B: nostrum E   honorificabo]
inlustrabo B   14 aemuler] ad aemulandum prouocem HG = Vg   ut] et HV =
Vg: et ut (ut *exp.*) G   15 quae] + est BHG   adsumptio nisi] adsumptionis BS
uitae BN$^{corr.}$ 16 delibatio] deliberatio B   est *om.* B   si^2] sit B
17 esses oleaster B   esses] sis G   socius] + factus es BV   ping. et rad. A
radices SRV   et *om.* B   factus es *om.* BV   18 aduersum B   si] + tu G
tu] tu* G   portat B   19 dices N   ergo] + si B   insererer B
20 propter incredulitatem] in incredulitate B: prop. incredulitate E   sunt] + rami M
sta HAG   22 bonitatem^2] + dei HGV = Vg   bonitate] bonitatem B

deris 23 sed et illi si non permanserint in incredulitate inserentur ·
potens est enim deus iterum inserere illos · 24 nam si tu ex naturali
excisus es oleastro · et contra naturam insertus es in bonam oliuam
quanto magis hii secundum naturam inserentur suae oliuae · 25 nolo
enim uos ignorare fratres · mysterium hoc · ut non sitis uobis ipsis
sapientes · quia caecitas ex parte contigit Istrahel · donec plenitudo
gentium intraret 26 et sic omnis Istrahel saluus fieret · sicut scriptum
est ueniet ex Sion qui eripiat et auertat inpietates ab Iacob · 27 et hoc
illis a me testamentum cum abstulero peccata eorum · 28 secundum
euangelium quidem inimici propter uos · secundum electionem
autem carissimi propter patres · 29 sine paenitentia enim sunt dona et
uocatio dei · 30 sicut enim aliquando et uos non credidistis deo · nunc
autem misericordiam consecuti estis propter illorum incredulitatem ·
31 ita et isti nunc non crediderunt in uestra misericordia · ut et ipsi
misericordiam consequantur · 32 conclusit enim deus omnia in
incredulitate · ut omnibus misereatur · 33 o altitudo diuitiarum
sapientiae et scientiae dei · quam incomprehensibilia sunt iudicia
eius · et inuestigabiles uiae eius · 34 quis enim cognouit sensum
domini · aut quis consiliarius eius fuit · 35 aut quis prior dedit illi et
retribuetur ei · 36 quoniam ex ipso et per ipsum et in ipso omnia · ipsi
gloria in saecula amen.

12: 1 obsecro itaque uos fratres · per misericordiam dei · ut exhibeatis corpora uestra · hostiam uiuentem sanctam · deo placentem ·
rationabile obsequium uestrum · 2 et nolite conformari huic saeculo
sed reformamini in nouitate sensus uestri ut probetis quae sit uoluntas
dei · quod bonum et beneplacitum et perfectum est · 3 dico enim per

23 sed et illi] et illi autem V   sed *om.* B   enim est H₂   iterum deus H₂
iterum] iter si B   24 ex *om.* R   es²] est MN   hii] hi BRCFV: *om.* MN
secundum] + suam B   25 enim] autem V   ign. uos B   mysterium] ministerium R*   uobis ipsis] ipsi uobis B: uobis ipsi SMNFV   ex parte *om.* V   contigit Istrahel] Ist. cont. B: cont. in Ist. HGV = Vg   26 et¹ *om.* V   sic *om.* ES
omnes H₁N*   saluos R*M   fierit MN*   sicut *om.* B   ueniat MN*   auertet
V = Vg   inpietates] captitates A: impietatem BHG   ab] *om.* A: ex B
28 secundum] *praem.* fratres B   inimici] amici B   carissimi] + sunt H₂
29 enim *om.* A*   30 et uos aliq. HG   credidisti G   incredulitatem] diffiden-
tiam BV   31 non *om.* E   uestram misericordiam BH₂G = Vg   32 omnia
deus B   incredulitatem A = Vg   omnium H = Vg   33 sapientiam A
incomprehensibilia] inscrutabilia G   iudicia] opera B   inuestigabilis AM   eius]
illius H₂   34 eius cons. BV   35 illi] ei B   et *om.* R*   retribuetur ei]
reddetur illi B   36 in ipso] + sunt BHG   saecula] + saeculorum BH₂G
amen *om.* H₂
12: 1 hostia A   uiuentem] uiuam B   rationabile] + sit G   . 2 confirmari
SR*N*   sensus uestri] mentis uestrae B   sit] est B   dei] domini R   quod...
est] bona et beneplacens et perfecta HG   et²] + quod V

gratiam quae data est mihi · omnibus qui sunt inter uos · non plus
sapere quam oportet sapere sed sapere ad sobrietatem · et unicuique
sicut deus diuisit · mensuram fidei · 4 sicut enim in uno corpore multa
membra habemus · omnia autem membra non eundem actum habent ·
5 ita multi unum corpus sumus in Christo singuli autem alter alterius
membra · 6 habentes autem donationes secundum gratiam quae data
est nobis differentes · siue prophetiam secundum rationem fidei ·
7 siue ministerium in ministrando · siue qui docet in doctrina 8 qui
exhortatur in exhortando · qui tribuit in simplicitate · qui praeest in
sollicitudine · qui miseretur in hilaritate · 9 dilectio sine simulatione
odientes malum adhaerentes bono · 10 caritate fraternitatis inuicem
diligentes · honore inuicem praeuenientes · 11 sollicitudine non
pigri · spiritu feruentes · domino seruientes · 12 spe gaudentes · in
tribulatione patientes · orationi instantes · 13 necessitatibus sanctorum communicantes · hospitalitatem sectantes · 14 benedicite
persequentibus uos benedicite et nolite maledicere · 15 gaudere cum
gaudentibus flere cum flentibus · 16 id ipsum inuicem sentientes ·
non alta sapientes sed humilibus consentientes · nolite esse prudentes
aput uosmet ipsos · 17 nulli malum pro malo reddentes · prouidentes
bona non tantum coram deo sed etiam coram hominibus · 18 si fieri
potest quod ex uobis est cum omnibus hominibus pacem habentes ·
19 non uosmet ipsos defendentes carissimi sed date locum irae ·
scriptum est enim mihi uindictam ego retribuam dicit dominus ·
20 sed si esurit inimicus tuus ciba illum si sitit potum da illi · hoc
enim faciens carbones ignis congeres supra caput eius · 21 noli uinci a
malo sed uince in bono malum.

13: 1 omnis anima potestatibus sublimioribus subdita sit · non est
enim potestas nisi a deo · quae autem sunt a deo ordinatae sunt ·

3 gratiam] + dei ERH₂GV   oportit V   sed sapere *om.* G*   sobrietatem]
prudentiam BG   4 mem. aut. omn. B   hab. act. B   actuum MN*
5 corpus *om.* V   Christo] + Iesu B   6 donationes] + diuersas B   differ-
entes] differentiae B   prophetia B: prophetiae H₁MNF   7 in¹ *om.* B
9 odientes] exsecrantes B   bonum RMN   10 caritatem H(R*N*)GV = Vg
fraternitatis] fraterna B   diligentes] benigni B   honorem SR*MV   inuicem²]
mutuo B   11 sollicitudinem H₁   12 in trib. pat. *om.* A   oratione SR*G
14 ben. pers. uos *om.* B   persequentes V   15 gaudete BG   flete BG
16 id] *praem.* in ES   inuicem] + de uobis B   prud. esse H₁G   17 nulli] noli
M: non N   reddentes ... *13: 12* abiciamus *om.* B   coram²] + omnibus SR = Vg
hominibus *om.* ERMNF   18 hominibus *om.* ERMNF   19 dicit dominus
om. V   20 sed *om.* V   esurierit SRH₂GV = Vg   sitat V   faciendo V
congerens E: congeris SRMNFG*V   supra] super HG = Vg   21 uince] uinci
MN*   bonum MN*
13: 1 est] estis V   potestas] + data H₂   ordinata ERNCFG

2 itaque qui resistit potestati dei ordinationi resistit qui autem resistunt ipsi sibi damnationem adquirunt · 3 nam principes non sunt timori boni operis sed mali · uis autem non timere potestatem · bonum fac et habebis laudem ex illa · 4 dei enim minister est tibi in bonum · si autem malum feceris time non enim sine causa gladium portat · dei enim minister est uindex in iram ei qui malum agit · 5 ideo necessitate subditi estote non solum propter iram sed et propter conscientiam · 6 ideo enim et tributa praestatis ministri enim dei sunt in hoc ipsum seruientes · 7 reddite ergo omnibus debita · cui tributum tributum cui uectigal uectigal · cui timorem timorem · cui honorem honorem · 8 nemini quicquam debeatis · nisi ut inuicem diligatis · qui enim diligit proximum · legem impleuit · 9 nam non adulterabis non occides non furaberis non concupisces et si quod est aliut mandatum in hoc uerbo restauratur diliges proximum tuum sicut te ipsum · 10 dilectio proximi malum non operatur · plenitudo ergo legis est dilectio · 11 et hoc scientes tempus quia hora est iam nos · de somno surgere · nunc autem propior est nostra salus quam cum credidimus · 12 nox praecessit dies autem adpropinquabit · abiciamus ergo opera tenebrarum et induamur arma lucis · 13 sicut in die honeste ambulemus · non in comisationibus et ebrietatibus non in cubilibus et inpudicitiis · non in contentione et aemulatione · 14 sed induite dominum Iesum Christum · et carnis curam ne feceritis in desideriis.

14: 1 infirmum autem in fide adsumite · non in disceptationibus cogitationum · 2 alius enim credit manducare omnia · qui autem infirmus est · holera manducet · 3 is qui manducat non manducantem non spernat et qui non manducat manducantem non iudicet · deus enim illum adsumpsit · 4 tu quis es qui iudices alienum seruum · suo

---

2 ordinationis S: ordinationem M: ordinatione G   adq. damn. N   damnationem *om.* M   3 principis G*   timoris H₁MNF   operis boni E: operi bono SG   malo G   autem] enim H₂   4 deus MN   enim¹] etenim A^corr.   si] se G*   male HGV = Vg   non ... est *om.* G   enim²] etenim A^corr.   male H₂   5 ideoque R   necessitati E*SR^corr.C^corr.   et *om.* H₁   6 ideo] + non G*   ipso HG   8 neminem H₁M: nemine G   quicquid G   proximum] + suum ESG   9 furaberis] furaueris V: + non falsum testimonium dices HG   in hoc uerbo *om.* V   restauratur] instauratur HG = Vg   diligis A*SR*MN*V   sicut] tamquam V = Vg   11 et *in ras.* G   autem] enim HGV = Vg   propior] proprior A*H₁MNFGV: propinquior C   credimus ER   12 adpropinquauit SRMNCF: appropriabit V   13 in³ *om.* A*   in⁴ *om.* A*V   14 induimini HG   feceritis] perficeritis H₁G   desideriis] concupiscentiis B

14: 2 enim] autem B   manducare] + se C   infirmus est] infirmatur B   holus AHV = Vg   3 is] *om.* B: his MNR*   non² *om.* H₁   spernet G*   manducat²] + et (*eras.*) A   deus enim] nam deus B   ads. illum B   4 qui] quis in (s *eras.*) G   iudicas BHG

domino stat aut cadit · stabit autem potens est enim deus statuere
illum · 5 nam alius iudicat diem inter diem alius iudicat omnem diem
unus quisque in suo sensu abundet · 6 qui sapit diem domino sapit · et
qui manducat domino manducat gratias enim agit deo · et qui non
manducat domino non manducat et gratias agit deo · 7 nemo enim
nostrum sibi uiuit et nemo sibi moritur 8 siue enim uiuimus domino
uiuimus siue morimur domino morimur siue ergo uiuimus siue
morimur domini sumus · 9 in hoc enim Christus et mortuus est et
resurrexit ut et mortuorum et uiuorum dominetur · 10 tu autem quid
iudicas fratrem tuum · aut tu qua re spernis fratrem tuum · omnes
enim stabimus ante tribunal dei · 11 scriptum est enim uiuo ego dicit
dominus quoniam mihi flectetur omne genu et omnis lingua confite-
bitur deo · 12 itaque unus quisque nostrum pro se rationem reddet
deo · 13 non ergo amplius inuicem iudicemus · sed hoc iudicate magis
ne ponatis offendiculum fratri uel scandalum · 14 scio et confido in
domino Iesu quia nihil commune per ipsum · nisi ei qui existimat quid
commune esse illi commune est · 15 si enim propter cibum frater tuus
contristatur · iam non secundum caritatem ambulas · noli cibo tuo
illum perdere pro quo Christus mortuus est · 16 non ergo blas-
phemetur bonum nostrum · 17 non est enim regnum dei esca et
potus · sed iustitia et pax et gaudium in spiritu sancto · 18 qui enim in
hoc seruit Christo placet deo et probatus est hominibus · 19 itaque
quae pacis sunt sectemur · et quae aedificationis sunt in inuicem
custodiamus · 20 noli propter escam destruere opus dei · omnia
quidem munda sunt · sed malum est homini qui per offendiculum
manducat · 21 bonum est non manducare carnem et non bibere̦

enim est C   enim] autem EG*   statue A*: stature B   5 diem inter diem]
alterno quoque die B   diem¹] + plus H₂ = Vg   alius] + autem B   diem³] + ut B
6 et¹ *om.* V   enim] autem B   non domino G*   8 domino² . . . morimur³ *om.*
A (*add. ms*)   ergo] ego A: *om.* B: enim V   9 enim] ergo EG: + uixit B   Chris-
tus] + et uixit V   et¹ *om.* SR   resurrexit] reuixit ESMNFG = Vg   mortuorum et
uiuorum] uiuentium et mort. B: uiuorum et mort. V   10 quid] qui ERG*
tuum¹] + in non manducando B   sprer E: spernas SR: spernes M   tuum²] + in
manducando B   omnes enim] nam omnes B   11 scriptum est enim] sicut
scriptum est H₁G   flectet ESMNR^{corr.}FGV = Vg: flectit R*   conf. omn. ling. BV
omnis] omni G*   deo] domino H₂   12 nostrum] nomen G*   reddat B: reddit M   deo *om.* B   13 inuicem *om.* A   offendiculum] offensionem B
14 commune¹] + cibum B   per] + se B   existimat] haec estimat G*   quid]
aliquid G^{corr.}   illi commune est *om.* B   15 si enim] nam si B   cibum] escam
B   cibo tuo] esca tua B   16 nost. bon. B   17 enim *om.* HGV = Vg
          18 homibus V   19 itaque] + ergo B   aedificationes SM*   in *om.*
BHG   custodiamus *om.* V = Vg   20 sunt *om.* B   offendiculum] offensionem
B   manducat *om.* MN   21 non est B*   non² *om.* G   bib. non B

uinum · neque in quo frater tuus offendit aut scandalizatur · aut
infirmatur · 22 tu fidem habes penes temet ipsum habe coram deo ·
beatus qui non iudicat semet ipsum in eo quo probat · 23 qui autem
discernit si manducauerit damnatus est · quia non ex fide · omne
autem quod non est ex fide peccatum est.

15: 1 debemus autem nos firmiores imbecillitates infirmorum sus-
tinere · et non nobis placere 2 unus quisque uestrum proximo suo
placeat · ad bonam aedificationem · 3 etenim Christus non sibi
placuit · sed sicut scriptum est improperia improperantium tibi
ceciderunt super me · 4 quaecumque enim scripta sunt ad nostram
doctrinam scripta sunt · ut per patientiam et consolationem scriptur-
arum spem habeamus · 5 deus autem patientiae et solacii · det uobis id
ipsum sapere in alterutrum secundum Iesum Christum · 6 ut unani-
mes uno ore honorificetis deum et patrem domini nostri Iesu Christi ·
7 propter quod suscipite inuicem · sicut et Christus suscepit uos in
honorem dei · 8 dico enim Christum Iesum ministrum fuisse circumcisionis propter ueritatem dei · ad confirmandas promissiones
patrum · 9 gentes autem super misericordiam honorare deum · sicut
scriptum est propter hoc confitebor tibi in gentibus et nomini tuo
cantabo · 10 et iterum dicit laetamini gentes cum plebe eius · 11 et
iterum dicit laudate dominum omnes gentes et magnificate eum
omnes populi 12 et rursus Isaias ait erit radix Iesse · et qui exsurget
regere gentes in eo gentes sperabunt · 13 deus autem spei · repleat uos
omni gaudio et pace in credendo · ut abundetis in spe in uirtute
spiritus sancti · 14 certus sum autem fratres mei et ego ipse de uobis ·
quoniam pleni estis dilectione · repleti omni scientia · ita ut possitis
alterutrum monere · 15 audacius autem scripsi uobis fratres ex parte ·
tamquam in memoriam uos reducens · propter gratiam quae data est

---

tuus *om.* B   offendet N*   22 fidem] + quam A   temet] te ER   semet]
se G   eo *om.* B   quod HGV   23 omne autem *om.* B   quod] quia B   est
om. B
    15: 2 uestrum *om.* BH₁G   ad bonam] in HG = Vg   3 sed *om.* BES
improperia *om.* A*   4 enim] autem HG   spem script. B   habeamus] + con-
solationis AV   5 sapere *om.* B   in alterutrum *om.* ESG*   Ies. Chr.] ipsum
Ies. B   6 unianimis EM   uno ore] in ore uno B: *om.* V   honorificemus V
7 et *om.* G   uos] nos B   honorem] gloriam B: honore G*   8 Ies. Chr. B
Iesum *om.* H₂   9 gente A*   misericordia EC   gentibus] + domine R
cant. nom. duo B   nomine E: in nomine SMNG: in nomini R   11 dicit] +
David A: *om.* HG = Vg   omn. gent. dom. H₁GV = Vg   12 rursus] iterum B:
rursum HG   ait] dicit B   exsurgit EM*N*V   gent. in eo sper. EG   eum
AᵐˢBRCV   13 pacem MN*   in³] et HG   14 autem sum B   autem]
enim R   fratres mei *om.* B   uobis] + fratres B   quoniam] + et ipsi HGV = Vg
possetis H₁MNFG   15 in … reducens] rememorans uobis B   uos *om.* ERG

mihi a deo · 16 ut sim seruiens Christo Iesu in gentibus · sanctificans
euangelium dei · ut fiat oblatio gentium accepta sanctificata in spiritu
sancto · 17 habeo igitur gloriam in Christo Iesu ad deum · 18 non
enim audeo aliquit loqui eorum quae per me non efficit Christus in
oboedientiam gentium · uerbo et factis 19 in uirtute signorum et
prodigorum in uirtute spiritus sancti · ita ut ab Hierusalem per
circuitum usque in Illyricum repleuerim euangelium Christi · 20 sic
autem hoc praedicaui euangelium non ubi nominatus est Christus ne
super alienum fundamentum aedificarem · 21 sed sicut scriptum est ·
quia quibus non est adnuntiatum de eo uidebunt et qui non audierunt
intellegent · 22 propter quod impediebar plurimum uenire ad uos ·
23 nunc uero ulterius locum non habens in his regionibus · cupiditatem autem habens ueniendi ad uos · ex multis iam praecedentibus
annis · 24 cum in Hispaniam proficisci coepero · spero quod praeteriens uideam uos et a uobis deducar illuc si uobis primum ex parte
fruitus fuero · 25 nunc igitur proficiscar in Hierusalem · ministrare
sanctis · 26 probauerunt enim Macedonia et Achaia collationem
aliquam facere · in pauperes sanctorum qui sunt in Hierusalem ·
27 placuit enim illis debitores enim sunt eorum · nam si spiritalium
eorum participes facti sunt gentiles debent et in carnalibus ministrare
eis · 28 hoc igitur cum consummauero et adsignauero eis fructum
hunc proficiscar per uos in Hispaniam 29 scio autem quoniam
ueniens ad uos in abundantiam benedictionis Christi ueniam ·
30 obsecro igitur uos fratres per dominum nostrum Iesum Christum

a deo *om.* C   16 seruiens] minister H_1MCFG = Vg: *om.* N   Iesu Christo A:
Christi Iesu HG = Vg   accepta *om.* BH_2 17 in *om.* G*   Christi G*
18 effecit R*M*N*   19 in[1] . . . prodigorum *om.* V   uirtute[1]] + eius B   sanc.
spir. H_2 ut] + compleretur B   per circuitum] *om.* B: in circuitu V   in[3]] *om.* B:
ad H_1G   repleuerim] et in circuitu B: repleuerint M   20 aedificem BV
21 sed . . . est *om.* V   adnuntiatum] nuntiatum BV   22 quod] + et HG = Vg
23 cupiditatem autem habens] cupio autem B   autem *om.* SR   ueniendi] uenire
BV   ex *om.* B   24 cum] *praem.* sed BHG   cum . . . coepero *om.* A*   prof.
coep. in Hisp. B   in *om.* G   Hispaniam] spaniam H_1: es paniam M: espianiam N:
ispianiam N[ms]   spero . . . praeteriens *om.* V   quod *om.* B   praeteriens] circuiens
B   uideam] uenire ad B   deducar] praemitti BV   si uobis] cum BV   fruitus]
fructus A   fuero] + uos V: + scio quia ueniens ad uos in complementum benedictionis Christi ueniam B; *uide u. 29 infra*   25 in *om.* HGV   ministrare sanctis *om.*
B   26 Machedonia A: Machedoniam G*   Achan B   sanctorum *om.* B   in
om. BHG   Hierusalem] + sanctis B   27 placuit enim illis *om.* BV   enim *om.*
G   illis] eis HG = Vg   deb. enim] et deb. HG = Vg   sunt] *om.* ES: sunnt V
nam] quoniam BV: + et H_2 si *om.* G*   spiritalem G*   et] + illi B
28 fructum hunc] factum tunc B   Spaniam H_1MNF   29 autem] enim B
quoniam] quod B   abundantia ESH_2V = Vg   benedictiones G*   30 igitur]
autem B   nostrum *om.* B

et per caritatem spiritus ut adiuuetis me in orationibus pro me ad deum · 31 ut liberer ab infidelibus qui sunt in Iudaea · et obsequii mei oblatio accepta fiat in Hierosolima sanctis 32 ut ueniam ad uos in gaudio per uoluntatem dei et refrigerer uobiscum · 33 deus autem pacis sit cum omnibus uobis amen.

16: 1 commendo autem uobis Foeben sororem uestram · quae est in ministerio ecclesiae quae est Cencris · 2 ut eam suscipiatis in domino digne sanctis et adsistatis ei in quocumque negotio uestri indiguerit etenim ipsa quoque adstitit multis et mihi ipsi · 3 salutate Priscillam et Aquilam adiutores meos in Christo Iesu · 4 qui pro anima mea suas ceruices subposuerunt quibus non solus ego gratias ago sed et cunctae ecclesiae gentium · 5 et domesticam eorum ecclesiam · salutate Epenetum dilectum mihi qui est primitiuus Asiae in Christo · 6 salutate Mariam quae multum laborauit in uobis 7 salutate Andronicum et Iuniam cognatos et concaptiuos meos qui sunt nobiles in apostolis qui et ante me fuerunt in Christo 8 salutate Ampliatum dilectissimum mihi in domino 9 salutate Urbanum adiutorem meum in Christo et Stachyn dilectum meum 10 salutate Appellen probum in Christo salutate eos qui sunt ex Aristobuli 11 salutate Erodionem cognatum meum salutate eos qui sunt ex

spiritus] + ac sollicitudinem B: + ut soll. V   ut *om.* BV   adiuuetis me] impertiamini mihi BV   me] pro me G   in . . . deum] ad dominum in orationibus (memorat S) H₁G   pro me] uestris BH₁G   deum] dominum BH₁G   31 et *om.* A   obsequii . . . sanctis] remuneratio mea quae Hierusalem est acceptabilis fiat sanctis suis B: ministerium meum quod (+ in N) Hierusolima defertur acceptabile sanctis fiat H₂   obsequiii mei A   oblatione G*   fiet EG*   in *om.* A   32 cum gaud. uen. ad uos B   gaudium H₁G*   dei] Christi Iesu BV   refrigerem B   33 uobis] nobis B   amen *om.* B
16: 1 Phebem BH₂: Phoebem H₁G — Vg: Foebem V   so***rorem A   uestram] nostram HGV — Vg: meam G (*sic Souter*)   Cheneris A*: Ceneris B: Cenchris HV — Vg: Chenchris G   2 susc. eam B   dignae G   sanctis] satis A^corr·H₂   et¹] ut B   quocumque] quibuscumque BV   negotio uestri indiguerit] desiderauerit nostri B: desid. uestri V   ipso G*   adstitit . . . ipsi] mihi et aliis adstitit B   adstitit] *praem.* ad A: adsistit H₁MNFG   3 Priscam HG* — Vg   4 ego solus B   solum HG   5 domestica memorum (m² *eras.*) A   eccl. eorum G   salutare B   Ephenetum A^ms SR*N^corr·CG^corr·: Ependitum B: Ephenium E: Ephenitum MN*G*: Epemen V   Christo] + Iesu H₁   7 Andronicam G*   Iuliam A^ms HG*: Iulium G^corr·   cognatus MN*   concaptiuuam in eos B: concaptiuus meus MN* in] inter MN   apostolos NC   qui] quia G   et³ *om.* B   Christo] + Iesu BSV 8 Ampleatum G*   dilectum B   9 meum¹] nostrum AG — Vg: mihi R in Christo *om.* M   Christo] domino B   Stachin BERCV: Stacin MN^corr·: Stacten N*: Stacihin G   meum² *om.* MN   10 Apellem B: Apellen SV — Vg: Appelen M salutatem G   ex] + domo BV   Aristoboli BEG — Vg: Arestobili E*: Arestopoli MN: Aristobolim V: + domo C   11 Herodionem BEG — Vg: Arudicionem M: Erudionem N   meum cogn. B   eos qui sunt *bis* B

Narcissi qui sunt in domino 12 salutate Tryphenam et Tryphosam
quae laborant in domino salutate Persidam carissimam quae multum
laborauit in domino 13 salutate Rufum electum in domino · et
matrem eius et meam · 14 salutate Asyncritum Phlegonta Hermem
Patrobam Herman et qui cum eis sunt fratres 15 salutate Philologum
et Iuliam Neream et sororem eius Olympiadem et omnes qui cum eis
sunt sanctos · 16 salutate inuicem in osculo sancto salutant uos omnes
ecclesiae Christi · 17 rogo autem uos fratres ut obseruetis eos qui
dissensiones et offendicula praeter doctrinam quam uos didicistis
faciunt et declinate ab illis 18 huius modi enim Christo domino
nostro non seruiunt sed suo uentri · et per dulces sermones et
benedictiones seducunt corda innocentium · 19 uestra enim oboedi-
entia in omnem locum prouulgata est · gaudeo igitur in uobis sed uolo
uos sapientes esse in bono et simplices in malo 20 deus autem pacis
conteret satanam sub pedibus uestris uelociter · 21 salutat uos
Timotheus adiutor meus et Lucius et Iason et Sosipater cognati mei
22 saluto uos ego Tertius qui scripsi epistulam in domino 23 salutat
uos Gaius hospes meus et uniuersa ecclesia salutat uos Erastus
arcarius ciuitatis et Quartus frater · 24 gratia domini nostri Iesu
Christi cum omnibus uobis amen · 25 ei autem qui potens est uos

---

Narcisci presbiteri B: Narcissi$_*$ G   sunt[2]] + presbyteri G   domino] Christo N
12 salute A*   Tryfernam B: Triphenam HG: Trifenam V: Tripherium G* *corr. in*
Triphenum *et postea in* Triphenam   Trifosam BV: Triphosam HG   quae[1]] qui G:
+ mecum multum B: + multum V   laborant] laborauerunt BV   Perfidam B
quae[2]] qui G*   13 electum] dilectum B: + meum HG   14 Asyncretum A[ms]:
Asmeritum B: Asencretum E*: Asincritum E[corr.]H₂G[corr.]V: Asincretum G*   Flegon-
tam BH₂: Pleconta[m] SR: Pleconta[m] E: Flegonta GV = Vg   Hermen B[corr.]HG =
Vg: Hermam R: Ermen V   Petrobam B   Herman] *om.* B: Hermam C[corr.] = Vg:
praem. et H₂   et] si V   sunt cum eis BV   eis] eius G   15 Filogum B: Philo-
cum ES: Philogum RM   Nereum HGV = Vg   eius] + et A*HG = Vg   Olimpi-
adem BH₁: Olibâ M: Olympam N: Olimpam C: Olymphiadem G   omnes *om.* B
sunt] omnes B   sanctis H₁G*   16 omnes *om.* B   17 ut obseruetis] dili-
genter obseruate B   dissensionis MN   dedicistis ESMNF   18 huius]
huiusce   domino nostro *om.* B   dulcis E*S   et benedictiones *om.* B
19 oboedientiam G*   omnem locum] omnes B: omni loco HG   prouulga A: diuul-
gata RH₂G = Vg: deuulgata ES   sed] et B   sapientes esse *bis* V   bonum
BH₁G*V   et simplices] sinceres autem B   malum BV   20 conterat HGV
Sathanam B: Satan M: Satanam N: Sathanan V   pedes uestros V   uestris *om.* A*
uelociter] + gratia domini nostri Iesu Christi uobiscum AH₂ = Vg; *uide u. 24 infra*: +
grat. dom. nos. uob. H₁G   21 salutat ... universa ecclesia (*u. 23*) *om.* A   salutant B   Lucas B   et Sosipater] pater G*   mei] + et ecclesia uniuersa Christi B
22 salutat B   Tereiius B   23 Gayus B   hospis E*V   uniuersa ecclesia]
uniu. eius eccl. C: uniuersae ecclesiae EG = Vg   Aristus A   et Quartus frater] *om.*
A   frater] superdispensator B   24 Iesu Christi *om.* H₁G   amen *om.* AV
25 ei] si B   potens] potest A*H₁G   est *om.* H₁G

confirmare · iuxta euangelium meum et praedicationem Iesu Christi · secundum reuelationem mysterii temporibus aeternis taciti 26 quod nunc patefactum est per scripturas prophetarum · secundum praeceptum aeterni dei ad oboeditionem fidei in omnes gentes cognitum 27 solo sapienti deo per Iesum Christum cui honor et gloria in saecula saeculorum amen.

confirmari H₁   secundum] iuxta B   tacete MN*   26 pactefactum B oboeditionem] obiectionem B   omnes gentes] cunctis gentibus AHG = Vg   cognito AHG = Vg: cogniti N^corr·F   27 soli BR^corr·N^corr·CG   cui] + est BH₂ honor et *om.* G   et gloria *om.* AHV = Vg   saecula] saela A*

Bibliography

I. SOURCES

Names of editor, short title (if necessary), and place and date of publication
are given only for editions which are not included in the series given in the list
of abbreviations at the beginning of the volume. Anonymous works are
entered under their abbreviated titles rather than under 'Anon.', which is here
reserved for the anonymous commentary on the Pauline epistles. The usual
reference for a commentary on an epistle of Paul is the abbreviated title of the
epistle in italics; these are to be distinguished from references to the epistles
themselves, which are in roman type.

Ambr. (Ambrose)

Abr.	*De Abraham* (CSEL 32)
Ep.	*Epistulae* (CSEL 82. 1, 3)
Esai.	*Expositio Esaiae prophetae* (CCSL 14)
Exam.	*Exameron* (CSEL 32)
Exc. Sat.	*De excessu fratris Satyri* (CSEL 73)
Fid.	*De fide* (CSEL 78)
Iac.	*De Iacob* (CSEL 32)
Luc.	*Expositio euangelii secundum Lucam* (CCSL 14)
Paenit.	*De paenitentia* (CSEL 73)
Ps.	*Explanatio super psalmos xii* (CSEL 64)
Ps. 118	*Expositio de psalmo cxviii* (CSEL 62)
Spir.	*De Spiritu Sancto* (CSEL 79)

Ambstr. (Ambrosiaster)

Quaest.	*Quaestiones ueteris et noui testamenti cxxvii* (CSEL 50)
Rom. (etc.)	*Commentarius in xiii epistulas Paulinas: ad Romanos* (etc.) (CSEL 81. 1)

Anon. (Anonymous) *Rom.* *Commentaria in epistulas apostoli Pauli, ad Romanos* (etc.), ed. H. J. Frede, *Ein neuer Paulustext und Kommentar*, i. *Untersuchungen* (Freiburg, 1973), ii. *Die Texte* (Freiburg, 1974)

Arnob. Iun. (Arnobius the Younger)
    Praed.   *Praedestinatus* (PL 53)

Athenag. (Athenagoras)
    Leg.   *Legatio*, ed. W. R. Schoedel (Oxford, 1972)

Aug. (Augustine)
    Ad Simpl.   *De diuersis quaestionibus ad Simplicianum* (CCSL 44)
    Agone chr.   *De agone christiano* (CSEL 41)
    Ciu.   *De ciuitate dei* (CCSL 47–8)
    Conf.   *Confessiones* (CCSL 27)
    Contin.   *De continentia* (CSEL 41)
    De gest. Pel.   *De gestis Pelagii* (CSEL 60)
    De grat. Chr.   *De gratia Christi et de peccato originali* (CSEL 60)
    De haer.   *De haeresibus* (CCSL 46)
    De mor.   *De moribus ecclesiae catholicae et de moribus Manichae-*
                             orum (PL 32)
    Diu. quaest.   *De diuersis quaestionibus lxxxii* (CCSL 44A)
    Duas ep.   *Contra duas epistulas Pelagianorum* (CSEL 60)
    En. in ps.   *Enarrationes in psalmos* (CCSL 38–40)
    Ep.   *Epistulae* (CSEL 44)
    Ep. fund.   *Contra epistulam Manichaei quam uocant fundamenti*
                             (CSEL 25)
    Exp. inch.   *Epistulae ad Romanos inchoata expositio* (CSEL 84)
    Exp. prop.   *Expositio quarundam propositionum ex epistula ad Ro-*
                             manos (CSEL 84)
    Faust.   *Contra Faustum Manichaeum* (CSEL 25)
    Fort.   *Contra Fortunatum Manichaeum* (CSEL 25)
    Gal.   *Epistulae ad Galatas expositionis liber i* (CSEL 84)
    Iul.   *Contra Iulianum* (PL 44)
    Lib. arb.   *De libero arbitrio* (CCSL 29)
    Maxim. Arian.   *Contra Maximium Arianum* (PL 42)
    Nat. bon.   *De natura boni contra Manichaeos* (PL 42)
    Parm.   *Contra epistulam Parmeniani* (CSEL 51)
    Pecc. merit.   *De peccatorum meritis et remissione et de baptismo*
                             (CSEL 60)
    Quaest. euang.   *Quaestiones euangeliorum* (CCSL 44B)
    Quaest. Gen.   *Quaestionum in Heptateuchum liber i: Quaestiones*
                             Genesis (CCSL 33)
    Serm.   *Sermones* (PL 38–9)
    Serm. dom.   *De sermone domini in monte* (CCSL 35)
    Solil.   *Soliloquia* (PL 32)
    Spir. et litt.   *De spiritu et littera* (CCSL 60)

Barn.   *Barnabae Epistula* (FP 1)

Bened. (Benedict of Nursia)
    Reg.   *Regula* (CSEL 75)

Caes. Arel. (Caesarius of Arles)
    Reg. mon.   *Regula monachorum* (PL 67)

Cas. (Cassiodorus)
    Inst.   *Institutiones* (PL 70)
    Rom.   *Expositio Pauli epistulae ad Romanos* (PL 68)

Cassian (John Cassian)
    Coll.   *Collationes* (CSEL 13)
    Inst.   *De institutis coenobiorum* (SC 109)

Celsus (A. Cornelius Celsus)
    Med.   *De medicina* (LCL 292)

Charisius
    Ars gramm.   *Ars grammatica*, ed. H. Keil, *Grammatici Latini* (Leipzig, 1957–80), vol. i

Chrom. (Chromatius of Aquileia)
    Serm.   *Sermones* (CCSL 9A)

Cic. (Cicero)
    De nat. deo.   *De natura deorum*, ed. A. S. Pease (Cambridge, Mass., 1955–8)
    Inu.   *De inuentione* (LCL 386)
    Re pub.   *De re publica* (LCL 213)
    Coll. Auell.   *Collectio Auellana* (CSEL 35)

Cypr. (Cyprian)
    Domin. orat.   *De dominica oratione* (CCSL 3A)
    Ep.   *Epistulae* (CSEL 3)
    Fort.   *Ad Fortunatum* (CCSL 3)
    Test.   *Ad Quirinum Testimoniorum libri iii* (CCSL 3)
    De cast.   *De castitate*, ed. C. P. Caspari, *Briefe, Abhandlungen und Predigten* (Christiana, 1890)
    De diu.   *De diuitiis*, ed. C. P. Caspari, *Briefe, Abhandlungen und Predigten* (Christiana, 1890)
    De diu. leg.   *De diuina lege* (PL 30)
    De indur. cord.   *De induratione cordis Pharaonis*, ed. G. Morin, in G. de Plinval, *Essai sur le style et la langue de Pélage* (Frieburg, 1947)
    Dial. Adam.   *Dialogus Adamantii* (GCS 4)
    Didasc. apost.   *Didascalia apostolorum*, ed. R. H. Connolly (Oxford, 1929)

Diog. Laert. (Diogenes Laertius)
    Vit. phil.   *Vitae philosophorum* (OCT)

Diomedes
    Ars gramm.   *Ars grammatica*, ed. H. Keil, *Grammatici Latini* (Leipzig, 1957–80), vol. i

Donatus
    Ars maior   *Ars maior*, ed. H. Keil, *Grammatici Latini* (Leipzig, 1957–80), vol. iv

Eus. Crem. (Eusebius of Cremona)
    Flor. Frising.   *Florilegium Frisingense* (CCSL 108D)

Greg. Naz. (Gregory of Nazianzus)
    Orat.   *Orationes* (SC 309)

Hil. (Hilary of Poitiers)
    Ps.   *Tractatus super psalmos* (CSEL 22)
    Trin.   *De trinitate* (CCSL 62–62A)

Iren. (Irenaeus)
    Demon.   *Demonstratio praedicationis apostolicae* (SC 62)
    Haer.   *Aduersus haereses* (SC 263–4, 293–4, 210–11, 100*–100**, 152–3)

Jer. (Jerome)
    Contra Rufin.   *Contra Rufinum* (CCSL 79)
    Ep.   *Epistulae* (CSEL 54–6)
    Esaiam   *Commentarii in Esaiam* (CCSL 73–73A)
    Gal. (etc.)   *Commentarii in iv epistulas Paulinas: ad Galatas* (etc.) (PL 26)
    Heluid.   *Aduersus Heluidium* (PL 23)
    Ioan.   *Liber contra Ioannem Hierosolumitanum* (PL 23)
    Iouin.   *Aduersus Iouinianum* (PL 23)

Just. (Justin Martyr)
    1 Apol.   *Apologia 1* (FP 2)
    Dial.   *Dialogus cum Tryphone Iudaeo*, ed. G. Archambault (Paris, 1909)

Lact. (Lactantius)
    Epit.   *Epitome diuinarum institutionem* (CSEL 19)
    Inst.   *Diuinae institutiones* (CSEL 19)
    Lib. pont.   *Liber pontificalis*, ed. L. Duchesne (Paris, 1955–7)

Mar. Merc. (Marius Mercator)
    Comm. super nom. Cael.   *Commonitorium super nomine Caelestii* (ACO 1. 5. 1)
    Lib. sub.   *Liber subnotationum in uerba Iuliani* (PL 48)

Mar. Vict. (Marius Victorinus)
    Adu. Arium   *Aduersus Arium* (SC 68)
    Gal. (etc.)   *Commentarii in epistulas Pauli: ad Galatas* (etc.)
                    (CSEL 83. 2)

Min. Fel. (Minucius Felix)
    Oct.   *Octauius*, ed. J. Beaujeu (Paris, 1964)

Novat. (Novatian)
    Cib. Iud.   *De cibis Iudaicis* (CCSL 4)
    Trin.   *De trinitate* (CCSL 4)

Orig. (Origen)
    Martyr.   *Exhortatio ad Martyrium* (GCS 2)

Orig.–Ruf. (Origen, as translated by Rufinus)
    Gen.   *Homeliae in Genesim* (GCS 29)
    Princ.   *De principiis* (GCS 22)
    Rom.   *Commentaria in epistulam Pauli ad Romanos* (PG 14)

Orosius
    Lib. apol.   *Liber apologeticus contra Pelagianos* (CSEL 5)

Ovid
    Amores   *Amores* (LCL)
    Met.   *Metamorphoses* (LCL 42–3)

Pel. (Pelagius)
    De nat.   *De natura* (CSEL 60)
    Lib. fid.   *Libellus fidei ad Innocentium* (PL 45)
    Rom. (etc.)   *Expositiones xiii epistularum Pauli: ad Romanos* (etc.),
                    ed. A. Souter, *Expositions*, vol. ii (Cambridge, 1926)

Prisc. (Priscillian of Ávila)
    Canones   *Canones in Pauli apostoli epistulas* (CSEL 18)

Prud. (Prudentius)
    Peristeph.   *Peristephanon* (PL 60)

ps.-Firm. Mat. (pseudo-Firmicus Maternus)
    Consult.   *Consultationes Zacchaei et Apollonii* (FP 39)

ps.-Hi. (pseudo–Jerome)
    Ep.   *Epistulae* (PL 30)
    Rom. (etc.)   *Commentaria in epistulas apostoli Pauli: ad Romanos*
                    (etc.), ed. H. J. Frede, *Ein neuer Paulustext und Kommentar*, i. *Untersuchungen* (Freiburg, 1973); ii. *Die Texte* (Freiburg, 1974)

Ruf. (Rufinus of Aquileia)
    Ad Anast.   *Apologia ad Anastasium Romae urbis episcopum* (CCSL 20)
    Apol.   *Apologia contra Hieronymum* (CCSL 20)

Ruf. Syr. (Rufinus of Syria)
    Lib. fid.   *Liber de fide*, ed. M. W. Miller (Washington, DC 1964)
    Sent. Sext.   *Sexti sententiae*, ed. H. Chadwick (Cambridge, 1959)

Tat. (Tatian)
    Orat.   *Oratio ad graecos*, ed. M. Whittaker (Oxford, 1982)

Tert. (Tertullian)
    An.   *De anima* (CCSL 2)
    Apol.   *Apologeticum* (CCSL 1)
    Bapt.   *De baptismo* (CCSL 1)
    Carn.   *De carne Christi* (CCSL 2)
    Coron.   *De corona* (CCSL 2)
    Ieiun.   *De ieunio* (CCSL 2)
    Iud.   *Aduersus Iudaeos* (CCSL 2)
    Marc.   *Aduersus Marcionem* (CCSL 1)
    Paenit.   *De paenitentia* (CCSL 1)
    Pud.   *De pudicitia* (CCSL 2)
    Scorp.   *Scorpiace* (CCSL 2)

Tycon. (Tyconius)
    Lib. regul.   *Liber regularum*, ed. F. Burkitt (Cambridge, 1894)

Zeno
    Tract.   *Tractatus* (CCSL 22)

Zosimus
    Ep.   *Epistulae* (CSEL 35)

2. SECONDARY LITERATURE

This list gives details of publication only for works cited in this volume. For a more complete, recent bibliography of Pelagian studies see Nuvolone, 'Pélage et pélagianisme: I. Les écrivains', *Dictionnaire de spiritualité*, xii. 2 (1986), 2889–923.

ABEL, MAURICE, 'Le "Praedestinatus" et le pélagianisme', *Recherches de théologie ancienne et médiévale*, 35 (1968), 5–25.
AFFELDT, WERNER, *Die weltliche Gewalt in der Paulus-Exegese: Rom. 13, 1–7 in den Römerbriefkommentaren der lateinischen Kirche bis zum Ende des 13. Jahrhunderts*

(Forschungen zur Kirchen- und Dogmengeschichte, 22; Göttingen: Vandenhoeck & Ruprecht, 1969).

ARBESMANN, RUDOLF, 'Fasten', in *Reallexicon für Antike und Christentum*, vii (Stuttgart: Anton Hiersemann, 1969), 447–93.

AUF DER MAUR, H. J., *Das Psalmenverständnis des Ambrosius von Mailand: Ein Beitrag zum Deutungshintergrund der Psalmenwendung im Gottesdienst der Alten Kirche* (Leiden: E. J. Brill, 1977).

BABCOCK, WILLIAM S., 'Augustine's Interpretation of Romans (AD 394–396)', *Augustinian Studies*, 10 (1979), 55–74.

BAMMEL, CAROLINE P. HAMMOND, 'The Last Ten Years of Rufinus's Life and the Date of his Move South from Aquileia', *Journal of Theological Studies*, NS 28 (1977), 372–429.

—— 'Philocalia IX, Jerome, Epistle 121, and Origen's Exposition of Romans VII', *Journal of Theological Studies*, NS 32 (1981), 50–81.

—— *Der Römerbrieftext des Rufin und seine Origenes-Übersetzung* (Vetus Latina: Die Reste der altlateinischen Bibel. Aus der Geschichte der lateinischen Bibel, 10; Freiburg: Herder, 1985).

—— 'Adam in Origen', in R. D. Williams (ed.), *The Making of Orthodoxy: Essays in Honour of Henry Chadwick* (Cambridge: Cambridge University Press, 1989), 62–93.

—— *Der Römerbriefkommentar des Origenes: Kritische Ausgabe der Übersetzung Rufins. Buch 1–3* (Vetus Latina: Die Reste der altlateinischen Bibel. Aus der Geschichte der lateinischen Bibel, 16; Freiburg: Herder, 1990).

BARDY, GUSTAV, 'Victorin de Pettau', in *Dictionnaire de théologie catholique*, xv. 2 (Paris: Letouzey et Ané, 1950), 2882–7.

BEATRICE, PIER FRANCO, *Tradux peccati: Alle fonti della dottrina agostiniana del peccato originale* (Milan: Università Cattolica de Sacro Cuore, 1978).

BERROUARD, MARIE-FRANÇOIS, 'L'exégèse augustinienne de Rom., 7, 7–25 entre 396 et 418 avec des remarques sur les deux premières périodes de la crise "pélagienne"', *Recherches augustiniennes*, 16 (1981), 101–95.

BESKOW, PER, 'Branding in the Mysteries of Mithras', in Ugo Bianchi (ed.), *Mysteria Mithrae: Proceedings of the International Seminar on the 'Religio-Historical Character of Roman Mithraism, with Particular Reference to Roman and Ostian Sources'*, Rome and Ostia, 28–31 Mar. 1978 (Études préliminaires aux religions orientales dans l'empire romain, 25; Leiden: E. J. Brill, 1979), 487–501.

Biblia Sacra iuxta Vulgatam Versionem, 3rd edn., ed. Bonifatius Fischer, 2 vols. (Stuttgart: Deutsche Bibelgesellschaft, 1983).

BISHCOFF, BERNHARD, 'Wendepunkte in der Geschichte der lateinischen Exegese im Frühmittelalter', *Sacris Erudiri*, 6 (1954), 189–279; rev. edn. in *Mittelalterliche Studien: Ausgewählte Aufsätze zur Schriftkunde und Literaturgeschichte*, i (Stuttgart: Anton Hierseman, 1966), 205–73. [English trans. in *Biblical Studies: The Medieval Irish Contribution*, ed. Martin McNamara (Proceedings of the Irish Biblical Association, i; Dublin: Dominican Publications, 1976), 73–160.]

BLUMENKRANZ, BERNHARD, *Juifs et chrétiens dans le monde occidental 430–1096* (École Pratique des Hautes Études—Sorbonne: Études Juives, 2; Paris and La Haye: Mouton & Co., 1960).

BOHLIN, TORGNY, *Die Theologie des Pelagius und ihre Genesis*, trans. Harald Buch (Uppsala universitetsårsskrift, 9; Uppsala: A.-B. Lundequist and Wiesbaden: Otto Harrassowitz, 1957).

BONNER, GERALD I., 'Les origines africaines de la doctrine augustinienne sur la chute et le péché originel', *Augustinus*, 12 (1967), 97–116; repr. in *God's Decree and Man's Destiny: Studies on the Thought of Augustine of Hippo* (London: Variorum Reprints, 1987).

—— *Augustine and Modern Research on Pelagianism* (The St Augustine Lecture, 1970; Villanova: Villanova University Press, 1972); repr. in *God's Decree and Man's Destiny: Studies on the Thought of Augustine of Hippo* (London: Variorum Reprints, 1987).

BORSE, UDO, *Der Kolosserbrieftext des Pelagius* (Bonn: Rheinische Friedrich-Wilhelms-Universität, 1966).

BROWN, PETER, *Augustine of Hippo* (1967; repr. Berkeley and Los Angeles: University of California Press, 1969).

—— 'Pelagius and his supporters: Aims and Environment', *Journal of Theological Studies*, NS 19 (1968), 93–114.

—— 'The Diffusion of Manichaeism in the Roman Empire', *Journal of Roman Studies*, 59 (1969), 92–103.

—— 'The Patrons of Pelagius: The Roman Aristocracy between East and West', *Journal of Theological Studies*, NS 21 (1970), 56–72.

—— 'Late Antiquity', in Paul Veyne (ed.), *A History of Private Life*, i. *From Pagan Rome to Byzantium*, trans. Arthur Goldhammer (Cambridge, Mass., and London: The Belknap Press of Harvard University Press, 1987), 235–311.

—— *The Body and Society: Men, Women, and Sexual Renunciation in Early Christianity* (New York: Columbia University Press, 1988).

BUONAIUTI, ERNESTO, 'Pelagius and the Pauline Vulgate', *Expository Times*, 27 (1916), 425–7.

BURKERT, WALTER, *Ancient Mystery Cults* (Cambridge, Mass., and London: Harvard University Press, 1987).

BURNS, J. PATOUT, *The Development of Augustine's Doctrine of Operative Grace* (Paris: Études Augustiniennes, 1980).

BURY, J. B., 'The Origins of Pelagius', *Hermathena*, 13 (1905), 26–35.

CADBURY, HENRY J., 'Erastus of Corinth', *Journal of Biblical Literature*, 50 (1931), 42–58.

CASPARI, C. P., *Briefe, Abhandlungen und Predigten aus den zwei letzten Jahrhunderten des kirchlichen Altertums und dem Anfang des Mittelalters* (Christiania: Mallingschen Buchdruckerei, 1890).

CAVALLERA, FERDINAND, 'Saint Jérôme et la bible', *Bulletin de littérature ecclésiastique*, 22 (1921), 214–27, 265–84.

—— *Saint Jérôme: Sa vie et son œuvre* (Spicilegium Sacrum Lovaniense: Études et documents, pt. 1, 2 vols.; Louvain and Paris: Champion, 1922).

CHADWICK, HENRY, *Priscillian of Avila: The Occult and the Charismatic in the Early Church* (Oxford: Clarendon Press, 1976).

—— 'Priscillien', *Dictionnaire de spiritualité*, xii. 2 (1986), 2353–69.

CHADWICK, NORA K., *Poetry and Letters in Early Christian Gaul* (London: Bowes & Bowes, 1955).

CHAPMAN, [H.] J., 'Pélage et le texte de s. Paul', *Revue d'histoire ecclésiastique*, 18 (1922), 469–81; 19 (1923), 25–42.

CHARLIER, CÉLESTIN, 'Cassiodore, Pélage et les origines de la vulgate paulinienne', *Studiorum Paulinorum Congressus Internationalis Catholicus, 1961* (Analecta Biblica, 17–18; Rome: Pontificio Institutio Biblico, 1963), ii. 460–70.

COLISH, MARCIA L., *The Stoic Tradition from Antiquity to the Early Middle Ages*, i. *Stoicism in Classical Latin Literature*; ii. *Stoicism in Christian Latin Thought through the Sixth Century* (Studies in the History of Christian Thought, 34–5; Leiden: E. J. Brill, 1985).

COURCELLE, PIERRE, *Connais-toi toi-même de Socrate à Saint Bernard*, 2 vols. in 3 (Paris: Études Augustiniennes, 1974–5).

COYLE, JOHN KEVIN, *Augustine's 'De moribus ecclesiae catholicae': A Study of the Work, its Composition, and its Sources* (Paradosis, 25; Fribourg: Fribourg University Press, 1978).

DE BRUYN, THEODORE S., 'A Translation, with Introduction and Notes, of Pelagius's "Commentary on Romans"' (diss. University of St Michael's College, 1987).

—— 'Pelagius's Interpretation of Rom. 5: 12–21: Exegesis within the Limits of Polemic', *Toronto Journal of Theology*, 4 (1988), 30–43.

—— 'Constantius the *tractator*: Author of an Anonymous Commentary on Romans?', *Journal of Theological Studies*, NS 43 (1992), 38–54.

DE BRUYNE, DONATIEN, 'Étude sur les origines de notre texte latin de saint Paul', *Revue biblique*, NS 12 (1915), 358–92.

—— Review of *Pelagius's Expositions of Thirteen Epistles of St Paul*, i. *Introduction*, by Alexander Souter: *BALCL* 1 (1921–8), No. 115 (pp. 57–9).

—— Review of *Pelagius's Expositions of Thirteen Epistles of St Paul*, ii. *Text*, by Alexander Souter: *BALCL* 1 (1921–8), No. 589 (pp. 242–4).

DECRET, FRANÇOIS, *Aspects du manichéisme dans l'Afrique Romaine: Les controverses de Fortunatus, Faustus et Felix avec saint Augustin* (Paris: Études Augustiniennes, 1970).

DE LABRIOLLE, P., *La Crise montaniste: Les sources de l'histoire du Montanisme. Texts grecs, latins, syriaques* (Paris, 1913).

DE SIMONE, RUSSELL, 'Modern Research on the Sources of Saint Augustine's Doctrine of Original Sin', *Augustinian Studies*, 11 (1980), 205–27.

DEWART, JOANNE MCWILLIAM, 'The Christology of the Pelagian Controversy', *Studia Patristica*, 17, ed. Elizabeth A. Livingstone (Oxford: Pergamon Press, 1982), 1221–44.

DILLON, JOHN M., *The Middle Platonists: A Study of Platonism, 80 B.C. to A.D. 220* (London: Duckworth, 1977).

DOIGNON, JEAN, "'J'acquiesce à la loi" (Rom. 7, 16) dans l'exégèse latine ancienne', *Freiburger Zeitschrift für Philosophie und Theologie*, 29 (1982), 131–9.

—— 'Les premiers commentateurs latins de l'Écriture et l'œuvre exégétique d'Hilaire de Poitiers', in Jacques Fontaine and Charles Pietri (eds.), *Le Monde latin antique et la Bible* (Bible de tous les temps, 2; Paris: Éditions Beauchesne, 1985), 509–21.

DÖLGER, FRANZ JOSEPH, 'Die religiöse Brandmarkung in den Kybele-Attis-Mysterien nach einem Texte des christlichen Dichters Prudentius', in *Antike und Christentum: Kultur- und Religionsgeschichtliche Studien*, 6 vols. (1929–50, repr. Münster: Aschendorff, 1974–6), i. 66–72.

DOMAGALSKI, BERNARD, 'Römische Diakone im 4. Jahrhundert: Zum Verhältnis von Bischof, Diakon und Presbyter', in Joseph G. Plöger and Hermann Joh. Weber (eds.), *Der Diakon: Wiederentdeckung und Erneuerung seines Dienstes* (Freiburg: Herder, 1980), 44–56.

DUMVILLE, DAVID, 'Late-Seventh- or Eighth-Century Evidence for the British Transmission of Pelagius', *Cambridge Medieval Celtic Studies*, 10 (1985), 39–52.

DUVAL, YVES-MARIE, 'Pélage est-il le censeur inconnu de l'Adversus Iovinianum à Rome en 393? ou: du "portrait-robot" de l'hérétique chez s. Jérôme', *Revue d'histoire ecclésiastique*, 75 (1980), 525–57.

ERDT, WERNER, *Marius Victorinus Afer, der erste lateinische Pauluskommentator: Studien zu seinen Pauluskommentaren in Zusammenhang der Wiederentdeckung des Paulus in der abendländischen Theologie des 4. Jahrhunderts* (Europäische Hochschulschriften, ser. 23: Theologie, 135; Frankfurt am Main: Peter D. Lang, 1980).

ESSER, HANS HELMUT, *Das Paulusverständnis des Pelagius nach seinem Pauluskommentar* (diss. Rheinische Friedrich-Wilhelmsuniversität, 1961).

—— 'Thesen und Anmerkungen zum exegetischen Paulusverständnis des Pelagius', in Ernst Wolf, with Helmut Gollwitzer and Joachim Hoppe (eds.), *Zwischenstation: Festschrift für Karl Kupisch zum 60. Geburtstag* (Munich: Chr. Kaiser, 1963), 27–42.

EVANS, ROBERT F., *Four Letters of Pelagius* (London: Adam & Charles Black, 1968).

—— *Pelagius: Inquiries and Reappraisals* (London: Adam & Charles Black, 1968).

FERGUSON, JOHN, *Pelagius: A Historical and Theological Study* (Cambridge: W. Heffer & Sons, 1956).

FISCHER, BONIFATIUS, 'Das Neue Testament in lateinischer Sprache', in Kurt Aland (ed.), *Die alten Übersetzungen des Neuen Testaments, die Kirchenväternzitate und Lektionare* (Arbeiten zur neutestamentlichen Textforschung, 5; Berlin and New York: Walter de Gruyter, 1972), 1–92.

FREDE, HERMANN JOSEF, *Pelagius, der irische Paulustext, Sedulius Scottus* (Vetus Latina: Die Reste der altlateinischen Bibel. Aus der Geschichte der lateinischen Bibel, 3; Freiburg: Herder, 1961).

—— 'Eine neue Handschrift des Pauluskommentars von Pelagius', *Revue Bénédictine*, 73 (1963), 307–11.

—— *Ein neuer Paulustext und Kommentar*, i. *Untersuchungen*; ii. *Die Texte* (Vetus Latina: Die Reste der altlateinischen Bibel. Aus der Geschichte der lateinischen Bibel, 7–8; Freiburg: Herder, 1973–4).

—— ed. *Kirchenschriftsteller: Verzeichnis und Sigel*, 3rd rev. edn. (Vetus Latina: Die Reste der altlateinischen Bibel, 1. 1; Freiburg: Herder, 1981).

—— ed. *Kirchenschriftsteller: Aktualisierungsheft* (Vetus Latina: Die Reste der altlateinischen Bibel, 1.1A; Freiburg: Herder, 1984).

FREUNDORFER, JOSEPH, *Erbsünde und Erbtod beim Apostel Paulus: Eine religionsgeschichtliche und exegetische Untersuchung über Römerbrief 5, 12–21* (Neutestamentliche Abhandlungen, 13. 1; Münster: Aschendorff, 1927).

GAGER, JOHN G., *The Origins of Anti-Semitism: Attitudes toward Judaism in Pagan and Christian Antiquity* (New York and Oxford: Oxford University Press, 1983).

GARCÍA-ALLEN, CARLOS, 'Pelagius and Christian Initiation: A Study in Historical Theology' (diss. Catholic University of America, 1978).

—— 'Was Pelagius Influenced by Chromatius of Aquileia?', *Studia Patristica*, 17, ed. Elizabeth A. Livingstone (Oxford: Pergamon Press, 1982), 1251–7.

GARCÍA-SÁNCHEZ, CARLOS: see García-Allen, Carlos.

GAUDEL, J., 'Péché originel, II. La tradition ecclésiastique avant la controverse pélagienne: Les Pères grecs; III. La tradition ecclésiastique avant la controverse pélagienne: Les Pères latins', *Dictionnaire de théologie catholique*, xii. 1 (Paris: Letouzey et Ané, 1933), 317–82.

GAUDEMET, JEAN, *L'Église dans l'empire romain (IVe–Ve siècles)* (Histoire du Droit et des Institutions de l'Église en Occident, 3; Paris: Sirey, [1958]).

GEERARD, M., and GLORIE, F., *Clavis Patrum Graecorum*, v. *Indices, Initia, Concordantiae* (Brepols: Turnhout, 1987).

GRANT, ROBERT M., *Early Christianity and Society* (San Francisco: Harper & Row, 1977).

GRESHAKE, GISBERT, *Gnade als konkrete Freiheit: Eine Untersuchung zur Gnadenlehre des Pelagius* (Mainz: Matthias-Grünewald-Verlag, 1972).

GRYSON, ROGER, *Le Ministère des femmes dans l'Église ancienne* (Recherches et synthèses, Section d'histoire, 4; Gembloux: J. Duculot, [1972]).

HADOT, PIERRE, *Marius Victorinus: Recherches sur sa vie et ses œuvres* (Paris: Études Augustiniennes, 1971).

HAMMOND, CAROLINE P.: *see* Bammel, Caroline P. Hammond.

HANSON, R. P. C., *Saint Patrick: His Origins and Career* (Oxford: Clarendon Press, 1968).

HELLMANN, SIGMUND, *Sedulius Scottus*, in Ludwig Traube (ed.), *Quellen und Untersuchungen zur lateinischen Philologie des Mittelalters*, i. 1 (Munich, 1906; repr. Frankfurt am Main: Minerva, 1966).

HUNTER, DAVID, 'Resistance to the Virginal Ideal in Late-Fourth-Century Rome: The Case of Jovinian', *Theological Studies*, 48 (1987), 45–64.

JAY, PIERRE, *L'Exégèse de saint Jérôme d'après son 'Commentaire sur Isaïe'* (Paris: Études Augustiniennes, 1985).

JAY, PIERRE, 'Jérôme et la pratique de l'exégèse', in Jacques Fontaine and Charles Pietri (eds.), *Le Monde latin antique et la Bible* (Bible de tous les temps, 2; Paris: Éditions Beauchesne, 1985), 523–42.

JOHNSON, D. W., 'Purging the Poison: The Revision of Pelagius' Pauline Commentaries by Cassiodorus and his Students' (diss. Princeton University, 1989).

JONAS, HANS, *Augustin und das paulinische Freiheitsproblem: Ein philosophischer Beitrag zur Genesis der christlich-abendländischen Freiheitsidee* (Göttingen: Vandenhoeck & Ruprecht, 1930).

JOUASSARD, G., 'La personnalité d'Helvidius', in *Mélanges J. Saunier* (Bibliothèque de la faculté catholique des lettres de Lyon, 3; Lyon: Facultés catholiques, 1944), 139–56.

JUDANT, DENISE, *Judaïsme et christianisme: Dossier patristique* (Paris: Les Éditions du Cèdre, [1969]).

JUNGMANN, JOSEF ANDREAS, *The Mass of the Roman Rite: Its Origins and Development* (*Missarum sollemnia*), trans. Francis A. Brunner, 2 vols. (New York: Benziger, 1951–5).

KASTER, ROBERT A., *Guardians of Language: The Grammarian and Society in Late Antiquity* (The Transformation of the Classical Heritage, 11; Berkeley: University of California Press, 1988).

KELLY, J. N. D., *Jerome: His Life, Writing, and Controversies* (London: Duckworth, 1976).

KELLY, JOSEPH F., 'Pelagius, Pelagianism and the Early Christian Irish', *Mediaevalia*, 4 (1978), 99–124.

KOCH, HUGO, 'Cyprian in den *Quaestiones Veteris et Novi Testamenti* und beim Ambrosiaster: Ein Beitrag zur Ambrosiasterfrage. Mit einem Anhang: Cyprian bei Pelagius', *Zeitschrift für Kirchengeschichte*, 45 (1926), 516–55.

LA BONNARDIÈRE, A.-M., 'Le verset paulinien *Rom.*, V. 5 dans l'œuvre de saint Augustin', in *Augustinus Magister: Congrès International Augustinien, Paris, 21–24 Septembre 1954. Communications* (Paris: Études Augustiniennes, [n.d.]), ii. 657–65.

LANDES, PAULA FREDERIKSEN, trans. *Augustine on Romans* (Chico, Calif.: Scholars Press, 1982).

LARDET, PIERRE, 'Introduction', in Jerome, *Apologie contre Rufin* (Sources Chrétiennes, 303; Paris: Les Éditions du Cerf, 1983), 1*–145*.

LEBEAU, PAUL, 'L'interprétation origénienne de Rm. 8. 19–22', in Patrick Granfield and Josef A. Jungmann (eds.), *Kyriakon: Festschrift Johannes Quasten*, 2 vols. (Münster: Aschendorff, 1970), i. 336–45.

Liber sacramentorum Romanae aeclesiae ordinis anni circuli (*Cod. Vat. Reg. lat. 316/Paris Bibl. Nat. 7193, 41/56*) (*Sacramentarium Gelasianum*), ed. Leo Cunibert Mohlberg, with Leo Eizenhöfer and Petrus Siffrin (1960; 3rd rev. edn. by Leo Eizenhöfer, Rome: Herder, 1981).

LIEU, SAMUEL N. C., *Manichaeism in the Later Roman Empire and Medieval China: A Historical Survey* (Manchester: Manchester University Press, 1985).

LINDEMANN, ANDREAS, *Paulus im ältesten Christentum: Das Bild des Apostels und die Rezeption der paulinischen Theologie in der frühchristlichen Literatur bis Marcion* (Tübingen: J. C. B. Mohr, 1979).

LOHSE, BERNHARD, 'Beobachtungen zum Paulus-Kommentar des Marius Victorinus und zur Wiederentdeckung des Paulus in der lateinischen Theologie des vierten Jahrhunderts', in Adolf Martin Ritter (ed.), *Kerygma und Logos: Beiträge zu den geistesgeschichtlichen Beziehungen zwischen Antike und Christentum* (Göttingen: Vandenhoeck & Ruprecht, 1979), 351–66.

LORENZ, RUDOLF, 'Zwölf Jahre Augustinusforschung (1959–1970)', *Theologische Rundschau*, 40 (1975), 97–149.

MACMULLEN, RAMSAY, *Christianizing the Roman Empire (A.D. 100–400)* (New Haven, Conn., and London: Yale University Press, 1984).

MANGENOT, E., 'Saint Jérôme ou Pélage éditeur des épîtres de saint Paul dans la Vulgate', *Revue du clergé français*, 86 (1916), 5–22, 193–213.

MARKUS, ROBERT A., 'The Legacy of Pelagius: Orthodoxy, Heresy, and Conciliation', in R. D. Williams (ed.), *The Making of Orthodoxy* (Cambridge: Cambridge University Press, 1989), 214–34.

—— *The End of Ancient Christianity* (Cambridge: Cambridge University Press, 1990).

MARROU, HENRI IRÉNÉE, *A History of Education in Antiquity*, trans. George Lamb (London and New York: Sheed and Ward, [1956]).

MARTIMORT, AIMÉ GEORGES, *Les Diaconesses: Essai historique* (Bibliotheca Ephemerides liturgicae, Subsidia, 24; Rome: C. L. V.-Edizioni Liturgiche, 1982).

MARTINETTO, GIOVANNI, 'Les premières réactions antiaugustiniennes de Pélage', *Revue des études augustiniennes*, 27 (1971), 83–117.

MEEKS, WAYNE A., *The First Urban Christians: The Social World of the Apostle Paul* (New Haven, Conn., and London: Yale University Press, 1983).

MERCATI, G., 'Two Leaves of a Sixth-Century MS of Pelagius on St Paul', *Journal of Theological Studies*, 8 (1906–7), 529–35.

MERKELBACH, REINHOLD, *Mithras* (Königstein: A. Hein, 1984).

METZGER, BRUCE M., *The Early Versions of the New Testament: Their Origin, Transmission, and Limitations* (Oxford: Clarendon Press, 1977).

MOMIGLIANO, ARNALDO, 'Impiety', in *Dictionary of the History of Ideas: Studies of Selected Pivotal Ideas*, ii (New York: Charles Scribner's Sons, 1973), 564–7.

MORRIS, JOHN, 'Pelagian Literature', *Journal of Theological Studies*, NS 16 (1965), 26–60.

MUNDLE, WILHELM, *Die Exegese der paulinischen Briefe im Kommentar des Ambrosiaster* (Marburg im Hessen: Christian Schaef, 1919).

MYRES, J. N. L., 'Pelagius and the End of Roman Rule in Britain', *Journal of Roman Studies*, 50 (1960), 21–36.

NAUTIN, P., 'La date des commentaires de Jérôme sur les épîtres paulin-iennes', *Revue d'histoire ecclésiastique*, 74 (1979), 5–12.

NELLESSEN, ERNST, *Untersuchungen zur altlateinischen Überlieferung des ersten Thessalonicherbriefes* (Bonner Biblische Beiträge, 22; Bonn: Peter Hanstein, 1965).

—— 'Der lateinische Paulustext im Codex Baliolensis des Pelagiuskommentars', *Zeitschrift für die neutestamentliche Wissenschaft und die Kunde der älteren Kirche*, 59 (1968), 210–30.

NEUMANN, CHARLES WILLIAM, *The Virgin Mary in the Works of Saint Ambrose* (Paradosis, 17; Fribourg: University Press, 1962).

NEUNHEUSER, BURKHARD, *Baptism and Confirmation*, trans. John Jay Hughes (Freiburg: Herder and Montreal: Palm Publishers, 1964).

NICHOLSON, M. FORTHOMME, 'Celtic Theology: Pelagius', in James P. Mackey (ed.), *An Introduction to Celtic Christianity* (Edinburgh: T. & T. Clark, 1989), 386–413.

NUVOLONE, FLAVIO G., 'Problèmes d'une nouvelle édition du *De induratione cordis Pharaonis* attribué à Pélage', *Revue des études augustiniennes*, 26 (1980), 105–17.

—— 'Pélage et pélagianisme, I: Les écrivains', *Dictionnaire de spiritualité*, xii. 2 (1986), 2889–923.

PELIKAN, JAROSLAV, *Development of Christian Doctrine: Some Historical Prolegomena* (New Haven, Conn., and London: Yale University Press, 1969).

—— *The Christian Tradition: A History of the Development of Doctrine*, i. *The Emergence of the Catholic Tradition (100–600)* (Chicago: University of Chicago Press, 1971).

PEPIN, JEAN, *Théologie cosmique et théologie chrétienne (Ambroise, Exam. I 1, 1–4)* (Bibliothèque de philosophie contemporaine: Histoire de la philosophie et philosophie générale; Paris: Presses Universitaires de France, 1964).

PIETRI, CHARLES, *Roma Christiana: Recherches sur l'Église de Rome, son organisation, sa politique, son idéologie de Miltiade à Sixte III (311–440)*, 2 vols. (Rome: École Française de Rome, 1976).

PIRENNE, ROGER, *La Morale de Pélage: Essai historique sur le rôle primordial de la grâce dans l'enseignement de la théologie morale* (Rome: Pontificia Universitas Lateranensis, 1961).

PLINVAL, GEORGE DE, 'Recherches sur l'œuvre littéraire de Pélage', *Revue de philologie, de littérature et d'histoire anciennes*, 60 (1934), 1–42.

—— *Pélage: Ses écrits, sa vie et sa réforme. Étude d'histoire littéraire et religieuse* (Lausanne: Payot, 1943).

—— *Essai sur le style et la langue de Pélage suivi du traité inédit* De induratione cordis Pharaonis, text ed. by Germain Morin (Collectanea Friburgensia, NS 31; Fribourg: Librairie de l'Université, 1947).

—— 'Précisions sur l'authenticité d'un prologue de Pélage: *Primum quaeritur*', *Revue des études augustiniennes*, 12 (1966), 247–53.

POSCHMANN, BERNHARD, *Penance and the Anointing of the Sick*, trans. Francis Courtney (Freiburg: Herder, 1964).

RB 1980: The Rule of St. Benedict in Latin and English with Notes, ed. Timothy Fry (Collegeville, Minn.: Liturgical Press, 1981).

REES, B. R., *Pelagius: A Reluctant Heretic* (Suffolk: Boydell Press, 1988).

RIGBY, PAUL, *Original Sin in Augustine's Confessions* (Ottawa: University of Ottawa Press, 1987).

RIVIÈRE, JEAN, *The Doctrine of the Atonement: A Historical Essay*, trans. L. Cappadelta, 2 vols. (London: Kegan Paul; Trench: Teubner & Co.; and St Louis: Herder, 1909).

—— 'Hétérodoxie des pélagiens en fait de rédemption?', *Revue d'histoire ecclésiastique*, 41 (1946), 5–43.

RUETHER, ROSEMARY RADFORD, *Faith and Fratricide: The Theological Roots of Anti-Semitism* (New York: Seabury Press, 1974).

Sacramentarium Veronense (Cod. Bibl. Capit. Veron. LXXXV [80]), ed. Leo Cunibert Mohlberg, with Leo Eizenhöfer and Petrus Siffrin (Rome: Herder, 1956).

SAGE, ATHANASE, 'Péché originel: Naissance d'un dogme', *Revue des études augustiniennes*, 13 (1967), 211–48.

—— 'Le péché originel dans la pensée de saint Augustin, de 412 à 430', *Revue des études augustiniennes*, 15 (1969), 75–112.

SAVON, HERVÉ, *Saint Ambroise devant l'exégèse de Philon le juif*, 2 vols. (Paris: Études Augustiniennes, 1977).

SAXER, VICTOR, 'La Bible chez les Pères latins du IIIe siècle', in Jacques Fontaine and Charles Pietri (eds), *Le Monde latin antique et la Bible* (Bible de tous les temps, 2; Paris: Éditions Beauchesne, 1985), 339–69.

SCHÄFER, KARL TH., 'Der Paulustext des Pelagius', in *Studiorum Paulinorum Congressus Internationalis Catholicus, 1961* (Analecta Biblica, 17–18; Rome: Pontificio Instituto Biblico, 1963), ii. 453–60.

SCHATKIN, MARGARET A., 'The Influence of Origen upon St. Jerome's Commentary on Galatians', *Vigiliae Christianae*, 24 (1970), 49–58.

SCHEFFCZYK, LEO, *Urstand, Fall und Erbsünde von der Schrift bis Augustinus* (Handbuch der Dogmengeschichte, 2, sect. 3a, pt. 1; Freiburg: Herder, 1981).

SCHELKLE, KARL HERMANN, 'Bruder', in *Reallexicon für Antike und Christentum*, ii (Stuttgart: Anton Hiersemann, 1954), 631–40.

—— *Paulus, Lehrer der Väter: Die altkirchliche Auslegung von Römer 1–11* (Düsseldorf: Patmos, 1956).

—— *Wort und Schrift: Beiträge zur Auslegung und Auslegungsgeschichte des Neuen Testamentes* (Düsseldorf: Patmos, 1966).

SCHUBERT, HANS VON, *Der sogennante Praedestinatus: Ein Beitrag zur Geschichte des Pelagianismus* (Texte und Untersuchungen zur Geschichte der altchristlichen Literatur, ed. Oscar von Gebhardt and Adolf Harnack, NS 9. 4; Leipzig: J. C. Hinrichs', 1903).

SIMON, MARCEL, *Verus Israel: Étude sur les relations entre chrétiens et juifs dans l'empire romain (135–425)* (Paris, 1948; 2nd, rev. edn. Paris, 1964).

SMITH, ALFRED J., 'The Latin Sources of the Commentary of Pelagius on the Epistle of St Paul to the Romans', *Journal of Theological Studies*, 19 (1917–18), 162–230; 20 (1918–19), 55–65, 127–77.

—— 'Pelagius and Augustine', *Journal of Theological Studies*, 31 (1929–30), 21–35.

SOUTER, ALEXANDER, *A Study of Ambrosiaster* (Texts and Studies, 7. 4; Cambridge: Cambridge University Press, 1905).

—— 'The Commentary of Pelagius on the Epistles of Paul: The Problem of its Restoration', *Proceedings of the British Academy*, 2 (1905–6), 409–39.

—— 'Pelagius and the Pauline Text in the Book of Armagh', *Journal of Theological Studies*, 16 (1914–15), 105.

—— 'The Character and History of Pelagius' Commentary on the Epistles of St Paul', *Proceedings of the British Academy*, 7 (1915–16), 261–96.

—— *Pelagius's Expositions of Thirteen Epistles of St Paul* (Texts and Studies, 9; Cambridge: Cambridge University Press), i. *Introduction* (1922); ii. *Text* (1926); iii. *Pseudo-Jerome Interpolations* (1931).

—— *The Earliest Latin Commentaries on the Epistles of St. Paul* (Oxford: Clarendon Press, 1927).

SPANNEUT, MICHEL, *Le Stoïcisme des pères de l'église: De Clément de Rome à Clément d'Alexandrie*, rev. edn. (Paris: Éditions du Seuil, 1957).

STANCLIFFE, CLARE, *St. Martin and his Hagiographer: History and Miracle in Sulpicius Severus* (Oxford: Clarendon Press, 1983).

STUDER, BASIL, and DALEY, BRIAN, *Soteriologie in der Schrift und Patristik* (Handbuch der Dogmengeschichte, 3, pt. 2a; Freiburg: Herder, 1978).

SWETE, H. B., *Theodori Episcopi Mopsuesteni in epistolas b. Pauli Commentarii: The Latin Version with the Greek Fragments, with an Introduction, Notes, and Indices*, 2 vols. (Cambridge: Cambridge University Press, 1880–2).

TESELLE, EUGENE, 'Rufinus the Syrian, Caelestius, Pelagius: Explorations in the Prehistory of the Pelagian Controversy', *Augustinian Studies*, 3 (1972), 61–95.

THEISSEN, GERD, *The Social Setting of Pauline Christianity: Essays on Corinth*, ed. and trans. John H. Schütz (Philadelphia: Fortress Press, 1982).

THIELE, WALTER, Review of Karl Th. Schäfer, 'Pelagius und die Vulgata'; id., 'Der Paulustext des Pelagius'; Franz Hermann Tinnefeld, *Untersuchungen zur altlateinischen Überlieferung des I. Timotheusbriefes*; Ernst Nellessen, *Untersuchungen zur altlateinischen Überlieferung des ersten Thessalonicherbriefes*; Udo Borse, *Der Kolosserbrieftext des Pelagius: Zeitschrift für Kirchengeschichte*, 77 (1966), 363–73.

—— 'Zum lateinischen Paulustext: Textkritik und Überlieferungsgeschichte', *Zeitschrift für die neutestamentliche Wissenschaft und die Kunde der älteren Kirche*, 60 (1969), 264–73.

TINNEFELD, FRANZ HERMANN, *Untersuchungen zur altlateinischen Überlieferung des I. Timotheusbriefes: Der lateinische Paulustext in den Handschriften D E F G und in den Kommentaren des Ambrosiaster und des Pelagius* (Klassisch-Philologische Studien, 26; Wiesbaden: Otto Harrasowitz, 1963).

TURNER, CUTHERBERT HAMILTON, 'Pelagius' Commentary on the Pauline Epistles and its History', *Journal of Theological Studies*, 4 (1902–3), 132–41.

—— 'Greek Patristic Commentaries on the Pauline Epistles', in *A Dictionary of the Bible*, ed. James Hastings with John A. Selbie (Edinburgh: T. & T. Clark, 1898–1904), v ('Extra Volume'), 484–530.

VALERO, JUAN B., *Las bases antropológicas de Pelagio en su tratado de las Expositiones* (Publicaciones de la Universidad Pontificia Comillas, Madrid, ser. 1: Estudios, 18; Madrid: Universidad Pontificia Comillas, 1980).

Vetus Latina: Die Reste der altlateinischen Bibel, xxiv. 1. *Epistula ad Ephesios*, ed. Hermann Josef Frede (Freiburg: Herder, 1962–4).

—— xxiv. 2. *Epistulae ad Philippenses et ad Colossenses*, ed. Hermann Josef Frede (Freiburg: Herder, 1966).

—— xxv. *Epistulae ad Thessalonicenses, Timotheum, Titum, Philemonem, Hebraeos*, pt. 1. *Einleitung. Epistulae ad Thessalonicenses, Timotheum*; pt. 2. *Epistulae ad Titum, Philemonem, Hebraeos*, ed. Hermann Josef Frede (Freiburg: Herder, 1975–82; 1983–91).

—— xxvi. 1. *Epistulae Catholicae*, ed. Walter Thiele (Freiburg: Herder, 1956–69).

VILLE, GEORGES, *La Gladiature en occident des origines à la mort de Domitien* (Palais Farnèse: École Française de Rome, 1981).

VOGELS, HEINRICH JOSEF, 'Der Pelagiuskommentar zu den Briefen des h. Paulus', *Theologische Revue*, 25 (1926), 121–6.

WERMELINGER, OTTO, *Rom und Pelagius: Die theologische Position der römischen Bischöfe im pelagianischen Streit in den Jahren 411–432* (Päpste und Papsttum, 7; Stuttgart: Anton Hiersemann, 1975).

—— 'Marius Mercator', in *Dictionnaire de spiritualité* (Paris: Beauchesne, 1980), 610–15.

WIESEN, DAVID S., *St. Jerome as a Satirist: A Study in Christian Latin Thought and Letters* (Ithaca, N.Y.: Cornell University Press, 1964).

WILLIAMS, HUGH, *Christianity in Early Britain* (Oxford: Clarendon Press, 1912).

WITHERINGTON III, BEN, *Women in the Earliest Churches* (Society for New Testament Studies, Monograph Series, ed. G. N. Stanton; Cambridge: Cambridge University Press, 1988).

WOLFGARTEN, E., 'Der dem Pelagiuskommentar zugrundellegende Text des Titusbriefes' (TS, Staatsarbeit, Bonn, [n.d.]).

ZIMMER, HEINRICH, *Pelagius in Irland: Texte und Untersuchungen zur patristischen Litteratur* (Berlin: Weidmann, 1901).

Index of Sources

1. BIBLICAL REFERENCES

References accompanied by an asterisk (*) are direct quotations.

2. CLASSICAL AND PATRISTIC REFERENCES

Index of Manuscripts

General Index

Abigail 153
Abraham 36, 39–40, 59, 63, 77, 84, 86–8, 92, 115–16, 120, 127 n. 17, 134
  descendants of 37, 46, 57–8, 86, 87, 89, 93, 116, 130
  example of 39–40, 88, 89
abstinence 15, 51–2, 140–3, 152
Adam 92–5, 97, 106, 110
  effects of 19–22, 41, 94–5
  example of 36, 40–1, 92–5
aduersus Iudaeos tradition 37, 47
African tradition 5–7
alms 138–9
Ambrose 4–5, 7
Ambrosiaster:
  anti-Manichaeism of 16
  commentaries of 1, 2, 4
  on faith 37, 39
  on free will 17
  on law 37, 47
  and prologues 9
  on sin 22–3, 41
  and *uetus latina* 7
Ananias 137
Anastasius 17
angels 109, 110, 115, 134
anonymous commentator 1, 2, 17
Apollinaris of Laodicea 3
Apollo 151
apostles 127, 148, 149
  marks of 53
  office of 59, 60
Aquila 53, 151
Arians 60 nn. 7, 9, 113, 131
Arius 60, 115
Arnobius the Younger 27
asceticism 12–13, 51–2, 128 n. 21, 137 n. 8
Asia 151
atonement, *see* Christ, death of
Augustine 5, 14
  on asceticism 12
  on election 20–1, 46–7
  on free will 17, 20–1

  on grace 20–1
  on original sin 19–22
  Pauline commentaries of 1, 6–7
  and Pelagius's commentary 26, 30, 51
authority 50–1, 136–7

baptism 33, 34 n. 222, 36, 39, 42, 96–8, 115
  of infants 19, 21–2, 94
  and justification 60, 81, 85, 95, 113
  ministers of 151
  second 97–8
  and works 83–4
Barnabas 59
Bible:
  commentaries on 1–7
  Latin versions of 7–9; see also *uetus latina*, Vulgate
  prologues to 9
Blesilla 12
body:
  and abstinence 140, 141
  health of 89
  renewal of 132
  and sin 16, 42–5, 49, 98, 104–5
  see also flesh, resurrection
Book of Armagh 7, 28
branding 66

Caelestius 18, 22, 24–5, 27, 34, 94 n. 34
call of God 21, 36, 45, 58, 112, 153
carnal life 36, 43–4, 103–4, 106, 107, 108, 141
Carterius 12
Cassiodorus 27–8, 30–1, 118 n. 17, 157
Cephas 59
charismatic power 113, 132, 133
Christ:
  baptism into 19, 39, 42, 96–7, 115
  body of 97, 106–7, 115, 132, 135, 146, 152
  conception of 12, 60, 93
  death of 39, 40, 42, 44, 62, 82, 90–1, 92, 97, 106–7, 113, 114, 121, 124, 126, 146